DATE DUE

BRODART, CO.

Cat. No. 23-221-003

THE STATE OF THE WORLD'S REFUGEES
2006

Human displacement in the new millennium

UNHCR

OXFORD
UNIVERSITY PRESS

OXFORD
UNIVERSITY PRESS

Great Clarendon Street, Oxford OX2 6DP

Oxford University Press is a department of the University of Oxford.
It furthers the University's objective of excellence in research, scholarship,
and education by publishing worldwide in

Oxford New York

Auckland Cape Town Dar es Salaam Hong Kong Karachi
Kuala Lumpur Madrid Melbourne Mexico City Nairobi
New Delhi Shanghai Taipei Toronto

With offices in

Argentina Austria Brazil Chile Czech Republic France Greece
Guatemala Hungary Italy Japan Poland Portugal Singapore
South Korea Switzerland Thailand Turkey Ukraine Vietnam

Oxford is a registered trade mark of Oxford University Press
in the UK and in certain other countries

Published in the United States by Oxford University Press Inc., New York

The opinions expressed in this book do not necessarily represent official UNHCR policy nor are
they necessarily endorsed by the internal advisors and the independent experts. Unless otherwise
stated, the book does not refer to events occurring after September 2005. The maps do not imply the
expression of any opinion on the part of UNHCR, concerning the legal status of any country, territory,
city or area, or the delimitation of frontiers or boundaries.

Unless otherwise stated, all maps are produced by the UNHCR Population and Geographic Data
Section (geographic data from Global Insight-1998 © Europa Technologies Ltd).

Unless otherwise stated, all statistics are provided by the UNHCR Population and Geographic
Data Section.

British Library Cataloguing in Publication Data
Data available

Library of Congress Cataloging in Publication Data
Data available

Typeset by SPI Publisher Services, Pondicherry, India
Printed in Great Britain
on acid-free paper by
Bath Press Ltd, Bath, Avon

ISBN 0-19-929094-6   978-0-19-929094-9
ISBN 0-19-929095-4 (Pbk.)   978-0-19-929095-6 (Pbk.)
1 3 5 7 9 10 8 6 4 2

Designed and laid out by Multimedia Design and Production, International Training Centre of the ILO, Turin, Italy

Editorial team

Managing editor and contributor
Nada Merheb

Co-editor and contributor
Sean Loughna

Language editor
Suresh Unny

Statisticians
Tarek Abou Chabake
Bela Hovy

Cartographers
Romain Leonarduzzi
Yvon Orand

Research assistants
Elena Bovay
Anna Tunkel

Produced by UNHCR's Division
of External Relations, under
the direction of
Anne Willem Bijleveld

Main contributing authors:

**Alexander Betts, B.S. Chimni,
Roberta Cohen, Sarah Collinson,
Jeff Crisp, María-Teresa Gil-Bazo,
Iain Hall, Gil Loescher, James Milner,
Anna Schmidt and Elca Stigter.**

Acknowledgements

The editorial team wishes to thank all those who contributed to the preparation of this book. For contributions to boxes: Sara Baschetti, Stephen Castles, Jubin Goodarzi, David Griffiths, Eva-Lotta Hedman, Mercedes Rose Jakupi, Loren B. Landau, Philippe Leclerc, Salvatore Lombardo, Ewen Macleod, Alejandra Martinelli, Eric Morris, Kathleen Newland, Gregor Noll, Susin Park, Paul Spiegel, Astri Suhrke, Elizabeth Tan, John Telford, and the International Organization for Migration (IOM).

For other editorial assistance and support: Ursula Aboubacar, Nadia Abu-Zahra, Geneviève Bador, Hamdi Bukhari, Anita Bundegaard, Beverley Byfield, Sheila Carey, Johan Cels, Nicholas Coussidis, Mohamed Dayri, Bryan Deschamp, Furio De Angelis, Michael Dell'Amico, Eva Demant, Jean-François Durieux, Daniel Endres, Ragnhild Ek, José H. Fischel de Andrade, Madeline Garlick, Ayman Gharaibeh, Hari Gupta, Susan Hopper, Jon Høisæter, Ardi Imseis, Salvatore Ippolito, Françoise Jaccoud, Peter Janssen, Arafat Jamal, Ninette Kelley, Anne Kellner, Anne-Marie Kerrigan-Deriche, Anja Klug, Khalid Koser, Frank Laczko, Brian Lander, Andrew Lawday, Mathijs Le Rutte, Johanna Lewis, Wei-Meng Lim-Kabaa, Karolina Lindholm-Billing, Sajjad Malik, Pablo Mateu, Michael McBride, Jozef Merkx, Emmanuelle Metral, Angelika Montillot, Terry Morel, Ruth Mukwana, Naoko Obi, Grainne O'Hara, Margaret Okole, Christian Oxenboll, Wendy Rappeport, Marc Rapoport, José Riera, Sholeh Safavi-Hemami, Jacob Rasmussen, Micheline Saunders-Gallemand, Yasser Saad, Solange Senaize, Bellings Sikanda, Paul Stromberg, Michael C. Tombs, Michèle Vieille, Alan Vernon, Suporn Vongchompoo, Jean-Noël Wetterwald, Steven Wolfson, Simone Wolken, Wendy Zillich, and the UN Relief and Works Agency for Palestine Refugees in the Near East (UNRWA).

Special thanks to Ruud Lubbers, former United Nations High Commissioner for Refugees, for his guidance during the preparation of this publication, and to Daniela Ionita for her editorial support.

The editorial team also wishes to thank the independent experts and UNHCR staff members who served as advisors.

Independent experts:

Yusuf Bangura, Research Coordinator, UN Research Institute for Social Development, Geneva
Jeff Crisp, Director, Policy and Research, Global Commission on International Migration, Geneva
Otto Hieronymi, Head, International Relations Program, Webster University, Geneva
Gil Loescher, Senior Research Fellow, Centre for International Studies, University of Oxford, Oxford
Irene Khan, Secretary-General, Amnesty International, London
Kathleen Newland, Director, Migration Policy Institute, Washington DC
Daniel Warner, Deputy to the Director for External Relations, Graduate Institute of International Studies, Geneva

UNHCR staff members:

Erika Feller, Director, Department of International Protection
Raymond Hall, Director, Division of Human Resources Management
Marjon Kamara, Director, Bureau for Africa
Ron Redmond, Head, Media Relations and Public Information Service, Division of External Relations
Judith Kumin, Regional Representative, Brussels
Eric Morris, Director and Special Advisor, New York

Contents

Contents

Page   *Page*

Figures

Preface

by the United Nations Secretary-General

It is difficult for anyone who has never been forcibly displaced to imagine what it is like to be a refugee. Yet, to fully respond to the needs of millions of displaced persons worldwide, that is what we must all try to do. Most refugees are ordinary people living extraordinary lives: driven from their homes by fear, conflict and persecution, they have had to give up jobs, possessions, dreams, even families in their struggle to survive. They remain some of the most vulnerable people in our societies. They need assistance and protection. And they need understanding.

For over fifty years the Office of the United Nations High Commissioner for Refugees has been at the forefront of efforts to respond to refugee needs. Today, in 115 countries, including many of the world's most difficult and dangerous places, UNHCR staff assist more than 19 million displaced persons. Most of these are people who desperately want to return home. It falls to the international community to help realize this hope or to enable refugees to start anew elsewhere.

The State of the World's Refugees is extremely timely in highlighting the work necessary to achieve refugee rehabilitation. It presents a detailed study of the plight of refugees the world over. It reviews efforts designed to ensure the safety and basic human rights of millions of displaced people. Above all, it places humanitarian action in its broader political context by examining the effects of increased national security concerns and migratory flows on asylum seekers, refugees and internally displaced persons worldwide.

At the 2005 World Summit, UN Member States directly addressed refugee concerns. They committed themselves to refugee protection and to resolving the plight of displaced persons. They reaffirmed the principles of solidarity and burden-sharing in assisting displaced populations and their host communities. They accepted responsibility, both individually and collectively, to protect populations from genocide, war crimes, ethnic cleansing and crimes against humanity. And they supported the establishment of a Peacebuilding Commission, which—by creating conditions conducive to refugee return and reintegration—promises to significantly enhance humanitarian responses to forced displacement.

The State of the World's Refugees sets forth the stark reality of refugee needs. It is a reality which must now be matched by our World Summit commitments. This book is crucial reading for all who care about the right of every person to live safely, peacefully and without fear in her own home. It serves as a tribute to the selfless dedication of all who work to protect and rehabilitate displaced persons. But foremost, it is a testament to the indomitable courage of the refugees who, in the face of overwhelming odds, somehow find the will to survive and to rebuild their lives.

Kofi A. Annan

Foreword

by the UN High Commissioner for Refugees

The years since the last edition of *The State of the World's Refugees* have witnessed the emergence of a number of trends that have significantly affected refugees and asylum. Since 2000, the number of refugees has fallen steadily, to just over nine million people at the beginning of 2005. This represents the lowest figure in almost a quarter of a century. This is partly due to the fact that in the last five years there were fewer refugee-producing crises and several conflicts came to an end thus allowing refugee return. Among the most significant repatriation movements is that of the four million Afghans who were assisted to return home since 2002.

Inter-state conflict is less prevalent today than internal strife and civil war, resulting in fewer refugee flows but more internal displacement. People who would otherwise seek safety in neighbouring states are more frequently compelled to remain within the borders of their own country, most often in similar conditions as refugees. Two long-running civil conflicts in Africa, the Democratic Republic of Congo and Sudan, accounted for an estimated 7.5 million internally displaced people in 2005.

Another trend has been the declining number of asylum seekers, which at the beginning of 2005 was at its lowest in recent years. Though many factors may contribute to this drop, one apparent cause is the increasingly restrictive measures states have taken to limit access to asylum as they attempt to manage migration and safeguard their security. In the context of the ever growing impact of mixed migration flows, asylum seekers are often using the same illicit channels as illegal migrants, and as a result are denied access to asylum procedures states are obliged to provide under international law.

In the context of the ever growing impact of globalization and mixed migration flows, preserving asylum requires that we be able to identify those in need of protection. In public opinion, there has been a blurring of illegal migration and security problems with asylum and refugee issues. This demonstrates the importance of combating intolerance and challenging the notion that refugees and asylum seekers are the agents of insecurity rather than its victims.

The past few years have also been characterized by efforts on the part of states, NGOs, the UN and other international organizations to respond to the new humanitarian challenges. In the area of refugee protection, UNHCR led several collaborative initiatives aimed at strengthening aspects of the international protection regime, ranging from providing specific aspects of protection to addressing root causes of displacement and policy development on issues not explicitly addressed by the 1951 UN Refugee Convention. Recent years have also seen a revival of efforts to bring an end to the refugee cycle through durable solutions, with special emphasis on bridging the gap between humanitarian and development assistance. Development plays a crucial role in ensuring that peace and economic recovery can take root in a post-conflict situation.

The growing recognition that the United Nations as a whole had to find a better way to protect and assist internally displaced persons led to a stride forward in September 2005, when the Inter-Agency Standing Committee attributed responsibilities in situations of internal displacement to various agencies. UNHCR was tasked to lead the response in the areas of protection, camp coordination and management, and emergency shelter. Addressing internal displacement is indeed an issue where flexible perspectives are needed from the international community as a whole, and UNHCR will be fully engaged in this effort.

This edition of *The State of the World's Refugees* examines these and other important issues in depth. Through critical analysis, it presents an account of key developments since 2000 and their impact on human displacement and the principle of asylum. The book also reviews the challenges states face as they reconcile legitimate national interests with their international legal and humanitarian obligations towards uprooted people. Finally, it assesses the impact of the complex and changing environment in which humanitarian organizations, including UNHCR, operate.

The many challenges to asylum and to humanitarian response require that we think anew. Never before has it been so important to ensure a multilateral dialogue and enhance our response capacity through greater burden and responsibility-sharing.

António Guterres

Introduction[1]

The turn of the Millennium marked the fiftieth anniversary of the creation of the Office of the United Nations High Commissioner for Refugees (UNHCR) and the adoption of the UN Convention relating to the Status of Refugees. The Convention sets out the basic principles on which international refugee protection is built: *non-refoulement*, which emphasizes that refugees should not be returned to any place where they could face persecution; and impartiality, whereby all refugees are provided protection without discrimination. Recently, these principles have come under increasing threat. In a world which has grown increasingly hostile to asylum and refugees, the very relevance of the Convention has been questioned.

Critics of the Convention allege that it is outdated, unworkable, irrelevant and inflexible. They label it a complication in the context of contemporary 'mixed migration'. For their part, many states argue that the Convention does not adequately address either their interests or the actual needs of refugees. Besides such criticisms, the refugee protection regime is being confronted by other developments with the potential to constrain refugee protection. These include states' greater emphasis on the economic costs of offering asylum; concerns about security in the context of the 'global war on terror'; fears regarding complex 'mixed migration' movements; and more restrictive asylum policies.

States that once had generous refugee policies now see the costs of asylum as outweighing its benefits. Admittedly, it was easier to welcome refugees who were culturally similar, fulfilled labour needs, arrived in manageable numbers and reinforced ideological or strategic objectives. With the end of the Cold War, however, many states saw refugees as a burden rather than an asset. Furthermore, since the 11 September 2001 attacks in the United States, state security concerns have come to dominate the migration debate, at times overshadowing the legitimate protection needs of individuals.

As governments have revisited their asylum systems from a security angle, they have instituted more restrictive procedures or substantially modified their policies to similar effect. Many states have broadened grounds for detention, and now focus more strongly on detecting potential security risks when reviewing asylum claims. In some situations, the post-11 September context has been used to extend the scope of exclusionary provisions of the Convention, allowing for refugees to be denied access to status determination procedures. In other cases, refugees have been subject to expulsion. These developments have taken place against a background of greater collaboration between the asylum and immigration authorities and intelligence and law enforcement agencies.

Uzbek refugees at the refugee camp outside the Kyrgyz village of Barash at the Uzbek-Kyrgyz border in May 2005. These refugees fled the military crackdown in Uzbekistan earlier the same month.
(Vyacheslav Oseledko/AFP/Getty Images)

States have serious concerns about 'uncontrolled' migration in today's era of globalization. In the view of governments aiming to minimize migration, asylum is an exemption that allows too many people through. Human smuggling and trafficking complicate the migration landscape; being smuggled to sanctuary has become an important option for asylum seekers, even though it carries a price beyond its financial cost. By resorting to the services of a smuggler, an asylum seeker seriously compromises his or her claim in the eyes of many states. This also leads to an imputation of double criminality: not only do refugees flout national boundaries, they consort with criminal gangs to do so. Therefore, it is argued, their claims must be bogus and measures to restrict their basic rights are justified. Such sentiments have played into the hands of politicians who have ridden the anti-foreigner sentiments that were aggravated by the 11 September attacks. This has fuelled xenophobic attitudes, to the detriment of refugees and asylum seekers.

As concerns about the costs of asylum, state security and 'uncontrolled' migration have led to a reshaping of asylum policies in many countries, two parallel trends have emerged. Both have had a negative impact on access to asylum and the treatment of refugees and asylum seekers. The first is an overly restrictive application of the Convention and its 1967 Protocol, which has led to an increase in detention and exclusion, besides lack of due process. The second is a proliferation of alternative protection mechanisms that guarantee fewer rights than those contained in the Convention. In some states there has been a gradual movement away from a rights-based approach towards more discretionary forms of refugee protection. Such mechanisms have included the notions of 'safe country of origin', 'internal flight alternative', 'effective protection elsewhere' and 'safe third country'.

While recognizing that states have legitimate concerns in the areas of security, uncontrolled migration and the costs of providing asylum, UNHCR has maintained that the fundamental principles of the Convention remain as valid and necessary as ever. It argues that the Convention has legal, political and ethical significance that goes well beyond its specific terms: legal, in that it provides the basic standards on which principled action can be founded; political, in that it provides a truly universal framework within which states can cooperate and share the burden resulting from forced displacement; and ethical, in that it is a unique declaration by states party to the Convention and/or its 1967 Protocol of their commitment to uphold the rights of some of the world's most vulnerable people.

In an attempt to bolster support for the international framework for protection principles and to search for new approaches to enhance protection, in 2001 UNHCR launched the Global Consultations on International Protection. The process aimed to promote a better understanding of protection dilemmas among both the beneficiaries of international protection and its providers. The outcome of the Consultations, which were a two-year process involving governments, NGOs, experts on refugee issues and UNHCR, was the Agenda for Protection. This focused on multilateral co-operation as a means to improve the protection of refugees and asylum seekers around the world.

The Agenda for Protection also comprises the Declaration of States Parties to the 1951 Convention relating to the Status of Refugees and/or its 1967 Protocol, which was adopted at the Ministerial Meeting in December 2001. The Declaration affirmed that the Convention remains the cornerstone of the international protection regime.

Although not a legally binding document, the Agenda for Protection has considerable political weight as it reflects a broad consensus on what can be done to achieve certain goals in refugee protection. Its programme of action identifies specific protection objectives within the context of broader migration movements, security concerns and the search for durable solutions.

The Convention does not suffice to achieve these goals. Rather than revising it, however, action was taken to build upon it through multilateral dialogue and arrangements to improve burden-sharing between countries in the North and South. This involved discussions on how to deal with situations of mass outflow and secondary movements. Some of these discussions gave priority to targeting development assistance in refugees' regions of origin more effectively; others sought multilateral commitments for the resettlement of refugees. These efforts are referred to as the Convention Plus initiative.

The Agenda for Protection does not address all the problems that the international protection regime has had to confront since 2000. Some of these are not new, but have been exacerbated by recent political, economic and social developments. Protracted refugee situations, for instance, have been receiving more attention partly due to the threats to national, regional and international security that they represent. Another area of concern has been the shrinking of humanitarian space as a consequence of violent attacks on humanitarian workers and the growing role of military forces in delivering assistance.

The start of the new century has seen a decline in armed conflict when compared with the 1990s. Consequently, there have been fewer and smaller outflows of refugees. The largest forced displacement emergency in recent years has been in Darfur (Sudan), where violence has driven hundreds of thousands of Sudanese to flee to neighbouring Chad. But a far greater number of people remain internally displaced in Sudan. The situation in Darfur, and others like it, have made the international protection regime pay greater heed to improving its response to situations of internal displacement. It is recognized that this is an area where there have been gaps in coordination, demarcation of responsibility and accountability.

In this regard, UNHCR has been involved in efforts to reinforce the inter-agency Collaborative Approach, which was initiated in the 1990s to offer protection to internally displaced persons and aid integration and development. This approach called for all available agencies to respond within their means and according to their mandates and expertise. To render the Collaborative Approach more effective, in 2005 the Inter-Agency Standing Committee allocated leading roles in specific sectors to various agencies. Based upon its expertise, UNHCR was designated the lead agency in the sectors of protection, camp coordination and management and emergency shelter in situations of internal displacement arising from armed conflict.

Figure 0.1   Total population of concern to UNHCR: by category and by region, *1 January 2005*

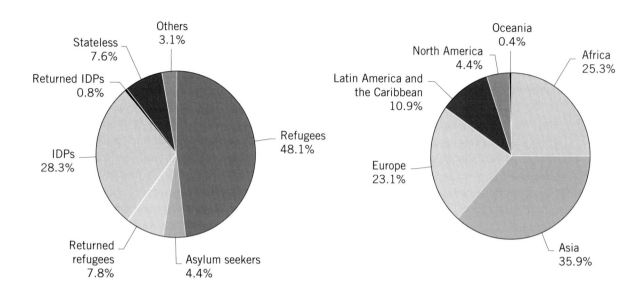

Stateless 7.6%
Others 3.1%
Returned IDPs 0.8%
IDPs 28.3%
Refugees 48.1%
Returned refugees 7.8%
Asylum seekers 4.4%

Oceania 0.4%
North America 4.4%
Latin America and the Caribbean 10.9%
Africa 25.3%
Europe 23.1%
Asia 35.9%

Source: UNHCR.

The State of the World's Refugees: Human Displacement in the New Millennium presents the challenges to refugee protection and assesses the response of the international community. The fifth edition in the series, it provides an overview of key developments related to forced displacement from 2001 to September 2005. The period covers the tenure of Ruud Lubbers as UN High Commissioner for Refugees and the start of António Guterres' term. Produced by UNHCR with input from other international organizations, NGOs, academics and independent experts, the book is divided into eight chapters, each focusing on a particular theme. Besides the main text, boxes in each chapter highlight specific issues.

Chapter 1 examines the growing complexity of population movements. It provides an overview of the current dynamics of forced displacement in the world and the numbers involved. The changing causes of conflict are linked to new patterns of displacement. In an ever more interconnected world, migration has become more complex and the distinctions between categories of migrants blurred. Migrants seeking better economic opportunities and refugees fleeing conflict and human rights abuses are increasingly using the same routes and intermediaries—including people smugglers. Many of them, particularly women and children, fall victim to human trafficking. Displacement induced by environmental degradation, natural and man-made disasters and development policies and projects is also addressed in this chapter.

The book moves on to look at efforts to strengthen international protection through enhanced inter-state cooperation. The Global Consultations on International Protection, the Regional Parliamentary Conference in Africa and the twentieth anniversary meeting of the Cartagena Declaration are some initiatives which have revived the international protection regime. However, as highlighted in Chapter 2, these developments have coincided with state concerns that have led to more restrictive policies which have had a negative impact on asylum seekers and refugees. Indeed, states face considerable challenges as they try to abide by their obligations under international refugee law while also meeting their security needs and improving border control. In this context, Chapter 2 goes on to examine the concepts of 'effective protection' and regional protection. It also looks at proposals on extraterritorial processing—which some perceive as geared more towards burden-shifting than burden-sharing.

The State of the World's Refugees also addresses recent developments related to refugee security. UNHCR and its partners have made the physical safety of refugees a priority, and have become more engaged in security issues. On the other hand, the emergence of new security concerns for states, particularly since the events of 11 September 2001, has led to the 'securitization' of asylum practices. Increasingly refugees and asylum seekers are perceived as harbingers of insecurity, rather than victims of it. In this context, the interdependent nature of the security threats in refugee situations is highlighted, and traditional perceptions of security purely in terms of a state's territorial integrity are linked to new concepts of human security.

Chapter 3 examines the security threats that refugees face and assesses responses to them. Under international law, it remains the state's obligation to ensure the physical protection of all those residing within its borders, including refugees. In reality, states often lack the capacity or the political will to provide such protection. In such cases, ensuring refugee protection necessitates and justifies international intervention at the political and military level. The chapter analyses the impact of state security concerns on refugee security, and also looks at sexual and gender-based violence, xenophobia and the impact of displacement on state and regional stability.

The international emergency response system continues to develop. Improvements have taken place in the areas of planning, human resources, supply stockpiles and early warning systems. Despite this, the response to the displacement crisis in Darfur, for example, was inadequate. This illustrates that gaps remain in the effectiveness of the international emergency response system. Chapter 4 notes that political will, funding levels and security issues determine the effectiveness of any emergency response. Recent developments, including an increase in the number and types of humanitarian actors, the bilateralization of aid and the constriction of humanitarian space have added to the challenges faced by the emergency-response sector.

Chapter 5 draws attention to the problem of protracted refugee situations. The majority of today's refugees continue to live in long-term exile with no prospect of a durable solution. Many of the conflicts that have led to refugee flows over the past 20 years remain unresolved. The chapter examines the factors that contribute to the prolongation of these situations and their implications for the human rights of refugees. Long-standing refugee populations have, in some cases, strained relations between host states and countries of origin. The long-term presence of refugee populations is argued to cause instability in neighbouring countries and trigger intervention and insurgency. In recent years, the problem of protracted refugee situations has been put back on the international agenda. The chapter reviews contemporary efforts to resolve such situations.

Voluntary repatriation, local integration in the country of first asylum or resettlement in a third country reflect the range of options available for the permanent resolution of the 'refugee cycle'. Over the years, the relative priority afforded to each of these durable solutions has changed, and accordingly new approaches to realizing them have been adopted. Chapter 6 discusses renewed efforts targeting development assistance, including the concepts of Development Assistance for Refugees and the 4Rs (Repatriation, Reintegration, Rehabilitation and Reconstruction), as well as the strategic use of resettlement. These initiatives have placed durable solutions within the context of a multilateral dialogue through which UNHCR attempted to strengthen burden and responsibility-sharing. The Zambia Initiative and the Uganda Self-Reliance Strategy are two pilot projects aimed at gearing development assistance towards attaining durable solutions for refugees while addressing state interests.

Like refugees, some internally displaced people are in need of international protection. These include victims of conflict and human rights violations who do not receive protection from their own governments and thus draw international attention to their plight. Chapter 7 examines an important shift in international thinking about the internally displaced. Today, it is widely recognized that people in need of aid and protection in their own countries have claims on the international community when their governments do not fulfil their responsibilities or where there is a breakdown of state authority. International intervention in such circumstances challenges the notion of state sovereignty. The chapter examines recent efforts to strengthen the international response to crises of internal displacement.

Chapter 8, the concluding chapter, brings together recent efforts and initiatives aimed at improving the international community's response to crises of forced displacement. Achievements are gauged and gaps recognized. The challenges ahead are identified. Of these, the first is to ensure that the core principles of international law, in particular that of *non-refoulement*, are adhered to. Another is to see that the burden is shared fairly when addressing the root causes of forced displacement and when responding to it. Finally, it suggests that the supervisory, accountability and partnership mechanisms of UNHCR, the lead organization in the field of human displacement, must be strengthened.

1 Current dynamics of displacement

At the turn of the century, UNHCR and its partners were struggling to cope with the massive population displacements unleashed by the ethnic conflicts that followed the end of the Cold War. No longer restricted to the care and protection of refugees who had crossed international borders, they were now much more widely engaged in the dangerous and uncertain task of trying to assist and protect displaced people *within* their countries of origin—usually in situations of continuing violence and political upheaval. Whether in the Balkans, Iraq, or Rwanda, this trend was accelerated by the greater willingness of powerful states to intervene in areas of strategic importance to them, or where gross human rights violations were taking place. The increasingly restrictive policies of potential asylum states also spurred the change.

These developments compelled UNHCR and its allied agencies to reassess their priorities and capacities. They renewed their efforts to seek durable solutions to displacement crises through better links between humanitarian relief and longer-term development and peace-building efforts. With the majority of new forcibly uprooted populations remaining within their countries of origin, more attention was focused on assisting and protecting the internally displaced.

There has been progress on many fronts: several violent conflicts have ended and large groups of refugees have returned home. But the dynamics of forced displacement remain complicated. Many protracted situations appear intractable. Hundreds of thousands of people continue to be uprooted by war and human rights abuses every year, and usually move within or between the poorest and least stable countries in the world. These people often find themselves in states that lack the capacity, willingness or resources to provide them even a minimal degree of assistance and protection. The efforts of humanitarian agencies to step into the breach are often impeded by dangerous political and security conditions.

This chapter highlights the main trends in forced displacement today. While the focus is on refugees and internally displaced persons uprooted by conflict and human rights abuse, forced displacement does not take place in isolation from other population flows. Millions of people are compelled to move within or out of their countries by a myriad of factors. Some are driven by poverty, fleeing to survive; others are drawn to real or perceived opportunities to better their lives away from home. This chapter also examines the plight of other displaced populations, including victims of trafficking; those involved in 'mixed migration'; and those displaced by natural disasters, environmental degradation and development projects.

A family of refugees returning from Pakistan to Afghanistan on their way to Pul-i-Charki, the main reception centre in Kabul. (UNHCR/N. Behring/2002)

Figure 1.1 Total population of concern to UNHCR by region of asylum and category, *1 January 2005*

Region	Refugees	Asylum seekers	Returned refugees	Others of concern				Total population of concern
				IDPs of concern to UNHCR	Returned IDPs	Stateless	Others	
Africa	3,023,000	207,000	330,000	1,200,000	33,000	120	67,000	4,860,120
Asia	3,471,000	56,000	1,146,000	1,328,000	62,000	724,000	113,000	6,900,000
Europe	2,068,000	270,000	19,000	900,000	51,000	731,000	391,000	4,430,000
Latin America and the Caribbean	36,000	8,000	90	2,000,000	-	-	26,000	2,070,090
Northern America	562,000	291,000	-	-	-	-	-	853,000
Oceania	76,000	6,000	-	-	-	140	-	82,140
Total	**9,236,000**	**838,000**	**1,495,090**	**5,428,000**	**146,000**	**1,455,260**	**597,000**	**19,195,350**

Sources: Governments; UNHCR.

Main trends

International efforts to improve refugee assistance and protection have been aided in recent years by the easing of some of the acute displacement crises that dominated the 1990s. Furthermore, there have been breakthroughs in the resolution of a number of long-running conflicts, allowing many refugees to return to their countries of origin. The global population of refugees of concern to UNHCR has declined in recent years, from nearly 18 million in 1992 to just over 9 million in 2004.[1] This is mainly due to a drop in the number of armed conflicts and several large-scale repatriations. But despite the reduction in the total number of refugees worldwide, the majority of those who remain live without any prospect of a durable solution to their plight. In 2004, there were some 33 situations of protracted refugee exile involving 5.7 million refugees. These figures do not include the millions of displaced Palestinians who come under the mandate of the United Nations Relief and Works Agency for Palestine Refugees in the Near East (UNRWA) (see Box 5.1).

Conflict-induced displacement

The world has witnessed a decline in armed conflict from a peak in the early 1990s.[2] There has also been a dramatic drop in the number of autocratic regimes—and a corresponding reduction in repression and political discrimination against ethnic minorities. The number of 'ethnonational' wars for independence—which dominated the decade following the end of the Cold War—is at its lowest since 1960. Since 2001, 13 major self-determination conflicts have been settled or contained, as against the emergence of six new or renewed campaigns, including Darfur (Sudan). In

Aceh (Indonesia), a protracted, low-intensity conflict that had grown more intense in recent years was defused following a ceasefire and negotiations in the wake of the tsunami of December 2004.

However, the post-11 September 2001 global 'war on terror' has introduced a new dynamic into a number of conflicts and refugee crises around the world, particularly where it has been used to justify new or intensified military offensives. This has been the case in Aceh, Afghanistan, Chechnya (Russian Federation), Georgia, Iraq, Pakistan and Palestine. People forcibly displaced by these conflicts have faced closed borders, extremely hostile and insecure conditions in exile and/or accelerated or involuntary returns due to 'anti-terror' measures in asylum states.

Interstate conflict is not as prevalent today as 'internal' strife and civil war, particularly in Africa.[3] However, foreign involvement in civil wars has continued to frustrate efforts to secure peace and stability in a number of areas—including the Great Lakes region of Africa centred on the Democratic Republic of Congo (DRC) as well as West Africa. Here, economic imperatives and commercial greed are intertwined with social and political grievances, all manipulated by political, commercial and military actors from within and outside the region.

In the DRC, for example, the exploitation of local resources became progressively militarized as a consequence of the conflict. Military groups used force to acquire and maintain control of mines and other natural resources. Forced labour was often used and populations forcibly displaced. Most of the profits from mineral extraction have been siphoned off by external military, political and commercial interests.[4]

Figure 1.2   Total population of concern to UNHCR, 1995-2004

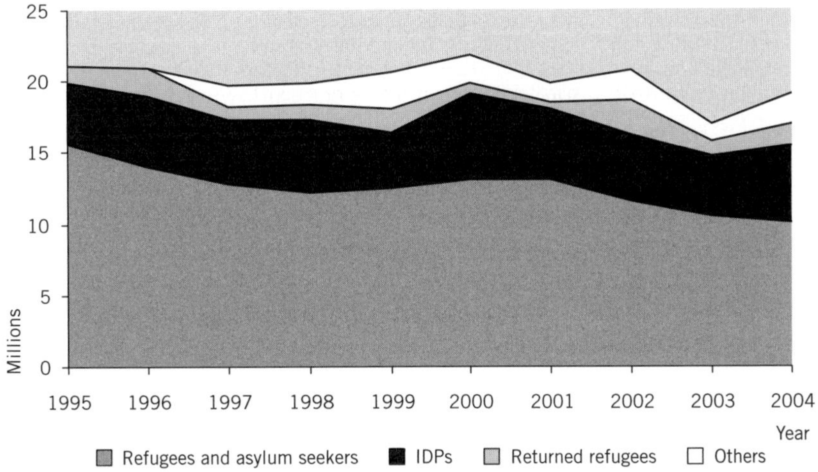

Note: The category 'Others' includes IDPs under UNHCR mandate who have returned to their place of residence during the year, stateless persons, etc. This type of data is not available for 1995-1996. For definition of categories see Annex 2.

All figures as at 31 December of each year.

Source: UNHCR.

Box 1.1

Globalization and migration

Globalization and international migration go hand in hand. As new areas of the world are pushed to forge links with the global economy, they often undergo massive social upheavals. These upheavals frequently lead to migration, which in turn can cause major changes in both sending and receiving areas. Indeed, an essential characteristic of globalization is large-scale flows of goods and services, financial assets, technology and people across international borders. Governments welcome economic flows—especially of finance and trade—but are more ambivalent about the movement of people. Rich economies lay out the welcome mat for highly skilled personnel, but often shut their doors to the less skilled and refugees.

Key trends

The world total of international migrants (defined as people living outside their country of birth for at least a year) grew from about 100 million in 1960 to 175 million in 2000. About half these migrants are women. Most of the increase has taken place in the period of rapid globalization since 1980. Much migration is within regions. North–North migration often involves skilled personnel, while South–South mobility usually sees workers move from areas with high unemployment

to where the jobs are. But migration from the South to the North is growing fast. The number of migrants in developed countries more than doubled in the last two decades of the twentieth century: in 1980 it stood at 48 million; by 2000 it had reached 110 million. In the same period, the number of migrants in developing countries has grown more slowly—from 52 million to 65 million (see Figure 1.3).

Only about 3 per cent of the world's population are migrants, but their concentration in certain regions often puts them at the forefront of social change. By 2000, 63 per cent of the world's migrants were in developed countries, where they made up 8.7 per cent of the total population. The remainder were in developing countries, where they constituted only 1.3 per cent of the total population. According to the latest figures from the Organization for Economic Cooperation and Development, there are 35 million immigrants in the United States, comprising 12.3 per cent of the total population. Western Europe has 32 million (9.7 per cent), Canada 5.7 million (19 per cent) and Australia 4 million (23 per cent). Migrants and their descendants seem to prefer large cities. In Toronto, for example, they comprise 44 per cent of the population. The comparable figure

for Brussels is 29 per cent, while one in four Londoners is a migrant or descendant of one.

How globalization shapes migration

Globalization has increased disparities in income and human security between North and South. Economic liberalization, the entry of multinationals into formerly closed areas of national economies and structural-adjustment policies are all instruments of social transformation. In many parts of the South, industrialization has lessened the value of traditional modes of production, forcing people to move from rural areas to cities. When workers do not find enough work in the cities, overseas migration may be the next step. Weak economies and weak states often go together, so impoverishment and outward migration are closely linked.

Globalization also creates the cultural and technical conditions for mobility. Global media beam idealized images of northern lifestyles into the poorest villages. Electronic communications allow easy access to information on migration routes and work opportunities. Long-distance travel has become cheaper and more accessible. Once migratory flows are established, they generate 'migration networks' in which the first to arrive

Figure 1.3   Stock of international migrants by major area, 1960-2000

Major area	Number of international migrants (millions)					International migrants as percentage of population		Distribution by major area (%)	
	1960	1970	1980	1990	2000	1960	2000	1960	2000
World	75.9	81.5	99.8	154.0	174.9	2.5	2.9	100.0	100.0
Developed countries	32.1	38.3	47.7	89.7	110.3	3.4	8.7	42.3	63.1
Developing countries	43.8	43.2	52.1	64.3	64.6	2.1	1.3	57.7	36.9

Source: United Nations Department of Economic and Social Affairs, *World Economic and Social Survey 2004: International Migration*, New York, United Nations, 2004, Table II.1.

help members of their families or communities who wish to follow.

Facilitating migration has become a major international business involving travel agents, bankers, lawyers and recruiters. Governments try to restrict the illegal side of the migration 'industry'—smuggling and trafficking. Yet the more governments try to control borders, the greater the flows of undocumented migrants appear to be. Governments remain focused on national migration controls, while migrants follow the transnational logic of globalized labour markets.

How migration shapes globalization

International migration is a major force for change. Some observers see it as an instrument for reducing global inequality and enhancing development. However, migration can also have negative effects, such as a 'brain drain' of highly qualified doctors, nurses and computer specialists. Governments of sending countries hope that migration will stimulate development through the money sent home by migrants and the transfer of skills. Indeed, global remittances were estimated at US$130 billion in 2002—considerably more than official development aid. Much of this money goes into consumption, but some is invested in health, education and productive activities. When it comes to the transfer of skills, however, sending countries do not always gain as much as they would like. Many migrants are employed in unskilled jobs and are unable to upgrade their skills. On the other hand, migrants in high-status jobs are unlikely to return to their home countries unless these offer stability, security and growth.

Migration leads to cultural and social change. In areas of origin, returnees may import new ideas that unsettle traditional practices and hierarchies. Receiving areas, on the other hand, are being transformed by unprecedented cultural and religious diversity. The multi-ethnic societies of Europe, North America and Oceania have introduced measures to integrate immigrant populations and to improve inter-group relations. But multicultural policies remain controversial, especially in view of security concerns that have arisen since September 2001. Policies on immigration have become highly restrictive—yet do not seem to have done much to reduce migration.

Migration can be a catalyst for political change in areas of origin, with diasporas supporting movements for democratization. (Diasporas may also provide the funds that fuel armed conflict.) In receiving countries, extremist politicians often depict migrants as threats to local livelihoods and cultural identities. Campaigns against immigrants and asylum seekers have become powerful mobilizing tools for the far right.

Towards international collaboration

The economic issues related to globalization come under the purview of multilateral institutions such as the International Monetary Fund, the World Bank and the World Trade Organization. Migration control, by contrast, has long been seen as a preserve of national sovereignty. As a consequence, the international community has failed to build institutions to ensure orderly migration, maximize the developmental benefits that could flow from it and protect the human rights of migrants. Though elements of an international framework already exist in International Labour Organization (ILO) conventions and the UN Convention on the Rights of Migrant Workers and Members of their Families, relatively few countries have ratified these instruments.

Some regional bodies have sought to cooperate on migration. The European Union has gone furthest by introducing free movement for citizens of its member states, and is working towards common policies on asylum seekers and immigration from outside the union. No other regional body has gone this far.

High-emigration countries are motivated by the need to reduce their labour surpluses and maximize remittances. Immigrant-receiving countries profit from cheap workers, and have been reluctant to take steps which might increase their costs. To safeguard the rights of migrant workers, more countries must implement ILO conventions and link them in a comprehensive framework. In addition, common policies on migration should be seen as an essential part of regional integration, and tied to policies on international cooperation and development.

Bilateral cooperation between states could also bring benefits; migrants could gain through better protection and social security. Emigration countries could benefit from the smoother transfer of remittances and restrictions on agents and recruiters. Immigration countries could gain a more stable and better-trained migrant workforce.

One significant move in this regard was the establishment in late 2003 of the Global Commission on International Migration. Mandated by UN Secretary-General Kofi Annan, the commission launched its report in October 2005. One of its key conclusions is that the international community has failed to realize the full potential of international migration or rise to its significant challenges. It recommends greater policy coherence at the national level, which can in turn result in more effective cooperation both regionally and globally. Besides specific recommendations on a range of issues, the report sets 'principles for action' to help states and other stakeholders formulate a more comprehensive and global response to migration.

The patterns of mobility and displacement in such protracted crises are complex. In many situations of severe instability, including those in Burundi, Colombia, Sri Lanka and northern Uganda, the dominant trend is one of short-term, short-distance, repetitive dislocation rather than large-scale displacement into camps. It is often extremely difficult to distinguish between displaced and non-displaced populations, or to differentiate movement as a coping mechanism from movement that is forced. Millions of people living in countries affected by conflict lack, or risk losing, even the most minimal levels of security, protection and support. Different levels of vulnerability and need affect communities and individuals in different ways, with those displaced not necessarily being the most vulnerable.

In Colombia, irregular armed groups have sought to control segments of the civilian population and prevent them from fleeing to safe areas so as to guarantee a supply of provisions and recruits. Such communities also provide cover for guerrillas, who effectively use them as human shields.[5] Within Afghanistan, non-displaced populations have been among the most vulnerable, with many of their members too weak or poor to flee.[6] In late 2001, Afghanistan had almost four times as many vulnerable non-displaced persons dependent on aid (4,150,000) as internally displaced people (1,200,000). Indeed, there were more vulnerable non-displaced people in the country than there were Afghan refugees abroad (3,695,000).[7]

Despite a decrease in the overall number of conflicts and those displaced across international borders, recent years have seen new refugee movements from lower-profile clashes. These include both new emergencies, such as in Côte d'Ivoire and the Central African Republic, and more protracted ones, including those in Burundi, Chechnya, the DRC, Myanmar, Somalia, and southern Sudan.

In a number of countries new refugee displacements were taking place at the same time as large-scale voluntary repatriations. Some states were generating refugee flows while simultaneously receiving refugees. For example, in 2004 the number of new Somali refugees arriving in Kenya, Tanzania, Yemen, and other countries of asylum outnumbered the 10,300 that returned to Somalia. Meanwhile, the return of 21,000 Liberians from Côte d'Ivoire was counterbalanced by the arrival of nearly 87,000 new Liberian refugees in Côte d'Ivoire, Ghana, Guinea and Sierra Leone. Another 22,200 refugees were displaced into Guinea and Liberia by the conflict in Côte d'Ivoire.[8]

Asylum and resettlement

Asylum applications in the rich industrialized countries have declined substantially. Following exceptionally large asylum flows in the early 1990s due to the conflicts in the former Yugoslavia and political crises in Albania, Armenia, Azerbaijan, Romania and other former Eastern bloc countries, asylum claims rose more gradually in Western Europe during the second half of the 1990s, levelling off at just below 400,000 in 2000.[9] Although some countries have witnessed small increases,[10] since 2001 the overall trend has been downwards. Member states of the European Union received nearly 20 per cent fewer asylum claims in 2004 than in the previous year, and 36 per cent fewer claims than in 2001. Most countries are now reporting their lowest annual

Figure 1.4 Major refugee arrivals in 2004

Origin	Main countries of asylum	
Sudan	Chad	130,000
	Uganda	14,000
	Kenya	2,300
	Other	240
	Total	**146,540**
Dem. Rep. of the Congo	Burundi	21,000
	Rwanda	11,000
	Zambia	4,300
	Uganda	1,600
	Other	260
	Total	**38,160**
Somalia	Yemen	17,000
	Kenya	2,400
	Other	130
	Total	**19,530**
Iraq	Syrian Arab Rep.	12,020
	Total	**12,020**
Côte d'Ivoire	Liberia	5,500
	Mali	460
	Other	10
	Total	**5,970**
Burundi	Rwanda	2,900
	United Rep. of Tanzania	1,100
	Other	190
	Total	**4,190**
Liberia	Sierra Leone	2,400
	Côte d'Ivoire	530
	Guinea	510
	Other	260
	Total	**3,700**
Rwanda	Malawi	410
	Other	140
	Total	**550**
Central African Rep.	Chad	500
	Total	**500**
Russian Federation	Azerbaijan	470
	Total	**470**

Note: This table refers to *prima facie* arrivals only.
Source: UNHCR.

total for several years. The number of applications lodged in Germany was 30 per cent lower in 2004 than in 2003, and the United Kingdom saw a drop of 33 per cent in 2004 when compared to the year before. New asylum claims fell by 26 per cent in North America and 28 per cent in Australia and New Zealand during the same period.[11]

Figure 1.5   Main origins of refugees, *1 January 2005*

Origin	Main countries of asylum*	
Afghanistan	Pakistan**	960,000
	Islamic Rep. of Iran	953,000
	Germany	39,000
	Netherlands	26,000
	United Kingdom	23,000
Sudan	Chad	225,000
	Uganda	215,000
	Ethiopia	91,000
	Kenya	68,000
	Dem. Rep. of the Congo	45,000
Burundi	United Rep. of Tanzania	444,000
	Dem. Rep. of the Congo	19,000
	Rwanda	4,700
	South Africa	2,100
	Canada	1,900
Dem. Rep. of the Congo	United Rep. of Tanzania	153,000
	Zambia	66,000
	Congo	59,000
	Burundi	48,000
	Rwanda	45,000
Somalia	Kenya	154,000
	Yemen	64,000
	United Kingdom	37,000
	United States	31,000
	Djibouti	17,000

Origin	Main countries of asylum*	
Palestinians***	Saudi Arabia	240,000
	Egypt	70,000
	Iraq	23,000
	Libyan Arab Jamahiriya	8,900
	Algeria	4,000
Viet Nam	China	299,000
	Germany	21,000
	United States	12,000
	France	9,100
	Switzerland	2,200
Liberia	Guinea	127,000
	Côte d'Ivoire	70,000
	Sierra Leone	65,000
	Ghana	41,000
	United States	20,000
Iraq	Islamic Rep. of Iran	93,000
	Germany	68,000
	Netherlands	28,000
	United Kingdom	23,000
	Sweden	22,000
Azerbaijan	Armenia	235,000
	Germany	9,200
	United States	2,600
	Netherlands	1,600
	France	680

* This table includes UNHCR estimates for refugees in industrialized countries on the basis of recent resettlement arrivals and recognition of asylum seekers.

** UNHCR figures for Pakistan only include Afghan refugees living in camps. According to a 2005 government census, the latest estimates available, there were an additional 1.9 million Afghans living in urban areas in Pakistan, some of whom may be refugees.

*** Palestinians under UNHCR mandate only.

Sources: Governments; UNHCR.

Most asylum seekers came from countries affected by conflict or widespread human rights abuses or both, such as Afghanistan, China, Colombia, the DRC, Georgia, Haiti, Iraq, Nigeria, the Russian Federation, Serbia and Montenegro, Somalia and Turkey.[12] Among the factors influencing the decision of individuals to apply for asylum in particular countries are historic, linguistic or cultural ties between states of origin and destination, settled immigrant communities in the destination country and migrant networks.[13]

The precise reasons for the fall in asylum application rates are unclear. Restrictive policies introduced by the destination countries since the early 1990s are certainly a significant factor, although it is difficult to attribute direct causal relationships between policies and outcomes. Direct pre-entry measures—such as carrier sanctions and visa requirements—might have had a greater impact on the number of asylum claims than indirect measures such as status-determination policies, recognition rates, detention and the withdrawal of welfare benefits. The political and economic situation in the home country is probably more significant than the characteristics of the receiving state; the movement of asylum seekers appears to be driven principally by protracted instability and conflict in regions of origin.[14]

Accordingly, a key factor in the recent drop in asylum claims in Western Europe seems to be the absence of emergencies on the region's borders. Another is shifts in the dynamics of some of the major refugee crises that had previously given rise to large asylum flows into the region. The number of Afghan asylum seekers arriving in Europe declined by 83 per cent between 2001 and 2004, while that of Iraqi asylum seekers declined by 80 per cent between 2002 and 2004.[15]

Refugee resettlement is far more susceptible to policy shifts than 'spontaneous' asylum flows because it is much more directly controlled by governments and humanitarian agencies, both in countries of first asylum and final destination. In the United States, for instance, new security controls introduced after the events of 11 September 2001 caused a sudden drop in the number of refugees resettled there in 2002, down to 26,800 from 65,400 in 2001.[16] But a subsequent reinvigoration of the resettlement programme led to the admission of twice that number in 2003 and in 2004.[17]

Against the backdrop of an increasing number of protracted refugee situations and growing resistance to unregulated asylum flows, recent years have seen new interest in refugee resettlement. Overall numbers remain low, however, with only some 55,500 persons admitted for resettlement to the ten main resettlement countries in 2003.[18]

Internally displaced people and other 'persons of concern'

In 2004, there were more than 17.5 million people in the broader category of 'persons of concern' to UNHCR, including internally displaced persons, returned refugees and 'stateless persons', in addition to refugees and asylum seekers.[19] This figure, though down from a peak of 27.4 million in 1994,[20] only encompasses a small minority of the world's internally displaced persons as it is restricted to those receiving assistance or protection from UNHCR.

While nearly 5.6 million internally displaced persons were 'of concern' to UNHCR in 2004, the total number of internally displaced persons worldwide was estimated at 25 million[21]—more than twice the number of recognized refugees (see Chapter 7 for a discussion of issues concerning the internally displaced). The preponderance within populations uprooted by violence and human rights abuse of the internally displaced is reflected in Sudan's Darfur region. Here, internally displaced persons—thought to number at least 1.6 million in 2004—far outnumber the 200,000 or so Sudanese who fled to neighbouring Chad.[22]

The estimated number of internally displaced people worldwide has remained more or less unchanged in recent years, with the figures for those returning home (approximately 3 million in 2004) nearly matching the numbers for new internally displaced populations.[23]

The apparently exponential increase in the number of internally displaced persons over the past two decades—from a little over a million in 1982 to at least 25 million today—is due to a number of factors. First, there has been growing international recognition of internally displaced persons as a group. Second, many potential asylum states have been restricting entry across their borders. Another key factor behind the increase is the nature of many intra-state conflicts today, where civilians are frequently targeted by warring groups. Most such wars of the past decade—including those in Bosnia and Herzegovina, Chechnya, Kosovo, Myanmar, Rwanda, and Sudan—have involved the deliberate displacement of populations.

Repatriation

In the past five years, long-standing conflicts have been brought to an end and human rights conditions have improved in a number of countries. These changes have provided new opportunities for the rebuilding of war-torn societies and the return of refugees and other displaced populations. The largest returns of recent years include the repatriation of more than 3.4 million refugees to Afghanistan and the return of over a million refugees and internally displaced persons to Bosnia and Herzegovina.[24]

In Africa, meanwhile, talks between the Sudanese government and the rebel Sudan Peoples Liberation Movement have triggered the spontaneous return home of nearly

Figure 1.6   Repatriation of refugees by region of origin, 1980-2004

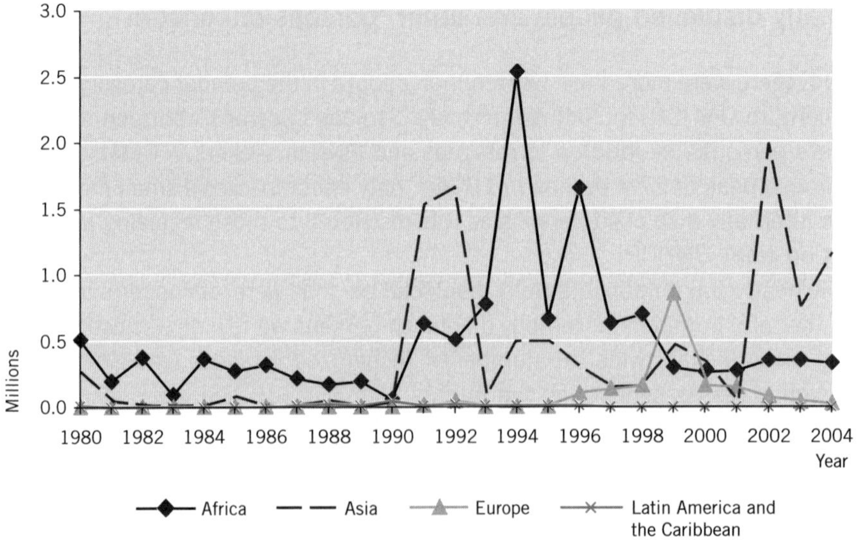

Source: UNHCR.

half a million refugees and internally displaced people in southern Sudan.[25] At least 300,000 refugees and 4 million internally displaced people have returned to their homes in Angola since the signing of the Luena Peace Accord in April 2002. And by the end of 2004, more than a quarter of a million refugees had returned to Sierra Leone.[26] Worldwide, more than 5 million refugees returned home between 2002 and 2004, including nearly 1.5 million in 2004.[27]

The cessation of hostilities often prompts the large-scale repatriation of displaced populations. But the security implications are often similar in scale to those posed by the initial exodus. Countries struggling to regain their footing in the immediate aftermath of conflict generally do not possess the capacity to absorb large returnee populations. Indeed, states emerging from internal armed conflicts are frequently characterized by deep social divisions, chronic instability, damaged infrastructure and hollowed-out economies. Even where large-scale repatriation programmes and other durable solutions have been successful, the situation could be reversed at any time by political instability and economic stagnation in areas that have suffered massive forced displacement. The reality for most refugees is a return to areas of persistent insecurity and poverty where longer-term development initiatives are patchy or, in some cases, non-existent.[28]

Uncertainty remains about the sustainability of large-scale returns of refugees and internally displaced persons, with the repatriation and reintegration period often proving the most difficult and dangerous. Returnees may face renewed violence, human rights abuse or extreme poverty, leading to further displacement in their search for safety or a viable livelihood. Indeed, security is a key factor in the success and safety of refugee returns. The necessary security and protection guarantees are least likely to be in place where returns are coerced or accelerated by 'push' factors in the asylum country, rather than by the 'pull' of peace and security in the country of origin. This has been the case for many Burundians returning from Tanzania and many Afghans returning from Iran.[29]

Repatriation is the beginning of a long process of reintegration that entails re-establishing ties with home communities and restoring normal and productive lives. It is a major challenge that can be as traumatic and difficult as the life of exile left behind. If returnees are not provided with adequate support and are not able to reintegrate, they may choose to flee again. This has been demonstrated time and again in regions such as West Africa, where chronic instability has hindered many repatriated refugees' efforts to reintegrate.

For instance, the return of Sierra Leonean refugees from Guinea in 2000 and Liberia in 2001, prompted by hostilities in the areas where they had sought asylum, has been likened to an emergency evacuation rather than an organized repatriation movement. Added to this, a review by UNHCR of the repatriation of Sierra Leonean refugees notes that the weak socio-economic structure in the country is not conducive to a rapid reintegration process.[30] Rather it is expected to be a lengthy and protracted one, highly dependent on the long-term commitments of the government and donors and the active engagement of humanitarian and development actors.

In Iraq, many refugees and internally displaced persons who returned in 2004 subsequently suffered renewed internal displacement due to limited local-absorption capacities and continuing conflict. In West Africa, UNHCR has expressed concern about the sustainability of returns due to continuing instability in the region. In Afghanistan, returnees have faced localized violence, persistent drought in some areas and lack of employment, basic social services and housing. Many have consequently headed for Kabul and other urban centres where security and livelihood opportunities are perceived to be better.[31]

Reflecting the importance of UNHCR's work in repatriation in recent years, the UN High Commissioner for Refugees has sometimes been referred to as the 'High Commissioner for Returnees'. Recognizing the challenges facing returnees in post-conflict situations, the organization and its partners are searching for balanced and integrated approaches to make returns durable. War-torn communities cannot absorb large numbers of returnees without first improving their capacity to meet the basic needs of citizens. As such, international development agencies must invest in reconstruction and reintegration programmes for local communities in areas of return as well as for returning refugees and internally displaced people.

Characteristics of refugee populations

Age and gender

Humanitarian actors and donors are becoming increasingly sensitive to the particular assistance and protection needs of different groups within displaced and returning populations. Programmes now target the specific needs of women, children and adolescents, older refugees and particular ethnic or social groups. According to 2003 demographic data relating to about 7.5 million persons of concern to UNHCR, children and adolescents under the age of 18 account for nearly half this number, with 13 per cent of these children under the age of five. This reflects high fertility rates and low life expectancy in many poor countries with high levels of forced displacement, particularly in Africa.[32]

The large number of young people among displaced populations has important implications for protection. Displaced children and adolescents are particularly vulnerable to threats to their safety and wellbeing. These include separation from families, sexual exploitation, HIV/AIDS infection, forced labour or slavery, abuse and violence, forcible recruitment into armed groups, trafficking, lack of access to education and basic assistance, detention and denial of access to asylum or family-reunification procedures. Unaccompanied children are at greatest risk, since they lack the protection, physical care and emotional support provided by the family.[33] Those accompanied by only one parent or carer may also be at higher risk than other children.

The vast majority of the world's refugee children seek sanctuary in poor countries. The proportion of children (under 18 years of age) among populations of concern was

Box 1.2

Displacement and natural disasters: the 2004 tsunami

The Tsunami Disaster of 26 December 2004 destroyed lives and coastal communities across the Indian Ocean. Minutes after an earthquake measuring 9.0 on the Richter scale occurred off the west coast of northern Sumatra in Indonesia, the first large tsunami hit nearby shores with devastating effect. It struck especially hard between the towns of Banda Aceh and Meulaboh in the province of Aceh. Triggered by the same earthquake, a massive upward shift in the seabed also caused tsunamis to strike coastal communities in parts of eastern India, Malaysia, the Maldives, south-western Myanmar, Sri Lanka and Thailand before reaching the coast of Africa. The damage to life and property was terrible: some 290,000 people were dead or missing, and more than 1 million displaced across 12 countries in the Indian Ocean. A third of the victims were children.

News of the disaster—which left some 5 million people in immediate need of assistance—sparked an extraordinary mobilization of resources. Governments, private citizens and corporations and NGOs in the affected countries and beyond were quick to respond with offers of money, supplies and manpower. The International Federation of Red Cross and Red Crescent Societies (IFRC) alone reportedly received US$2.2 billion. The United Nations estimated that some US$6.8 billion was pledged towards post-tsunami relief and recovery, with US$5.8 billion coming from government sources and the rest from corporate and private donations.

The international machinery for the coordination and delivery of relief in complex humanitarian emergencies was revved up. A report to the UN's Economic and Social Council noted that 16 UN agencies, 18 IFRC response teams, more than 160 international NGOs and many private and civil-society groups were involved in delivering emergency relief. The large number of organizations involved posed tremendous challenges for the UN's Office for the Coordination of Humanitarian Affairs. In some areas

the sheer scale of the destruction posed formidable logistical difficulties. In many cases, relief operations were undertaken, at least in part, by national or foreign military forces using their own transport and equipment. Thirty-five different armed forces were involved in the relief effort, and in Indonesia and Sri Lanka the UN Joint Logistics Centre assisted in the coordination of military support.

Unsurprisingly, relief efforts had to be tailored to different situations in the affected countries, each with its own pre-tsunami political and socio-economic conditions. In the Maldives, where some 5–10 per cent of the population was initially displaced, the limited presence of UN organizations or international NGOs in the country prior to the tsunami presented challenges for those seeking to mobilize international assistance. In Somalia, where the greatest destruction to life and property occurred in Puntland, a self-declared autonomous region, the lack of a central government complicated relief efforts. The importance of military-strategic considerations in some of the worst affected areas, most notably Aceh, the northern and eastern provinces of Sri Lanka and to some extent in the Andaman and Nicobar Islands of India added another dimension to the emergency response.

While disaster relief is not part of its mandate, UNHCR joined in the emergency response to the tsunami. The sheer scale of the destruction and the fact that many of affected populations were of concern to the organization prompted the move. Responding to requests from the UN Secretary-General and UN Country Teams, UNHCR concentrated on providing shelter and non-food relief. In Sri Lanka, UNHCR's presence in the country prior to the tsunami allowed for a comparatively swift and sustained humanitarian intervention—including efforts focused on the protection of internally displaced persons. In Somalia, where some 290 people died and some 54,000 were displaced by the disaster, UNHCR and the United Nations Human

Settlements Programme were primarily responsible for coordinating the provision of shelter and non-food relief. The UN's Children's Fund and the World Food Programme coordinated much of the other emergency assistance.

In Aceh, UNHCR established temporary field locations in the provincial capital, Banda Aceh, and three other hard-hit towns on the west coast. It withdrew from the province on 25 March 2005, the official expiry date for the emergency phase as declared by the Government of Indonesia. (UNHCR has since been invited to return to assist the Indonesian Government in the rehabilitation of the province, as outlined in a memorandum of understanding signed in June 2005.)

A range of protection concerns were identified in the aftermath of the tsunami, including access to assistance, enforced relocation, sexual and gender-based violence, safe and voluntary return, loss of documentation and restitution of property. The tsunami response also underlined weaknesses in the areas of shelter, water and sanitation and camp management. Problems of coordination among NGOs, and between NGOs and UN agencies, pointed to the need to strengthen local and regional capacities.

The protection of displaced populations was especially urgent in areas of protracted conflict and internal displacement in Aceh, Somalia and Sri Lanka. Furthermore, there was concern for some affected populations whose governments declined offers of international aid, such as the Dalits (formerly known as untouchables) of India and Burmese migrant workers in Thailand; it was feared they might be discriminated against and their protection needs compromised. In short, the broad range of challenges across a dozen countries in the aftermath of the tsunami underlined the importance of effectively protecting affected populations and defining the obligations of local and national governments—as set out in the UN's Guiding Principles on Internal Displacement.

54 per cent in Africa, 46 per cent in Asia, but only 25 per cent in Europe.[34] The low number of refugee children reaching industrialized countries may be partly the result of age-selective asylum migration,[35] including the 'secondary' movements of asylum seekers from poor refugee-hosting regions to richer countries.

The 2003 demographic data indicate a relatively equal gender balance in most regions hosting large displaced populations. It hovers around 50 per cent across most of the world, and only falls significantly below this level (to 41 per cent) in North America, Latin America and the Caribbean,[36] where young male asylum seekers constitute a higher proportion of those of concern to UNHCR. Where, as is the case in Africa, half of the refugee population consists of females and half are children and adolescents, roughly a quarter of the refugee population is composed of girls under 18. Meanwhile, roughly a quarter of refugees and internally displaced persons worldwide are women of reproductive age, and around one in five is likely to be pregnant.[37]

These statistics have important implications for protection policies, since women and girls are the principal targets of sexual and gender-based violence and exploitation, and are therefore disproportionately vulnerable to associated risks such as trafficking, HIV/AIDS transmission and abduction. In the DRC, a surge in HIV/AIDS infection among the general population, including those displaced internally, has been linked to extensive sexual violence by paramilitary groups and foreign troops.[38] With less access to information and education than non-displaced people, many of the displaced have very little knowledge of how HIV/AIDS is contracted or avoided.[39]

Camps and settlements

The highly varied conditions of exile for different displaced populations have equally diverse implications for their access to protection and assistance, and for their prospects for local integration, return or resettlement. In protracted refugee situations, many of the displaced have remained confined to refugee camps, sometimes for decades. They are marginalized in the country of asylum, unable to return home in safety, and cannot look forward to resettlement elsewhere. In some situations, those located in camps lack many fundamental rights—such as freedom of movement and the right to work—due to their forced exclusion from mainstream society. They are often exposed to high levels of violence and human rights abuse because of poor security within or around the camps.

According to UNHCR's 2003 demographic data, of the 13.1 million displaced persons of concern to the organization, some 36 per cent were located in camps or centres, 15 per cent were living in urban areas, and 49 per cent were either dispersed in rural areas or living in an unknown type of settlement.[40] In Africa, almost half the people of concern to UNHCR are in camps, as compared to less than a quarter in Asia.

However, these figures do not capture the overall situation of displaced populations, since they exclude internally displaced people who are not assisted by UNHCR and incalculable numbers of 'self-settled' refugees worldwide. Many internally displaced persons and self-settled refugees are in countries where the

Box 1.3

Protection for victims of trafficking

The perception of trafficking as a human rights violation, rather than a security issue, has gained prominence in recent years. This has been accompanied by the recognition that trafficked persons should not be seen as offenders, but rather as victims in need of protection and assistance. Along with prevention and prosecution of traffickers, the protection of those victimized by trafficking has become part of a three-pronged approach to the larger fight against trafficking in persons. The 2000 UN Protocol to Prevent, Suppress and Punish Trafficking in Persons, especially Women and Children, recognizes this and includes provisions for the protection of victims.

It is widely accepted that it is extremely difficult to obtain reliable data on the scope and magnitude of people-trafficking. However, the 2004 *Trafficking in Persons Report* of the US Department of State estimates that each year 600,000 men, women and children are trafficked across international borders. Other estimates of international organizations and NGOs put the number much higher. Asylum seekers and refugees have been identified as populations vulnerable to trafficking.

Just like asylum seekers and refugees, trafficked persons are often in need of protection. Many victims are afraid to return home for fear of retribution from their traffickers, are deeply traumatized by their experience and in need of medical and psychological support. Effective prosecution of traffickers relies, for now, on the cooperation of those trafficked, but providing evidence can put the victim in danger of reprisals. Increasingly, for those countries that have no specific legislation for the protection of trafficked persons, it has been suggested that victims be offered asylum, though it should be emphasized that this should only be used as a last resort for trafficking victims.

Protection programmes have developed substantially over the past decade, and many states now offer victims protected-status visas if they are afraid to return home. Protection of trafficking victims requires that they are identified quickly, and not automatically charged as criminals and/or deported. While asylum systems rely on claimants being aware of their rights, the majority of trafficked persons are unaware that they might be entitled to protection—a fact exploited by traffickers. Proactive identification of trafficking victims by law enforcement and immigration authorities is vital, but the similarity of some trafficking scenarios to smuggling and illegal employment makes this a difficult task. As a result, many countries have created screening processes, established referral mechanisms and trained police and social workers to spot possible trafficking cases.

Though swift action can be critical when prosecuting traffickers, the trauma of the trafficking experience can leave victims unfit to assess their own interest. Some countries, such as Belgium, Germany, Italy and the Netherlands offer victims a short reflection period. They are provided with medical attention, safe shelter, legal advice and time to consider the options available to them. This method offers essential breathing space and may ultimately lead to improved cooperation with the authorities.

Many trafficking victims want to return home immediately. For those who wish to stay, few states offer permanent-residence status. An exception is the United States' T-visa, which allows certain victims of trafficking to remain and, after three years in 'T' status, to apply for permanent residency. But there is a limit to the number of such visas that may be issued each year. More common is a short-term residence permit. While in some countries this permit is renewable, eligibility for renewal is usually linked to criminal proceedings against the trafficker.

In the majority of countries where residence permits are available, they are conditional upon the victim's ability and willingness to cooperate with authorities. This puts pressure on a victim afraid to return to his or her country of origin, and can create mistrust between the victim and the authorities. Regardless of whether they cooperate or not, victims need medical, psychological and social support. However, many of the assistance programmes available in destination countries are tied to cooperation with criminal investigations.

Italy provides a model for effective protection of trafficked persons. Temporary residence permits are offered to all victims, regardless of whether they cooperate or not. The six-month permit is renewed for the victims who cooperate, are deemed to be at risk, attending an education programme or employed when the permit expires. Victims can access social services and find jobs, and are required to attend social-assistance and reintegration programmes run by local organizations. It is important to note that encouraging victims to testify—rather than putting pressure on them to do so—has not adversely affected prosecution of traffickers.

Given that there are few channels for permanent settlement in destination countries, the vast majority of victims return home eventually. As a result, countries of origin (in cooperation with NGOs and bodies such as the International Organization for Migration) have begun to develop support programmes for victims who return home.

Avoiding conditionality between protection schemes and counter-trafficking investigations, and offering social assistance at home as well as in host countries, give victims a real choice as to how they rebuild their lives. Trafficking is a modern form of slavery. Freedom to choose is thus a vital element of rehabilitation for victims of trafficking.

government is either indifferent or actively hostile to their assistance and protection needs. In at least 13 countries in recent years, including Myanmar, Sudan and Zimbabwe, state forces or government-backed militia have attacked displaced and other civilian populations.[41]

'Mixed migration', trafficking and smuggling

The combination of poverty, marginalization and politically induced displacement is critical in explaining the high levels of mixed migration in every part of the world. The phenomenon covers migrant workers uprooted by sudden changes in economic or political conditions in the country where they are working. It also includes internally displaced persons, refugees and other forced migrants moving on after their initial displacement to seek better protection and livelihood opportunities in other countries or regions. The number of international migrants in 2005 has been estimated at about 175 million,[42] of which asylum seekers and refugees constitute only a small part. The rapid growth of such migration has been attributed to the advances in communications and transportation brought about by globalization.

Modern migratory patterns make it increasingly difficult to distinguish between the various groups on the move. Population flows are not homogeneous but of a mixed, composite character. The immediate causes of forced displacement may be identified as serious human rights violations or armed conflict. But these causes often overlap with, or may themselves be provoked or aggravated by, economic marginalization and poverty, environmental degradation, population pressure and poor governance.

Asylum seekers and refugees may use the same modes of travel as undocumented migrants and resort to, or be exploited by, smugglers and traffickers. In some cases, refugees may use these channels to leave one country of asylum and move to another to escape insecurity or economic hardship. On the other hand, persons who do not qualify for international protection may resort to claiming asylum in the hope of being allowed to stay abroad.

The motives behind the secondary movement of many forcibly displaced persons and 'voluntary' migrants are numerous, and cannot be easily categorized. For example, initial displacement may lead subsequently to 'secondary' migration or displacement as part of individuals' or households' coping and livelihood strategies. In Afghanistan, for instance, complex transnational patterns of displacement and migration have become an essential feature of coping mechanisms in a harsh and insecure environment, with many families seeking to enhance economic opportunities through the migration of family members.[43]

One of the most important supports for many refugees and internally displaced persons in protracted displacement crises is money sent to them by family members living abroad. A recent report on Liberian refugees in Ghana notes how, with the assistance they receive from UNHCR dwindling, remittances have proved crucial to their survival.[44] Indeed, the importance of remittances should not be underestimated;

not only do they sustain many displaced populations, they also support—and thus possibly prevent the displacement of—many communities living in protracted crisis situations.

In Colombia, decades of conflict have forced the movement of millions of people, with many heading from rural to urban areas to seek both protection and better economic opportunities. Once settled in towns and cities, they may be difficult to differentiate from the wider populations of the urban poor.[45]

Migrant workers may become vulnerable to forced displacement when there are sudden changes in local political or economic conditions, or where they are employed in the informal sector and lack legal status or effective protection from the state in their country of residence. For instance, the situation of Burmese workers in Thailand was particularly insecure following the tsunami in December 2004. In Côte d'Ivoire, where migrant workers constitute 30 per cent of the population, Burkinabe, Guinean and Malian workers within refugee populations have been displaced by the recent conflict, triggering large-scale returns to their countries of origin.[46]

The poorest and most marginalized people are particularly vulnerable to abduction, forced military recruitment and trafficking. This vulnerability is heightened in situations of displacement and armed conflict, where people are separated from their homes, families, communities and livelihoods.

There is now growing evidence of large-scale trafficking of persons within and between every continent by organized criminal networks. The evidence suggests that such trafficking is highly diverse and varied in terms of routes and destinations. Some of it takes place within countries—as when women and children are forced away from rural areas into domestic work or prostitution in urban centres—and some takes place internationally, across regions and continents.

Children and young women are disproportionately affected by international trafficking, since much of it is linked to the sex industry. Such trafficking is also often associated with severe physical and mental abuse and exploitation. Displaced people are also more vulnerable to trafficking due to their relative poverty and separation from homes, families, communities and livelihoods—with displaced children and women especially at risk.

Although some of the same criminal networks might be involved, the smuggling of migrants and asylum seekers is a separate phenomenon from trafficking. People-smuggling is primarily concerned with enabling individuals to evade controls at borders where legal entry would be difficult or impossible. Although smugglers provide a clandestine service sometimes used by both forced and voluntary migrants, smuggling is not a form of forced migration *per se*. Many asylum seekers now use smuggling networks to try and enter industrialized countries, since the introduction of visa restrictions and other controls makes it difficult for them to do so any other way. While many succeed, unknown numbers perish as a result of unsafe conditions, such as unseaworthy or overloaded boats.

Box 1.4

Prevention and reduction of statelessness

Estimates of the number of stateless persons in the world vary between 9 and 11 million. The 1954 UN Convention relating to the Status of Stateless Persons is the international instrument which defines a stateless person and sets out his or her rights and obligations. UNHCR has a specific mandate relating to the prevention and reduction of statelessness and the protection of stateless persons, as specified by the UN General Assembly in 1974 and 1976. That mandate has been expanded by resolutions of the General Assembly and UNHCR's Executive Committee. In February 1996 the General Assembly requested UNHCR to actively promote accession to the 1954 Convention and the 1961 Convention on the Reduction of Statelessness. The Assembly also directed UNHCR to help interested countries prepare nationality legislation and called upon states to adopt such laws to reduce statelessness. However, despite UNHCR's efforts only 57 states have ratified the 1954 Convention.

Activities contributing to resolving statelessness

In its search for durable solutions for the displaced, UNHCR has helped determine the nationality status of many stateless refugees, particularly in the context of voluntary repatriation programmes or implementation of the refugee cessation clause. (In the latter, refugee status is withdrawn when there is no longer any recognized need for international protection.) For some refugee groups such as Black Mauritanians, or Feili Kurds from Iraq, arbitrary deprivation of nationality had been the main reason they have been recognized as refugees. The implementation of reintegration programmes in Mauritania and voluntary repatriation programmes in Iraq guaranteed refugees' right to recover nationality upon return.

More generally, UNHCR tries to ensure that in repatriation agreements between countries of asylum and countries of origin, children born in

the former are considered nationals of the latter. These provisions complement the efforts of UNHCR and countries of asylum to ensure the systematic registration of births of refugee children. Such a registration system has been implemented for the enormous Afghan refugee populations in Pakistan and Iran. But in other situations, even when the reasons which forced refugees to flee their home countries come to an end and the cessation clause is envisaged, refugees who have developed strong ties with the country of asylum are allowed and helped to apply for citizenship.

For instance, many stateless refugees who did not opt for voluntary repatriation to Tajikistan were granted nationality by Kyrgyzstan and Turkmenistan in 2004 and 2005. The Government of Kyrgyzstan has been granting citizenship to Tajik refugees since 2000, and more than 5,000 Tajiks have become citizens. Similarly, presidential decrees adopted in 2005 granted Turkmenistan citizenship to 13,245 people, most of them stateless refugees who fled Tajikistan during that country's 1992–97 civil war.

Other situations involving stateless refugees have not progressed as well. Muslims from northern Rakhine State in Myanmar who have returned home have not been able to gain citizenship and remain stateless. Similarly, many refugees from Bhutan who were deprived of citizenship languish in camps in Nepal and foresee little chance of returning home or reacquiring their citizenship.

Prevention of statelessness

When states consider enacting or revising citizenship legislation—or administrative procedures related to citizenship—UNHCR tries to provide legal and technical advice to help prevent statelessness. In the last five years, the organization has provided advice to many states, in particular in Central and Eastern Europe, but also to Armenia, Bosnia and Herzegovina, Cyprus, the Democratic Republic of Congo, The former

Yugoslav Republic of Macedonia, Georgia, Iraq, Mexico, Montenegro, Serbia, Timor Leste, Turkmenistan and Viet Nam, among others.

In addition to the 1961 UN Convention on the Reduction of Statelessness, there are regional instruments which further contribute to the prevention, reduction and elimination of statelessness. One is the 1997 European Convention on Nationality. There is also a draft protocol on the avoidance of statelessness in relation to state succession which should be adopted by the Council of Europe and open for ratification by the beginning of 2006. The protocol was drafted in an effort to avoid statelessness through state succession, which may occur as a result of a transfer of territory from one state to another, unification of states, dissolution of a state, or separation of part or parts of a territory.

Elaborating on the convention's general principles on nationality, the draft protocol contains specific rules on nationality in cases of state succession. Its 21 articles provide practical guidance on such issues as the responsibilities of the successor and predecessor states, rules of proof, the avoidance of statelessness at birth, and the easing of acquisition of nationality by stateless persons.

Finding solutions to protracted situations

In October 2004, taking into account the findings of the first global survey on statelessness conducted by UNHCR, the organization's Executive Committee requested it to continue to provide technical and operational support to states and to pay more attention to situations involving protracted statelessness. The challenges before UNHCR are many, and include trying to end situations of protracted statelessness which leave millions without effective citizenship. It will have to give priority to situations where the stateless live in extreme poverty but must also address those in which the stateless enjoy almost all the rights of citizens.

Some long-standing situations of statelessness have recently ended due to the political will of the states concerned and the assistance of UNHCR and national or local NGOs. Some examples:

- In Sri Lanka, 190,000 stateless persons acquired citizenship in 2004 on the basis of the 'Grant of Citizenship to Persons of Indian Origin Act', unanimously approved by Parliament in October 2003. This benefited persons who during British colonial rule were brought from India to work on Sri Lanka's tea and coffee plantations. UNHCR and the Sri Lankan authorities designed an information campaign to ensure that stateless persons could apply for citizenship in a fair and transparent manner, and without long or complicated administrative procedures.

- In Ukraine, a new legal framework allowed acquisition of citizenship by the formerly deported Crimean Tatars and their descendants. Between October 2004 and the end of March 2005, more than 2,800 returnees from Uzbekistan were able to acquire Ukrainian citizenship under the favourable provisions of a new citizenship law. The number of Crimean Tatars who still need to obtain Ukrainian citizenship has reached a record low; hundreds of thousands of

them were able to acquire citizenship in the last decade.

- In The former Yugoslav Republic of Macedonia, amendments to a citizenship law adopted in 2004 allowed long-term residents to regularize their citizenship status. The Ministry of Interior, in cooperation with UNHCR and the Organization for Security and Cooperation in Europe, organized a campaign to disseminate information on the procedures for residents to regularize their citizenship status. The campaign included dissemination of brochures and TV spots in the languages of the Albanian and Roma populations considered most at risk of statelessness.

In other areas of the world too there was some progress on issues of statelessness. In Estonia and Latvia, every year more of the large population of permanent residents rendered stateless by the collapse of the Soviet Union apply for naturalization and gain citizenship. In addition, children born to stateless parents are granted Estonian or Latvian nationality through a simple declaration. In the Russian Federation, as well as in most other members of the Commonwealth of Independent States, citizenship legislation and bilateral dual-citizenship treaties are dealing with the consequences of the dissolution

of the Soviet Union. One exception: despite many interventions at the federal and local level, the situation of the Meskhetians of Krasnodar has not been settled. Most of the 17,000 members of this community in Russia have not gained citizenship and the majority are being resettled in the United States.

In the Democratic Republic of Congo, a new citizenship law enacted in November 2004 provides the legal basis to solve the nationality status of the Banyarwanda population. In December 2003, Ethiopia enacted a new citizenship law which should allow many ethnic Eritreans living in the country to reacquire the nationality they were deprived of in the late 1990s.

Despite these improvements, many protracted situations of statelessness remain, leaving millions of persons disenfranchised and with few rights. Some of these communities are the Biharis in Bangladesh; the Bidoons in Kuwait, the United Arab Emirates, Iraq and Saudi Arabia; some Kurds in Syria; and the Muslim populations of Myanmar, in particular those residing in or originating from northern Rakhine State. Thailand and many other Asian countries such as Brunei, Cambodia, Malaysia and Viet Nam also host populations with undetermined nationality. All are part of UNHCR's casebook for the coming years.

Environmental and natural disasters

This broad category includes millions of people displaced directly or indirectly by environmental degradation and natural or man-made disasters. The rise in the number of victims of natural disasters over the past decade and ever-greater levels of displacement caused by development projects have added millions to the number of forcibly displaced people in the world. According to the International Federation of the Red Cross and Red Crescent Societies, the total number of people affected by natural disasters has tripled over the past decade to 2 billion people, with the accumulated impact of natural disasters resulting in an average of 211 million people directly affected each year.[47] This is approximately five times the number of people thought to have been affected by conflict over the past decade.

It is increasingly recognized that the recent escalation in the numbers of those affected by disasters is due more to rising vulnerability to hazards than to an increase in the frequency of hazards *per se.* However, it is recognized that climate change may be playing a part in intensifying the number and severity of natural hazards.[48]

In many ecological and economic crises, mobility and migration represent crucial survival strategies. It can therefore be very difficult to distinguish between forced disaster-induced displacement and mobility linked to people's coping mechanisms. Sometimes, restrictions on mobility are a major factor in the development of famine, as was seen when Eritrea's borders with Kenya and Sudan were closed.

Displaced populations and other migrants are often disproportionately vulnerable to disasters because their normal livelihoods have already been disrupted or destroyed, or because their presence has contributed to environmental degradation in their areas of refuge. Where disasters occur in conflict zones, the destruction of infrastructure and lack of state services can seriously hamper the provision of relief and recovery assistance.

The tsunami of December 2004 exemplified the interaction between politics and the impact of natural disasters. In the Indonesian province of Aceh, conflict, violence and a massive counter-insurgency campaign by the Indonesian military against separatist rebels had displaced more than 300,000 people since 1999. A further half-million or so Acehnese—12 per cent of the population—were displaced by the tsunami. Relief efforts were complicated by the fluid and complex displacement that resulted from the combination of political causes and the immediate devastation of the tsunami.[49]

'Self-settled' refugees and internally displaced persons living in urban areas are often highly vulnerable to the impact of natural disasters; many live in informal and unsafe settlements where they have no legal entitlement to their homes and are not served by any risk-reduction measures. But all those displaced by disasters have specific needs, including access to assistance, protection from violence, and the restoration of their livelihoods. The UN's Guiding Principles on Internal Displacement suggest that those uprooted by natural or man-made disasters are entitled to protection and assistance. However, this does not apply to those displaced by development policies and projects.

Development-induced displacement

The World Bank has estimated that forcible 'development-induced displacement and resettlement' (DIDR)—including the forced movement of people to make way for large infrastructure projects such as dams, urban developments and irrigation canals—now affects an average of 10 million people per year. India is thought to have the largest number of people displaced by such projects, at least 33 million. It is calculated that for every large dam (of which there are 3,300 in India) around 44,000 people are displaced.[50]

As with disaster-induced displacement, there is often a link to political factors, since the most impoverished and marginalized ethnic groups often bear the brunt of the dislocation caused by development projects. For example, in India, Adivasis (tribal people) account for 40–50 per cent of communities affected by DIDR, though they constitute only 8 per cent of the country's population.[51]

Growing awareness of the problem in the 1980s led the World Bank to attach conditions to its loans designed to ensure compensation and appropriate resettlement for displaced communities.[52] While the major donors now generally impose such conditions, they are difficult to enforce[53] and the compensation is often inadequate. As a consequence, the result for those displaced is often dispossession of land and resources, violation of their human rights and a lowering of living standards.[54]

There are many more people displaced by development projects than there are refugees. But unlike refugees, the millions displaced by development do not have an adequate protection regime. They often face permanent poverty and end up socially and politically marginalized.[55] Many of them drift into urban slums, or become part of floating populations which may spill over into international migration.[56]

Looking ahead

The return of millions of refugees and internally displaced persons to their homes following years of exile, the recent reduction in asylum flows to industrialized countries and the fall in overall refugee numbers worldwide represent a shift in the dynamics of forced displacement. Especially when compared to the mass refugee crises of the 1990s, the picture is undoubtedly a positive one for the large numbers of people who now have the chance to return home and rebuild their lives.

Yet the recent reduction in refugee numbers does not indicate a significant decline in forced displacement *per se*. While progress has been made towards solving a number of major conflicts around the world, many protracted conflicts continue to prevent millions of refugees from returning home. Peace, where achieved, is almost always uncertain. Violence and abuse continue to cause displacement and suffering, with many of those affected unable to seek or find effective protection.

Most forced displacement—whether caused by human rights abuses, natural disasters or development projects, or in the form of trafficking or abduction—takes place in poor countries, and has the greatest impact on the poorest and most vulnerable people in those societies. In some countries, entire populations are caught up in a pernicious cycle of extreme poverty and violence in which displacement and mobility have become part of complex coping and survival mechanisms. The efforts of humanitarian actors and the wider international community to mitigate such conditions have proved entirely inadequate.

Addressing the human rights abuses, development failures and conflicts that force so many millions to leave their homes remains an immense challenge. A better understanding of the local and global factors behind forced displacement and greater respect for the rights of uprooted populations is essential if prevention and protection efforts are to be effective. Also needed is greater cooperation between the many political, humanitarian and development actors concerned. Ultimately, the success of global efforts to reduce poverty and achieve the Millennium Development Goals will depend on the success of the international response to the crisis of forced displacement.

2 Safeguarding asylum

The notion of asylum is a remarkably constant feature of human history. Throughout the ages and in every part of the world, societies with very different cultures and value systems have recognized that they have an obligation to provide safety and support to strangers in distress. In the twentieth century, this longstanding social convention was progressively incorporated into international law, culminating in the establishment of the 1951 Refugee Convention relating to the Status of Refugees and its 1967 Protocol. These statutes set out the rights and obligations pertaining to people who have been obliged to leave their own country and are in need of international protection because of a 'well-founded fear of persecution' on account of their 'race, religion, nationality, membership of a particular social group or political opinion.'

By the second half of 2005, no fewer than 146 of the 191 member states of the United Nations had acceded to these international instruments, which, under the terms of its mandate, are promoted and supervised by UNHCR. Many countries have also recognized their obligations towards refugees by becoming parties to relevant regional agreements, including the Organisation of African Unity's (OAU) 1969 Convention governing the Specific Aspects of Refugee Problems in Africa; the 1984 Cartagena Declaration on Refugees in Latin America; and a variety of European agreements (see Box 2.1).

While the principles of asylum may be firmly established in normative, legal and institutional terms, their practical application remains imperfect. Indeed, recent years have witnessed a growing degree of 'asylum fatigue' in many parts of the world, a process that has threatened and in many cases undermined the protection that the 1951 UN Refugee Convention was intended to provide to refugees and asylum seekers.

In developing countries, where more than two thirds of the world's refugees are to be found, states which are struggling (and often failing) to meet the needs of their own citizens express growing concern about the pressures placed on them by the prolonged presence of large populations of refugees. Confronted with weak economies, inadequate infrastructures, environmental degradation and the HIV/AIDS pandemic, many of these countries believe that they receive inadequate support from the world's more prosperous nations in their efforts to assume responsibility for so many refugees.

Governments and local communities in the developing world also point out that the presence of refugees exposes them to security threats such as cross-border attacks, besides placing undue burdens on their administrative structures. In too many cases, moreover, national and local politicians have sought to mobilize electoral support by promoting xenophobic sentiments, exaggerating the negative impact of hosting

Asylum seekers in Pavshyno detention center near Mukachevo in Ukraine, close to the border with Hungary, Poland, and Romania. Asylum seekers arriving in Ukraine originate mainly from Afghanistan, Bangladesh, India, Iraq and the Russian Federation (UNHCR/L. Taylor/2004).

refugees and ignoring the fact that refugees can actually attract international assistance and investment to an area, creating new jobs and trading opportunities.

In industrialized states, the challenge to refugee protection derives primarily from the arrival of asylum seekers from poorer regions of the world. While the number of such asylum seekers has diminished significantly in recent years, and while the majority originate from countries that are affected by armed conflict and political violence, governments and electorates in the developed world tend to perceive these new arrivals in very negative terms. They are seen as people who submit 'bogus' claims to refugee status, threaten the sovereignty of the state by entering it in an illegal manner and force governments to spend large amounts of money on asylum and welfare systems. Furthermore, these arrivals are widely believed to put unacceptable pressure on scarce resources such as jobs, housing, education and healthcare. Finally, it is a commonly held perception that even if their application for refugee status is rejected, most asylum seekers will remain illegally in the country.

During the past decade, and more specifically since the 11 September 2001 attacks in the United States, the problem of asylum fatigue in both developing countries and industrialized states has been exacerbated by a growing concern that foreign nationals and members of ethnic minorities represent a potential threat to national security and public safety. As a result, asylum seekers and refugees have come under a growing degree of public suspicion and are subject to increasingly

Figure 2.1   Number of states party to the 1951 UN Refugee Convention and the 1967 Protocol, 1950-2005

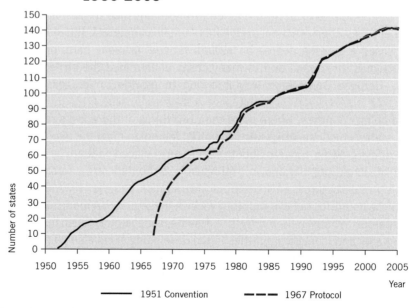

Note: As at 20 May 2005.
Source: UNHCR.

rigorous state controls. In a context where governments and electorates are unable to draw a clear distinction between the victims of persecution and the perpetrators of terrorist violence, there is an evident need to safeguard the principle of asylum. This chapter examines a number of areas in which refugee protection must be strengthened, while Chapter 3 looks at issues specifically associated with the physical safety and security of refugees.

Challenges to protection

States have consistently reaffirmed their commitment to refugee protection. However, there remain a number of gaps, mostly arising from long-standing problems such as violations of the principle of *non-refoulement*; lack of admission and access to asylum procedures; detention practices that violate international standards; lack of registration and documentation; and shortcomings in refugee status determination procedures.

Refoulement and border closures

At the very heart of the international asylum and refugee protection regime is the right of people whose lives and liberty are at risk to seek safety and security in another state. This principle underpins the notion of *non-refoulement*, which protects people from being returned to the frontiers of a country where they would be placed at risk on account of their race, religion, nationality, membership of a particular social group or political opinion. This principle is now recognized as a component of customary international law and is therefore considered binding on all states, including those that are not signatories to the 1951 UN Refugee Convention.

Despite the well-established nature of this principle, recent years have seen many instances in which asylum seekers have been rejected at borders or forcibly removed to countries where their safety cannot be assured.[1] In 2001, for example, thousands of Afghans fleeing the bombing of their country found that the borders of neighbouring states, which had hosted millions of Afghan refugees for over two decades, were closed.[2] Some refugees were eventually able to find their way across an international border, primarily to Pakistan. But thousands of others had no alternative but to remain in camps in the unstable border area.

In 2002, in the Great Lakes Region of Africa, tens of thousands of refugees from the Democratic Republic of Congo were returned to their country of origin under conditions that were far from secure.[3] In 2003, several hundred refugees fleeing renewed fighting in the Indonesian province of Aceh were removed from neighbouring Malaysia on the grounds that they were illegal migrants.[4] In the same year, South America witnessed a number of efforts to remove Colombian refugees from countries where they enjoyed temporary protection.[5]

Box 2.1

Towards a common European asylum system

The first phase in establishing a common European asylum system is almost complete. The 1997 Treaty of Amsterdam set the legal framework. It prescribed legally binding instruments for refugee protection and set minimum standards in a number of areas. The purpose was to harmonize national asylum systems. A 1999 European Council meeting in Tampere, Finland, set the political agenda to inform this legislative process. European Union member states agreed at the highest levels to work towards a common asylum system. They confirmed that the system should be based on absolute respect for the right to seek asylum and full application of the 1951 UN Refugee Convention.

The first phase—Instruments on minimum standards adopted

The deadline for adoption of the first legally binding instruments was set for five years after entry into force of the Treaty of Amsterdam, a period which expired at the end of April 2004. This deadline coincided with the enlargement of the European Union on 1 May 2005, when 10 new states joined as members. The legislation sets minimum standards for a European Union-wide temporary-protection regime; reception conditions for asylum seekers; and eligibility criteria for those given the status of refugees and others in need of international protection. Political agreement has been reached on minimum standards for procedures to determine or withdraw refugee status, though this is pending final

consultations with the European Parliament.

Regulations have been established to determine which state would be responsible for examining an asylum application lodged in a European Union member state by a third-country national—the so-called Dublin II Regulation—and a fingerprints database has been set up. A European Refugee Fund and other financial instruments supporting European Union asylum systems and initiatives have been established. Migration legislation adopted in this period also contains provisions relevant to asylum including *inter alia,* the directive on family reunification and migration control measures, such as carriers' sanctions and measures against trafficking and smuggling.

In principle, European asylum legislation is applicable to all member states of the Union. However, the United Kingdom and Ireland have only acceded to specific instruments, while Denmark has opted out of all asylum-related mechanisms.

The outcome of the first phase is mixed. The adopted legislation reflects some best practice in refugee protection, such as recognition of persecution by non-state actors. It also grants subsidiary protection status to individuals who do not fall within the definition of refugees in the 1951 UN Refugee Convention but are protected against removal by international human rights law. Furthermore, the legislation obliges

member states to provide a minimum standard of support to asylum seekers during the determination procedure, including healthcare, accommodation and other benefits.

However, member states found it particularly difficult to agree on procedures to determine just who should qualify for international protection and what rights they should enjoy. Most member states sought to maintain their existing asylum systems, as well as accommodate the conflicting interests arising in the post-11 September climate. The result often was agreement at the level of the lowest common denominator.

In this context, the European Union's draft Asylum Procedures Directive has been severely criticised by the European Parliament, NGOs and UNHCR for falling short of international standards in refugee and human rights law and best practice. Indeed, questions have been raised about their ability to set a framework which could lead to a common European asylum system.

The 1951 UN Refugee Convention and the 1950 European Convention for the Protection of Human Rights and Fundamental Freedoms are considered part of the *acquis* to which all European Union members should conform. The Charter of Fundamental Rights of the European Union of 2000, although not yet legally binding, also enshrines the right to asylum and the prohibition of both the collective expulsion of aliens and *refoulement.*

Restrictions on access

Large-scale *refoulement* and border closure are generally associated with developing countries affected by rapid and large-scale refugee influxes. Governments in such countries often do not have the capacity to establish more sophisticated forms of control over the presence of foreign nationals on their territory. In the industrialized world, where asylum seekers tend to arrive in smaller numbers and over longer periods of time, states have a broader array of measures to obstruct or deter the arrival of people seeking international protection.

The second phase—The Hague Programme

The elements of the second phase of a common European asylum system were prescribed in the Hague Council in November 2004. The Hague Programme, a plan to develop the European Union into an area of freedom, security and justice, sets out a political agenda for the development of asylum law and policy. It reiterates that the common asylum system should be based on absolute respect for the right to seek asylum.

An extensive evaluation by the European Commission of the instruments related to asylum is expected by 2007. Still, the way in which the instruments are being transposed in at least some member states seems to confirm the fears of UNHCR and others that the agreed minimum standards may become a maximum to be achieved. Given the extensive and severe criticism encountered in relation to at least some of the legislation, future progress may depend on the courts, in particular the European Court of Justice.

Following adoption by the Hague Council of the Directive on Family Reunification, the European Parliament brought an action against the Council before the European Court of Justice in December 2003. It claimed that fundamental rights had been breached by the directive. It is conceivable that the European Parliament may do the same in relation to other instruments in future. Questions and cases may be directed towards the court from national institutions as well.

The stated aim of the second phase is the establishment of a common asylum procedure and a uniform status for those granted protection, based on the full and inclusive application of the 1951 UN Refugee Convention and other relevant treaties. The second-phase instruments are to be adopted by 2010, after evaluation by 2007 of the legal instruments adopted in the first phase. The establishment of appropriate structures involving the national asylum services of the member states would facilitate cooperation. While separate national asylum systems may be maintained, the Hague Programme also calls for a study on the possibility of joint processing of asylum applications within the Union.

The draft Constitutional Treaty for Europe should provide the legal basis for the development of the common European asylum system. The Charter of Fundamental Rights would also be incorporated, making its standards binding on European Union member states. It will, however, remain to be seen what happens to the draft Constitutional Treaty following its rejection in France and the Netherlands.

Cooperation with third countries

While steps are taken towards completing the European Union asylum system, cooperation on asylum and migration matters with third countries has become a high priority. The Hague Programme acknowledges the need for the European Union to contribute in a spirit of shared responsibility to a more accessible, equitable and effective international protection system in partnership with third countries. Regional protection programmes, resettlement, return standards and readmission policies are to be strengthened in the coming years. Readmission agreements, maritime border controls and capacity-building in regions of origin and transit are current priorities of the Union in the field of asylum and migration. In this context—and more controversially—the Hague Programme also seeks to look at the implications of processing of asylum applications outside the European Union.

The interest in protection in regions of origin could serve to make additional resources available to countries that are carrying particularly heavy burdens in hosting refugees. In addition, there has been increasing interest in resettlement as a durable solution and tool for international protection, which is a positive development when not seen as a substitute for the grant of protection to spontaneous arrivals. However, in view of the challenges it faces in developing its asylum system, Europe will have to show that its cooperation with third countries is based on burden-sharing, not burden-shifting, and that it is able and willing to establish a common European asylum system that is in line with international standards and best practice.

Passport and visa requirements are a primary case in point. Many refugees leave their home countries suddenly, without the opportunity to secure the documents they need to travel and enter another country. Others escape from countries that are in such a state of conflict and upheaval that such travel documents are impossible to secure. Even those with valid passports are frequently unable to secure the visa needed to enter an asylum country, since visas are not generally issued for protection reasons and may even be denied if it is thought that the applicant intends to seek asylum when she or he has reached the country concerned. Asylum seekers may consequently resort to the use of false or altered documents and engage the services of professional smugglers in order to make their escape. Significantly, the 1951 UN Refugee Convention recognizes the necessity of such actions, stating that a person who is in need of international protection shall not be penalized for unlawful entry to another country.[6]

Passport and visa requirements are by no means the only method employed to obstruct or limit access to potential countries of asylum. During the past two decades, many countries have imposed sanctions on airlines and other international carriers that transport improperly documented travellers, a strategy that has obliged the carriers to instigate their own checks and controls. A number of industrialized states have also deployed their immigration officials to foreign airports, primarily in countries known to produce significant numbers of asylum seekers and irregular migrants.

In their efforts to identify and apprehend individuals who are travelling without the requisite documents, states are exercising their legitimate and sovereign rights to control their borders, safeguard national security and ensure public safety. In an era of international terrorism, it is entirely understandable that politicians and the public should place such concerns at the top of their agenda.[7] Nonetheless, there is a need to recognize that the measures employed to protect national sovereignty and security can be very blunt instruments, preventing people who are in need of protection from gaining access to the territory and asylum procedures of another state. In some cases,

Figure 2.2   Asylum applications submitted in industrialized countries, 1990-2004

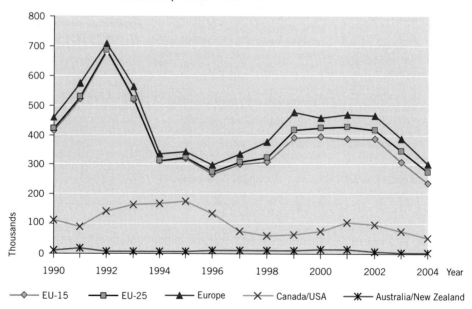

Note: EU-15 refers to member states of the EU prior to 1 May 2004; EU-25 refers to member states of the EU as of 1 May 2004. Europe includes EU-25, Bulgaria, Iceland, Liechtenstein, Norway, Romania, Switzerland and Turkey.

Source: Governments; UNHCR.

the outcome of such measures is that people are refused admission and are removed to a country where their security is placed in jeopardy, thereby violating the principle of *non-refoulement*.

Denial of access to a potential country of asylum can also occur as a consequence of the 'safe third country' concept, whereby asylum seekers are refused admission to a state's territory and/or asylum procedures if they have arrived from a country that is considered to be safe or where they could have submitted an application for refugee status.[8] At first sight, this concept does not seem an unreasonable one, in the sense that it appears to prioritize the availability of protection over the asylum seeker's choice of destination. But in practice its application raises serious concerns, especially if the asylum seeker is not provided an opportunity to rebut the presumption of safety in the country from which she or he has arrived, and if that country is unable to consider the asylum seeker's claim to refugee status in a manner that is consistent with international protection standards.

While some states provide exceptions to the application of the safe third country concept, and do not invoke it when the asylum seeker has family members in the third country or when the person concerned is an unaccompanied minor, these exceptions are not the norm. Indeed, some countries have designated all of their neighbours as 'safe countries' for the purpose of asylum applications. This means that any asylum seeker who arrives by land is considered ineligible to submit a claim to refugee status and is liable to summary rejection and return at the border.

In the past five years, a number of governments and politicians in the industrialized states have suggested that it might be possible to prevent asylum seekers from gaining access to their territory, without at the same time denying them access to an asylum procedure and, if they are found to be in need of it, international protection. The favoured means of achieving these objectives is to be found in the notion of 'offshore' or 'extraterritorial processing', whereby certain categories of asylum seeker are removed from the territory of the state in which they have arrived and are transferred to a facility in another country or region pending an assessment of their claim to refugee status.[9] A more detailed analysis of such proposals and their implications for asylum and refugee protection is provided in Box 2.2.

Such policies and measures have compelled many asylum seekers to resort to people smugglers and to enter a country illegally or under a different pretext and claim asylum once they get in. Some asylum seekers who have entered illegally refrain from claiming asylum in an attempt to avoid deportation or restrictions being imposed on them, and instead choose to live as undocumented workers.[10]

Interception

Arrivals by sea have become common in the Caribbean, the South Pacific and the Mediterranean, directing attention to the issue of interception and rescue at sea. The arrival of asylum seekers by boats brings into question states' obligations towards refugees, freedom of navigation and the control of coastal borders.[11]

Box 2.2

Outsourcing refugee protection: extraterritorial processing and the future of the refugee regime

Are affluent states about to outsource refugee protection to low-cost, no-frills countries? Some observers would affirm that this is already happening, with the deflection policies of the North leaving the South with a disproportionate share of the protection burden. The recent European debate on processing asylum claims in regions of origin or transit indicates that a radical change to the asylum regime is looming.

In 2003, the governments of Denmark, the Netherlands and the United Kingdom engaged in a review of asylum policies which culminated in a 'New Vision for Refugees'. Its central tenet was that certain classes of asylum seekers would be removed to centres outside Europe or at its fringes. This initiative effectively imported the so-called 'Pacific Solution' of the Australian Government into the European context. The Pacific Solution entailed the transfer of asylum seekers to, and the processing of their asylum claims in, third countries in the Pacific.

The European proposals

The United Kingdom's paper entitled New International Approaches to Asylum Processing and Protection, circulated in early 2003, was the core document in the European debate on the issue. Essentially, it consisted of four elements:

1. The creation of 'regional protection areas' (RPAs) to improve protection in the region. UNHCR would be responsible for providing 'protection and humanitarian support' to refugees, and would have to ensure that the prohibition of inhuman treatment in Article 3 of the European Convention on Human Rights was not contravened. This meant safeguarding asylum seekers from threats within RPAs as well as removing such threats.

2. The return of spontaneous arrivals in the United Kingdom or cooperating countries to an RPA. This would discourage 'economic immigrants using asylum applications as a migration route into third countries' and bring down the number of applications in the United Kingdom (provided the RPAs had sufficient geographical coverage).

3. International recognition of the need to intervene to reduce flows of genuine refugees and enable refugees to return home. Options in this regard ranged from assistance to countries of origin to military intervention.

4. An assumption that the main way in which refugees would move to a third country would be through RPAs, where managed resettlement schemes would add some options for onward movement. 'Although not all refugees would be accepted for resettlement, this would enable countries who currently accept asylum seekers to share the refugee burden but in a managed way'. Refugees who did not gain a resettlement place would be helped to integrate locally in their region of origin.

In its subsequent deliberations at the international level, the United Kingdom introduced an important distinction between RPAs in the region of origin and Transit Processing Centres closer to the external borders of the European Union.

Shortly after the United Kingdom informed its partners about its new vision, UNHCR attempted to take the lead in the evolving debate by presenting a three-pronged model to deal with the issue. The three prongs encompassed solutions in the region, improved domestic asylum procedures and the processing of manifestly unfounded cases in European Union-operated detention centres within the Union's borders.

They were met with little enthusiasm by European governments.

While Denmark, the Netherlands, Italy and Spain were outspoken supporters of the idea, a number of member states, including Sweden, Germany and France, were clearly opposed. By mid-2003 it had emerged that the United Kingdom could not muster enough support for a radical reformulation of the protection system.

Nonetheless, a number of experimental pilot projects with a regional protection component were launched in collaboration with the European Union, interested member states and UNHCR. In 2004, the German government changed its earlier stance for an appropriation of its idea. Later that same year Italy deported boat arrivals from the island of Lampedusa to Libya, which is not a signatory to the 1951 UN Refugee Convention. It seemed as if a crude version of the British government's 'vision' was being implemented, with Italy taking the lead. 'Outsourcing' had clearly grasped the imagination of the European Commission, which decided to sketch plans for 'Regional Protection Programmes'. However, unlike the United Kingdom's plan, the programmes would include the transformation of third countries to safe ones.

The barbed wire conundrum

What, then, is the problem with 'regional protection areas' or 'transit processing centres'? Essentially, it is the necessity for barbed wire. An RPA or processing centre must offer human rights protection on a level roughly equivalent to that within the European Union. This would be necessary to satisfy European courts that removal to such centres is in accordance with human rights and refugee law. Then, barbed wire is needed to keep out the local population of the country where the centre is located. On the other hand, if an RPA or processing centre offers human rights protection below the European Union level its migrant inhabitants will continue their efforts to reach the Union. Barbed wire would be needed to keep them in.

Can extraterritorial processing offer an effective response to human smuggling? Not as long as such processing is based on the use of force rather than on convincing migrants that states offer better alternatives than smugglers. Confined to a camp or transit centre, asylum seekers are expected to swap the right not to be *refouled* for the privilege of a place in the resettlement queue. Some will see this as their only chance in circumventing the camps and trying to access the informal labour markets in the North. Refugees and other migrants will be at least as desperate to use the services of smugglers under a camp regime as they are today. We can reasonably assume that they will move to destination states in the same numbers as before, but perhaps abstain from filing an asylum application.

Processing in camps: the legal issues

Processing in camps raises intricate legal and practical issues. The most pressing one is about state responsibility: which state will bear the legal responsibility for offshore processing? Will it be the territorial state where the processing camp is located? Or the state financing and removing asylum seekers there? Or will it be both? The right answer will depend on a number of factors, and presumes the existence of a precise blueprint of how the processing camps are to work. Yet this much is clear: under Article 1 of the European Convention on Human Rights, states cannot evade legal responsibility for their actions abroad.

Then again, will the asylum seeker understand this? And if so, will there be access to a lawyer at the camp?

Will that lawyer be able to work the human rights mechanism of another continent? The answer in all three cases is: not likely. European governments might dilute their responsibility further by employing international organizations and private enterprise as operative partners. Media will find it difficult to access camps and follow their operation, which will remove the fate of its inhabitants from television screens and newspapers. In effect, judicial monitoring and public awareness will be significantly reduced.

Which groups of asylum seekers should be removed for processing in camps? This question reveals a grave dilemma. To move almost all processing and much of the protection work outside European Union territory and to deter spontaneous arrivals, a large majority of such arrivals would need to be targeted for removal. However, to deliver on international legal obligations, persons to be removed after screening would need to be very carefully screened in accordance with their protection needs, thus undermining the objectives of volume, speed in processing and deterrent effect. Either the scheme will hardly make a difference in terms of migration control, or it will violate international law by exposing individuals and groups to discriminatory treatment.

What safeguards are applicable at the removal stage? First, it will be necessary to operate screening procedures before removing asylum seekers to an offshore processing camp. In cases where removal would arguably amount to a violation of rights and freedoms under the European Convention on Human Rights, some form of legal remedy is indispensable.

What are the protection standards to be applied in the processing camps? The minimum elements of physical safety and shelter are necessary, yet insufficient from the perspective of

international law if the individual needs of persons reallocated to such camps are not taken into account. Invariably, there must be an element of legal protection. In the 2000 case of *T.I. vs. The United Kingdom* before the European Court of Human Rights, the respondent government argued that the applicant was safe in Germany, among other things because the country was party to the European Convention on Human Rights. Any violation of its Article 3 by German authorities, it was averred, could be brought before the Strasbourg judges again. The same logic would apply to the return from the United Kingdom or another contracting state to an offshore processing camp. There must be an effective legal remedy to avert violations of human rights.

Finally, consider a situation where a refugee in a processing camp finds that all resettlement quotas are exhausted, local integration is unavailable and voluntary repatriation inconceivable due to persistent risks in the country of origin. Such a refugee would be confined to indefinite detention, which would fly in the face of international refugee and human rights law.

Interception at sea represents one of the most direct means whereby states seek to prevent asylum seekers from gaining access to their territory and domestic asylum procedures. This approach came to particular prominence in the second half of 2001, when a number of boats carrying asylum seekers were intercepted as they approached Australia. Controversially, the occupants of these boats were not allowed to land on Australian territory but, in the context of an 'extraterritorial processing' initiative which became known as the Pacific Solution, were transferred to other countries (Indonesia, Nauru and Papua New Guinea) where their claims to refugee status were examined (see Box 2.3).

Interception at sea has assumed a variety of different forms and has been practiced in a number of regions. During the Indochinese exodus of the 1970s and 1980s, boats carrying asylum seekers from Viet Nam and Cambodia were routinely apprehended and towed out to the sea by Southeast Asian countries of first asylum. For many years the US Coast Guard has intercepted ships carrying asylum seekers and unauthorized migrants, primarily from Cuba and Haiti. When permitted, access to US asylum procedures has consisted of a summary interview on-board the Coast Guard vessel. Defending its actions, the United States has stated that such interceptions are not in violation of the *non-refoulement* principle, which it considers to apply only to refugees within the territory of the state, and not to asylum seekers at sea.

In the Mediterranean region, the issue of interception and rescue at sea has arisen in response to the growing number of people transiting through North Africa before seeking entry by boat to the European Union. In June 2004, for example, a German-flagged vessel, the *Cap Anamur*, rescued a group of 37 people in the Mediterranean. The incident involved three European Union member states: Malta, Italy and Germany. When confronted with the plight of the *Cap Anamur*, Italy and Germany stated that they considered it an absolute duty to respect the international norm that imposes an obligation to lodge an asylum application in the country of first arrival (which they considered to be Malta, as the ship had crossed its territorial waters) and argued that a derogation of such a norm could open the door to numerous abuses.[12] After several days during which the vessel was not allowed to disembark at any port, and following the intervention of UNHCR and a number of NGOs, the boat was finally allowed to let its rescued passengers off in Sicily on humanitarian grounds.[13]

The occupants of boats intercepted in the Mediterranean have generally been taken for processing to a European port where they have been given the opportunity to submit an asylum claim. But instances have come to light in which vessels have been escorted into international waters with no provision made for the disembarkation of passengers. It should be noted that interception measures that effectively deny refugees access to international protection, or which result in them being returned to the countries where their security is at risk, do not conform to prevailing international guidelines and may even amount to a violation of the 1951 UN Refugee Convention.[14]

Box 2.3

The Tampa Affair: interception and rescue at sea

Some of the most searing images from the last quarter-century have been pictures of refugees and would-be migrants in grave peril on foundering boats. From the aftermath of the Viet nam war till today, images of 'boat people' have highlighted the desperate measures that people will take to escape their homelands. Unseaworthy and overcrowded vessels, often carrying mixed groups of refugees and migrants organized by unscrupulous smugglers, have become all too common in the Mediterranean, the Caribbean and the South Pacific regions.

No one knows how many boat people have died, but thousands have been rescued at sea. In the reality of dangerous journeys undertaken to gain access to reluctant coastal states, the time-honoured maritime traditions of rescue at sea collide with the growing determination of states to prevent illegal entry to their territory.

A recent renowned rescue at sea was carried out by the Norwegian merchant ship *Tampa* in August 2001. Sailing from Perth, Australia under the command of Captain Arne Rinnan, the freighter of the Wallenius Wilhelmsen Line received a call for assistance from the Rescue Coordination Centre of the Australian Maritime Safety Authority. The Tampa changed course and was guided by an Australian coastal search airplane to reach an Indonesian boat crowded with passengers and in acute distress. The boat was breaking up in heavy seas as the *Tampa* arrived just in time to transfer the 433 people on board to its own decks. The Norwegian ship had facilities on board for only 50 people, including its crew of 27.

The closest port to the site of the rescue was on Christmas Island, an Australian territory, but Australia's Immigration Department forbade the *Tampa* to enter Australian territorial waters. The Australian government was determined to stop unauthorized arrivals of asylum seekers, and so refused to disembark the Tampa's passengers and permit the vessel to proceed on its scheduled route. After long and tense negotiations—during

which conditions on board the Tampa reached crisis proportions—a complicated and costly arrangement saw the passengers forcibly removed from the ship and dispersed to camps in Nauru, a small state nearby. Some 132 unaccompanied minors and families were accepted by New Zealand, where almost all received refugee status. None went directly to Australia. In this long process, the owners and agents of the Tampa incurred substantial losses.

At the time, the obligation to render assistance to vessels in distress was codified in international maritime law in such instruments as the UN Convention on the Law of the Sea (1982) and the International Convention on Maritime Search and Rescue (1979). The obligation to extend aid applies without regard to the nationality, status, or circumstances of the persons in distress. Under these rules, ship owners, ships masters, coastal nations and flag states (the states where ships are registered) all have responsibilities for search and rescue.

The International Convention on Search and Rescue mandates that a rescue is not complete until the rescued person is delivered to a place of safety. That could be the nearest suitable port, the next regular port of call, the ship's home port, a port in the rescued person's own country, or one of many other possibilities. The convention provides that 'a situation of distress shall be notified not only to consular and diplomatic authorities but also to a competent international organ if the situation of distress pertains to refugees or displaced persons.' The ship itself cannot be considered a 'place of safety'—indeed, carrying a large number of unscheduled passengers could endanger the crew and passengers themselves, owing to overcrowding, insufficient food and water and the tensions of life at close quarters.

The inability to disembark rescued passengers in a timely fashion and return to scheduled ports of call lead to strong reluctance in the maritime industry to engage actively in search and rescue missions. For their

principled actions in the face of such profound disincentives, in 2002 UNHCR gave the captain, crew and owner of the *Tampa* its highest award, the Nansen Refugee Award.

The Tampa affair helped focus international attention on the question of who has responsibility for accepting asylum seekers rescued at sea, adjudicating their claims, and providing a place of safety for those who are confirmed in their need for international protection. In 2002, the general assembly of the International Maritime Organization (IMO) adopted a resolution seeking to identify any gaps, inconsistencies and inadequacies associated with the treatment of persons rescued at sea. IMO solicited the input of a number of UN agencies in a search for a coordinated approach to the issue.

Consequently, in 2004 IMO's Maritime Safety Committee adopted pertinent amendments to the International Convention for Safety at Sea and the International Convention on Maritime Search and Rescue. (These amendments are to enter into force on 1 July 2006.) At the same session, the committee adopted the current Guidelines on the Treatment of Persons Rescued at Sea. The purpose of these amendments and the current guidelines is to ensure that persons in distress are assisted, while minimizing the inconvenience to assisting ships, and to safeguard the continued integrity of the International Convention on Maritime Search and Rescue.

The amendments impose upon governments an obligation to cooperate to ensure that captains of ships that have rescued persons in distress at sea are released from their obligations with the minimum further deviation from the ship's intended route. The government or party responsible for maritime safety and rescue where survivors are recovered is responsible for ensuring that a place of safety is provided. The guidelines, on the other hand, aim to help governments and masters of ships fulfil their legal and humanitarian obligations to persons rescued at sea.

Asylum seekers from various countries at the Sangatte Red Cross Centre near Calais, France before attempting to cross the border into the UK via the Channel Tunnel. (UNHCR/H. J. Davies/2002)

Reception and detention

Those refugees and asylum seekers who are able to leave their own country and enter another state often find themselves in a very vulnerable situation. They are likely to be in need of life-sustaining material assistance including food, water, shelter, sanitation and healthcare. In many situations they will be vulnerable due to the traumatic experiences they have gone through, their separation from family members and friends, and their arrival in a country with an unfamiliar language, culture and bureaucracy. In such circumstances, unaccompanied minors, refugee children and adolescents, female heads of household and the elderly and infirm are often at particular risk of hardship and abuse.

In practice, the reception conditions experienced by asylum seekers and refugees vary widely and often fail to meet minimum standards. In the last five years, serious cases of rejection at borders or forcible return of refugees and asylum seekers have been reported.[15] In developing countries, refugees frequently arrive in remote and isolated border regions of their asylum country where resources are scarce, where government bodies, international agencies and NGOs have a limited presence, and where the local population is barely able to eke out a living. All too frequently, refugees who cross a border in order to escape from turmoil in their own country find themselves in areas where the rule of law barely exists and which are characterized by high levels of crime, banditry, social unrest and political violence.

Even in more prosperous states, asylum seekers and refugees may encounter many difficulties in meeting their basic needs. In many of the industrialized states, the assistance that they receive from the state and other bodies may be subject to restrictions and provided on a time-limited basis. While waiting for their status to be determined they may be prohibited from entering the labour market, and therefore feel obliged to accept casual and illegal work in the informal sector where they are vulnerable to exploitation by their employers. In the worst cases, they may resort to more dangerous, illicit activities in order to survive, thereby exposing themselves to the risk of arrest and imprisonment.

The necessary public support for the reception of asylum seekers has continued to be hampered by the tendency of certain elements in the media and some politicians to mix the issues of illegal migration and refugees without sufficient concern for accuracy.[16] Areas of concern include the summary dismissal of asylum claims deemed manifestly unfounded on the basis of very broad criteria and unduly restrictive interpretations of what defines a refugee. The latter include very narrow and restricted notions of what amounts to persecution, who qualify as agents of persecution and what constitutes effective state protection. Furthermore, appeals procedures are often inadequate.[17]

One issue that gives rise to particular concern in the context of reception standards is that of detention. While the legal framework of refugee protection does not forbid governments from holding asylum seekers in detention, various conclusions of UNHCR's Executive Committee have recognized that detention must be regarded as an exceptional act, used only, for example, to establish a person's identity, to ascertain elements of their asylum claim or to protect national security and public order. The manner and duration of detention should be proportionate to these ends, and should also be subject to judicial or administrative review.

In some instances, all illegal entrants, including refugees and asylum seekers, continued to be detained on a mandatory basis. States have cited national security and public order as justification for such detention, and emphasize the need for such measures to determine identity and nationality and to deter other potential asylum seekers.[18]

Many countries detain refugee claimants and their children at various points of the asylum process. Most disturbingly, asylum seekers can be detained for failing to arrive with the necessary travel documents, and can remain in detention for the entire length of the asylum process. And while many states have established special holding centres for asylum seekers and irregular migrants, in other countries they are detained in regular jails, alongside common criminals.

Identification, registration and documentation

For the principle of asylum to be effective, people who are in need of international protection have to be identified, registered and provided with appropriate documentation. The need to strengthen registration as a protection tool has been increasingly recognized. The proper registration and documentation of refugees and asylum seekers are important in assessing and monitoring assistance needs. They are also significant protection tools, notably against *refoulement* and arbitrary detention. Registration facilitates access to basic rights and family reunification, enables identification of those in need of special assistance, and supports the implementation of appropriate durable solutions.

Where registration procedures are weak or ineffective, the practical consequences can be severe. Unregistered and undocumented refugees may be at risk of arrest, detention, *refoulement* or deportation, may be denied the material assistance they need in terms of food, water, shelter and healthcare, and may be unable to benefit from the family tracing and family reunion activities that are normally established in the aftermath of a refugee emergency. Such refugees are also disadvantaged when it comes to the establishment of voluntary repatriation, local integration and resettlement programmes that are intended to provide lasting solutions to their plight. In addition, the children of refugees and asylum seekers who are unable to register marriages and births may find themselves effectively stateless, and thereby deprived of rights both in their country of asylum and in their nominal country of origin.

Lack of official documentation continues to impede access to residence permits, public healthcare and social assistance, and to result in *refoulement*, arrest and detention. In some countries refugees were either not given any identity documentation or received documents valid for limited purposes and not necessarily recognized by the police, security forces or other government elements. In these situations, the lack of proper documentation made refugees more vulnerable to denial of rations and other assistance as well as to abuse, including beatings, extortion, arbitrary arrest and detention, and widespread intimidation.

The heightened focus on registration has yielded positive developments. It has encouraged efforts in many countries to register adult refugees individually, to provide more comprehensive demographic profiles of populations and to issue documentation on a more systematic basis. Some participating countries are Colombia, Côte d'Ivoire, Georgia, Ghana, Guinea, Sierra Leone, Tanzania, Uganda, Uzbekistan and Yemen.[19]

Status determination

In order to benefit from the provisions of the 1951 UN Refugee Convention, a refugee must first be recognized as someone who has a well-founded fear of persecution in her or his country of origin and is therefore in need of international protection. This process of identification and status determination takes place in two principal ways. When large numbers of people from a conflict-affected country cross an international border and seek asylum in another state, it is common for them to be recognized as refugees on a group, or *prima facie,* basis. This means that each individual does not have to be assessed on his or her need for protection.

In situations where asylum seekers arrive in smaller numbers and over longer periods of time, however, they are usually required to undergo a refugee status

Figure 2.3   Asylum applications submitted in the top five European receiving countries, 2000-2004

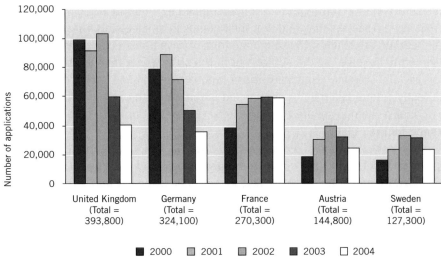

Note: The figure for France for 2000 excludes applications by minors.
Source: Governments.

Figure 2.4   Main origins of asylum applicants in the top 10 European receiving countries, 2000-2004

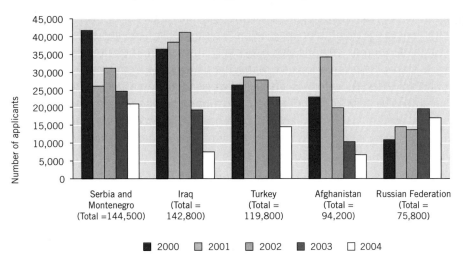

Note: The top 10 receiving countries in Europe during 2000-2004 were Austria, Belgium, France, Germany, Italy, Netherlands, Norway, Sweden, Switzerland and the United Kingdom.
Source: Governments.

determination process, in which their need for international protection is assessed. In certain countries such procedures have attained a relatively high degree of sophistication, thoroughness and fairness. In many others, however, the process of status determination continues to be characterized by limitations and weaknesses.

First, asylum seekers may find that their claims to refugee status are not given a full or fair hearing, especially if they originate from or have transited through a country that is deemed to be 'safe' by the authorities in the state where they are seeking asylum. Other asylum seekers, especially those whose applications are considered to be 'manifestly unfounded' may be channelled into accelerated asylum procedures which do not enable them to secure adequate legal representation or to produce supporting evidence for their claim.[20]

Second, asylum seekers do not always have an adequate opportunity to appeal against the rejection of their claim to refugee status. And in some countries they are not allowed to remain pending the outcome of their appeal, but are returned to third countries or to their countries of origin before the appeal decision has been rendered. The benefit of a successful appeal will evidently be lost in such cases if the person concerned has already been exposed to lasting harm.

Third, the quality of the process used to assess asylum applications is not always adequate, often because states lack the capacity to undertake this task effectively and because they are unable or unwilling to invest sufficient resources in it. Adjudicators in many countries are poorly paid, inadequately trained and insufficiently motivated, and do not have access to the reliable country-of-origin information that is needed to assess an asylum application fairly and thoroughly. In many countries, moreover, the state's limited capacity has led to the growth of substantial asylum backlogs, requiring asylum seekers to live in precarious circumstances for months or years while waiting for a final decision on their case. States in developing regions are especially limited in their ability to undertake refugee status determination. In many instances they cede much or all of that function to UNHCR, which is also hard-pressed to undertake such a time- and labour-intensive task with the human and financial resources at its disposal.

Fourth, asylum decisions lack consistency, with acceptance rates for refugee claimants varying significantly from one country of asylum to another. In 2002, for example, the overall recognition rate for asylum seekers in Canada was 58 per cent, while in Greece it was less than 1 per cent.[21] Such variations can be partially explained by the fact that asylum countries have different caseloads, some of which are more likely to have *bona fide* claims than others. However, this does not explain why the acceptance rate for Chechen asylum seekers varies from virtually zero in some countries to close to 100 per cent in others.[22] Such inconsistencies arise because of varying interpretations of the criteria for refugee status and because the standard of proof required differs substantially from one country to another. Thus, while decision-makers in some states recognize that refugees often have difficulties in obtaining lawful travel documents, decision-makers elsewhere consider the use of false documents to be an indication of the asylum seeker's lack of credibility.

In recent years, certain groups of refugees in both large-scale influx situations and individualized asylum systems have been singled out and stigmatized on account of their ethnicity, beliefs or nationality.[23] A number of states in various regions effectively discriminated against asylum seekers when they denied them access to asylum procedures on the basis of their country of origin, because they came via certain countries or were from a particular minority.

In some countries, the absence of an appeal on the judgement of the merits of a claim weakens the credibility of the refugee status determination procedure. In addition, a number of restrictive measures have strengthened barriers to admission and thus access to asylum procedures. Shortcomings in procedural safeguards related to refugee status determination remain, most notably in accelerated procedures and the use of the 'safe third country' concept, both of which result in increasing restrictions on access to asylum procedures and infringement of the right to seek asylum. The increase in the use of alternative forms of protection at the expense of recognition under the 1951 UN Refugee Convention leaves asylum seekers and refugees in a state of uncertainty as to the duration and content of the protection afforded.

Restricted rights

Refugees who are recognized on a *prima facie* basis may not be obliged to submit individual asylum applications, but this is not to suggest that their protection and welfare is guaranteed because they have been admitted to and allowed to remain in a country of asylum. This chapter has already referred to the material hardships that are frequently experienced by refugees in developing countries, while the following chapter examines the many threats that exist in relation to the physical security of such refugees. Above and beyond these difficulties, many of the displaced, especially those living in protracted refugee situations, are confronted with serious restrictions on their human rights in areas such as:

- Freedom of movement: Refugees are often confined to camps or to other designated areas and can leave them only with special permission. They may be subject to fines and even penal sentences if they fail to comply with such regulations.
- Civil and political rights: In many situations refugees are barred from engaging in political activities, from holding mass meetings and from establishing their own associations and organizations.
- Legal rights: Refugees in developing countries often lack a clearly defined legal status, do not have long-term residence rights and have no prospect of seeking naturalization in their country of asylum.
- Socio-economic rights: A further right denied to many refugees is the ability to engage in agricultural, wage-earning and income-generating opportunities. They do not have access to land, they are not allowed to enter the labour market, they cannot take out loans, and restrictions on their freedom of movement make it difficult for them to engage in trade.

- Freedom of choice: Refugees living in camps frequently find themselves under the control of authoritarian political and military leaders within their community. This situation further limits their ability to exercise basic human rights, including the right to return to their country of origin at a time of their own choosing.[24]

Responses

Confronted with this wide range of challenges, and considering them to be far more serious today than they were at any time since the establishment of the 1951 UN Refugee Convention, some commentators have suggested that the international refugee protection regime is breaking down and have even predicted its imminent demise.

Such a conclusion would be mistaken for three reasons. First, it would be wrong to believe that there was ever a 'golden age of asylum' in which states and other actors unfailingly respected the notions of asylum and refugee protection. Indeed, many if not all of the protection problems now encountered by refugees and asylum seekers, including *refoulement*, the closure of borders, interception at sea, detention and restricted rights have a host of historical precedents.

Second, while there is certainly a need to focus on the challenges that exist in relation to asylum and refugee protection, there is also a need to acknowledge the continuing achievements of the refugee protection regime. In the past five years alone, millions of refugees and asylum seekers throughout the world have been able to escape from life-threatening circumstances in their own country, to benefit from international protection and to find a lasting solution to their plight, whether by means of voluntary repatriation, local integration in their country of asylum or resettlement in a third country.

Third, while governments have sometimes responded to their economic, political and security concerns by acting in a manner that has negative consequences for refugees and asylum seekers, they have also acknowledged the need for a multilateral response to refugee problems. They have reaffirmed their commitment to the 1951 UN Refugee Convention and have endorsed an agenda that provides them with a coherent set of protection goals, activities and indicators.

In 2001, UNHCR initiated the Global Consultations on International Protection. This process evolved around three 'tracks', with the overall goal of reinvigorating the refugee-protection framework. The first track sought to strengthen the commitment of states to respect the centrality of the 1951 UN Refugee Convention and its 1967 Protocol in the international refugee protection system. The second track provided a forum to take stock of developments in refugee law and to clarify disputed notions through a series of expert discussions on the interpretation of the Convention and its Protocol.[25] The third track was structured around a number of protection policy matters to address contemporary challenges.[26]

The commitment to refugee protection and the relevance of the 1951 UN Refugee Convention and its 1967 Protocol were reaffirmed in December 2001 at the end of the first track of the Global Consultations by the adoption of the Declaration of States Parties to the 1951 Convention and/or its 1967 Protocol relating to the Status of Refugees.[27] The Declaration was an important achievement, not only because it was the first statement of its type in the 50-year history of the Convention, but more significantly because it was issued at a time when some governments had started to ask whether the Convention was relevant to current realities. The Declaration reaffirmed the contemporary relevance of the Convention and underscored the importance of the legal norms on which it is based.

The Global Consultations tried to resolve areas of inconsistent interpretation and state practice. The process attempted to identify new approaches that would bridge gaps in refugee protection in a cooperative manner to ensure that burdens and responsibilities were more equitably shared. Following the Consultations, and in order to provide for the implementation of the 2001 Declaration, the Agenda for Protection was adopted to guide action by UNHCR, states, NGOs and other partners in furthering protection objectives in the years ahead.[28]

The Agenda for Protection provides a framework for fulfilling the commitments reaffirmed by states in the Declaration. It sets out six inter-related goals and details actions for achieving them. The goals focus on issues that are inadequately covered by the Convention. These include, for example, the issue of refugee registration, the protection of refugee women and children, protection responses in situations of mass influx and expanded opportunities for durable solutions.

Since the conclusion of the Global Consultations and establishment of the Agenda for Protection, new efforts have been made to mobilize support for asylum and refugee protection at the regional level. In 2003, for example, a memorandum of understanding was signed by UNHCR and the African Commission on Human and Peoples' Rights,[29] aimed at strengthening cooperation between the parties in order to promote and protect more effectively the human rights of refugees, asylum seekers, returnees and other persons of concern. Another recent initiative is the Regional Parliamentary Conference on Refugees in Africa: the Challenges of Protection and Solutions, held in Cotonou (Benin) in June 2004. The conference was attended by parliamentarians of 26 African countries and adopted a Declaration and a Programme of Action.[30] This Programme of Action is aimed at implementing the commitments contained in the Declaration by developing concrete objectives and strategies to support African parliaments in their work in favour of protecting refugees and finding durable solutions.

In the Latin American context, representatives of 18 countries in the region gathered in Mexico City in November 2004 to commemorate the 20th anniversary of the adoption of the Cartagena Declaration on Refugees. The meeting resulted in the adoption of the Mexico Declaration and Plan of Action to Strengthen the International Protection of Refugees in Latin America.[31] The Declaration reaffirms the fundamental right to seek and receive asylum, the enduring validity of the principles and norms

Box 2.4

Urban refugees

As the world's urban population has grown, so has the number of urban refugees. Within two decades even sub-Saharan Africa—the world's most rural region—will see more than half its population living in urban areas. Declining state services in rural areas, the removal of agricultural subsidies and changing family structures have encouraged the trend. As for refugees, more of them are moving to urban areas to escape the restrictive encampment schemes instituted by host countries. The percentage of the total refugee population that lives in urban, rather than rural areas is highest in Europe and Latin America. However, the absolute numbers of urban refugees in Asia and Africa make them a significant group in those regions as well. A sizeable number of urban refugees are in countries of first asylum. For instance, some 2 million Afghans, many of whom may be refugees, live in Pakistan's cities.

Urban refugees include people trading the assistance they receive when in camps for the freedom to participate in urban labour and commodity markets. This pattern is particularly pronounced in sub-Saharan Africa, where internally displaced persons forced off rural holdings by conflict, persecution or famine are moving to cities. In Europe, North America and Australia most (but not all) urban refugees have been resettled from other parts of the world and receive assistance from international, national and private organizations.

The presence of refugees and displaced persons in urban areas raises significant protection concerns, especially when refugees self-settle outside the purview of official programmes. Camp-based refugees are formally distanced from many of their host communities' socio-economic and political processes, but those in urban settings have no option but to engage with local populations, markets and institutions. Given the prevailing conditions in the cities (or neighbourhoods) where they typically settle, refugees share many challenges with citizens: public health hazards, urban violence and lack of housing, education and health services. These challenges are heightened as levels of domestic migration and urbanization almost invariably outpace job creation and improvements to urban services and infrastructure.

Urban refugees—and other immigrant communities—also face challenges linked to their position as outsiders. Local officials and host populations may prevent them from accessing even those services to which they are legally entitled. Where refugees have religious or ethnic ties with marginalized or persecuted local populations they may face even greater difficulties.

Two other protection concerns emerge from refugees' limited access to documentation, services and jobs. The first is critical for urban refugees who rely almost exclusively on existing social services, compete in labour and housing markets and are subject to the same regulatory regimes as host populations. Although papers designating an individual's refugee status and right to residence are critical, these do not ensure protection. Whereas camp-based refugees primarily interact with specially trained staff, urban refugees depend on civil servants who may be unfamiliar with, or simply not respect, their papers. Moreover, full access to education, housing, employment and financial services often requires documents not always available to refugees,

contained in the 1951 UN Refugee Convention and its 1967 Protocol, and the importance of using the norms and principles of other international instruments of humanitarian and human rights law to strengthen international protection. The Declaration also recognizes the non-derogative nature of the principle of *non-refoulement*, including non-rejection at the border, and the commitment of Latin American countries to keep their borders open to those in need of international protection.

The Mexico Plan of Action is intended to address the region's principal protection challenges. These include the development of asylum systems, the strengthening of protection capacities among governments and NGOs, and the plight of refugees who have settled in urban centres and are struggling to attain self-sufficiency. The Plan proposes concrete projects ranging from research and doctrinal development of international refugee law to institutional capacity building, as well as programmes on durable solutions promoting the self-reliance and local integration of refugees.

One of UNHCR's primary concerns over the past five years has been to ensure that the commitments made in the Declaration of States Parties to the 1951 Convention such as professional qualifications, school or banking records and birth certificates. Without these, urban refugees are hindered in accessing services and markets and are vulnerable to exploitation, police abuse, arbitrary arrest and deportation. Refugees' inability to speak local languages may further limit their options and their ability to protest abuse from employers, landlords, police or citizens.

Difficulties accessing local markets and services are mirrored in urban refugees' relationships with voluntary agencies and other NGOs. While there may be more such agencies in urban areas than in purpose-built settlements, few may be explicitly committed to refugee protection. In many instances, local NGOs and religious organizations give priority to assisting citizens or exclude non-nationals (including refugees). Even where local organizations accept responsibility for refugees, they may lack specialized skills for assisting with asylum claims, monitoring cases or advocating for the displaced. Furthermore, refugees' tendency to relocate frequently further hampers service providers' attempts to track and assist vulnerable groups.

The attitudes prevalent among host governments, international aid/donor agencies and host populations add to protection challenges. There is, for example, a tendency to treat those arriving in cities with considerable suspicion. This often emanates from a belief that urban refugees are mainly 'irregular movers' who have surrendered protection, usually in rural camps, to search for opportunities elsewhere. Depending on national policy, those fitting this description may not be entitled to asylum or assistance. In other cases, policies explicitly confine refugees to camps or only allow urban settlement under strict conditions.

In almost all instances, refugees must prove their right to be in the city. They may also need to address hostility from urban residents who do not distinguish between refugees and growing numbers of unwelcome economic migrants, both domestic and international. In such contexts, government officials may concentrate on regulating rather than assisting refugees to prevent the asylum process from becoming a way around normal immigration channels. Even those who formally establish their rights as refugees may become

scapegoats for politicians, unions and others.

To address these and other challenges, in December 1997 UNHCR introduced a Policy on Refugees in Urban Areas. While it represented an important step in protecting the rights of urban refugees, the policy has been difficult to implement. For one, urban refugees' *de facto* integration (or invisibility) has made it difficult to develop specialized programmes for them. Moreover, those programmes that do exist are relatively expensive and difficult to fund, given the generalized suspicions outlined above. Engaging directly with metropolitan governments is an additional challenge for an organization such as UNHCR that is more familiar with negotiations and advocacy at the national level. Recognizing these concerns, UNHCR is currently reviewing its urban-refugee policy in consultation with relevant stake holders.

and or its 1967 Protocol and Agenda for Protection are effectively operationalized. Significant improvements have been made, for example, in the way that refugees and asylum seekers are registered and provided with documents that attest to their status. Such efforts have helped to protect them from *refoulement* and arbitrary detention, have improved access to assistance and family reunification and contributed to the search for durable solutions, especially voluntary repatriation and resettlement.

In addition, a variety of initiatives have been taken to meet the protection needs of particular refugee groups, including women, children, victims of sexual and gender-based violence and those affected by HIV/AIDS. With regard to refugee children, for example, UNHCR has established counselling programmes that provide younger refugees with a better understanding of their rights, thereby helping to protect them against military recruitment, forced labour and sexual exploitation. Significant attention has also been given to the provision of primary and secondary education, especially for refugee girls, who are generally under-represented at school.

Refugee protection and globalization

Governments and UNHCR are currently striving to formulate appropriate and effective responses to the challenge of asylum in a rapidly changing international environment. While there is a broad consensus within the international community concerning the continued relevance of the 1951 UN Refugee Convention, demonstrated by the positive outcome of the Global Consultations, there is also a recognition that the world has changed significantly in the past five decades. The number of states has proliferated as a result of decolonization and the demise of the communist bloc. The process of globalization has created an enormous amount of new wealth, but has distributed that wealth in a highly uneven manner. Developments in communications and transportation have led to unprecedented levels of human mobility and facilitated the instantaneous transfer of information and money from one part of the world to another. And serious new threats have arisen in the form of transnational terrorist and criminal networks.

Such developments have had major effects on the dynamics of human displacement and have generated an intense and sometimes polarized debate with regard to the way that refugees, asylum seekers and other uprooted people can be most effectively protected, while at the same time safeguarding the legitimate interests of states. The following sections examine three of the issues that have been most prominent in that debate: the relationship between national security, asylum and refugee protection; the asylum–migration nexus; and the challenge of building protection capacities in countries of asylum.

National security and asylum

While the trend of implementing ever more restrictive policies towards asylum seekers and refugees had started well before the events of 11 September 2001,[32] the new climate of heightened security concerns served to legitimise these practices. It also allowed for closer cooperation among states in criminal matters at the risk of the protection needs of refugees being overlooked.

Indeed, just a few days after 11 September, the UN Security Council adopted a resolution calling upon states to take appropriate measures under the relevant provisions of national and international law before granting refugee status to ensure that the asylum seeker has not been involved in terrorist acts.[33] It further called on states to ensure that refugee status is not abused by those involved in terrorist acts, and that asylum claims should not be grounds for refusing requests for the extradition of alleged terrorists.[34]

Since that time, the security concerns of states have increasingly been invoked as a justification for the introduction of laws and policies which impinge upon the principle of asylum and the protection of refugees. Border controls have been tightened in many parts of the world, while the grounds for the detention, exclusion, expulsion and extradition of foreign nationals have been broadened. Security considerations have also prompted some states to restrict access to asylum procedures and resettlement opportunities. More generally, in their efforts to strengthen national security and safeguard public safety, governments have paid less heed to the principles of multilateralism, due process and fundamental human rights—precisely those principles on which the refugee protection regime is founded.[35]

The perception persists that asylum provides a convenient cover for terrorists and their sympathizers. While this view may be based to a significant extent on the unfair stereotyping of asylum seekers (especially those who have travelled in an irregular manner, who are young and male, and who originate from countries that are associated with political violence and religious extremism) it cannot be entirely discounted. Asylum systems are not immune to abuse, and it would be naïve to believe that terrorists have ignored the opportunity to consider how the systems might be exploited.

At the same time, the security threat posed by the movement and presence of asylum seekers must be put into perspective. Asylum seekers are, for example, amongst the most closely scrutinized of all foreign nationals; they are routinely fingerprinted and checked against national and international security databases. Those who arouse any suspicion are liable to be detained, and to be monitored upon their release. If a terrorist wishes to enter and remain in a country undetected, submitting an application for asylum would not appear to be the most promising means of achieving that objective.

It is also essential to point out that the international refugee protection regime incorporates some robust mechanisms to prevent the abuse of asylum by those responsible for serious crimes. Article 1F of the 1951 UN Refugee Convention, for example, provides for the exclusion from refugee status of those responsible for war crimes, crimes against peace and humanity and serious non-political crimes committed outside the country of refuge prior to their admission to that country.[36] People who have engaged in acts contrary to the purposes and principles of the United Nations are also excluded from the protection of the Convention. In addition, the Convention allows for an exception to the principle of *non-refoulement*, permitting states to expel refugees from their territory if there are reasonable grounds for regarding them as a danger to national security, or if they have been convicted of a serious crime which constitutes a danger to that country.

The danger in the current international context is that states will use the issue of terrorism to legitimize the introduction of restrictive asylum practices and refugee policies, a process which began well before the events of 11 September 2001.[37] Indeed, there is already evidence to suggest that the exclusion clauses of the 1951 UN Refugee Convention are being invoked more frequently, using low thresholds of proof and without adequate due-process protections. Terrorism is, of course, a matter of life and death, and it is incumbent upon states to ensure that their citizens enjoy the highest possible level of safety and security. At the same time, when decisions about the fate of asylum seekers are taken in haste, are made on the basis of inadequate evidence and are not open to public or judicial scrutiny, there is the serious risk of a miscarriage of justice which could place the life and liberty of those asylum seekers at serious risk.[38]

Map 2.1   Refugees and asylum seekers by country of asylum,
1 January 2005

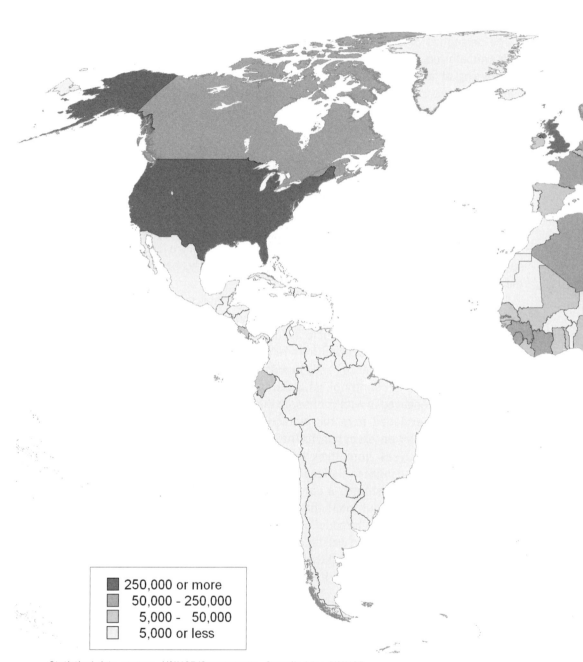

■	250,000 or more
■	50,000 - 250,000
■	5,000 - 50,000
□	5,000 or less

Statistical data sources: UNHCR/Governments. Compiled by: UNHCR.
The boundaries and names shown and the designations used on this map do not imply official endorsement or acceptance by the United Nations.
Geographical data sources: UNHCR, Global Insight digital mapping - © 1998 Europa Technologies Ltd.

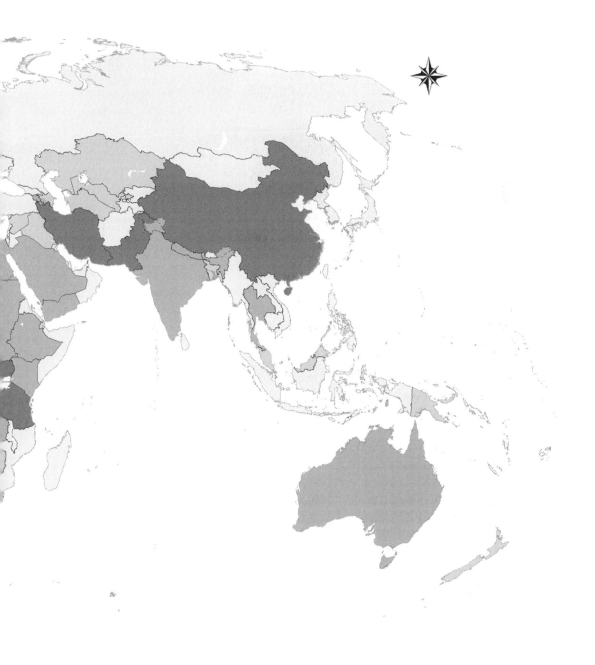

These Liberian refugees have been resettled in the UK as part of a resettlement programme for vulnerable families. Here they are being provided with orientation by a Migrant Helpline aid worker. (UNHCR/H. J. Davies/2004)

The asylum–migration nexus

In recent years, the issues of asylum and refugee protection have become inextricably linked with the question of international migration, especially those migratory movements that are undertaken in an irregular, undocumented or clandestine manner. That linkage is manifested in three principle ways. First, many migrants who are looking for work and who are not in need of international protection submit asylum applications once they have arrived in another country, hoping they might be granted refugee status because they have no other legal means of entering and remaining in that state, even on a temporary basis. Second, population movements from a single country may include some people who have a genuine claim to refugee status and others who do not, especially when that country is simultaneously affected by persecution, armed conflict, political instability and economic collapse. Third, many refugees and asylum seekers are obliged to move from one country to another irregularly because they are unable to obtain the passports, visas and tickets they need to travel in an authorized manner. Such phenomena are often referred to collectively as 'mixed migrations' or the 'asylum–migration nexus'.[39]

The new linkages that exist between asylum and migration derive from several dimensions of the globalization process: the growing disparity in standards of living and levels of human security in different parts of the world; the growth of global transportation, communication and social networks; and the ease with which capital and goods can now flow from one country and continent to another, while the movement of labour remains subject to strict controls.[40]

States, especially those in the developed world, have responded with some alarm to the issue of mixed migration, pointing to the relatively low proportion of asylum seekers who qualify for refugee status, the expense of maintaining their asylum procedures and social welfare systems, the difficulty of deporting those asylum claimants whose applications are rejected, and the security risks associated with the growth of irregular migration and human smuggling.[41]

Their primary response to this situation has been to introduce a raft of measures intended to obstruct or deter the arrival of irregular migrants in general and asylum seekers in particular, including those who have a *bona fide* claim to refugee status. In exercising their sovereign and legitimate right to control their borders and safeguard national security, states have made it increasingly difficult for people to 'seek and enjoy asylum in another state', a right guaranteed by the Universal Declaration of Human Rights. The number of asylum seekers registered in 50 European and non-European industrialized countries dropped by 40 per cent from 2001 to 2004.[42] While the drop may in part be due to a stabilization of the situation in war-torn countries such as Afghanistan, the Democratic Republic of Congo, Liberia and Sierra Leone, it also seems that the restrictive measures introduced by the world's more prosperous states have had their intended effect.

A principal goal of the Agenda for Protection is that of 'protecting refugees within broader migration movements.' If that objective is to be realized, it is essential to ensure that the principle of asylum is not undermined by the effort to stem irregular migration. First, states must respect Article 31 of the 1951 UN Refugee Convention, which states that refugees must not be penalized on account of their illegal entry or presence in a country, 'provided they present themselves without delay to the authorities and show good cause for their illegal entry or presence.' Second, police officers, border guards, immigration and asylum officials must be trained and convinced to uphold the principles of international refugee law. Third, states should establish fair, thorough and efficient refugee status determination procedures, so that asylum seekers are quickly informed of the outcome of their case. In situations of mass influx, the provision of *prima facie* refugee status to new arrivals has proven to be a particularly valuable means of safeguarding asylum and refugee protection. Fourth, if the integrity and credibility of asylum systems are to be preserved, steps must be taken to ensure the departure of those asylum seekers whose applications for refugee status are rejected after a full and fair examination of their case. In this respect, unsuccessful asylum seekers have a particular obligation to respect the law and to respect the wishes of the authorities when they are asked to leave the country. Fifth, there is a strong case to be made for the industrialized states, many of which are confronted with the prospect of diminishing and ageing populations and whose economies increasingly rely on illegal and casual migrant labour, to establish regular migration programmes.

Unless they are able to access the labour markets of the North by legal means, migrants from the South will continue to submit invalid claims to refugee status, further undermining public confidence in the whole notion of asylum. Similarly, an expansion of refugee resettlement programmes would allow more people who are in need of international protection to move in an orderly manner to, and gain residence rights in, a country which offers them a more promising future.

Finally, action is required to address the issue of 'onward movements', whereby refugees and asylum seekers move in an irregular manner from a country where they have already been granted (or had the opportunity to seek) asylum, often because they are unable to find an adequate degree of protection or standard of living in that state, and have no prospect of finding an early solution to their plight.[43] As demonstrated by the recent experience of sub-Saharan Africans who have moved to the countries of North Africa in the hope of gaining access to the European Union, the people involved in such movements have to spend large amounts of money for the services of human smugglers, and are then obliged to undertake very hazardous journeys in which their lives and liberty are at constant risk. Even then they have no guarantee that they will reach their destination. It is for this reason that UNHCR gives such priority to building protection capacities in countries of asylum.

Enhancing protection capacities

The notions of asylum and refugee protection mean very little unless people who are obliged to seek sanctuary in another state are able to enjoy an adequate degree of physical, legal, material and psychological security in that country. Sadly, that is frequently not the case. Too many refugees are obliged to live in precarious conditions, receiving inadequate assistance, unable to establish their own livelihoods, deprived of freedom of movement and at risk of detention, exploitation and violence. Desperate to escape from such difficult conditions, and without any means of moving by authorized means, they readily become prey to human smugglers and traffickers.

The debate around enhancing protection capacity in regions of origin of refugees, and thus preventing onward movement towards industrialized states, has been overshadowed by suspicions about the motives of the states seeking to legitimize policies of forced removal to countries in the region of origin. Strengthening protection capacities in countries/regions of origin is consistent with the 1951 UN Refugee Convention. The Convention recognizes that international cooperation for the protection of refugees is necessary in order to palliate the heavy burdens on certain countries as a result of granting asylum. It also calls on governments to continue to receive refugees in their territories and to act in a spirit of international cooperation in order that these refugees find asylum and the possibility of resettlement.[44] However, it has been argued that recent initiatives on regional protection proposed by some states are more geared towards burden-shifting rather than burden-sharing.

To address these problems, greater efforts are required to enhance protection capacities in countries of asylum. This is especially the case in developing and middle-income countries, many of which have acceded to the 1951 UN Refugee Convention and given sanctuary to large numbers of refugees but which simply do not have the legal, institutional and economic means to provide them with a safe haven. This approach was epitomized by a United Kingdom proposal in 2003 for the

Box 2.5

The Comprehensive Plan of Action for Somali Refugees

The Comprehensive Plan of Action (CPA) for Somali Refugees aims to address one of the most protracted and neglected refugee situations in Africa. More than 16 years of conflict have resulted in population displacement on a massive scale. At the start of the civil war in 1988, internal opposition to the Somali dictator, Siad Barre, led to the flight of some 400,000 refugees from north-west Somalia to Ethiopia and Djibouti. Following the overthrow of the Barre regime in 1991, more than half the Somali population was displaced. By 2005, despite the repatriation of more than 1 million refugees to Somalia over the previous 12 years (485,000 of these with UNHCR assistance) there remained some 350,000 refugees in neighbouring countries and the wider diaspora. Of Somalia's 400,000 and more internally displaced people, many are women and children. The scale of the ongoing humanitarian situation in Somalia requires an integrated, comprehensive response from the international community.

Two other factors reinforce the need for a CPA in Somalia. The first is the relative stability in particular areas of the country. Despite ongoing conflicts in the southern and central regions, by the end of the 1990s working administrations had been established in Somaliland (1991) and Puntland (1998). The second factor is the peace process. In May 2000 a new round of peace talks between warring Somali factions opened at Arta, Djibouti. In October 2000 the Transitional National Government was established with a view to forming a national government towards the end of 2003. In October 2004 Abdullahi Yusuf Ahmed was proclaimed president of the new Somali Transitional Federal Government.

The Somalia CPA was initiated by UNHCR in collaboration with the Somali authorities, regional host states, the European Commission, Denmark, the United Kingdom and the Netherlands in mid-2004. The objectives of the CPA are to provide effective protection and a range of durable solutions to Somali refugees and internally displaced persons. The CPA aims to develop an integrated approach by using all three of the durable solutions to refugee displacement: repatriation, local integration and resettlement.

The main focus of the CPA is on the repatriation programme underway in Somalia since the early 1990s to ensure the sustainability of returns and reintegration. Within Somalia, the CPA also seeks to identify durable solutions for the internally displaced. With regard to the host states in the region, it seeks to explore and support any possibility of improving refugees' access to local integration, which until now has been extremely limited. The resettlement component of the CPA, which aims to move the most vulnerable groups of Somalis from countries of first asylum, is currently limited in scope, although there is growing interest in resettlement schemes on the part of several European Union states with significant Somali populations. Where durable solutions are not immediately available, the CPA seeks to improve the prospects for refugee self-reliance pending eventual return, and to enhance the quality of protection and assistance available in Djibouti, Ethiopia, Kenya and Yemen.

The CPA Preparatory Project, based on a 'gaps analysis' and national consultations with governments in the region, has formed the basis of negotiations on the CPA. Work on the drafting of the CPA is now fully underway and, following further consultations with the widest possible group of stakeholders, the final document will be presented to the international community. On the basis of commitments made to specific programme areas at this conference, projects will be developed and implemented by UNHCR and its partners from 2006.

The CPA is related to the wider UN Joint Needs Assessment (JNA)/Somali Reconstruction and Development Programme which is being developed and led by the United Nations Development Group and the World Bank at the request of the International Community and the Transitional Federal Government of Somalia. Both the JNA and the CPA involve the same stakeholders: Somali counterparts, the UN, NGOs, returnees and IDPs. The priorities identified in the JNA consultations with stakeholders point to many of the same areas identified by the CPA consultations and to be addressed by the latter. Consequently, these two processes will be mutually reinforcing and closely coordinated. However, the CPA aims to focus on programmes that will be implementable irrespective of the direction of the ongoing peace process.

One of the most pressing problems facing the CPA is the continuing political instability in central and southern Somalia and the obstacle this presents to voluntary repatriation. The Transitional Federal Government, which moved from Kenya to Somalia in June 2005, must now overcome its internal divisions and establish viable state institutions. Reaching agreement on the status of Somaliland, which is seeking to assert its independence from Somalia, represents a significant part of ensuring a consolidated peace.

No less significant is the reluctance of the international community to provide the funding and political support to lay the foundations of a comprehensive humanitarian and development programme in Somalia. A vital component of a civil peace in Somalia is the disarmament and demobilization of the countless military factions spawned by 16 years of war. External political initiatives and scrutiny of the demobilization process are necessary ingredients of security in Somalia.

The outcome of the Somalia CPA has internal, regional and global implications. Continued population displacement inside Somalia has the potential to destabilize the region as a whole. The global effects of continuing insecurity in Somalia are also evident in the large number of Somalis now living in North America and Europe. What is currently lacking, but sorely needed, is the political will in the international community to develop an integrated approach to Somalia spanning security, economic development and humanitarian assistance.

establishment of 'regional protection areas' in locations close to countries that produce significant numbers of refugees and asylum seekers.[45]

The proposal sparked concern among NGOs and UNHCR, and became the subject of inter-governmental negotiations at the European level. In the case of extraterritorial processing, there has been extensive criticism that such practices may threaten the human security of refugees,[46] given the historical human rights consequences of the precedence of third-country processing centres and the use of concepts such as 'safe havens' and containment.[47] Furthermore, such practices demonstrate illegalities and impracticalities (see Box 2.2).

In 2003, the European Commission proposed a similar approach enabling people to enjoy effective protection as quickly and as close to their own country as possible, thereby averting the need for them to seek such protection elsewhere.[48] The Commission subsequently affirmed the crucial role of European Union member states and other industrialized countries in assisting countries of first asylum to establish such conditions.[49] On this basis, in 2005 the Commission adopted a communication on 'regional protection programmes' which entails enhancing the protection capacity of areas in regions of origin and creating the conditions in which refugees can benefit from the durable solutions of voluntary repatriation, local integration or resettlement.[50]

Attempts to strengthen the capacity of asylum countries in regions of origin have long been on UNHCR's agenda. Making the most of the impetus of these initiatives, in August 2004 UNHCR launched the Strengthening Protection Capacity project, which develops in three stages and focuses on four countries: Benin, Burkina Faso, Kenya and Tanzania.[51] An essential component of the project was the development of a Framework for Identifying Gaps in Protection Capacity. This analytical framework is being used more widely in other countries. For instance, it has been adopted by the Central Asia Protection Gaps Initiative, and for the Preparation of Gaps Analysis and Action Plans for Asylum Building in CIS (Commonwealth of Independent States) Countries. It is also being used by the Preparatory Project for a Somali CPA (comprehensive plan of action).[52] Needless to say, efforts of this type are unlikely to prove effective unless they receive financial support from the world's more prosperous states and unless refugee-hosting countries pursue policies that are conducive to protecting refugees and their rights.

The notion of 'protection in regions of origin' is a potentially valuable one that can be used to mobilize the support needed to provide refugees with better conditions of life and improve their prospect of finding durable solutions. But it is not a panacea. Many of the areas in which large numbers of refugees are to be found—northern Kenya, northern Uganda, western Tanzania and eastern Chad, to give just four African examples—are all confronted with serious economic, infrastructural and security problems, and do not provide the conditions in which to provide a high standard of refugee protection. It is equally clear that a good proportion of the world's refugees will be unable to find an early solution to their plight within their region of origin, and that the onward movement of refugees and asylum seekers will continue to take place while standards of living and levels of human security differ so greatly from one part of the world to another.

Given that some 70 per cent of the world's 9.2 million refugees are to be found in developing countries,[53] there is also a risk that the effort to improve protection in regions of origin will require poorer states to assume responsibility for an even greater proportion of the world's refugees. For these reasons, UNHCR considers it essential for the industrialized states to maintain equitable and effective asylum systems, to admit a larger number of refugees by means of resettlement programmes, and to provide tangible support to the notions of burden and responsibility-sharing, as endorsed by the Global Consultations on International Protection.

The way forward

The provision of international protection, and the application of international human rights and humanitarian principles on which it is based, are being increasingly challenged by political, social and economic realities. Core elements of refugee status, and the rights and responsibilities therein, are being questioned. More and more, asylum seekers are portrayed not as refugees fleeing persecution and entitled to sanctuary, but rather as illegal migrants, potential terrorists and criminals—or at a minimum as 'bogus'. Increasingly, asylum policies are being driven by security concerns and the need for enhanced migration management. Consequently, asylum policy has become alienated from refugee policy.

A key facet of globalization is the increasing mobility of the world's population. In response, control of migration has become an important aspect of national policy and international cooperation. This has led to a tendency to criminalize migrants, including asylum seekers, by associating them with people smugglers and traffickers. International legal instruments and institutions originally established to assist refugees are increasingly being used to stem unwanted migration. While it remains the prerogative of states to control their borders, they remain obliged to provide basic safety and assistance to those deemed in need of international protection. Therefore, the imperative should not be to prevent movement, but rather to balance effectively the security concerns and political interests of states and the aspirations for economic betterment of migrants in a manner that protects the interests of both.

In this context, strengthening protection remains a primary objective for the international community. To achieve this, more support should be provided to enhance protection capacity. This should include ensuring procedures are in place to provide access to appropriate, fair and efficient assessments of protection needs and to provide durable solutions thereafter. In turn, this necessitates more investment in national asylum systems and enhanced multilateral cooperation so that burdens and responsibilities are shared equitably.

3 Addressing refugee security

Of all the reasons that drive refugees to flee their homes, none is as great as fear. It may be fear of direct physical attack, or of a conflict where rape, torture and ethnic cleansing are part of military strategy. In their attempts to escape refugees may dodge bullets in a war zone, be chased by human traffickers or risk their lives crossing stormy seas on leaky boats. Even if they survive these dangers and make it to another country, they may find that their fears continue to dog them. The conflict they tried to escape may have followed them, and their lives and dignity may still be threatened.

Ensuring the physical safety of refugees is one of the most pressing concerns of UNHCR and its partners. The refugee protection regime was created by the international community to shelter those fleeing direct threats to their lives. But this very fact has meant that refugee protection has always been profoundly affected by larger security issues. Real and perceived security threats not only influence the willingness of states to provide asylum to refugees, they also determine the quality of the refuge provided. At another level, insecure environments weaken the ability of UNHCR and allied humanitarian agencies to assist and protect refugees—and thus to uphold their basic rights.

The beginning of the twenty-first century has seen a number of new developments with regard to refugee security. For one, UNHCR has become much more involved in security issues, especially as they affect ongoing operations. For another, the emergence of new security concerns for states, such as terrorism, has led to the 'securitization' of practices related to asylum. Lastly, issues of migration, development and relief have become more closely linked to security.[1] Indeed, there is an increasingly widespread view that the viability of the refugee protection regime hinges on its real and perceived impact on international security.[2]

This chapter will outline the importance of security in refugee protection and illustrate the increasing interconnectedness of refugee, state and global security. It describes recent legal and operational developments related to security both at the inter-state level and on the ground. The concluding part of the chapter highlights the ways in which preventive and 'soft' measures integrated into refugee protection and assistance can help defuse many of the security threats faced by refugees and their hosts alike.

In Sri Lanka, UNHCR-supported 'open relief centres' have been maintained in areas of conflict since 1990. The civilian character of these centres has been respected due to an informal understanding between UNHCR, the Government of Sri Lanka and the Liberation Tigers of Tamil Eelam. (UNHCR/M. Kobayashi /1999)

Security and refugee protection

Refugees have always been a by-product of war, which is still the most clearly identifiable and direct threat to national security. Within the global refugee protection regime, security concerns motivate state responses to refugee flows and are of primary importance in UNHCR's operations. The linkage of national and international security concerns and humanitarian assistance and asylum is not new. It can be seen in accounts of the emergence of organized refugee assistance in Europe following the Second World War.[3] In the 1960s and 1970s, African governments in particular attached considerable importance to security concerns arising from refugee movements.[4]

Aware of the potential of conflicts to spill over borders via refugee flows,[5] the international community has always emphasized that asylum must be recognized as a neutral, non-political act embedded in a system of multilateralism. In addition to this most fundamental norm, the 1951 UN Refugee Convention contains an explicit system of checks and balances which address states' security concerns.[6] The system serves to provide protection to individuals and to defuse potential interstate tension.

But the challenge of integrating the differing security interests and strategies of the various parts of the international refugee regime has grown more complex. The problems arising from operating in war zones and continuing protection concerns related to refugees in protracted situations are partly responsible. So too is the rise of xenophobia and fear of asylum seekers in many countries, which has led to a tendency to see refugees not as victims but as perpetrators of insecurity. That kind of thinking has inspired more aggressive interception measures, higher barriers to entry and indiscriminate detention, all of which pose new security risks to refugees. Meanwhile, many states see their responsibility for refugees as shared with the international community. While some see this practice as an offloading of state responsibility, it also reflects recognition that the security concerns of states as well as refugees are best met by ensuring that the multilateral and humanitarian character of refugee protection is maintained.

Human security: establishing linkages

All involved in refugee protection, be they states, host populations or humanitarian organizations, share some broad security concerns. Yet how they interpret these concerns can differ widely. To account for such differences, traditional perceptions of security purely in terms of a state's territorial integrity have increasingly been linked to new concepts of human security. This new thinking has been adopted by many members of the United Nations family and incorporated into the foreign-policy agendas of countries such as Canada and Japan.[7]

The new view of human security highlights the interdependent nature of the security threats in refugee situations. It recognizes that long-term state security is ultimately dependent on the security provided to non-state actors such as refugees and that, inversely, refugee protection may be impossible in situations of acute and continuous state insecurity.[8] The new perspective on human security also links the security concerns of individuals and communities to a wider range of threats including, but not restricted to, physical violence. Indeed, the concept of effective protection has evolved along with changes in the perception of the various dimensions of human security. For instance, protection now means safeguarding not just the physical integrity but also the human dignity of every refugee.

Refugee security

Threats to the physical security of refugees emanate from a variety of sources, including organized crime, errant military and police forces, anti-government militants, local populations and the refugee community itself. The vulnerability of refugees is magnified where they have limited material and financial resources and their family and community structures have been strained or destroyed. The physical threats to refugees range from theft, assault and domestic violence to child abuse, rape and human trafficking. Furthermore, in their vulnerable state refugees may be easily manipulated for political ends.

The presence of armed elements in refugee flows and settlements poses a fundamental threat to the civilian and humanitarian character of asylum, creating serious security concerns for refugees, host communities, local authorities and humanitarian workers alike.[9] The task of identifying combatants within a mass influx is made harder by the vast numbers involved. Besides, members of militia groups rarely identify themselves, and often hide their weapons in order to blend in with the civilian population.

Armed groups in refugee situations have been known to divert humanitarian aid from those who need it most, either through outright theft or through voluntary and involuntary 'taxation'. Both methods have been linked to malnutrition among refugees when increased rebel activity demands higher contributions. Rebels may also engage in forced recruitment of young men and children or use refugee camps as rest and recuperation sites. Many of these problems are exacerbated when refugees reside for long periods in countries of asylum where they lack educational and economic opportunities.

The presence of armed elements can also increase the risk of armed attacks on refugee settlements by opposing forces. In some cases, armed elements may challenge the implementation of durable solutions such as voluntary repatriation and local integration. For example, in the aftermath of the 1999 East Timor crisis, pro-Indonesian militiamen used violence and false information about conditions in East Timor to try and prevent refugees in West Timor from returning home.[10]

Box 3.1

Sexual and gender-based violence

War magnifies the everyday injustices that many women live with in peacetime. During periods of armed conflict, all forms of violence increase, particularly violence against women and girls. Women forced to flee their homes are often caught in a vicious cycle of abuse, exposed to sexual exploitation throughout the refugee experience. Sexual and gender-based violence ranges from harassment, domestic violence and rape to female genital mutilation and the withholding of food or other essentials unless paid for with sex.

It is now acknowledged within the humanitarian community that displacement has very specific gender dimensions, and that the protection concerns of refugee women and girls differ in many respects from those of men. For instance, in addition to being disproportionately affected by sexual and gender-based violence, women often do not get equal access to humanitarian assistance and asylum opportunities.

Protection concerns

Sexual and gender-based violence can occur at every stage of the refugee cycle: during flight, while in the country of asylum and during repatriation. For example, in Darfur (Sudan) where civil war has displaced more than a million people, gender-based violence has been rampant. In 2004, Amnesty International conducted interviews with hundreds of internally displaced and refugee women from Darfur, who had suffered rape, abduction, sexual slavery and torture. With the majority of displaced people still trapped across the border, and the widespread stigma of rape keeping many women silent, those interviewed comprised but a small fraction of the total number of victims.

Unfortunately, camps may not always be safe havens for women. Separated from the security offered by extended networks of family and community, unaccompanied women and girls may be regarded by camp guards and male refugees as sexual prey. Those who are lucky enough to flee with their family often find that the tremendous strains of refugee life increase the incidence of domestic violence. Poorly planned camps that do not take into account the needs of women and girls can also expose them to abuse; attacks are more common when women are forced to travel unprotected to remote areas in search of food, water and firewood.

When food and other necessities are in short supply, women may not get a fair share of what is available. The United Nations Development Fund for Women (UNIFEM) has warned that women in camps get less of everything from plastic sheeting to soap. If men are the sole distributors of food and supplies, the likelihood of sexual exploitation is much higher. Sadly, there have been cases where humanitarian workers and peacekeepers, the very people responsible for the well-being and protection of refugees, have abused their power.

Prevention and response

Due to powerful socio-cultural and legal obstacles, sexual and gender-based violence is one of the most challenging issues for a humanitarian organization. It is an extremely under-reported crime in countries where victims of sexual assault are stigmatized. Women and girls remain silent due to shame and the acute fear of being shunned by their families and communities. Moreover, traditional justice systems do not always provide the victim with protection; verdicts can sometimes

The new concept of human security also raises awareness of threats to the physical security of refugees other than direct attacks or military activity. These include an understanding of the existential insecurity introduced by insufficient or irregular supplies of food because of ration cuts or other restrictions. Such shortfalls not only threaten lives but are linked to an increase in domestic or sexual violence and other crimes in protracted refugee situations. In other circumstances urban refugees, who often lack any assistance or secure legal status, may be targeted for crimes and abuse by the host population (see Box 2.4).

State security strategies within and across borders

In the late 1990s a number of UN Security Council resolutions marked the increasing attention of states to security issues arising from refugee movements. In these resolutions, states recognized that massive population displacement could constitute a threat to regional and international peace and stability, and even represent a result in further human rights violations. In some cultures a woman can be forced to marry her attacker.

Many countries of asylum have failed to incorporate into domestic law the provisions in international or regional human rights instruments—which they ratified—on the protection of women. Combined with gender-biased provisions in domestic law, they work to minimize women's opportunities to seek legal recourse.

Throughout the 1990s, UNHCR supported initiatives which addressed sexual and gender-based violence. Published in 1991, UNHCR's *Guidelines on the Protection of Refugee Women* went beyond conventional ideas of protection by stressing two very important points: the intrinsic relationship between protection and assistance, and the notion that the participation of refugees in the decision-making process promotes protection. Following the *Guidelines,* UNHCR came out with a guide for protection officers on sexual and gender-based violence, increasing awareness of the issue, and established legal and counselling services in the field.

In 1993, the Women Victims of Violence Project in Kenya, later passed on by UNHCR to CARE-Kenya, established drop-in centres that enabled women to report sexual violence. In order to reduce the vulnerability and exposure of women to assault while collecting firewood, UNHCR and its implementing partners carried out the Firewood Project in 1997. This assisted with firewood distribution, covering 30 per cent of household firewood consumption in the Dadaab camps in Kenya. In Guinea, the government collaborated with UNHCR and NGOs on education campaigns on women's issues within the refugee community. In the refugee camps for Burundians in Tanzania, UNHCR and its implementing partners focused on awareness-raising and the provision of proper legal, medical and psycho-social support to victims of sexual violence. Efforts were also made to involve more women in health and education activities.

Conclusion

Addressing sexual and gender-based violence has proven a challenge for the humanitarian community, though considerable progress has been made on the issue. While there have been significant efforts over the last two decades to place sexual and gender-based violence on international and national policy agendas, glaring gaps in the protection of women against abuse still exist. According to UNHCR, in 2004 alone 157 incidents of sexual and gender-based violence were reported in Bhutanese refugee camps in Nepal, 259 cases were recorded in the Dadaab refugee camp area in Kenya, and more than 1,200 cases were documented in refugee camps in Tanzania. These are just some of the instances where women have suffered violence with little recourse to medical, psychological or legal help.

Today, UNHCR is working towards a more coordinated approach to combat sexual and gender-based violence. Known as the multi-sectoral approach, it seeks change through the involvement of all actors who provide services to the survivors of sexual and gender-based violence. This approach recognizes that such women and girls may need the support of a number of sectors, including health and community services, the judiciary and law enforcement. When it comes to violence against women, all have a role to play both in preventing it and responding to it.

deliberate strategy of war. More concretely, the Security Council linked population displacement to threats to international peace and security and considered such threats grounds for international action in Haiti, Iraq, Kosovo, Liberia, Rwanda and Somalia.[11]

Displacement has certainly contributed to the endemic instability in Africa's Great Lakes region. The volatility here is to some extent the result of a tradition among refugee warriors of allying themselves with political factions—whether in government or opposition—in their host state and becoming entangled in that state's internal politics (see Box 3.2).[12] Here and elsewhere, refugees have become linked to the foreign-policy strategies of states, undermining the very notion of the non-political nature of asylum.[13] Indeed, while many states do not possess the resources to identify and disarm combatants within refugee groups, others actively encourage such armed elements on their soil, using them as a bargaining chip in relations with the country of origin.[14]

Box 3.2

The Great Lakes: regional instability and population displacement

It is estimated that at least 3.5 million people have perished in eastern Congo since 1998. At present, one thousand die there each day as a result of violence, starvation and disease. More than 3 million Congolese, Burundians and Rwandans remain displaced in the region. Furthermore, according to UN estimates, some 20,000–40,000 child soldiers have been recruited into the ranks of warring groups and more than 40,000 women have been victims of sexual violence. Overall, some two-thirds of the population in the Democratic Republic of Congo (DRC) suffers from malnutrition. Approximately 70 per cent of the children in the country do not go to school.

The unrest continues to revolve around the rivalries among the Tutsi, Hutu and other ethnic groups in the area that have been exploited by the governments of the DRC and its neighbours to advance their respective agendas. Porous national borders and ethnic, cultural and historical links between the inhabitants of these countries have transformed intra-state unrest into inter-state conflicts. These have assumed a regional dimension and produced massive population displacements within and across borders.

Concern about continued political instability and population displacement in the region has prompted a number of outside actors to try and contain or resolve the political and humanitarian tragedy. Beginning in 1999, the UN Security Council created a peacekeeping mission (MONUC) for the DRC. The mission's mandate and size were gradually expanded, and by 2004 it had become the largest UN peacekeeping operation in the world. Furthermore, between 1999 and 2003, mediation efforts led by South Africa prompted neighbouring states such as Angola, Burundi, Namibia, Rwanda, Uganda and Zimbabwe to withdraw their troops from the DRC.

Despite these initial steps, the cycle of violence and displacement in the DRC intensified. The country's eastern neighbours continued to exploit ethnic cleavages and used Congolese proxies to pursue their objectives. The scale of the fighting and population displacement was particularly extensive in Ituri, adjacent to Uganda. MONUC established a limited presence in Ituri to monitor the situation. But humanitarian agencies in the region faced many obstacles in gaining access to victims because of the vastness of the territory, poor infrastructure, the impenetrability of the rain forest where many displaced people sought refuge, and intimidation and violence by armed elements. Between 1999 and 2003, more than 50,000 people were killed and some 600,000 displaced in Ituri alone, with 10,000 refugees entering Uganda. The population displacement peaked in mid-2003, by which time a total of 3.4 million Congolese had been forced to flee their homes.

A significant milestone was reached in July 2003 with the creation of the Government of National Unity and Transition in Kinshasa which included the various Congolese political factions. This arrangement was brokered with the assistance of South Africa. As a consequence, hundreds of thousands of internally displaced persons and refugees returned to their homes. Meanwhile, negotiations between the Burundian government and several rebel groups bore fruit, resulting in a ceasefire agreement that paved the way for the return of thousands of refugees and internally displaced persons.

But in spite of the positive developments, the cycle of violence and displacement in the eastern part of the DRC continued. In South Kivu, a mutiny by Congolese army units in May 2004 prompted tens of thousands of people to flee the fighting, crossing into Burundi and Rwanda. Only weeks later, in July, armed clashes in Ituri between local militias led to the displacement of 35,000 Congolese. Furthermore, when Rwandan forces launched cross-border operations in the DRC to pursue Rwandan Hutu insurgents in late 2004, more than 100,000 people were displaced by the fighting; some 40,000 became refugees in Burundi and Rwanda.

The violence and displacement in eastern Congo continue to threaten regional security and the welfare of the entire population of that area. Some progress is being achieved on the political, humanitarian and security fronts, albeit in a gradual manner. Extricating the region from the spiral of destruction and displacement entails the disarming of militias by the Congolese military and MONUC. Also required are a political process that fosters reconciliation and generous measures of humanitarian assistance and development investment.

Another facet of the interplay between refugee flows and states relates to internal security and stability. This is linked to the greater availability of small arms in conflict zones, as well as potential conflicts over resources created by the presence of large groups of refugees. Rapid and massive refugee flows can aggravate instability in states facing economic problems, political uncertainty and ethnic or social tensions. Tensions between refugees and their host population may be the result of actual or

Map 3.1 The Great Lakes Region, *June 2005*

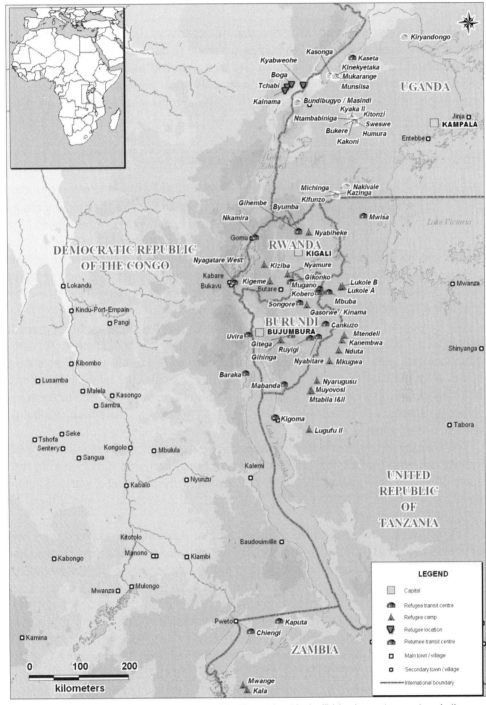

perceived competition for resources or of resentment when refugees are seen as privileged in relation to their poorer hosts. This has been the case in Kenya, for instance.

These tensions may lead to other security concerns. In Ethiopia, Kenya and Tanzania, the areas around refugee camps are prone to banditry, the blame for which often falls on refugees. Such problems are aggravated in poor states and those in which a weak governing authority is unable to exercise sovereignty effectively.[15] In such places, the security threats faced by refugees and the local population are often the same.

Host communities and humanitarian workers

Protracted refugee situations pose additional difficulties, especially when uprooted people lack educational and economic opportunities and where their prospects for durable solutions are limited. This is often the case in host countries where local inhabitants also struggle to survive. Some 90 per cent of the world's refugees live in developing nations, where economic stagnation and unemployment are high and general opportunities low. The resulting competition, be it real or perceived, for scarce resources leads to friction between refugees and the local population. The latter often blame the former for a variety of problems, including increases in crime.

The existence of a link between high crime rates and the presence of refugees is widely accepted, even though the nature of this link is often unclear. In some situations refugees resort to illegal activities as a result of general economic scarcity—or to fill breaks in their food supply. Yet crime rates are influenced not only by refugees but also by changing patterns of conflict across borders. Furthermore, refugees' attempts to breach restrictions on their freedom of movement, economic activity or self-reliance are sometimes labelled crimes.

The security threats that host populations and refugees often share, such as rebel activity, ongoing conflict and scarcity may also bring them into direct conflict with each other. Where existing problems are exploited by politicians with intolerant agendas, the result in both rich and poor countries is xenophobia and attacks on refugees (see Box 3.4).

Conflict-prone environments also endanger the humanitarian workers who help refugees. The surge in attacks on such workers risks undermining the fundamental viability of humanitarian assistance in many of today's conflict zones. Staff of various UN agencies, the International Committee of the Red Cross (ICRC) and NGOs have been intimidated, physically threatened, kidnapped or killed while trying to carry out their duties (see Box 3.3). The UN Security Council has stressed that guaranteeing the security of aid workers is a major challenge when providing assistance to populations of concern.[16]

Yet, although humanitarian workers in war zones are at risk, their presence can also discourage attacks on the displaced. This was frequently the case in the Balkans and in the African Great Lakes region in the 1990s.[17] The dangers faced by humanitarian personnel have raised difficult questions about the role of the military and other security forces in refugee protection. More recently, in Afghanistan and Iraq, ongoing political conflict and military intervention have risked undermining the perceived neutrality of aid workers, with direct consequences for their security.

Developing responses

Some of the security threats outlined above are of long standing. However, in recent years there has been more awareness of the interconnectedness of various threats as well as a more concerted effort to address them. Conceiving of security as a shared concern also means conceiving of it as a shared responsibility. Under international law, a state is obliged to ensure the physical protection of all those who reside within its borders—refugees included—and it remains the responsibility of the host state to prevent the militarization of refugee-populated areas. At the same time, the security of refugees and their hosts is also a collective endeavour, both to prevent dangerous situations from occurring and to stop their escalation.

The principle of shared responsibility for refugee security among all multilateral and bilateral actors was inscribed in UNHCR's Executive Committee Resolution 58 of 1987, when international concern was focused on armed attacks on refugee camps.[18] Recent years have seen further acceptance of this principle both in multilateral forums and in operational practice. This acceptance can also be seen as a response to new concerns such as terrorism or sexual and gender-based violence, all of which threaten the security of refugees in multiple ways. At its worst, however, it can mean an outsourcing of state responsibility to international actors.

Enlarging the multilateral mandate

Since the early 1990s and the crises in Bosnia and Herzegovina and Rwanda in particular, security has become a bigger issue in refugee assistance. At the United Nations, this shift is reflected in Security Council resolutions 1208 (1998) and 1296 (2000), which directly address the security and neutrality of refugee camps.[19] Among other things, these resolutions establish the legal parameters for authorizing action under the UN Charter, which could involve the deployment of international military forces and monitors to address insecurity in camps. In line with expanded notions of security, the resolutions also aim to link up humanitarian, political and military activities.

Security has also been the subject of informal discussions among governments following UN Secretary-General Kofi Annan's report on the causes of conflict in Africa and his two reports on the protection of civilians in armed conflict.[20] During this process states have called on UNHCR to provide advice, training and technical assistance to host states to help them discharge their responsibilities to refugees.

UNHCR's Executive Committee concluded in 1993 that the organization 'may monitor the personal security of refugees and asylum seekers and take appropriate

Box 3.3

Security of humanitarian workers

A survey of the period 1985–98 registered a total of 256 humanitarian workers[i] killed in the line of duty, or an average of 18 per year. For later years the counts are higher, estimates ranging from an annual average of 22 to 41 violent deaths over a seven-year period. Combined with front-page media reports of dramatic security incidents, such figures have contributed to the widespread notion that humanitarian workers today are at greater risk of violent death than before. But what do these numbers mean?

Has the security risk increased?

Statistics in this area are notoriously poor, making it difficult to determine trends and assess risk. It is indicative that the only two careful studies done in recent years arrive at very different conclusions. A report published by the European Commission's Humanitarian Office (ECHO) in 2004 counted 158 violent deaths among humanitarian workers in the period 1997–2003; an annual average of 22.[ii] Given the vast growth in humanitarian activities—there has been a fivefold increase in international humanitarian aid in the past two decades—the conclusion must be that the security risk to the individual worker has decreased substantially. However, a similar report undertaken by the Geneva-based Centre for Humanitarian Dialogue (CHD) in 2005 and covering the same period found almost twice as many violent deaths, i.e. 291.[iii] Even allowing for the increase in humanitarian workers worldwide, a doubling of the annual rate of violent deaths (i.e. from 18 to 41) compared to earlier years studied suggests very significant risk.

The different conclusions demonstrate the depth of the assessment problem. There are no statistics on the number of humanitarian workers worldwide and no common reporting procedures for different agencies. The definition of what constitutes violence against humanitarian workers differs. For example, should it include a scuffle with a security guard or an assault on a local driver on short-term hire? Analysts can apply very different definitions and arrive at very different conclusions, as is apparent above. Nevertheless, some conclusions seem reasonable:

- *The increasing number of deaths reflects above all the expansion of humanitarian activities in or near conflict zones.* The most marked increase in humanitarian aid occurred after the Cold War, when the number of civil wars and new possibilities for collective

Figure 3.1   Estimates of humanitarian workers killed 1997-2003

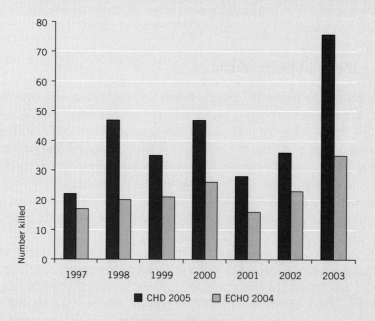

Sources: Centre for Humanitarian Dialogue, *No Relief*, Geneva 2005;
ECHO, *Report on Security of Humanitarian Personnel*, 2004;
both based on D. King, 'Chronology of Humanitarian Aid Workers Killed in 1997-2003', 15 January 2004.

Figure 3.2 Humanitarian aid 1971-2003

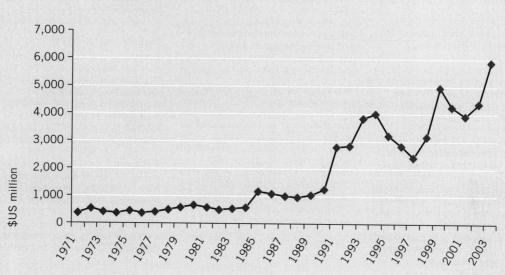

Source: OECD/DAC, Paris. Values in constant 2003 dollars.

intervention brought more aid operations into theatres of conflict.

- *The security risk to individual humanitarian workers has probably decreased.* Humanitarian aid—and therefore probably humanitarian operations as well as the number of workers in the field—has expanded faster than the incidence of violent death among humanitarian workers, even if we use the high death estimates for recent years. This is especially clear from the late 1990s and onwards (except in 2003). In good years, the security risk to individual staff members was by any measure very low. For instance, by the beginning of this century, the United Nations had some 60,000–70,000 staff around the world.[iv] In 2001, according to the Secretary-General, three were killed; the following year the number rose to six (not including three who died in a helicopter crash).

- *The security risk is not evenly spread.* One crisis could have a

major impact not only on the media and public opinion, but—given the overall small numbers—on the casualty statistics as well. Thus, the relative stability and even decline in violent deaths among humanitarian workers since 1997 was abruptly broken by the events of 2003. The bombing of the UN headquarters in Baghdad and violence in Afghanistan accounted for about half of the deaths of humanitarian workers that year. A decade earlier, events in two countries—Bosnia and Herzegovina, and Rwanda—similarly made the death count rise sharply in one year (1994). Overall, however, Africa is the region where the most aid workers have been intentionally targeted in recent years.

Threats and targets

Most humanitarian workers who die on the job are intentionally killed. Accidents (such as airplane and car crashes), bombing raids and landmines account for the rest. This

has been the pattern since the mid-1980s, but with one main difference—traffic accidents have declined dramatically from 16 per cent of the violent deaths in the 1985–98 study to only 3 per cent in later years. Increased road-safety consciousness among humanitarian organizations has evidently made a difference.

Most security incidents do not end with death. Humanitarian workers face a range of threats, variously motivated and accompanied by different kinds of violence. Banditry remains a major worry, involving theft of office property and vehicles, the ransacking of warehouses and hijacking of relief convoys. Hostage-taking, bomb threats and harassment are also widespread. A recent survey of security incidents experienced by UN agencies and four major NGOs recorded almost 3,500 in one year alone, not including accidents. According to the CHD 2005 report, most frequent were cases of theft (1,833), unspecified non-lethal violence and assault on the agency or its personnel (1,166), harassment (302), bomb threats (40) and deaths (37).

Deadly violence takes different forms in different regions. In Iraq, humanitarian workers are most likely to be killed or injured by bombs. In Afghanistan, they face ambushes and executions. In Angola, they risk running across landmines. More local staff are killed than internationals—information from 1997–2003 suggests about twice as many,[v] but there is little systematic data to explain why. The number of local staff may be larger at the outset, or more exposed in the field, as in the case of security guards and drivers. Agencies may employ more national than international staff in high-risk areas such as Iraq. Local employees may be more vulnerable for political reasons than expatriates.

Until recently, most of the humanitarian workers killed were UN staff—only a third worked for NGOs.[vi] This started to change in 1999, and soon the pattern was reversed, with two NGO staff killed for every UN employee who suffered the same fate.[vii] Lack of systematic information makes it difficult to provide precise explanations for the difference, but there may be several.

The expansion of NGO activities started in the early 1990s. However, the simple increase in numbers—and the addition of inexperienced people in the field—tells only part of the story. Different security strategies are also important. As the security environment deteriorated in the early 1990s, UN agencies sought protection by 'hardening targets' (erecting outer compound walls, requiring two vehicles for field missions, etc.). This may have reduced the casualty rate even before the minimum operating security standards (MOSS) were instituted in 2001. Most NGOs, however, continued to rely on good

relations with the local population for protection, using the so-called 'acceptance' approach. From another perspective, this appeared as a greater willingness to take risks.

Security and neutrality

Violence against humanitarian workers does not strike only at the new and inexperienced. Nor does it spare agencies that stringently adhere to the neutrality principle—the ICRC headquarters in Baghdad was bombed. Some NGOs, by contrast, have long expressed the primacy of solidarity over strict neutrality—a tradition that goes back to the Biafra war of the late 1960s—and have not been targeted for that reason. Rather, the growing violence against humanitarian workers reflects the changing context and nature of warfare as well as an assertive and expanding humanitarian response.

Not only did the international humanitarian regime grow in the 1990s, it also began to mount more

Figure 3.3   Intentionally killed humanitarian workers, 1997-2003, by region

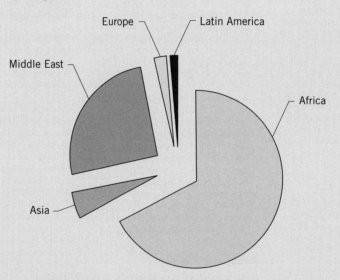

Source: D. King, 2004.

operations within areas of conflict. More humanitarian agencies moved from assisting refugees safely behind battle zones to working on the typically shifting front lines of conflict. Meanwhile, paramilitary forces and militias attacked civilian populations without respecting the Red Cross and Red Crescent symbols. State military forces also violated international humanitarian law.

In wars where population movement and relief supplies were strategic assets, humanitarian workers became part of the struggle. As the political element of humanitarian action became more explicit, neutrality—and the safety it was thought to provide—eroded. Seeking protection from international military forces or even UN peacekeepers, as some humanitarian workers did, further underlined the tension between the need for security and the principle of neutrality.

Since the first Gulf War (1991), military forces have taken on more humanitarian tasks. Western military forces provided critical logistical functions in the Rwanda refugee crisis in 1994 and built refugee camps and organized relief supplies during the Kosovo crisis in 1999. US and NATO forces have explicitly combined humanitarian, political and military operations through joint civilian–military teams deployed in insecure areas, as in Afghanistan. This militarization of humanitarian space has reduced the perceived neutrality of aid workers.

Western military intervention for purposes of regime change has intensified the neutrality dilemma of humanitarian agencies. If humanitarian workers entered in the wake of controversial and contested interventions, they risked being perceived as partisan even if their intentions were strictly

humanitarian. Funding from intervening states accentuated this perception, and insecurity increased markedly. It is striking that more humanitarian workers were victims of targeted killings in 2003—the year of high casualties in Iraq and Afghanistan—than in the three preceding years taken together.

Whether humanitarian action is perceived as a fig leaf for political inaction, as in Bosnia and Herzegovina, or as bandaging the wounds after military action, as in Iraq, the security of aid workers is compromised. Aid agencies have responded in varied ways—by withdrawing or suspending aid, hardening targets, or seeking protection from the military. But none of the responses comes without cost, and some entail limits on humanitarian action.

Figure 3.4   Humanitarian workers killed 1997–2003, cause of death

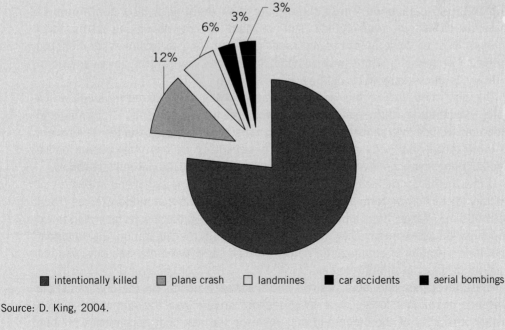

| ▪ intentionally killed | ▨ plane crash | ☐ landmines | ▪ car accidents | ▪ aerial bombings |

Source: D. King, 2004.

action to prevent or redress violations thereof.' Security Council Resolution 1208 also stressed the need for refugee-hosting countries to develop institutions and procedures to implement the provisions of international law. The resolution repeatedly called for the location of camps away from borders to prevent the involvement of refugees in the conflict from which they fled.

Furthermore, in 2002 UNHCR's Executive Committee called on the agency to develop mechanisms to ensure the demilitarization of refugee camps. The Rwandan emergency in the mid-1990s pushed this enlarged security agenda forward by bringing home the security challenges confronting refugee operations in the absence of an existing security apparatus, be it of the host government or the United Nations.

The 'ladder of options' and beyond

Wherever armed elements or combatants might be present, assuring the civilian and humanitarian character of asylum and of the areas hosting refugee populations involves a range of measures. These include disarming and demobilizing armed exiles, preventing the flow of arms between refugees, protecting refugees from attack and intimidation, and separating combatants or war criminals from refugees.

There are various ways in which the international community has tried to address this challenge, most prominently by developing the so-called 'ladder of options'.[21] The ladder represents an assessment-and-response tool. It describes a series of possible and ideally *multilateral* responses to escalating threats to the civilian and humanitarian character of refugee camps and to the security of refugees and humanitarian personnel. These threats are then dealt with by a continuum of measures ranked in order of their 'soft' or 'hard' nature, depending on the local context. Most of these measures represent different ways to assure separation and exclusion of persons who—mainly because of their continuing involvement in military conflict—cannot be defined as refugees.

The 'soft' measures of the ladder include preventive and corrective steps which build cooperation with national law-enforcement mechanisms. 'Intermediate' measures include international support for national security forces and the deployment of international fact-finding missions and observers as well as international police forces. 'Hard' methods involve the use of regional or international military forces.

Under the harder measures, once a mandate is secured, regional and international military forces may perform a number of roles alongside national military forces. Their activities may range from monitoring and intelligence-gathering to reconnaissance and situation assessment. They may also be involved in the separation, disarmament and demobilization of combatants; border control; camp-perimeter security; and the training of national military forces.

These measures have both positive and negative aspects. On the one hand, the presence of military forces in a refugee camp undermines the humanitarian and civilian character of the camp and may increase the risk of it becoming a military

UN aid workers, escorted by Australian peacekeepers, board a helicopter to evacuate the border town of Atambua in West Timor, Indonesia, on 7 September 2000. Dozens of foreign aid workers fled West Timor that day after a mob led by pro-Indonesian militia gangs killed three UN workers and three local people. (AP Photo/UN/P. Green/2000)

target. On the other, the presence of a well-disciplined and well-equipped military force in the vicinity of a camp may act as a deterrent against attack and the militarization of the camp.

The deployment of ECOMIL (Economic Community of West African States Mission in Liberia) troops in August 2003 had an immediate impact, reducing security fears in and around the camps for refugees and internally displaced people in the vicinity of the Liberian capital, Monrovia. It secured the camps and forced armed militiamen to withdraw. Arguably, the rapid deployment of humanitarian and security personnel in and around refugee-populated areas during the initial phase of a humanitarian emergency helps deter armed elements from infiltrating the population or targeting refugees. The ECOMIL troops were eventually replaced by international civilian police officers.

In Nepal, the introduction in 2003 of a well-equipped security force in the area around refugee camps has reduced the movement of unidentified groups at night and prevented attacks on the camps. In Uganda, on the other hand, the lack of a fully effective military force in the north of the country has allowed the Lords Resistance Army rebels to attack settlements of refugees and internally displaced people.

The use of international civilian police (CIVPOL) monitors, authorized under the UN Charter to train and assist police in ensuring camp security, is one way the international community can support refugee security when it cannot be guaranteed by the host state. CIVPOL monitors may be deployed—without the express permission of the host state—as part of a multinational peacekeeping or peace-building force. However, they will be less effective if the host state does not acknowledge their mandate. The United Nations authorized such monitors for Angola, Bosnia and Herzegovina, Cambodia, East Timor, Haiti, Kosovo, Mozambique and Somalia. CIVPOL officers were involved in these interventions as advisers, monitors and instructors. Later, in Kosovo and East Timor, CIVPOL was replaced by armed law-enforcement officers with full executive authority, including the right to use deadly force.[22]

Security packages

The aim of the ladder of options is to enhance the effectiveness of responses to security threats in refugee situations. In practice its application has been largely restricted to operations which fall broadly under the 'soft' end of the ladder. Frequently, due to the absence of states with the capacity or willingness to engage themselves, so-called 'security packages' have been implemented by UNHCR in consultation with host governments and some bilateral donors. In the best-case scenario such programmes are aimed at building and sustaining the capacity of a host state to provide and promote refugee security. However, where relationships among all actors deteriorate, these measures may introduce new security problems.

During the Rwandan refugee crisis in the mid-1990s, UNHCR hired a contingent of Zairean soldiers to support security in the Congolese camps. The move was initially successful; later, however, these troops became embroiled in the conflict as well. In Kosovo, UNHCR issued guidelines for quasi-national security forces, and in the late 1990s more formal arrangements to improve refugee security based on security packages were concluded, first with Tanzania and then with Kenya and Guinea. These experiences paved the way for similar strategies in other countries, among them Ghana, Liberia, Sierra Leone and, most recently, Chad.

Broadly, the aim of security packages is to reduce the level of insecurity and criminality in refugee camps and safeguard their civilian and humanitarian character. The packages increasingly contain specific references to a reduction in sexual and gender-based violence. They are linked to the deployment of specially trained police officers both in and around refugee settlements who collaborate with international

Field Safety Advisors (FSAs). The FSAs also liaise with the law-enforcement authorities at the district and regional levels on all security matters, monitor the deployment of police officers and their performance, and participate in the training of new police contingents. Ideally the underlying agreement with the host government also includes commitments to instruct both refugees and hosts on the refugee–related laws and regulations in the country as well as international refugee law. Security packages may be linked to provisions for joint screening and the separation of armed combatants from refugees.

The responsibilities of police in such packages include the disarmament of refugees prior to their admission to camps; the maintenance of controls to prevent the entry of arms into camps; and the identification, arrest and prosecution of criminals. The hope is that their presence alongside humanitarian actors may deter criminal or rebel activity, besides providing recourse to law when crimes are committed. Law-enforcement personnel may include national police, paramilitary forces and refugee security guards. Where such a presence does not exist, the problems are all too apparent. In Nepal, it is very difficult to get the police or members of a joint-security force to a refugee camp at night—the area around the camps is considered too insecure.[23] With the police reluctant to show up, crime in the camps has increased.

Another challenge is that of aligning police practices with protection. It has been shown in both Guinea and Tanzania that when security forces are trained to understand refugee law and issues related to sexual and gender-based violence they are better able to provide camp security. Codes of conduct for the police are used to define appropriate behaviour and contribute to greater accountability within the force.

With proper supervision and training, security mechanisms that involve refugee guards, wardens, patrols and watch teams can be highly effective. But such teams can be successful in maintaining security and order only if their roles and responsibilities are clearly defined, and they have good relations with the host country's law-enforcement authorities. Refugee participation is seen in a system of refugee security volunteers (*Sungu-sungus*) in Tanzania, community-watch teams in Liberia and a neighbourhood-watch system in Ghana.[24]

In Zambia, which hosts Angolan and Congolese refugees, neighbourhood-watch programmes have led to a reduction in crime, the identification of armed elements and improvements in aid distribution. In Sierra Leone, the active cooperation of Liberian refugee wardens with the local police has improved camp security. Overall, refugee security mechanisms function effectively when they complement or supplement the general law-enforcement system of the host country. However, if not monitored properly, both such refugee-empowerment initiatives and the introduction of external police could lead to vigilante justice or harassment of less-powerful refugees.

In this context, attention must be paid to the criteria by which activities may be judged detrimental to the civilian and humanitarian character of camps in order to prevent arbitrary arrest or punishment. Finally, such programmes cannot succeed without continuous coordination, exchange of information and monitoring of performance.

Defining obligations and strengthening the rule of law

Because of the sometimes very different interests of the many actors involved in refugee security, statements of intent are essential if policies are to be effective. Indeed, they are an essential tool in defining obligations and responsibilities and in formalizing the commitments of all actors involved. Such declarations are generally followed by agreements outlining the rights and responsibilities of the various parties. They also provide a means by which international bodies can define the extent of their support for a host country. That support may include developmental and financial components, such as provisions for training, protection workshops, the payment of allowances and the donation of vehicles and communication equipment. The statements also reaffirm the host state's responsibility for promoting the best interests of the refugee population.

When primarily financed internationally, security packages help to acknowledge and reduce the burden on the host government. However, international funding can also create dependence on the part of the host state, sometimes generating unrealistic expectations. Moreover, in some security packages operational and legal lacunae have been identified in the processing of separated combatants and the management of facilities.

Ultimately, policing alone does not provide effective security, and the range of issues linked to security packages has expanded. UNHCR is now engaged in helping with reform of the legal sector and prisons in various countries. Measures under the soft end of the ladder are increasingly used to deal with the daily issues of physical protection relating to crime, low-level violence and harassment, particularly of women. At the same time, UNHCR is focusing less on issues related to the exclusion of those deemed not entitled to protection and separation of combatants. This is partly due to the political and practical difficulties associated with exclusion and separation processes, but it also reflects an awareness of the broader range of security threats affecting refugees and their hosts. This awareness was heightened following revelations of sexual violence and exploitation of refugee women and children in East and West Africa. Those revelations made it painfully evident that a security package has to be complemented by protection and community-service activities.

The deployment of poorly paid and undisciplined police and security forces may exacerbate security problems, sexual abuse and the looting of relief supplies. State capacities to safeguard refugee security cannot therefore be enhanced without bettering the quality of law enforcement and the judiciary and promulgating appropriate legislation. The judicial system has two primary roles: it continues and concludes the work of the police and it checks for potential flaws or abuse, tackling problems that may arise. The rule of law provides an impartial arbitrator in what are

Box 3.4

Xenophobia and refugees

Host communities sometimes view refugees with suspicion and mistrust. Refugees are perceived as a threat to their hosts' economic prosperity, social stability and cultural identity. Even where the local population welcomes refugees, their compassion can falter if refugees increase pressure on housing, social services and the environment, or if they stay for longer than anticipated. Such conditions can create fertile ground for the emergence of xenophobia and intolerance. Furthermore, the situation could be exacerbated by irresponsible news media and manipulation of the refugee issue by self-serving politicians.

Over the past several years, conditions have deteriorated in certain countries. There has been an increase in violent attacks on refugees and harsh rhetoric from politicians who use refugees as scapegoats, blaming them for social ills and economic problems. This trend gathered pace following the events of 11 September 2001, especially in the West, where refugees from Muslim countries were vulnerable to xenophobia and discrimination. In the European Union, where there are ongoing efforts to harmonize asylum policies, media reports and public debates quite often blurred the distinction between issues such as asylum, economic migration and terrorism.

These developments prompted UNHCR to list ten areas of 'most concern'. Among them were the threat of increased xenophobia and racism, and the possibility that governments would introduce legislation that would discriminate against refugees from particular religious, ethnic, national or political backgrounds. In late 2001, UNHCR expressed deep concern about xenophobia and discrimination against Muslims, and urged 'governments and politicians to avoid falling into the trap of making unwarranted linkages between refugees and terrorism.' It also asserted that 'genuine refugees are themselves the victims of terrorism

and persecution, not its perpetrators.' Similar concerns were echoed by the UN High Commissioner for Human Rights, emphasizing the need to combat xenophobia and cautioning against weakening the international refugee protection regime.

Even in countries that have had a tradition of extending a warm welcome to refugees, a change in political, economic or social conditions can lead to the emergence of xenophobia. The case of Côte d'Ivoire serves as a poignant example. Until 2002, this was one of the most stable countries in West Africa, renowned for its vibrant economy, ethnic and religious diversity, and hospitality towards the 70,000 refugees from Liberia in the country. The Liberians, who had arrived in 1989, had been well received and been allowed to reside in villages in the western provinces of Côte d'Ivoire rather than in refugee camps. Moreover, they enjoyed access to work, education and healthcare, and were free to move about the country.

But things changed in September 2002, when a coup attempt against President Laurent Gbagbo provoked a full-scale civil war that severely affected the western provinces. Suspicions that foreign countries, including Liberia, had been involved in the attempted coup led to the rise of anti-foreigner sentiment among Ivorians. Some Ivorian politicians and newspapers added fuel to the fire by accusing the refugees of aiding the rebels. UNHCR tried to ensure the safety of 43,000 Liberian refugees by relocating them away from the conflict areas and resettling the most vulnerable in third countries. Many refugees were the victims of torture, murder and forcible recruitment by both the Ivorian rebel and government forces. In spite of a subsequent peace agreement between the government and rebels, the situation remains fragile and Liberian refugees in Côte d'Ivoire now live in precarious conditions.

Across the Atlantic Ocean, two decades of conflict between the Colombian government and rebel groups has created the worst humanitarian situation in the Western Hemisphere. Some 3 million Colombians have been internally displaced, while as many as 700,000 have fled to neighbouring Venezuela, Ecuador, Panama and Costa Rica. In recent years, political and economic problems coupled with the destabilizing spillover effects of the unrest in Colombia have given rise to xenophobia in these countries. The involvement of Colombian guerrillas in violence, kidnapping and drug trafficking in the border regions has not helped.

UNHCR has pursued a regional strategy to strengthen protection and assistance for Colombian refugees and asylum seekers and counter xenophobia. It has tried to boost public awareness of the refugees' plight through radio advertisements, photo exhibits and educational programmes.

The fight against xenophobia is a global struggle. But substantive moves in the right direction have been taken by the international community. In 2001, the final Declaration and Program of Action adopted by the UN-sponsored World Conference against Racism and Xenophobia contained 15 paragraphs relating to refugees. They dealt with root causes, respect and equitable treatment, durable solutions, responsibility sharing and upholding the 1951 UN Refugee Convention and its 1967 Protocol. Furthermore, in 2003 the Organization of American States adopted a resolution at its general assembly in Santiago, Chile, calling on member states to establish national mechanisms to protect refugees and asylum seekers and combat xenophobia and racism. However, there will be no end to discrimination against refugees until politicians encourage positive attitudes towards diversity and the displaced.

frequently emotionally or politically charged environments. Both refugees and locals are more likely to feel that justice is done if they have access to a fair and impartial judicial system.

Beyond training and material support, in some cases accessibility to justice has been improved by the introduction of mobile courts which convene periodically in a camp, or through the construction of new courts close to refugee-populated areas. In this respect there is a need to ensure that refugees are aware of their rights and the appropriate channels to turn to when these rights have been disregarded. They must also be made aware of their obligations to conform to the laws of the country of refuge and abstain from actions that would compromise the security and neutrality of their camp or settlement.

Preventive strategies

The challenge for the international community and host states is to comprehend the ways in which refugee policies and assistance may themselves help to reduce security threats. Understanding these connections has become an important step in the search for refugee security.

Separating militants from the general refugee population is frequently not as important as addressing the root causes of refugee involvement in crime, violence and military or subversive activities. Some argue that more effort should go towards ensuring good camp management and providing general physical protection to refugees. This necessitates increasingly comprehensive approaches to security measures, and strategies for a broad range of refugee situations which engage key actors at every stage of the humanitarian effort.[25]

Information channels

One of the most effective strategies in reducing security risks for refugees is the effective dissemination of reliable information. Dependable information is the basis of an effective early warning and assessment system which improves refugee security by ensuring that appropriate assistance measures are put in the right place at the right time.

At the country or regional level, early warning of impending emergencies can provide an indication of the composition and needs of refugee groups. Early assessment of the general situation will help gauge requirements regarding the size and location of transit facilities, camps or settlements and other assistance centres. It will allow local and international actors to prepare for potential conflicts or risks. Ideally, it prevents security problems from arising, rather than just dealing with them when they occur. The early assessment of the security situation in the Presevo Valley in Kosovo, for instance, helped prevent an outbreak of violence in the area (see Box 4.1).

Of equal importance to refugee protection are specific assessment and reconnaissance missions designed to provide a detailed evaluation of the security situation, determine the extent of infiltration by armed elements and recommend appropriate measures. For example, a security plan would document the best means to distinguish armed elements or combatants from *bona fide* refugees; identify traditional conflicts or grievances within the refugee population or between refugees and local groups; and indicate the location of landmines or unexploded ordnance in the vicinity of settlements, among other things.

The development of effective and objective information channels as well as reporting and complaint mechanisms is crucial to refugee assistance and protection. Camp situations are often breeding grounds for rumour and misinformation. Credible information channels are therefore vital to give refugees the accurate information required to defuse tensions. Regular and non-confrontational discussions between camp authorities, humanitarian agencies and representatives of host and refugee communities would allow grievances to be voiced and develop a forum for constructive dialogue.

Keeping information channels open is a priority if programmes addressing sexual and gender-based violence are to succeed. An atmosphere of awareness is a precondition when creating an environment in which vulnerable women and children can air their concerns without fear of retribution or social stigma.

Relationships of trust are the most basic building blocks of preventive security strategies. Trust relies not only on transparent procedures but also on direct and easy access to humanitarian and protection personnel, encouraging refugees to report security incidents and fears. This in turn provides a more accurate picture of the security situation and reinforces understanding and respect for mutual responsibilities and obligations under the law.

Another dimension of information is its transformative and educational force. This applies to efforts to accurately inform host populations about the plight of those arriving in their midst, thereby helping to combat prejudice and xenophobia. In many refugee situations peace-education programmes serve a crucial role in helping to resolve conflict at all levels. Such initiatives often require that governments and humanitarian workers alike recognize the importance of refugee self-expression, and challenge them to distinguish between illicit political activity and the necessary and legitimate expression of human concerns. Efforts which aim to engage refugees in peace processes in their home countries may help prevent armed conflict by allowing the channelling of grievances peacefully and by re-establishing constructive relationships between their former homes and places of exile.

National legislation

All states that have acceded to the international instruments relating to the protection and assistance of refugees have an obligation to implement national legislation which is consistent with those instruments. Where a country has not acceded to these instruments, it may still have laws that support the protection of refugees and formalize the customary international norm of *non-refoulement.*

Where national legislation ignores the rights of refugees, it limits their ability to become self-reliant. For example, restrictive legislation in Kenya and Tanzania does not allow refugees to leave camps; as a result, most refugees in these countries remain entirely dependent on international assistance. Besides putting a large financial burden on the international community, this dependence contributes to a climate of idleness and apathy in the camps which may push refugees into crime or military activity.

The same dangers exist in richer countries. Here, government policies which risk undermining the principle of *non-refoulement* or take greater recourse to the detention of asylum seekers present new risks to refugee security.[26] Indeed, as a result of states' increasing fears of international terrorism, many countries have passed restrictive legislation that has made it more difficult for genuine refugees to reach safety. This forces refugees to turn to human smugglers and take ever greater risks in an attempt to reach safety. Indiscriminate detention poses a direct threat to the security of individuals and drives genuine refugees underground. It also links refugees and common criminals in the public mind, increasing prejudice and xenophobic responses. This is just one example of the way in which national refugee policy can create conflicts between refugees and local populations.

Put in simple terms, governments have two options in dealing with refugees: one is to restrict contact between them and the host community; the other is to enhance mutual understanding and thereby help in the creation of common control mechanisms. In this respect, the efforts of some governments to restrict refugee movement do not seem to have had the desired effect of reducing tensions with the local population. Rather, the opposite seems to be the case. Sudanese refugees have been targeted by local communities in Kenya and Uganda. In the former, the majority of the Sudanese belong to an ethnic group that has a history of enmity with the local Turkana people over cattle-rustling. In the latter, the Sudanese Acholi people have traditionally been disliked by the local population.

In contrast, in some areas of Pakistan the government has successfully established a number of informal community-cooperation arrangements to enhance relations between encamped refugees and surrounding communities. In Sierra Leone, where locals have generally regarded the refugee population with suspicion, the separation of armed elements and the direction of resources towards local communities have defused these tensions.

Refugee camps

Camps may be a convenient way to channel and distribute humanitarian aid to large groups of refugees. At the same time, they are unnatural, closed environments which can leave refugees vulnerable to manipulation and exploitation, with the danger

Box 3.5

HIV/AIDS and refugees

While the refugee status should not be equated with an increased risk of contracting HIV, the nature of a refugee environment may increase the vulnerability of people—especially women, adolescents and children—to the disease. HIV/AIDS spreads faster where there is poverty, lawlessness and social instability; these are the conditions that often give rise to, or accompany, forced displacement.

The link between the respect and protection of human rights and effective HIV/AIDS programmes is clear. People will not seek HIV-related counselling, testing, treatment and care if lack of confidentiality, discrimination, *refoulement*, restrictions on freedom of movement or other negative consequences could follow a positive diagnosis. For these reasons, an essential component in refugee protection is the creation of a legal and ethical environment which is protective of the human rights of HIV/AIDS victims. Towards that aim, in June 2004 UNHCR became the tenth co-sponsor of UNAIDS, thereby helping to broaden and strengthen the UN response to the global epidemic. Since then, UNHCR has collaborated with other organizations to advocate the inclusion of refugee issues in countries' plans, proposals and policies related to HIV/AIDS.

Examples of such cooperation include:

- Nigeria: UNHCR received funds from UNAIDS for an HIV/AIDS prevention project at Oru Camp.

- Pakistan: UNHCR and other sponsors provided funds to support a National HIV/AIDS programme officer for three years.

- Indonesia: Training of asylum seekers on HIV/AIDS prevention was supported by UNAIDS.

- Yemen: A joint UNAIDS–UNHCR mission to assess the prevalence of HIV/AIDS among refugees in Yemen was undertaken.

- Great Lakes Initiative on AIDS: The UNAIDS Secretariat, the World Bank and governments in the region have cooperated extensively on this innovative and important sub-regional initiative.

- Mano River Union (MRU) Initiative on AIDS: UNHCR has increased collaboration with the UNAIDS Secretariat, UNFP, the African Development Bank and the Governments involved in the MRU.

Given the movements of displaced populations, UNHCR emphasizes a sub-regional approach linking countries of asylum and origin. These initiatives acknowledge two key points. The first is that refugees and other migrant populations have frequent and sometimes sustained interactions with surrounding host communities. This regular contact places both groups at increased risk of contracting or transmitting HIV. The second is the inherent mobility of these populations. The frequent movements of refugees and other migrant populations often make it more difficult to provide them with the HIV services they require. The creation of regional and/or sub-regional plans will help to ensure that refugees, returnees and other migrant populations find care throughout their travels, potentially reducing the risk of HIV transmission in the host-country population.

Sub-regional and regional HIV/AIDS plans provide services to people who might not otherwise receive regular care. They allow more mobile populations, such as refugees and those in the transport sector, to continue to be treated. More comprehensive interventions, such as anti-retroviral therapy, are also made possible. The ability to provide and sustain such treatment has become increasingly important in moving toward the goal of providing access to HIV/AIDS treatment to all those who need it.

increasing where such situations are prolonged.[27] Where encampment cannot be avoided in the first instance, planning is essential to ensure that the size, layout and organization of a refugee camp are conducive to the maintenance of security, especially for vulnerable groups such as female-headed households, single women, unaccompanied children and the elderly.

Here size and location can make a difference. In Kenya, the huge refugee camp of Kakuma, with 90,000 refugees, and the three camps of Dadaab (Dagahaley, Ifo and Hagadera) with more than 35,000 people each, are quite difficult to manage in terms of aid distribution and oversight.[28] To mitigate some of the adverse effects of encampment, guidelines advise that a camp's population should not exceed 20,000 and that it should provide at least 45 square metres per person.[29]

Furthermore, adequate access to basic services such as water, latrines, distribution points and educational facilities can help enhance security, as can proper lighting at night.

Placing or relocating refugee camps a significant distance from national borders or areas of lawlessness helps improve security. But this can only be done with the approval of the host government. In 2003, the Government of Guinea accepted the relocation of refugees from the south to more central locations in order to reduce the threat posed by combatants infiltrating the settlements.[30] In Panama and Chad, relocation has helped ease security concerns for Colombian and Sudanese refugees, respectively.[31] Often, however, host governments are reluctant to have camps moved to, or established in, locations away from the border for political reasons. They may fear that the further from the border the refugees are, the more difficult it will be to send them home.

In some contexts, resistance to relocation may come from the refugees themselves. They may share ethnic, linguistic, religious or cultural traits with local communities closer to the border, making assimilation or cohabitation easier. Indeed, locating camps in areas where a sense of community can be fostered is beneficial to both local and refugee populations. The trade-offs inherent in such decisions must be carefully evaluated in consultation with the refugees.

Improving refugee–host relations

Real or perceived competition for scarce resources is bound to breed mistrust and intolerance and sometimes open aggression. In this sense, effective refugee protection needs to address the relationship between refugees and their hosts; ideally it would integrate the needs and rights of both populations to the greatest extent possible. In developing countries this means minimizing disparities between the standards of living of refugees and host populations. Improvements to the infrastructure for water, sanitation, health and roads must benefit the entire local community if refugees are not to be perceived as a privileged group and thereby resented. Communication strategies must link material assistance to the themes of co-existence and respect for human rights, while public-information programmes teach the local population about refugees.[32] Local authorities should be helped to communicate with refugee representatives to promote trust between the communities and provide a mediation mechanism in case of conflict.

The establishment of programmes to raise ecological awareness in large refugee populations can help stimulate the local economy and minimize the impact of refugees on the environment, thereby reducing potential conflicts with the local population. Programmes in which firewood is harvested from sustainable sources or purchased from local contractors and supplied to the camps may help to dissuade refugees from sourcing it themselves, again reducing conflicts with the local community.

Empowerment of refugees

Ultimately, the ability of people to act on their own is critical to human security.[33] It enhances the credibility of information and allows people to exercise their potential as individuals and to re-establish or reintegrate into peaceful and functioning communities. The participation of refugees in the physical planning and management of a camp is thus as essential as their involvement in the mechanisms governing assistance and protection. This applies to the smallest unit of human organization, the family unit, which is a vital mechanism for security and stability in a refugee camp. Parental responsibility enhances the safety and discipline of children and youths. Moreover, it increases the protection of women and children from sexual abuse and prevents the recruitment of youths for military purposes.

In this context, educational opportunities and training programmes not only provide opportunities for the future but also help prevent the recruitment of youths by armed and subversive elements. In protracted refugee situations primary and secondary education, vocational training and income-generating programmes help refugees become economically self-sufficient and restore their self-esteem. Such initiatives are generally seen to have a positive impact on security both in the short and long term.

Future concerns

UNHCR's mandate is to uphold the human rights of people who lack national protection. It has remained constant since the organization was established in 1950. Yet the challenges it meets in addressing these basic principles have changed over time, and past experiences have provided lessons for the future. The refugee protection regime was not established to address the root causes of conflict that create refugees, but the nature of the task of refugee protection will ensure that security issues will always be an integral part of it.

Today, security has multiple and interdependent dimensions. Expanded notions of human security recognize the importance of non-state agents and redefine a range of interventions as relevant to security. The awareness of these dimensions is fundamental to addressing the security concerns involved in refugee assistance. However, it risks evaluating the problems of refugees purely through the lens of security.

It is also important to remember that the many dimensions of security cannot always be integrated into one response. Almost all refugee-security strategies underline the need of the host state to fulfil its obligation to protect refugees within its borders. If a host state is unwilling or unable to do so, United Nations practice suggests that some type of international response may be an option. Security packages, while ameliorating some threats, often risk trying to do too many things at once. They cannot, ultimately, respond to the problems of militarization of refugee camps or cross-border conflict. These are issues which cannot be resolved solely through humanitarian response, but rather require intervention at the political level.

4 Responding to emergencies

If the past is any guide, the world can expect a big emergency involving human displacement every 16 months—and a massive one every two years. In the past 15 years there have been seven of the latter, each of which has resulted in the displacement of more than 1.5 million people.[1] Since the 1991 Gulf War the international emergency-response system, in which UNHCR plays a major role, has been strengthened in the areas of planning, human resources, supply stockpiles and early warning systems. But despite these efforts, its effectiveness has been uneven.

The reasons for that patchy record include the reluctance of the international community to take strong action to defuse conflict, funding shortfalls, insecurity in areas of humanitarian operations, and the inaccessibility of some of those in need of assistance. Matters have also been complicated by an increase in the number of humanitarian and political actors involved in emergency assistance, the trend towards 'bilateralization' of aid and a constriction of the neutral humanitarian space within which aid personnel can work safely. This chapter looks at how these challenges have spurred the review and reformulation of policies to improve emergency responses in the future.

Historical overview

The establishment of UNHCR in 1951 coincided with the onset of the Cold War. Initially, the agency's main stage of operations was Western Europe, which received refugees fleeing communist regimes. At its inception, UNHCR's work was limited to legal issues, helping governments to adopt laws and procedures to implement the 1951 UN Refugee Convention. Its first major challenge was responding to the exodus of some 200,000 refugees from Hungary in 1956, following the Soviet suppression of the Hungarian uprising.[2]

During the 1960s, as decolonization in Africa gained momentum, UNHCR grew into a refugee agency with a global mandate. The process began when it assisted Algerians who had fled their country's war of independence and sought refuge in neighbouring Tunisia and Morocco and helped them to repatriate at the end of the conflict. The Algerian crisis marked UNHCR's first involvement in Africa. Subsequently UNHCR was exposed to many new challenges and dangers in providing assistance and protection to Rwandan refugees in the Great Lakes region of Africa. By

Refugees from Darfur, Sudan arriving at camps close to the border in Chad. (UNHCR/B. Heger/2004)

1969, about two-thirds of UNHCR's global programme funds were being spent in African countries.[3]

Decolonization and post-independence civil conflicts ranged across much of Africa and Asia in the 1970s and 1980s. The 1971 Bangladesh crisis marked UNHCR's first large-scale involvement in South Asia. As on numerous occasions thereafter, the UN Secretary-General called on UNHCR to play the role of 'focal point' for the overall relief operation. Involving about 10 million refugees, the Bangladesh crisis saw the largest single displacement of people in the second half of the twentieth century. This period was also characterized by the involvement of the Cold War superpowers in internal wars—in the Horn of Africa, Latin America, and Asia—which generated large flows of refugees. UNHCR grew rapidly as it tried to respond to emergencies on three continents.[4]

In the 1990s new conflicts of a different nature arose, and with them came shifts in perceptions about refugees. Western countries in particular began to see refugees as a burden, and turned their efforts to trying to contain them within their region of origin. Consequently, UNHCR became more involved in situations of ongoing armed conflict, necessitating greater cooperation with military forces. This was illustrated by UNHCR's major operation when Kurds fled northern Iraq at the end of the first Gulf War in 1991. Another major and long-term emergency operation started the same year when the violent break-up of the former Yugoslavia led to the largest refugee crisis in Europe since the Second World War.

Other crises in the 1990s which were characterized by large-scale human displacement included those in the Great Lakes region of Africa, West Africa, Southeast Asia and the Horn of Africa. But as the interest of the major donors waned, many crisis areas virtually disappeared from the international political and media maps; at the beginning of the twenty-first century several forgotten refugee situations continued to fester.[5] In Africa in particular, the major powers were reluctant to get involved unless their strategic interests were at stake.

Since 2000, several new or intensified emergencies have made significant demands on humanitarian agencies. These have occurred in Afghanistan, Iraq, Sudan and the countries affected by the tsunami of December 2004.

Preparedness capacity

Over the past decade the international community has paid more attention to emergency preparedness to improve the quality of its response to crises. Self-examination has been a part of this process. The 1996 inter-agency evaluation of the humanitarian response in Rwanda pointed out that aid agencies lacked consistent working definitions of preparedness measures and contingency planning. The report noted that it was important to conceive preparedness broadly to include the advance placement of key technical and logistics staff and adequate mapping and communications equipment.[6]

Some progress has been made, and is reflected in an increase in the number of professionals with emergency-response expertise on humanitarian rosters. User-friendly and efficient emergency procedures and clear standards and guidelines have been instituted. Emergency supplies have been stockpiled, with stand-by purchase arrangements and delivery mechanisms that can be activated rapidly to ensure rapid deployment. Such pre-positioning occurs at the international and regional levels, though the latter tends to have more limited stockpiles.[7] UNHCR has its international stockpiles in Copenhagen and Abu Dhabi and a few regional ones in Africa to cover 500,000 people. Required items can be airlifted within 48 hours in the event of an emergency.[8]

For an emergency involving half a million people UNHCR can deploy between 60 and 125 international staff, depending on the needs and capacities of governments, host communities and partner organizations.[9] Such teams ideally possess the required technical expertise, experience, language skills and gender balance and can be mobilized within 72 hours.[10] This enhanced capacity was well-demonstrated by the rapid response to the tsunami of 2004. However, delays in responding to the crisis in Sudan's Darfur region and the influx of refugees into neighbouring Chad demonstrate that gaps remain.[11]

Early-warning mechanisms and contingency-planning processes provide situation-specific preparedness at the national and regional levels. The contingency-planning process envisions different scenarios on the basis of possible political developments and potential displacement patterns. These are then combined with estimates of staffing and technical need, funding requirements and a demarcation of the responsibilities of different agencies. Lines of authority and communication are specified to ensure smooth coordination. Early warning mechanisms have failed in the past because they were based upon most likely, rather than worst case, scenarios.

Though of crucial importance, the maintenance of a high level of preparedness requires the diversion of resources away from ongoing activities. This can be particularly onerous when agencies face funding shortages and no major emergencies are visible on the horizon to provide immediate justification for the diversion of resources. The dilemma of choosing whether resources should be allocated to emergency-response mechanisms or to regular functions surfaces time and again. It was seen during the Kosovo emergency, when budget cuts had a negative effect on UNHCR's emergency capacity.[12]

Ideally, early warning would lead to interventions that mitigate conflict and halt human rights violations. During the 1990s, alongside its humanitarian operations, UNHCR played an increasingly important role in international political negotiations and exerted leverage over states.[13] Since 2000, the early-warning task force of the Inter-Agency Standing Committee (IASC) has been at the forefront in keeping track of political developments that could require high-level interventions.

The government of the country affected by an emergency has the primary responsibility and authority to coordinate and direct international assistance. As was

Box 4.1

Presevo Valley: preventing another disaster in the Balkans

Towards the end of 2000, clashes between Yugoslav security forces and the Liberation Army of Presevo, Medvedja and Bujanovac (UCPMB) in southern Serbia forced thousands of Albanian villagers from the area to move into neighbouring Kosovo. Although at the time the number of displaced persons was relatively small and the conflict was confined to a five-kilometre-wide strip between Serbia and Kosovo, the hopes for finally achieving peace and stability in the region hung on the line. There was also a danger that the conflict erupting in southern Serbia would have serious implications for Serbs remaining in Kosovo.

In June 1999, following the cessation of NATO's bombing campaign and the return of hundreds of thousands of ethnic Albanian refugees from neighbouring countries to Kosovo, reprisals against the Serb population in the province began. Scores of Serb civilians were forced to flee their homes. Those brave enough to stay behind could not move about freely and had to be under constant guard by NATO. Around the same time, some of the Yugoslav security forces implicated in war crimes in Kosovo were redeployed in the predominantly Albanian municipalities of Presevo,

Medvedja and Bujanovac, referred to by the international community as the Presevo Valley.

An agreement between the Yugoslav security forces and NATO led to the establishment of a five-kilometre-wide buffer zone between Kosovo and southern Serbia which was meant to prevent accidental clashes between the two armies. The establishment of the Ground Safety Zone, as it was called, along with the redeployment of the Yugoslav security forces set the stage for the eventual outbreak of violence in the area.

By the fall of 2000, the reprisals in Kosovo—though far from over—had begun to decline. UNHCR was working with NATO and the UN Mission in Kosovo on 'putting in place the conditions' for Serb returns. Negotiations were underway with the Albanian political leadership to encourage them to recognize the right of the Serbs to return to their homes. There was also a new, more moderate government in Belgrade under the leadership of Yugoslav President Vojislav Kostunica.

It was in this cautious but hopeful environment that the armed struggle of the UCPMB and counter-insurgency operations by the Yugoslav security forces began in

southern Serbia. UNHCR responded immediately to the influx of Albanian villagers into Kosovo and began contingency planning for further displacement. Concerned about possible repercussions on the Serb population in Kosovo, UNHCR's special envoy to the region made a number of assessment missions to southern Serbia to explore means to defuse the conflict.

The Albanians in the Presevo Valley feared the Yugoslav forces from Kosovo operating in the area, whom they accused of intimidation, harassment, the occupation of housing and destruction of property. There was also a history of discrimination against ethnic Albanians in the Presevo Valley which was aggravating the situation and had provoked the rise of the UCPMB. The lack of representation in the local police force—most of the Albanian police had been dismissed by the former regime—was the leading concern, though there were a number of other problems related to education, employment and the media. As the Albanians were also under-represented in the government, they asserted that they were unable to resolve their grievances through the appropriate political structures.

highlighted in the response to the Asian tsunami, the international community does not always adhere to the principle of subsidiarity—whereby larger multilateral institutions do not take on tasks that can be adequately performed by local or regional organizations—during the initial stages of the humanitarian effort.[14] International humanitarian organizations are expected to meet basic needs when governments cannot—or will not for political reasons.[15] This calls for efforts to strengthen the preparedness of regional and sub-regional organizations, which can also operate as part of an effective early warning system.[16]

UNHCR's special envoy drew up a list of confidence-building measures to address these grievances and defuse the situation. He presented these to President Kostunica and the Deputy Prime Minister of Serbia, Nebojsa Covic, who was designated as Belgrade's main interlocutor on the crisis. He also stressed the importance of ending hostilities as soon as possible, given the negative consequences for the Serb population in Kosovo and prospects for the return of those who had fled. The steps that would follow and eventually lead to a peace agreement were achieved through the combined efforts of a remarkable network of partners, including the United Nations, NATO, inter-governmental and regional organizations, and concerned governments.

In early 2001, the Secretary-General's Special Envoy to the Balkans, Carl Bildt, warned that the crisis was the 'most serious threat to stability in the Balkans'. Meanwhile, the High Commissioner for Refugees wrote letters to the Secretary-General of NATO, Lord Robertson, and the Secretary-General of the Council of the European Union, Javier Solana, appealing for international help to prevent the conflict from spiralling out of control. He called on the European Union to send monitors to the region and engaged the Organization for Security and Cooperation in Europe to establish a multi-ethnic police force for southern Serbia. UNHCR also established a full-time presence in the Presevo Valley and encouraged other UN agencies and NGOs to do the same.

Back in Belgrade, Deputy Prime Minister Covic began work on a plan that would incorporate the confidence-building measures proposed by the special envoy. These included the integration of ethnic Albanians into the political, governmental and social structures in southern Serbia, and a step by step demilitarization of the Ground Safety Zone. Covic's plan also included an amnesty for the Albanian fighters. Meanwhile, NATO sent in a representative to facilitate direct talks between Covic and the UCPMB.

By the spring of 2001, a demilitarization agreement was reached by the two parties. UNHCR proposed that the demilitarization begin in Lucane, a small village in Bujanovac Municipality, which had been partially occupied by Yugoslav forces. On 17 May, UNHCR was present alongside NATO representatives, EU monitors, Deputy Prime Minister Covic and the commander of the UCPMB to witness the disarmament of the rebel movement and the historic withdrawal of Yugoslav forces from the village. The process was repeated village by village until the entire area was demilitarized and there was a complete cessation of hostilities.

On the humanitarian side, UNHCR and other UN agencies and NGOs began to implement programmes that included repairing homes and other forms of assistance to boost the confidence of the population. The combined efforts of all of these players paved the way for the return of some 15,000 displaced persons to their homes. When fighting broke out in the neighbouring former Yugoslav Republic of Macedonia in the spring and summer of 2001, the same actors came together to resolve the conflict, averting another potential disaster in the Balkans. These experiences demonstrate that effective partnerships and preventive measures work when the international community shows the political will and mobilizes the necessary resources.

Nature of the response

A problem often encountered in emergencies is the lack of a formal mechanism to trigger a significant and timely response by the humanitarian community. In Darfur, for instance, where people have been killed and displaced on a massive scale by violence, the humanitarian response has been criticized as deficient. The inaccessibility of Darfur, and the unwillingness of some governments to criticize the Sudanese government so as to not risk the peace process in the southern part of the country, were two of the reasons for this inadequate response. But widespread public outrage and extensive media coverage appear to have had an impact: governments have changed their stance and donors have stepped up funding to assist the internally displaced in Darfur and refugees in neighbouring Chad.

Non-refoulement

Non-refoulement is a dominant principle of international law. It stipulates that states should not reject, return, or expel persons to territories where they would face persecution and violence.[17] Most relevant in the context of an emergency is that states allow entry to asylum seekers. In recent years, many states have become reluctant to allow asylum seekers to cross their borders. As a consequence of the hardening of asylum policies, the principle of *non-refoulement* has been undermined. For instance, in 2001 Pakistan refused to allow a new influx of Afghan refugees onto its territory. The government deemed that the international community had not provided it with sufficient assistance to deal with the millions of refugees who had poured into the country since the end of the Cold War.[18]

In the initial phase of an emergency response, the principal focus is on diplomatic efforts to allow free passage of refugees. In 1999, during the Kosovo emergency, humanitarian evacuation and transfer programmes transported refugees to 28 countries outside the region, thereby fairly apportioning the burden.[19] These programmes attempted to relieve the pressure on Macedonia and encourage it to continue admitting refugees from neighbouring Kosovo. In resolving the crisis, it helped that the media gave the Kosovo exodus a high profile, that the international community was willing to act decisively and that developed states close to the region were willing to shoulder a fair share of the refugee burden.

Humanitarian logistics

Logistics bridges emergency preparedness and response, yet this function tends to be disregarded in high-level decision-making processes.[20] The swiftness of the response to an emergency is dependent on the ability to procure and transport supplies to where they are needed. Various evaluations have highlighted gaps in these procedures, putting the lives of the displaced at risk.[21] Disruptions in the flow of goods can be caused by a lack of funding, high levels of insecurity and limited access, and competition among agencies to obtain the same relief goods at the same time. In the response to the 2004 tsunami damaged infrastructure, customs delays and heavy demands for transportation caused congestion at airports and on roads. The donation of unsolicited items added to the load on already stretched supply lines.[22]

Humanitarian logistics must also see to the timely deployment of appropriate staff. The logistical effort required to bring workers to an emergency area is immense: arrangements for transport, visas, accommodation and other services must be made in good time.[23] Due to the complex and insecure working environment, there is often a high turnover of staff, resulting in the frequent shifting of responsibility, lengthy induction periods, limited institutional memory and fragmented coordination efforts.[24] Aid teams often need to be set up in remote locations where establishing basic administration and communication systems may take a long time, thereby hindering their security and efficient coordination.[25]

Devastation in Banda Aceh in Indonesia following the tsunami of 26 December 2004. (UNHCR/J. Austin/2005)

High standards of capacity and coordination are required not only for the logistics of emergency response but also for the efficient management of the onward movement of a displaced population. In some instances, displaced populations may need to be moved out of conflict zones to safe areas. For such operations to be successful a sufficient number of large vehicles and adequate supplies of fuel, food, water, sanitation and shelter are needed.[26] This was the case in Chad, where in 2003–2004 more than 150,000 Sudanese refugees were relocated into eight newly created camps under difficult circumstances, given the size of the population and the hostile desert environment. This relocation away from the border area guaranteed a degree of protection against incursions by militants from Darfur.[27]

The protection–assistance nexus

Responses to emergencies should be driven by a clear assessment of need rather than available or anticipated levels of funding, but this is not always the case.[28] Whenever possible, assessments should be made and clear benchmarks set to determine priority areas of response. However, it must be noted that in many cases massive caseloads or extreme insecurity make it impossible to make reliable needs assessments. As a result, the overall quality of needs-driven assessments has been poor.[29]

Emergency responses tend to emphasize assistance over protection. Particularly in mass-influx situations, immediate needs such as food and health are given more attention than protection. This is partly because the former are easily identified. Sometimes, however, inexperienced protection staff are unable to identify protection needs. As a result, in some situations protection and human rights take a back seat to assistance.[30] Protection needs could also be left unaddressed if senior protection staff do not formulate a protection strategy in the critical early stages of an emergency.

In the 1990s, UNHCR formulated a 'ladder of options' to provide security to displaced populations. The first step is to be in the presence of those who have been displaced. The second is to provide medium-term alternatives such as training and support to build national law-enforcement capacity and/or the deployment of international civilian or police monitors. The top of the ladder involves international peacekeeping missions, including regional arrangements such as in Afghanistan, the Democratic Republic of Congo and Liberia. Due to personnel constraints, the second option has not received much attention. However, in Darfur staff of the African Union have been deployed to provide protection and security along the routes taken by the displaced and in their camps.[31]

Over time, the United Nations and NGOs have moved towards encapsulating the wide variety of assistance activities in an all-encompassing human rights framework. Socio-economic and cultural rights have been of particular importance in providing a yardstick for the quality of life of displaced persons. These include the right to adequate housing, food, health and education services. Such rights make victims of conflict 'claimants of rights' rather than objects of charity, and thus contribute to preserving their dignity.[32]

Indeed, humanitarian discourse has veered away from perceiving displaced persons as passive, aid-dependent victims and towards the view that they are in charge of their own lives. Even under the harshest personal circumstances the displaced try to help themselves.[33] Thus, the need for a development-oriented approach in the initial stages of the humanitarian response has received more attention. This means the involvement of displaced people in the decisions that affect their lives. Humanitarian assistance can then support their coping mechanisms, strengthen available assets and build capacity wherever necessary to promote self-reliance in the longer term.

Gender and age

In emergency situations, pre-existing inequalities tend to be exacerbated and vulnerable groups tend to be more at risk. The main threats that women face during an emergency include sexual and gender-based violence, trafficking and increased exposure to HIV/AIDS. The rights and needs of displaced women have been receiving increased attention since the 1990s, and sensitivity to gender and age issues has been incorporated into mainstream emergency-response guidelines and programmes. This includes providing displaced women with individual identification or registration cards to facilitate their freedom of independent movement.

Gender mainstreaming has even been applied to food distribution; supplies are distributed to women instead of men so as to ensure more even allocation within families. Gender concerns also come to the fore when considering camp design and layout. If a camp has no light at night in those areas used by women, or if there is a lack of material to close entrance ways, the risks of being attacked at night might increase. Strong efforts are made to involve women in the decision-making process, and to prevent and respond to gender-based violence.

A growing number of agencies mainstream gender throughout their programmes, but responses continue to be fragmented. While progress has been made in sensitizing humanitarian staff to gender issues, it can be difficult to hire enough women, particularly at the national level. Moreover, the prevention of, and response to, gender-based violence is often considered to be a culturally sensitive issue as it deals in part with violations occurring in the private sphere.[34] This explains the hesitation or refusal of some host governments to address gender issues.

In emergency settings children, particularly those who are unaccompanied, have special protection needs. Displaced minors are often at an increased risk of malnutrition, disease, physical danger, emotional trauma, trafficking, exploitation and abuse.[35] Significant progress has been made in this field, particularly during the 1990s, and since 1998 children's issues have increasingly been put on the international peace and security agenda.[36] However, significant gaps in child protection remain, partly due to a lack of awareness among humanitarian workers of the threats facing children and their protection needs.[37] The roles and responsibilities of agencies working with children are not always clearly defined, and there are sometimes gaps and/or overlaps in their activities. The needs of children have not been given enough priority, particularly when funds are short or new arrivals overwhelm existing assistance capacities.

Recent developments

Changes in the humanitarian sector in the 1990s, such as the bilateralization of aid, uneven funding, an increase in operations in conflict areas and a proliferation of actors have had a significant impact on the nature of humanitarian response. While

Box 4.2

Democratic Republic of Congo: a forgotten crisis

The Democratic Republic of Congo (DRC) presents an example of a protracted and complex crisis. It is characterized by a collapsed state, high levels of violence and human rights abuse, many international aid actors, limited funding and lack of the political will to alter the situation. A proliferation of arms, pervasive banditry and crime have further aggravated the situation, in particular in the eastern part of this vast and ethnically diverse country. The humanitarian crisis in the DRC has been described as one of the worst in the world, and is regularly referred to as 'forgotten'.

Ethnic demands and economic interests, especially in those areas rich in natural resources, have provoked an inter-ethnic conflict that also involves international players. In 1997, President Mobutu Sese Seko was overthrown by Laurent Kabila, with the military aid of Rwanda and Uganda. Kabila was subsequently opposed by the rebels who took control of about a third of the country in the east. Kabila was supported by Angolan and Zimbabwean troops, while the rebels were backed by Burundi, Rwanda and Uganda. A 1999 ceasefire signed in Lusaka allowed the United Nations to establish a peacekeeping mission (MONUC) in the country. But the ceasefire was repeatedly violated by all signatories, and violence continued, particularly in the north and east.

Laurent Kabila was assassinated in January 2001, and succeeded by his son, Joseph Kabila. The young Kabila's leadership ushered in a period of hope for peace and stability, as he was willing to implement the provisions contained in the 1999 Lusaka Peace Accords. He adopted a series of bold economic measures and withdrew troops from the front. In 2002, peace agreements were signed by the warring groups in the DRC and between the governments of the DRC, Rwanda and Uganda. The 2002 Sun City Agreement led to

the establishment in July 2003 of an all-inclusive transitional government, which officially reunified the country.

In 2003, power vacuums created by the withdrawal of troops in North and South Kivu and in the mineral-rich Ituri district led to renewed violence. In Ituri, much of the fighting has an ethnic dimension, namely between the Hema pastoralists and the Lendu agriculturalists. Both have, at different times, been backed by Uganda. The violence only ended when French troops intervened. Tens of thousands of people have died and more than 500,000 have been displaced since 1999 as a result of fighting in Ituri.

The endless years of strife and conflict have had dramatic consequences for the civilian population. Poverty, accentuated by the conflict, has increased peoples' vulnerability on a massive scale. The crumbling state infrastructure in health and other sectors, inflation and high levels of unemployment have further exacerbated the negative effects of the conflict. The fighting has led to appalling levels of hunger, disease and death, and to countless abuses of human rights. Many thousands of women and men, girls and boys have become victims of sexual and gender-based violence, compounding the human impact of a conflict that has resulted in the death of more than 3.8 million civilians since 1998. In 2005, there were more than 1.5 million internally displaced people and over 400,000 refugees in the country, multiplying the strains on available resources.

For several years the international community paid only minor attention to the DRC. Funding for the crisis remained low, compared to that for higher-profile cases such as Afghanistan and Iraq. In 2001, with the hope that Joseph Kabila's leadership would usher in an era of peace-building, international confidence increased. Thus, while

the Consolidated Appeal was only funded 32 per cent in 2000, it increased in the following years, going from 67 per cent in 2001 to more than 72 per cent in 2004. But the international community has not made consistent efforts to help the country address its political challenges.

Under the leadership of Joseph Kabila, the country has opened up towards the humanitarian community. By September 2005, MONUC was fielding over 16,000 police and military personnel with the authority to use force. However, despite the increase in security due to the MONUC deployment, humanitarian access has remained fragmented because of continued violence. This has frequently led to the evacuation of humanitarian workers and the suspension of aid programmes. In addition, the sheer size of the country and the poorly developed—sometimes nonexistent—infrastructure continue to pose operational and logistical challenges.

In 2005, the UN Security Council adopted Resolution 1592, which extended MONUC's mandate and explicitly stated that its main objective is peace enforcement. Some progress has been made towards disarming the various militias and implementation of the Sun City Agreement. Yet, in 2005, continued insecurity in the East remains closely linked to the political impasse in Kinshasa. The government still appears to be a conglomerate of different factions rather than a coherent entity. Elections set for the summer of 2005 were postponed, and the creation of integrated national-security services and the promulgation of a constitution and a new electoral law remain pending. Besides the continued support of the international community, a long-term solution for the DRC will require stability in neighbouring countries and throughout the region.

Map 4.1   Democratic Republic of Congo, *June 2005*

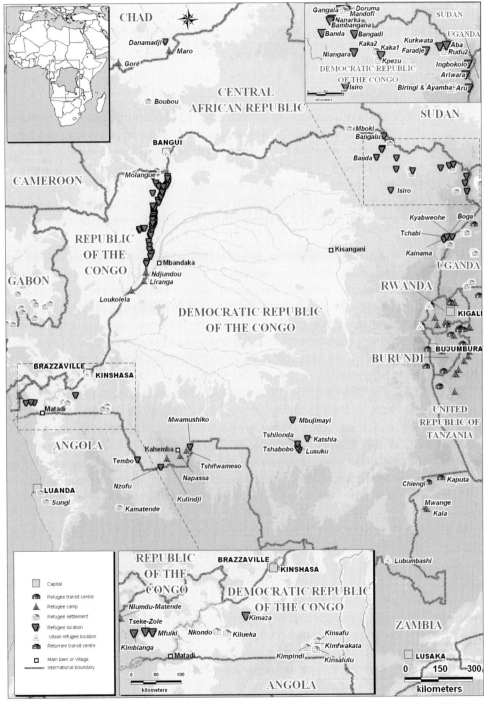

The boundaries and names shown and the designations used on this map do not imply official endorsement or acceptance by the United Nations. Geographical data sources: UNHCR, Global Insight digital mapping - © 1998 Europa Technologies Ltd.

the overlap between humanitarian and political agendas has always shaped relief responses, a shift towards greater unilateral interventionism in some countries has led to greater synchronization of their political, military and humanitarian objectives.[38] In some cases decisions concerning emergency responses have been driven by media attention and public opinion.

Funding

The post-Cold War era witnessed a major restructuring of aid budgets among principal donors, partly due to demands for more transparency regarding public expenditures. Generally, international emergency response has remained the preserve of large Western agencies and the United Nations. In some Western countries attempts at greater coherence between political and humanitarian action has led to significant changes in humanitarian policy.[39] Indeed, in some cases humanitarian assistance has been used as a tool of state policy rather than to support conflict prevention and resolution.[40]

As a result of the linking of states' political and humanitarian agendas, total aid budgets have increased since the beginning of the 1990s—but the proportion available to multilateral agencies has gone down. The demands for increased accountability and the conflation of political and humanitarian agendas have prompted some donors to use aid funds to promote their own visibility, especially at the field level. Indeed, the tendency of many donors to work outside the UN system in the Kosovo crisis is widely believed to have had a negative impact on multilateral humanitarian institutions.[41]

Meanwhile, disparities in funding seriously question international impartiality. Aid budgets have multiplied where states' strategic and humanitarian interests overlap, such as in Afghanistan and Iraq, while they have been squeezed in other crisis areas. For instance, in the Kosovo emergency of 1999 the quality and quantity of aid delivered far outstripped that provided to refugees in many African countries.[42] The impact of state interests on humanitarian response was also illustrated by the case of Iraq, for which a funding appeal was launched at a time when other equally—if not more—urgent crises were under-funded.[43]

In addition to contingency planning, preparedness and joint needs assessments, the principal mechanism for achieving a multilateral coordinated response is the UN Consolidated Appeal Process (CAP). Consolidated appeals are consistently under-funded, even though donors declare their commitment to the process. In 2004, only 60 per cent of humanitarian assistance requested by the CAP was actually received.[44] Moreover, the high degree of earmarking of funds by donors precludes the allocation of resources in proportion to need. This forces UNHCR and other UN agencies to constantly reprioritize their proposed activities at the cost of adherence to their respective mandates, and on occasion introduces or increases competition between agencies.[45]

For their part, donors have important concerns about the effectiveness of responses and the lack of institutional learning, leading to demands for greater accountability. This has resulted in more evaluation studies, as well as numerous manuals and guidelines on good practice.[46] Some of these evaluations have adopted a participatory approach, including consultations with refugees and humanitarian workers at different stages of the process.[47] Ultimately, however, the accountability agenda must be driven by humanitarian principles and the needs of displaced persons rather than donor interests.[48]

The role of the military

The increased role of military forces in humanitarian emergencies has been received as a mixed blessing. In many emergencies such forces have turned out to be crucial in getting help to insecure and difficult-to-access areas. Military forces tend to be highly skilled, organized and well equipped. During the Kosovo crisis, they took on the critical task of constructing shelters for the large number of refugees. In the aftermath of the 2004 tsunami, local and international military forces were hailed for their assistance in helping get aid to those affected by the disaster.

Authoritative coordination by military commands can facilitate a rapid response, then gradually make way to a consensual one driven by the host government and humanitarian actors. Partnerships with military actors can be of crucial importance to ensure security and direct access to affected populations, as well as to separate militants and other elements that pose a security threat. Increasingly, such operations are conducted in failed (or failing) states which are experiencing high levels of insecurity.

But the linking of humanitarian agencies with military forces has resulted in a dilution of the former's neutrality in insecure and politically charged environments. Humanitarian workers have been facing more violence and intimidation. Between July 2003 and July 2004 at least 100 civilian United Nations and NGO personnel were killed.[49] Such violence often triggers the suspension of operations and evacuation of humanitarian workers, halting the critical flow of aid. Since the presence of humanitarian agencies often affords civilians a degree of security, attacks against aid workers have consequently reduced this basic level of protection.[50]

Challenges ahead

Even though each emergency is unique and poses a new set of challenges, a strong emergency-preparedness capacity can facilitate a rapid and effective response that saves lives. Allocating responsibility for specific sectors to particular lead agencies is one way to ensure a more effective approach. Moreover, support functions such as

Box 4.3

A host-country perspective: the case of Tanzania

At the end of 2004, Tanzania was host to more than 400,000 refugees spread over 11 refugee camps in western Tanzania and an estimated 200,000 in refugee settlements in the areas of Mishamo, Ulyankulu and Katumba. The majority of the refugees in Tanzania are Burundians and Congolese. As Africa's leading refugee-hosting country, Tanzania is a key actor in the global refugee regime. Since independence, it has received refugees from more than nine countries and was widely praised for its hospitality to refugees who, until the emergencies of the 1990s were hosted under a rural-settlement approach that served as a model across the continent. However, under the political and material pressures arising from these emergencies, the settlement approach was replaced by a camp-centred and repatriation-focused model that continues today. More than a decade later, the political, economic and operational/organizational legacies of this period continue to weigh heavily on all aspects of refugee policy in Tanzania.

Instability in the programmes recurs despite the absence of large-scale and rapid refugee inflows. Continued movement of refugees both in and out of the country combines with a highly fluctuating capacity and/or willingness of both the host country and international actors to respond to the simultaneous challenges of new arrivals and the longer term presence of refugees. The Government of Tanzania believes that concerted efforts to find a solution to the refugee problem should focus on addressing the reasons that have led to displacement. To this end, it is supporting peace efforts in the Democratic Republic of Congo (DRC) and Burundi. These efforts culminated in the signing of the Arusha Peace Accord of 2002; this formed the basis of the Transition Government in Burundi and paved the way for the repatriation of Burundian refugees, albeit on a limited scale. Political changes within Tanzania, most notably decentralization and greater liberalization, add to a situation in which political, humanitarian and economic imperatives are frequently seen as conflicting.

Security policies and improved regional relations

Increasing tension between Burundi and Tanzania in the early years of the decade was significantly eased by a number of diplomatic initiatives, including a mission by the UN Executive Committee on Humanitarian Affairs to Tanzania and the establishment in 1999 of the so-called 'security package'. This programme funds special Tanzanian police and up to three UN field safety advisers to strengthen law and order, improve the safety of refugees and local communities and maintain the civilian and humanitarian character of the camps. Independently, the Tanzanian military increased its presence along the border. Another innovation, based upon experience in Latin America, sought to involve refugee representatives in the Burundi peace negotiations, but this met with limited success.

While the most pressing concerns related to international security could therefore be tempered, new issues emerged. These included difficulties arising from a growing 'securitization' of refugee issues in Tanzania, where policy is perceived almost exclusively through the lens of crime and law enforcement. The government's reaction to security incidents has been to tighten restrictions on the movement and economic activity of refugees. The programme has also struggled with the issues of sexual exploitation and sexual and gender-based violence. The security package is ultimately a temporary

logistics, administration and telecommunications have demonstrated their core value on many occasions, and should therefore be provided with sufficient funding.

Humanitarian space can be widened by adopting concrete measures to better protect staff. Partnerships with UN peacekeeping and civilian missions, as well as with regional organizations, could facilitate a regional response to the protection of displaced persons. Meanwhile, the implications of using military personnel must be assessed on a case-by-case basis to better gauge their impact on humanitarian neutrality.

Working in partnership with potentially affected states goes beyond inter-agency coordination and memorandums of understanding. The United Nations, NGOs and donors have a role when states fail, or are unable, to take on a central humanitarian role. At a minimum, this would see international aid bodies working closely together to measure that cannot replace the important role of the police, judiciary and immigration authorities in ensuring the security and effective protection of refugees at the district level.

Basic needs and minimum standards

In the past, the long-standing nature of the refugee programme in Tanzania made it a place in which new, innovative methods could be explored. More recently, however, continued budget cuts and repeated breaks in the supply of food have fostered a sense of instability. Although refugees continue to have a fair level of access to primary education, healthcare, water and sanitation, there has been a shortage of food and some non-food items. This, coupled with restrictions on refugee movement, lack of sufficient farmland and employment opportunities has meant that basic operational challenges persist and very little movement away from the immediate post-emergency phase has been possible. Within the framework of the Strengthening Protection Capacity Project, of which Tanzania is one of the four pilot countries, the government has agreed to consultations on the feasibility of introducing share-cropping and/or agro-forestry to increase refugee self-reliance.

To help deal with this situation, donor coordination has been re-energized. Donors now participate in the annual WFP–UNHCR joint assessment mission. Similarly, a grouping of national and local NGOs has strengthened its efforts to achieve mutually beneficial solutions for both the refugee and local populations as well as meet the concerns of the government. Recently, the group funded and publicized a study of the refugee impact on the country.

Policy change and continuity

Although Tanzania is a supporter of the Agenda for Protection, it has also campaigned for a revision of the 1951 UN Refugee Convention, whereby 'safe havens' in the countries of origin can replace the need for asylum. In 2003, the government issued its first-ever national refugee policy. This provides for asylum seekers to be admitted to the country for one year, within which time arrangements should be made to take them back to established safe zones in the countries of origin. The policy makes local integration very difficult.

Tanzania's legislative and policy framework concerning refugees is not fully consistent with the provisions of the 1951 Refugee Convention. They provide only for temporary asylum, restrict refugee movement and do not allow for judicial review when asylum applications are rejected. The government has indicated that it is in the process of reviewing the policies. In a bid to improve refugee reception and status-determination procedures and avoid *refoulement*, in 2005 the government established ad hoc committees to interview new arrivals from Burundi and the DRC. Rejected cases were to be referred to the National Eligibility Committee, which conducts refugee-status determination. But implementation varies from district to district, and concerns have arisen about the continuing validity of *prima facie* refugee status in the country.

Refugees are often portrayed as a burden to Tanzania. The government frequently says there has been no tangible benefit from hosting them, only a drain of its limited resources. In the government's view the differences in the quality of refugee protection in the country are provoked by a failure of global burden sharing and insufficient efforts to address the root causes of displacement.

provide funding, technical assistance and, when requested, leadership to states that are affected by conflict-induced displacement.

Finally, with hostility towards migrants and refugees on the rise, the containment approach remains attractive to many governments. Continuous efforts will therefore be needed to remind states of their responsibilities under the 1951 UN Refugee Convention to ensure that borders are not sealed off.

5 Protracted refugee situations: the search for practical solutions

The majority of today's refugees have lived in exile for far too long, restricted to camps or eking out a meagre existence in urban centres throughout the developing world. Most subsist in a state of limbo, and are often dependent on others to find solutions to their plight. Their predicament is similar to that of the tens of thousands of refugees who stagnated in camps in Western Europe in the 1950s and 1960s. The High Commissioner for Refugees at the time, Gerrit van Heuven Goedhart, called those camps 'black spots on the map of Europe' that should 'burn holes in the consciences of all those privileged to live in better conditions'.[1] If the situation persisted, he said, the problems of refugees would fester and his office would be reduced to 'simply administering human misery'.[2] The issue of displaced persons in Europe was finally settled some 20 years after the end of the Second World War; today's protracted refugee crises, however, show no signs of being resolved in the near future.

Since the early 1990s, the international community has focused largely on refugee emergencies. It has delivered humanitarian assistance to war-affected populations and supported large-scale repatriation programmes in high-profile areas such as the Balkans, the Great Lakes region of Africa and, more recently, Darfur (Sudan) and Chad. Yet more than 60 per cent of today's refugees are trapped in situations far from the international spotlight. Often characterized by long periods of exile—stretching to decades for some groups—these situations occur on most continents in a range of environments including camps, rural settlements and urban centres. The vast majority are to be found in the world's poorest and most unstable regions, and are frequently the result of neglect by regional and international actors.

Refugees trapped in these forgotten situations often face significant restrictions on their rights. At the same time, their presence raises political and security concerns among host governments and other states in the region. As such, protracted refugee situations represent a significant challenge both to human rights and security. 'The consequences of having so many human beings in a static state,' argues UNHCR, 'include wasted lives, squandered resources and increased threats to security'.[3] Taken independently, each of these challenges is of mounting concern. Taken collectively, and given the interaction between security, human rights and development, the full significance of protracted refugee situations becomes more apparent.

Karen refugees from Myanmar in the Tham Hin camp, Ratchaburi Province, Thailand. Many of the ethnic Karen refugees in this camp fled their homeland in 1997. (UNHCR/K. Singhaseni/1997)

Despite the gravity of the problem, protracted refugee situations have yet to feature prominently on the international political agenda. In the vacuum, humanitarian agencies such as UNHCR try to care for forgotten populations and mitigate the negative effects of prolonged exile. These efforts are not enough, however. In the past, similar crises in Europe, Southeast Asia and Latin America were resolved through comprehensive plans of action involving humanitarian agencies as well as political, security and development actors. Such an integrated approach is also needed today.

Nature and scope of the problem

The difficulty of defining protracted refugee situations has arguably frustrated efforts to formulate effective policy responses, and a more detailed understanding of the global scope and importance of the problem is clearly necessary. UNHCR defines a protracted refugee situation as 'one in which refugees find themselves in a long-lasting and intractable state of limbo. Their lives may not be at risk, but their basic rights and essential economic, social and psychological needs remain unfulfilled after years in exile. A refugee in this situation is often unable to break free from enforced reliance on external assistance'.[4]

In identifying the major protracted refugee situations in the world in 2004, UNHCR used the 'crude measure of refugee populations of 25,000 persons or more who have been in exile for five or more years in developing countries'.[5] The study excluded Palestinian refugees, who fall under the mandate of the UN Relief and Works Agency for Palestine Refugees in the Near East (UNRWA), and represent the world's oldest and largest protracted refugee situation.

The definition above accurately describes the condition of many refugees in protracted situations. What it does not reflect is that many of these refugees are actively engaged in seeking solutions for themselves, either through political and military activities in their countries of origin or through onward migration to the West. Furthermore, evidence from Africa and Asia demonstrates that while population numbers in a particular protracted situation may remain relatively stable over time, the composition of a population often changes.

A definition of protracted refugee situations should therefore include not only the humanitarian elements of the phenomenon but also its political and strategic aspects. In addition, a definition must recognize that countries of origin, host countries and the international community are all implicated in the causes of protracted refugee situations.

In protracted situations, refugee populations have moved beyond the emergency phase—where the focus is on life-saving protection and assistance—but cannot expect durable solutions in the foreseeable future. These populations are typically, but not necessarily, concentrated in a specific geographic area, and may include camp-based and urban-refugee populations. The nature of a protracted situation will be the result of conditions in the refugees' country of origin, the responses of and

Figure 5.1   Major protracted refugee situations, *1 January 2005*

Country of Asylum	Origin	end-2004
Algeria	Western Sahara	165,000
Armenia	Azerbaijan	235,000
Burundi	Dem. Rep. of Congo	48,000
Cameroon	Chad	39,000
China	Viet Nam	299,000
Congo	Dem. Rep. of Congo	59,000
Côte d'Ivoire	Liberia	70,000
Dem. Rep. of Congo	Angola	98,000
Dem. Rep. of Congo	Sudan	45,000
Egypt	Occupied Palestinian Territory	70,000
Ethiopia	Sudan	90,000
Guinea	Liberia	127,000
India	China	94,000
India	Sri Lanka	57,000
Islamic Rep. of Iran	Afghanistan	953,000
Islamic Rep. of Iran	Iraq	93,000
Kenya	Somalia	154,000
Kenya	Sudan	68,000
Nepal	Bhutan	105,000
Pakistan	Afghanistan*	960,000
Rwanda	Dem. Rep. of Congo	45,000
Saudi Arabia	Occupied Palestinian Territory	240,000
Serbia and Montenegro	Bosnia and Herzegovina	95,000
Serbia and Montenegro	Croatia	180,000
Sudan	Eritrea	111,000
Thailand	Myanmar	121,000
Uganda	Sudan	215,000
United Rep. of Tanzania	Burundi	444,000
United Rep. of Tanzania	Dem. Rep. of Congo	153,000
Uzbekistan	Tajikistan	39,000
Yemen	Somalia	64,000
Zambia	Angola	89,000
Zambia	Dem. Rep. of Congo	66,000

Note: This table refers to refugee situations where the number of refugees of a certain origin within a particular country of asylum has been 25,000 or more for at least five consecutive years. Industrialized countries are not included. Data does not include Palestinian refugees under the mandate of the UN Relief and Works Agency for Palestine Refugees in the Near East (UNRWA).

* UNHCR estimate.

Source: UNHCR.

conditions in the host countries and the level of engagement by the international community. Furthermore, as the experience of the Sudanese refugees scattered across eight African countries indicates, members of the same displaced group in different host countries will experience different conditions.

Politically, the identification of a protracted refugee situation is a matter of perception. If a displaced population is seen to have existed for a significant period of time without the prospect of solutions, then it may be termed a protracted refugee situation. Indeed, it is important that the crude measure of 25,000 refugees in exile for five years should not be used as a basis for excluding other groups. For example, of the Rohingya who fled from Myanmar to Bangladesh 12 years ago, 20,000 still remain. Similarly, there are 19,000 Burundians in the Democratic Republic of Congo, 16,000 Somalis in Ethiopia, 19,000 Mauritanians in Senegal, 15,000 Ethiopians in Sudan and 19,000 Rwandans in Uganda.

Long-staying urban refugees are not typically included in an understanding of protracted refugee situations. Yet tens of thousands live clandestinely in urban areas, avoiding contact with the authorities and bereft of legal status. There are almost 40,000 Congolese urban refugees in Burundi, more than 36,000 Somali urban refugees in Yemen and almost 15,000 Sudanese urban refugees in Egypt. Nearly 10,000 Afghan urban refugees live in India and more than 5,000 Liberian urban refugees remain in Côte d'Ivoire. These are only some of the largest caseloads. In addition, there are hundreds of thousands of Palestinian refugees throughout the Middle East.

Trends in protracted refugee situations

Chronic and stagnating refugee situations are a growing challenge for the international community. Their total number has increased dramatically over the past decade, and host states and regions of origin feel their effects more keenly. More significantly, protracted refugee situations now account for the vast majority of the world's refugee population.

During the 1990s, a number of long-standing refugee groups that had been displaced by Cold War conflicts in the developing world went home. In southern Africa, large groups of Mozambicans, Namibians and others were repatriated. In Indochina, Cambodians in exile in Thailand returned home, while Vietnamese and Laotians were resettled in third countries. With the end of fighting in Central America, the vast majority of displaced Nicaraguans, Guatemalans and Salvadorans returned to their countries.

Nonetheless, in 1993 there remained 27 protracted refugee situations and a total population of 7.9 million refugees. Indeed, even as older refugee populations were being repatriated, new intra-state conflicts resulted in massive refugee flows. Conflict and state collapse in Somalia, the Great Lakes region of Africa, Liberia and Sierra Leone in the 1990s generated millions of refugees. Millions more were displaced by ethnic and civil conflict in Iraq, the Balkans, the Caucasus and Central Asia. As the global refugee population mushroomed in the early 1990s, the pressing need was to respond to the challenges of simultaneous mass influx situations in many regions of the world.

More than a decade later, many of these conflicts and refugee situations remain unresolved. Indeed, the number of protracted refugee situations now is greater than at the end of the Cold War. In 2004 there were 33 protracted refugee situations with a total refugee population of more than 5.5 million (see Figure 5.1). While there are fewer refugees in protracted situations today, the *number* of such situations has greatly increased. In addition, refugees are spending longer periods in exile. It is estimated that 'the average of major refugee situations, protracted or not, has increased from nine years in 1993 to 17 years at the end of 2003'.[6]

In 1993, 48 per cent of the world's 16.3 million refugees were caught in protracted situations. At the end of 2004, the number of refugees had come down to 9.2 million—but more than 61 per cent of them were in protracted situations. And, as illustrated by Map 5.1, they are found in some of the most volatile regions in the world.

East and West Africa, South Asia, Southeast Asia, the Caucasus, Central Asia and the Middle East are all plagued by protracted refugee situations. Sub-Saharan Africa has the largest number, with 17, involving 1.9 million refugees. The countries hosting the biggest groups are Guinea, Kenya, Tanzania, Uganda and Zambia. In contrast, the geographical area covering Central Asia, South West Asia, North Africa and the Middle East hosts only eight major protracted situations but nonetheless accounts for 2.5 million refugees. At the end of 2004 the overwhelming majority of these—approximately 2 million—were Afghans in Pakistan and Iran. In Asia (China, Thailand, India and Nepal) there are five protracted situations and some 676,000 refugees. Europe faces three major protracted situations involving 510,000 refugees, primarily in the Balkans and Armenia.

Causes of protracted refugee situations

Long-standing refugee populations originate from the very states whose instability lies at the heart of chronic regional insecurity. Most of the refugees in these regions—be they Somalis, Sudanese, Burundians, Liberians, Iraqis, Afghans or Burmese—come from countries where conflict and persecution have persisted for years.

While there is increasing recognition that international policy-makers must pay closer attention to these countries of origin, it is also clear that resolving refugee situations must be a central part of any solution to long-standing regional conflicts. It is essential to recognize that chronic and unresolved refugee situations have political causes, and therefore require more than humanitarian solutions.

Protracted refugee situations stem from political action and inaction, both in the country of origin (the persecution and violence that led to flight) and in the country of asylum.[7] These situations are the combined result of the prevailing conditions in the country of origin, the policy responses of the country of asylum and the lack of sufficient donor engagement. They arise when peace and security actors fail to address conflict or human rights violations in the country of origin and donor

Map 5.1   Major protracted refugees situations*, *1 January 2005*

Legend:
- 500,000 or above
- 200,000 to 500,000
- 100,000 to 200,000
- 25,000 to 100,000

*Refugee situations numbering 25,000 or more persons of a certain origin, which have existed for five or more consecutive years.

Industrialized countries are not included. Data includes both UNHCR assisted and non-assisted refugees. Data does not include Afghans in urban areas.
Statistical data source: UNHCR, 2004.
The boundaries and names shown and the designations used on this map do not imply official endorsement or acceptance by the United Nations.
Geographical data sources: UNHCR, Global Insight digital mapping - © 1998 Europa Technologies Ltd.

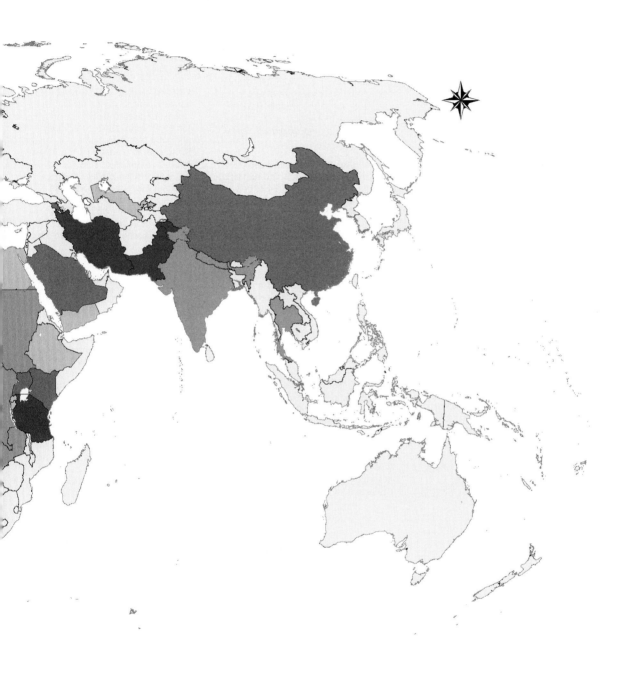

Box 5.1

Palestinian refugees

By far the most protracted and largest of all refugee problems in the world today is that of the Palestine refugees, whose plight dates back 57 years. The UN General Assembly's Resolution 181 of November 1947 recommending the partition of Palestine led to armed clashes between Arabs and Jews. The conflict, which lasted from November 1947 to July 1949, led to the expulsion or flight of some 750,000-900,000 people from Palestine, the vast majority of them Arabs. The General Assembly's subsequent Resolution 194 of December 1948 stating that those 'refugees wishing to return to their homes and live in peace with their neighbours should be permitted to do so at the earliest practicable date, and that compensation should be paid for the property of those choosing not to return and for loss or damage to property,' was never implemented. Israel refused to allow the repatriation of Arab refugees, most of whose villages had been destroyed.

More Palestinians were displaced in the wake of the 1967 Arab-Israeli war and the 1982 Israeli invasion of Lebanon. Israel's on-going construction of a barrier between its territory and the occupied West Bank is creating 'a new generation of Palestinian refugees', says John Dugard, the UN

Special Rapporteur on the situation of human rights in the Palestinian territories occupied by Israel since 1967. Today, more than 4.2 million Palestinian refugees are dispersed across areas of the Middle East in which their forefathers originally took refuge, with others dispersed across the world.

Responding to the crisis created by the partition resolution and subsequent conflict, in December 1949 the General Assembly created the United Nations Relief and Works Agency for Palestine Refugees in the Near East (UNRWA). Its brief was to 'carry out in collaboration with local governments . . . direct relief and works programmes' for refugees from Palestine. The Assembly recognized that 'continued assistance for the relief of Palestine refugees is necessary to prevent conditions of starvation and distress among them and to further conditions of peace and stability' without prejudice to the rights of the refugees as affirmed in Resolution 194. This provided UNRWA with a broad humanitarian mandate. Over time, that mandate has evolved to focus on four main programmes: education, health, relief and social services, and microfinance. The agency operates in three states—Jordan, Lebanon and Syria—as well as the West Bank and the Gaza Strip. In the absence of a just and durable resolution of the Palestine refugee

problem, the General Assembly has repeatedly renewed UNRWA's mandate.

UNRWA defines a 'Palestine refugee' as 'any person whose normal place of residence was Palestine during the period 1 June 1946 to 15 May 1948 and who lost both home and means of livelihood as a result of the 1948 conflict.' This is a working definition for the purpose of determining eligibility for UNRWA services. There are other groups of Palestinians who do not meet this definition but are refugees nonetheless, such as the thousands who were displaced by the 1967 war.

UNHCR's mandate does not extend to the majority of Palestinian refugees by virtue of Paragraph 7 (c) of the organization's Statute which excludes persons who continue to receive from other organs or agencies of the United Nations protection or assistance. A similar provision excludes these refugees from the scope of the 1951 UN Refugee Convention. Article 1D of the Convention provides that it 'shall not apply to persons who are at present receiving from organs or agencies of the United Nations other than the United Nations High Commissioner for Refugees protection or assistance.' Because refugees have to be physically present in UNRWA's area of operations to benefit from its

governments do not help the host country. Failure to address the situation in the country of origin means that refugees cannot return home; a reluctance to aid the host country reinforces the perception of refugees as a burden and a security concern, leading to encampment and a lack of local solutions. Humanitarian agencies are then left to shoulder the burden.

The protracted presence of Somali refugees in East Africa and the Horn, for instance, is the result of the failed intervention in Somalia in the early 1990s and the inability of the international community to help rebuild a failed state. As a result, hundreds of thousands of Somali refugees have been in exile in the region for more than a decade. In the face of increasingly restrictive host-state policies, humanitarian agencies are left responsible for the care and maintenance of the refugees.

assistance, stateless Palestine refugees living beyond that area get no assistance from the agency. Therefore, under the terms of the 1951 UN Refugee Convention they are entitled to assistance and protection from UNHCR. This leaves a 'protection gap' affecting Palestinian refugees who are not registered with UNRWA but live in its area of operations. In most cases they do not receive protection or assistance from UNHCR or UNRWA.

With the exception of a small number of international staff, UNRWA's 26,000-strong labour force is drawn almost exclusively from the Palestine refugee community. Because of the prolonged nature of the Palestine refugee problem, the agency's efforts to provide education and health care have been pivotal in developing the refugees' full human potential. Indeed, education is the largest of UNRWA's main programmes, accounting for approximately 54 per cent of its General Fund Budget in 2005. The agency makes a special effort to maintain gender parity in primary and preparatory education.

UNRWA's Health programme accounted for approximately 18 per cent of its General Fund Budget in 2005. Among other services, the programme provides primary care focusing on the needs of women and children. The programme has been crucial to improving environmental health. Some 10 per cent of UNRWA's 2005 budget went to its Relief and Social Services programme. This aims to alleviate poverty and hunger and fosters community-based efforts to promote gender equality. Another key programme is that of Special Hardship Case. It provides direct material and financial aid to families without a male adult able to earn an income or any other means of support. About 6 per cent of refugees require this assistance.

Finally, UNRWA's Microcredit and Microenterprise programme, created in 1991, offers credit to create employment. It provides loans to existing and start-up enterprises. The programme has developed credit products to improve the economic and social conditions of poor micro-entrepreneurs, small businesses, impoverished women and working-class families.

Since 2000, UNRWA programmes in the occupied territories have also tried to protect vulnerable refugees from the worst effects of the ongoing conflict and occupation. These effects have included death and injury, with more than 3,700 Palestinians killed and 29,000 injured; widespread destruction of property—both housing and agricultural land—and infrastructure; and the crippling of the local economy by Israel's complex system of checkpoints and restricted access. The last also makes delivery of humanitarian aid more costly and difficult.

UNRWA's efforts to mitigate the socio-economic effects of the situation have included emergency job creation, whereby the agency both funds and directs temporary work projects to try and mitigate the socio-economic crisis. Between January and March 2005, UNRWA offered 6,449 temporary employment contracts under direct hire. The agency's emergency assistance to households in need of food and money has contributed to nutritional and financial security, particularly in the event of the death or injury of a principal breadwinner or the destruction of a home. The agency also helps homeless families by repairing or rebuilding shelters, through cash grants and self-help projects. Between September 2000 and June 2005 UNRWA had rebuilt 775 dwelling units for 831 families in the Gaza Strip.

The humanitarian aid and assistance that UNRWA provides to the Palestine refugees can never be enough. But it will be required as long as the issues of statelessness, prolonged military occupation, economic marginalization and vulnerability characteristic of the Palestinian refugee crisis are not addressed.

The failure of the international community and regional players to consolidate peace can generate a resurgence of conflict and displacement, leading to a recurrence of protracted refugee situations. For example, the return of Liberians from neighbouring West African states in the aftermath of the 1997 elections in Liberia was not sustainable. A renewal of conflict in late 1999 and early 2000 led not only to a suspension of the repatriation of Liberian refugees from Guinea, Côte d'Ivoire and other states in the region, it also gave rise to a massive new refugee exodus. Following the departure into exile of Liberian strongman Charles Taylor in 2003, there has been a renewed emphasis on return for the hundreds of thousands of Liberian refugees in the region. Though large-scale facilitated repatriation began in late 2004, it does not appear as if the lessons of the late 1990s have been learned. Donor support for the demobilization and reintegration of Liberian combatants has been limited, and there is growing fear of fresh conflict as former combatants are again being recruited into rival factions.

As these examples illustrate, the primary causes of protracted refugee situations are to be found in the failure to engage in countries of origin and the failure to consolidate peace agreements. These examples also demonstrate how humanitarian programmes have to be underpinned by enduring political and security measures if they are to result in lasting solutions for refugees. Assistance to refugees in protracted situations is no substitute for sustained political and strategic action. More generally, the international community cannot expect humanitarian actors to resolve protracted refugee situations without the sustained engagement of the peace, security and development agencies.

Declining donor support for long-standing refugee populations in host countries has also contributed to the rise in protracted refugee situations. A marked decrease in financial contributions to these groups has security implications, as refugees and local populations begin to compete for scarce resources. The lack of donor support has also reinforced the perception of refugees as a burden on host states, which now argue that the displaced put additional pressure on the environment, services, infrastructure and the local economy. With the international community less willing to share the burden, host countries are reluctant to find local solutions to protracted refugee situations.

This trend first emerged in the mid-1990s, when UNHCR experienced budget shortfalls of tens of millions of dollars. These shortfalls were most acutely felt in Africa, where contributions to both development assistance and humanitarian programmes fell throughout the 1990s. Of greater concern is the tendency of donor governments to give vastly disproportionate amounts of aid to a few cases in the media glare and far less to dozens of other less-publicized refugee caseloads.[8] Declining donor engagement with long-standing refugee populations, or donor fatigue, has left many host states with fewer resources with which to address the needs of refugees and respond to increased pressure on local environments and services. According to UNHCR, 71 per cent of the world's asylum seekers, refugees and others of concern to the agency were hosted in developing countries at the end of 2004.[9] Given that these states are themselves heavily dependent on official development assistance to meet the needs of their own citizens, the additional burden of large refugee populations becomes all the more significant. Such concerns are exacerbated by the pressures of externally imposed democratization, economic liberalization and rising local expectations.

Human rights implications

An increasing number of host states respond to protracted refugee situations by containing refugees in isolated and insecure refugee camps, typically in border regions and far from the governing regime. Many host governments now require the vast majority of refugees to live in designated camps, and place restrictions on those

Figure 5.2   Longest protracted situations: major Palestinian refugee populations in the Middle East

Country/Area	Number of Palestinian Refugees
Gaza	962,000
Jordan	953,000
West Bank	688,000
Syria	425,000
Lebanon	401,000
Saudi Arabia*	240,000
Egypt*	70,000
Iraq*	23,000

Sources: UNRWA as at 31 March 2005; *UNHCR as at 1 January 2005.
This table includes only Palestinian refugee populations of 10,000 or more.

seeking to leave the camps for employment or education. This trend, recently termed the 'warehousing' of refugees, has significant human rights and economic implications.[10]

As highlighted by the US Committee for Refugees and Immigrants, levels of sexual and physical violence in refugee camps remain of great concern. UNHCR has argued that 'most refugees in such situations live in camps where idleness, despair and, in a few cases, even violence prevails. Women and children, who form the majority of the refugee community, are often the most vulnerable, falling victim to exploitation and abuse'.[11]

The prolonged encampment of refugee populations has led to the violation of a number of rights contained in the 1951 UN Refugee Convention, including freedom of movement and the right to seek wage-earning employment. Restrictions on employment and the right to move beyond the confines of the camps deprive long-staying refugees of the freedom to pursue normal lives and to become productive members of their new societies. Professional certificates and diplomas are often not recognized by host governments, and educational, health and other services are limited. Faced with these restrictions, refugees become dependent on subsistence-level assistance, or less, and lead lives of poverty, frustration and unrealized potential.

UNHCR has noted that the prolongation of refugees' dependence on external assistance 'also squanders precious resources of host countries, donors and refugees',[12] while 'limited funds and waning donor commitment lead to stop-gap solutions'.[13] It adds that spending on care and maintenance 'is a recurring expense and not an investment in the future'.[14] Refugees in camps cannot contribute to regional development and state-building.[15] In cases where refugees have been

Box 5.2

Bhutanese refugees in Nepal

Approximately 103,000 Bhutanese Lhotshampas have been confined to several refugee camps in south-eastern Nepal since 1990. This protracted refugee situation is a source of regional tension between Nepal, Bhutan and India. If left unresolved, it may set a dangerous precedent in a region rife with ethnic and communal tension.

The Lhotshampas are descendents of Nepalese who moved to the southern lowlands of Bhutan in the nineteenth century. The Hindu Lhotshampas remained largely unintegrated with Bhutan's Buddhist Druk majority. However, under Bhutan's Nationality Law of 1958 they were allowed to hold government jobs and enjoy Bhutanese citizenship. By the 1980s, however, Bhutan's king and the ruling Druk majority expressed concern over the rapidly growing Lhotshampa population. The 1988 census revealed that Bhutan's population was 48 per cent Buddhist, 45 per cent Nepali and 7 per cent 'other'. Concerned about the influx of Nepali migrants into Bhutan and the higher birth rate of the Lhotshampas, the Druks feared that this demographic shift threatened their privileged position and traditional Buddhist culture.

During the 1980s, the Bhutanese authorities adopted a series of ethno-nationalist policies. In 1985, the government established new eligibility requirements for Bhutanese citizenship that effectively disenfranchized many ethnic Nepalis, depriving them of their citizenship and civil rights. In addition, the government introduced measures to enforce rigidly the Druk dress code and forbid the use of Nepali in the educational curriculum. Special permission was required for admission to schools and to sell cash crops.

When the Lhotshampa minority in southern Bhutan began to organize politically in the late 1980s to lobby against restrictive legislation, the authorities declared these activities subversive and unlawful. Some Lhotshampas became activists in the Bhutanese People's Party, which called for Bhutan's democratization. Large-scale protests broke out in 1990, resulting in violent clashes with the police and army and mass arrests.

The authorities increased their intimidation of the Lhotshampas in southern Bhutan by destroying their property and arbitrarily detaining and torturing activists. Individuals were

forced to sign 'voluntary migration certificates' before being expelled from the country. In December 1990 the authorities announced that Lhotshampas who could not prove they were residents of the country before 1958 must leave. Consequently, tens of thousands of Lhotshampas were made stateless and fled to Nepal and the Indian state of West Bengal.

Since the early 1990s more than 100,000 Lhotshampas have been confined to seven refugee camps in south-eastern Nepal. Donor governments have spent approximately US$20m per year on assistance and protection programmes. Children are provided with education to the secondary-school level and the Lhotshampa leadership takes an active part in administering the camps. However, despite the relatively high standard of the camps, there is considerable frustration among the refugees over their prolonged exile. These frustrations are particularly pronounced among young people, who constitute the highest proportion of the refugee population and for whom there are few opportunities for further education and employment. As protracted exile has continued,

allowed to engage in the local economy, they have had 'a positive impact on the [local] economy by contributing to agricultural production, providing cheap labour and increasing local vendors' income from the sale of essential foodstuffs'.[16] When prohibited from working outside the camps, refugees cannot make such contributions.

Political and security implications

One of the most significant political implications of long-standing refugee situations is the strain that they often place on diplomatic relations between host states and the refugees' country of origin. The prolonged presence of Burundian refugees in Tanzania, coupled with allegations that anti-government rebels were based within the suicide rates have increased in tandem with domestic violence, alcoholism and the trafficking of women and children.

There is only limited integration of the refugees with the local population. The Lhotshampa provide cheap labour, particularly in the construction industry, and have increased the quantity of goods in local markets. The local populace also benefit from access to health care in the Lhotshampa camps. Still, local villagers complain that the refugees compete for employment and drive down wages, depress prices in the markets by selling their food rations, and contribute to crime and prostitution.

A solution to the protracted refugee situation in Nepal remains as elusive as ever. Since 1993 there have been more than a dozen high-level meetings between the governments of Bhutan and Nepal to try and resolve the crisis. In December 2001, the two sides finally agreed on a joint nationality-verification process and began work in one refugee camp. However, the process has been plagued by problems and was severely criticized by observers for failing to meet international standards. The verification process

excluded UNHCR and involved only representatives of the governments of Bhutan and Nepal.

More than 70 per cent of residents in the only camp verified so far were classified as voluntary migrants on the grounds that they signed voluntary migration forms when leaving Bhutan. Yet most refugees claim that they were forced to sign such forms before being permitted to leave. In some cases, members of the same family were placed in different categories, risking separation in the event of eventual repatriation. Some refugees who were minors in Bhutan and did not possess identity documents before they fled were classified as non-Bhutanese even though their parents possessed identity papers. UNHCR was denied access by the government of Bhutan to areas of potential return.

UNHCR announced in 2003 that it would encourage and promote local integration in Nepal as the preferred solution for the Lhotshampas and support resettlement initiatives for vulnerable cases. It would also phase out care and maintenance assistance in the camps and encourage targeted assistance for self-reliance pending durable solutions.

As of mid-2005, however, it was unclear how effective this policy would be. The government of Nepal opposed local integration, preferring to work towards the refugees' eventual repatriation to Bhutan. The plan is also opposed by the majority of refugee leaders in Nepal; they too view repatriation as the only durable solution. International observers, particularly human rights organizations, say Bhutan's behaviour towards the Lhotshampas is ethnic cleansing. They believe that accepting such state actions would set a dangerous precedent for the region and might result in the expulsion of minorities from other South Asian countries.

UNHCR has recently started to promote resettlement for the most vulnerable categories in the camps. A comprehensive solutions package in which various options would be implemented simultaneously would be preferable. But lack of progress on repatriation and local integration should not block the possibility of resettlement, even though this will benefit a relatively small number.

refugee camps, led to a significant breakdown in relations between the two African neighbours in 2000-02, including the shelling of Tanzanian territory by the Burundian army. The presence of Burmese refugees on the Thai border has been a frequent source of tension between the governments in Bangkok and Rangoon. In a similar way, the elusiveness of a solution to the plight of Bhutanese refugees in Nepal has been a source of regional tension, drawing in not only the host state and the country of origin but also regional powers such as India (see Box 5.2).

Protracted refugee populations are a critical element in continuing conflict and instability and have obstructed peace and undermined economic development.[17] The long-term presence of large refugee populations has engendered conflict by causing instability in neighbouring countries, triggering intervention, and sometimes spurring armed elements within camps to begin insurgencies or form resistance and terrorist movements. The militarization of refugee camps creates a security problem for the country of origin, the host country and the international community. Arms trafficking, drug smuggling, trafficking in women and children, and the recruitment of child soldiers and mercenaries occur in some of the camps hosting long-standing refugee populations.

Prolonged refugee crises not only raise direct security concerns but also have indirect security implications. Tensions between refugees and the local population often arise from the belief that refugees receive preferential treatment. This is especially the case when local people have difficulty accessing health, education or other services while such services are readily available to refugees in camps. As donor support for camp-based refugees decreases, however, competition between refugees and the host population for scarce resources creates insecurity. In the same way, reductions in assistance in the camps may lead some refugees to turn to banditry, prostitution and theft.

Protracted refugee situations are no less dangerous sources of instability than other more conventional security threats. The outbreak of conflict and genocide in the Great Lakes Region of Central Africa in the early 1990s serves to show what can happen if solutions are not found for long-standing refugee populations. Tutsis who fled Rwanda between 1959 and 1962 and their descendants filled the ranks of the Rwandan Patriotic Front which invaded Rwanda from Uganda in October 1990. Many of these refugees had been living in the region for more than three decades. In the aftermath of the Rwandan genocide, it was widely recognized that the failure of the international community to find a lasting solution for the Rwandan refugees from the 1960s was a key factor behind the events that led to the genocide in 1994. According to UNHCR, 'the failure to address the problems of the Rwandan refugees in the 1960s contributed substantially to the cataclysmic violence of the 1990s'.[18] But more than a decade after the genocide it appears as though the lesson has not been learned; dozens of protracted refugee situations remain unresolved in highly volatile and conflict-prone regions.

Meanwhile, many host states, especially in Africa, see long-standing refugee populations as a security concern synonymous with the spill-over of conflict and the spread of arms. Indeed, host states are increasingly unwilling to see refugees as victims of persecution and conflict; rather, they are perceived as a potential source of regional instability.

The nature of less developed states and their often-peripheral place in the international system make them especially vulnerable to external shocks.[19] Given the regional dynamics of many conflicts in Africa and Asia and the inability of states in these regions to insulate themselves from the spill-over of conflict, the prolonged presence of refugees becomes an increasingly important political issue.

Comprehensive solutions: lessons from the past

The contemporary response to protracted refugee situations stands in stark contrast to the international reaction to some of the major refugee crises during the Cold War. Then, the geopolitical interests of the West led to engagement with these crises and their resolution. This engagement resulted in comprehensive plans of action that drew on the three durable solutions of repatriation, local integration and third-country resettlement. Such an approach was central to resolving the situation of displaced people in Europe long after the Second World War, and of millions of Indochinese and Central American refugees in the 1980s. When dealing with the protracted refugee crises of today it is important to remember that by understanding the particular characteristics of each situation and by considering the needs of all the countries concerned, the international community has successfully resolved numerous refugee situations in the past half-century.

Towards the end of the 1950s, concerned individuals drew attention to the plight of the tens of thousands of people displaced within Europe by the Second World War who were still in need of durable solutions. Calls for action by refugee advocates, NGOs and UNHCR resulted in 1959 being declared 'World Refugee Year' by the United Nations and the initiation of a comprehensive response to those remaining both in camps and outside.[20] Following UNHCR's appeal to governments to provide funds and resettlement quotas, this protracted refugee problem was resolved by the mid-1960s.

The response to the European refugees was motivated by humanitarian concern for the people left behind after successive selection missions had picked those who were young and healthy and met rigid resettlement criteria.[21] It illustrates the potential of a comprehensive resettlement effort to address the needs of protracted and neglected refugee caseloads. This programme is an often-forgotten precedent for addressing the durable-solutions and protection needs of refugees for whom neither local integration nor repatriation are viable options.

The international response to the Indochinese refugee crisis in Southeast Asia is another important example of a comprehensive solution. It came in response to a public outcry over the dire conditions faced by the thousands of 'boat people' fleeing Viet Nam and refugees from Cambodia and Laos. Following dramatic steps by countries in the region to withhold sanctuary by preventing the entry of the asylum seekers, concerned states gathered at a conference on Indochinese refugees in Geneva in July 1979.[22] Western states agreed to dramatically increase the number of refugees they resettled from the region. In exchange, it was agreed that the boat people would be recognized as refugees *prima facie*, that illegal departures would be prevented, and that regional processing centres would be established. The result was a formalized *quid pro quo*: resettlement in Western states in exchange for assurances of first asylum in the region.

The immediate results were positive. But by 1988 the number of asylum seekers began to rise dramatically, drawn by the prospect of resettlement. The new arrivals were a mix of refugees and economic migrants, and it was clear that a satisfactory solution could not be achieved without the co-operation of a wide range of actors. A second conference on Indochinese refugees was convened in June 1989 and concluded by adopting the Comprehensive Plan of Action (CPA) for Indochinese Refugees.

The CPA contained five mechanisms through which the countries of origin, countries of first asylum and resettlement countries cooperated to resolve the refugee crisis in Southeast Asia. These were an Orderly Departure Program to prevent clandestine departures, guaranteed temporary asylum by countries in the region, individual refugee status determination for all new arrivals, resettlement in third countries for those recognized as refugees, and facilitated return for rejected claimants.[23] Notwithstanding a number of criticisms,[24] by and large the CPA achieved its objectives of reducing the number of clandestine departures, managing the flow of migrants and finding extra-regional durable solutions for recognized refugees.

Unlike the CPA, which identified resettlement as the primary durable solution, the International Conference on Central American Refugees (CIREFCA), also convened in 1989, placed the greatest emphasis on return and reintegration.[25] Following peace agreements that ended more than a decade of conflict in El Salvador, Nicaragua and Guatemala, CIREFCA was an integral part of the wider objective of consolidating peace in the region. Through a series of development initiatives for returning refugees, capacity-building projects targeting states and NGOs, and the integration of refugees and returnees into national and regional development strategies, CIREFCA formulated a comprehensive solution appropriate to regional priorities.

These three examples demonstrate how comprehensive solutions could respond to the challenges of protracted refugee situations. While each approach used different combinations of the three durable solutions, all three shared the feature of concerted efforts by a wide range of actors to address particular refugee crises. This lesson is highlighted in UNHCR's Agenda for Protection, which emphasizes the need for 'more coherence in integrating voluntary repatriation, local integration, and resettlement, whenever feasible, into one comprehensive approach.' Furthermore, such an approach must be implemented 'in close cooperation among countries of origin, host States, UNHCR and its humanitarian and development partners, especially NGOs, as well as refugees.'[26]

Towards a more effective response

Throughout the 1990s, given its focus on refugee emergencies, the international community largely ignored the challenge of formulating comprehensive responses to protracted refugee situations. While significant progress was made in developing the responsiveness of each of the three durable solutions, as outlined in the following chapter, little attention was paid to their complementary nature or how they could be applied in the comprehensive resolution of long-standing refugee crises. With the exception of a few key studies in the early 1980s, the problem of protracted refugee situations also failed to attract the attention of the research community.[27]

Developments within UNHCR

The problem of protracted refugee situations was brought back onto the international policy and research agenda in 2000 and 2001. Supported by renewed donor interest in the question, UNHCR commissioned a number of studies to better understand the dynamics and implications of contemporary long-term refugee problems, including those of Sudanese in Kenya,[28] Sierra Leoneans in Guinea,[29] and Liberians in Côte d'Ivoire[30] and Ghana.[31] A summary of their findings was published as a UNHCR working paper.[32]

These studies contributed to the development of a working definition of protracted refugee situations and a better understanding of their causes, consequences and the necessary elements of a solution. In particular, the studies shed important light on the distinction between a 'basic needs' and 'minimum standards' approach to long-term refugee populations, and highlighted the benefits that could be derived from enhancing the refugees' own coping strategies. However, it was noted, 'it would be highly misleading to suggest that there are any quick or easy solutions to the problem of protracted refugee situations in Africa'.[33]

It was in the context of these studies that the question of protracted refugee situations in Africa was addressed by UNHCR's Executive Committee in October 2001. Participants acknowledged that these situations 'pose serious challenges to the host country, the international community and the refugees themselves'.[34] At the same time, UNHCR highlighted its desire to 'improve responses by formulating a comprehensive and coherent strategy to address protracted refugee situations'.[35]

Three months later, in December 2001, more focused discussions took place on the question of protracted refugee situations in Africa during a ministerial meeting in Geneva. The discussions emphasized the need to place the problem within a historical and political context, to address the root causes of refugee movements, to support national capacity-building, and the importance of sustained donor engagement to resolve chronic refugee problems.[36]

The 2004 Standing Committee Paper is UNHCR's most comprehensive policy document on protracted refugee situations and includes a number of important innovations.[37] While highlighting that UNHCR is not a political actor, the paper argues that the agency must be aware of the political context of its work. The study also presents a number of options for responding to long-term refugee problems, including the need to focus on refugee well-being in the short term and the importance of linking a broad coalition of actors in the search for solutions.

The development of more systematic and structured responses to long-standing refugee problems has also been one of the stated objectives of UNHCR's Convention Plus initiative. There have been efforts to identify the roles that the agency and other governmental and non-governmental actors should play and the lessons that should be

Box 5.3

The story of one Somali refugee in Dadaab, Kenya

More than 2 million refugees in Africa are trapped in protracted situations. One of them is a young Somali student named Abass Hassan Mohamed.

Abass is the second of six children. His family and some 300,000 other people fled to Kenya in the midst of the violent implosion of Somalia in 1991–92. He was only ten years old when he fled his home. He says very little about his early days in the refugee camp, but remembers that it was dusty, hot and violent, and that people died daily.

Death and malnutrition rates in the Somali refugee population soared through 1992, while cross-border raids by Somali elements posed a significant security threat to refugees and aid workers. Malnutrition rates were as high as 54 per cent in some refugee camps. Death rates reached 100 a day per 100,000 refugees, five times the average level. At the same time, almost daily attacks by Somali bandits, known as *shiftas,* resulted in alarming numbers of murders and rapes.

Thirteen years later, Abass still lives in one of three remaining refugee camps near Dadaab in north-eastern Kenya, just 80 kilometres from the border with Somalia. The camps house some 135,000 other refugees. Abass' experience in Dadaab highlights the hardships faced by those trapped in forgotten refugee situations—but it also demonstrates the courage of individual refugees, the human potential they represent, and the dramatic difference when a solution to their plight is found.

In February 2004, Abass received his results from national secondary-school exams. Competing against students from across the country, Abass sat for exams in subjects as diverse as English, Chemistry, Commerce and Swahili, a language widely spoken in East Africa. His results were extraordinary. He ranked first in Kenya's Northeast Province and eighth in the whole of Kenya.

Although he does not brag, Abass overcame incredible odds to achieve this remarkable result. Of the 44 students in his class, only 32 graduated. His days were full of activities such as football, the debating club and the school environment club, but also with more demanding tasks such as standing in the blazing sun and 45-degree heat for hours to receive the family's fortnightly food rations. He tried to do his homework at night by the light of the family's only kerosene lamp, but his family often could not afford the fuel.

Abass learned to survive in one of the most violent camps in Africa, where rape, murder and armed robbery were almost daily occurrences. Physical and material insecurity have plagued the Dadaab camps for years. The refugees in these camps have existed with no legal status for well over a decade, compounding the challenge of finding a durable solution. In addition, they are required to remain within the camps and are, as a result, totally dependent on international assistance. This assistance is dwindling; refugees receive only 80 per cent of their food requirements and have limited access to water. Half the shelters in the camps are dilapidated.

Abass faced incredible challenges growing up as a refugee in Dadaab. He remained determined, however, not to let these difficulties get in his way. Throughout the long years in the camp, he tried to view his situation as temporary, and think instead of the day he would be able to leave to start a new life. Abass dreams of studying medicine. In a community with only one doctor for 135,000 people, he believes that is the best way to help his people.

Once again, Abass has beaten the odds and come one step closer to realizing his dream. In August 2005, he left Dadaab for the United States, where he will enrol at Princeton University with a full scholarship.

Abass is one of the very few Somali refugees in Dadaab who have found a solution to an otherwise protracted situation. He leaves behind a family and community whose future is far more uncertain. Given the prevailing insecurity in southern and central Somalia, the region of origin of many of the refugees in the Dadaab camps, there are no prospects for their repatriation in the foreseeable future. Their lack of legal status and the policies of the Kenyan government mean they are unable to support themselves—let alone integrate—locally. Finally, there have been extremely limited resettlement opportunities for ethnic Somalis from the Dadaab camps in recent years.

As a result of the lack of solutions, some 135,000 refugees in the Dadaab camps live in limbo. Abass is one of the lucky few who will be able to start afresh. The rest can do little more than wait, try to survive on rapidly dwindling international assistance, and pin their hopes on the international community to resolve their situation.

There are some signs of encouragement. A range of programmes introduced by UNHCR and its partners in the late 1990s have seen a dramatic decline in the level of violent crime in the camps. From a high of more than 300 incidents involving rape, murder and armed robbery in 1998, cases of serious crime fell to just 36 in 2003. There have also been some positive developments, albeit tentative, in the restoration of a central government in Somalia. Finally, there has been some revival of donor interest in formulating a comprehensive response to the situation of Somali refugees in the region as a whole.

However, these positive developments are just a beginning. Abass' story demonstrates the incredible challenges faced by refugees in protracted situations, the skills and abilities that these refugees possess, and their desire to play an active role in rebuilding their lives. With the sustained support of the international community, they may yet realize their dreams.

Somali refugees in the El Nino school in one of the camps in Dadaab, Kenya. Somali refugees have been living in these camps since they were set up in 1991. (UNHCR/B. Press/July 1999)

drawn from past experience to develop a more systematic approach to comprehensive solutions.[38]

Efforts have been made to apply these conceptual developments to two of the world's most complex and protracted refugee situations, those of Afghans in South West Asia and Somalis in East Africa and the Horn of Africa. The hope is that through pilot projects to address these two situations, the 'strengths and shortcomings of the frameworks should be identified and necessary adjustments made' before their application to other protracted refugee situations.[39]

'Afghanistan Plus' initiative

Launched in 2003, this initiative's goal is to build a comprehensive framework to manage population movements in the region. Specifically, UNHCR aims to reach agreement on key policy issues, such as repatriation, reintegration, migration, assistance, protection and institutional development. It hopes to achieve this through consultation and cooperation with governments of the region, key donors, technical-cooperation agencies such as the International Labour Organization and the International Organization for Migration as well as a range of civil-society groups.

These approaches have been based on the understanding that population movements to and from Afghanistan are now primarily economic and migratory in nature and consequently require different administrative responses. The Afghanistan Plus initiative emphasizes the importance of sensitizing donors to the need for continued international engagement and support, especially for programmes within Afghanistan. The initiative also aims to build further consensus among regional actors on the need for new bilateral and regional mechanisms for both migration and repatriation. Finally, UNHCR has emphasized that development-assistance programmes and funds should play a bigger role in assisting reintegration inside Afghanistan and improving the conditions of long-staying Afghans still outside the country and their host communities (see Box 6.2).

Somalia CPA

As with the Afghanistan Plus initiative, the lessons learned from a CPA for Somali refugees could be applied to other protracted situations. Its objectives are to identify durable solutions for Somali refugees living in the region's host countries. Given the continuing instability in southern and central Somalia, the focus of the CPA is on repatriation to Somaliland and Puntland, where conditions for returnees are more secure than in southern and central Somalia. However, it is widely recognized that for sustained returns more emphasis on reintegration and post-conflict recovery is required.

The second objective of the CPA is to examine how human rights and economic conditions for Somali refugees can be improved in host countries such as Kenya, Ethiopia, Yemen and Djibouti. Local experts in the region will determine the gaps in protection and assistance that need to be addressed by the CPA. Given the difficult prospects for sustainable peace in Somalia, addressing the protection and assistance gaps in countries of asylum in the region would meet the short- to medium-term needs of Somali refugees (see Box 2.4).

Limitations

The Somali-refugee CPA and the Afghanistan Plus initiative are commendable efforts to try and engage the international community. However, they do not adequately link humanitarian factors with underlying economic, political and security issues.

Resolving the problem of long-standing Somali refugees requires the restoration of stability in southern and central Somalia. Similarly, a solution for Afghan refugees requires the sustained engagement of development actors in rebuilding Afghanistan.

The lessons from past CPAs, such as those in Indochina and Central America, are that humanitarian efforts must be closely linked to political, diplomatic and development initiatives. Past CPAs also required the active involvement of viable and functioning countries of origin so that internal conflicts and refugee problems would not recur. Finally, successful CPAs relied on external political initiatives that preceded and laid the foundations for humanitarian and development programmes. Without strong political support and successful peace negotiations there is little prospect of resolving protracted refugee crises such as the Afghan or Somali situations.

The need for an integrated approach

It is important to recognize that humanitarian actors cannot address the political dimensions of protracted refugee situations on their own. While it is essential that refugee-protection agencies are sensitive to host governments' security concerns, actions by humanitarian agencies without the support of both development agencies and the UN Security Council will not beget truly comprehensive solutions. As long as discussions on protracted refugee situations remain exclusively within the humanitarian community and do not engage the broader peace, security and development communities, they will be limited in their impact.

Despite the need for a multifaceted approach, the overall response of policy makers remains compartmentalized. Security, development and humanitarian issues are usually discussed in different forums, each with their own institutional arrangements and independent policy approaches. There is almost no strategic integration of approaches and little effective coordination in the field. Neither the United Nations nor the donor community has adequately integrated the resolution of recurring refugee problems with the promotion of economic and political development, conflict resolution and sustainable peace and security. International involvement in nation-building, reconstruction, and rehabilitation in war-torn regions is still piecemeal and under-resourced. Meaningful comprehensive solutions must overcome these divisions.

Such an approach needs to be rooted in an understanding of the relationship between forced migration and security since the end of the Cold War and the security concerns of Third World states. The nature of protracted refugee situations in the developing world has changed. During the Cold War, these situations were addressed because of the interest of the superpowers, primarily the United States. In recent years, however, declining donor engagement coupled with a new sense of vulnerability in host states has led to a changed environment within which solutions must be crafted. In this sense, it is important to emphasize that the task is not simply to replicate past solutions, but to fashion new ones that draw on the lessons of the past but are appropriate to the new environment.

First, from the *peace and security* sector, sustained engagement is necessary not only from the UN Security Council and the Department of Peacekeeping Operations (DPKO) but also from the African Union, the Economic Community of West African States, the South Asian Association for Regional Cooperation, the Association for Southeast Asian Nations and foreign and defence ministries in national capitals. Second come *development* actors. Ranging from the UN Development Programme, the World Bank and international NGOs to national development agencies, they would play an important role at all stages of a comprehensive solution. Finally, *humanitarian agencies* such as UNHCR, the UN Office for the Coordination of Humanitarian Affairs and NGOs need to bring their particular skills and experience to bear.

These three sets of actors should engage in a related set of short, medium and long-term activities to form a CPA. These activities should include a thorough analysis of the situation and the interests of the various stakeholders. This analysis should form the basis of related action plans for the three groups, which must be fully supported by the international community.

In the short term, the CPA should focus on the stabilization of the current situation, the establishment of dialogue between key stakeholders, and confidence-building activities in the country of origin and in host countries. Next should come a consolidation phase, focusing on a resolution to the conflict, the rehabilitation of refugee-populated areas and preparation for the various durable solutions. Once this groundwork has been laid, the CPA can be implemented. This would lead to a durable peace in the country of origin, the execution of long-term development strategies and the realization of a comprehensive solution through the complementary use of the three durable solutions.

Such an integrated approach to addressing refugee situations has been explored in the past. In fact, UNHCR, DPKO and the United Nations Development Programme all have experience of working together. While the effectiveness of such partnerships has sometimes been questioned, it is important to examine why some have been more successful than others. More generally, it is important to recognize that a solution cannot truly be comprehensive without the sustained engagement of all the three types of actors.

Addressing protracted refugee situations in a more consistent and comprehensive manner is one way for the United Nations system as a whole to demonstrate its relevance and usefulness. The decision of the UN General Assembly at the 2005 World Summit to create a Peacebuilding Commission is a step in this direction.[40] The main purpose of the commission is to bring together all relevant parties within and outside the United Nations to address the needs of a troubled nation. The commission is to improve planning for sustained recovery after war as well as coordination of the many post-conflict activities.

However, the success of such an integrated approach will depend entirely on the commitment of the international community to see it succeed. Comprehensive solutions are the best way to address the concerns of Western states, meet the protection needs of refugees and respond to the concerns of countries of first asylum. In the long term, governments must consider how their trade, aid and development policies and strategic and diplomatic concerns may be brought to bear not only on addressing refugee flows but also on preventing them. Ultimately, it must be recognized that the most efficient, effective and humane approach to refugee situations is their prevention. The international community must realize that by engaging with failing states today, it is preventing the refugee crises of tomorrow.

6 Rethinking durable solutions

It is not acceptable, former High Commissioner Ruud Lubbers said in 2001, that refugees spend years of their lives in confined areas.[1] Yet the political failure to find durable solutions for refugees leads to precisely the kinds of protracted situations that degrade the displaced. Unable to return to their homeland, settle permanently in their country of first asylum or move to a third state, many refugees find themselves confined indefinitely to camps or holding areas, often in volatile border zones.[2] Such restrictive conditions are a denial of rights under the 1951 UN Refugee Convention and a waste of human talent.[3] Furthermore, the prevalence in prolonged refugee situations of idleness, aid-dependency, a legacy of conflict and weak rule of law can induce fresh cycles of violence, threatening human security.[4] With more than 6 million refugees stranded in a 'long-lasting and intractable state of limbo' at the end of 2004, it is imperative that the search for durable solutions be intensified.[5]

Three durable solutions—voluntary repatriation, local integration in the country of first asylum or resettlement in a third country—are the options available for the permanent resolution of the 'refugee cycle'. All three are regarded as durable because they promise an end to refugees' suffering and their need for international protection and dependence on humanitarian assistance.[6] The search for durable solutions has been a central part of UNHCR's mandate since its inception. The organization's statute commands the High Commissioner to seek 'permanent solutions for the problem of refugees by assisting Governments . . . to facilitate the voluntary repatriation of such refugees, or their assimilation within new national communities'.[7] However, the role of the three durable solutions and the relative priority accorded to each has changed with time.

The search for durable solutions

During the Cold War and the national-liberation struggles of the 1960s and 1970s, those who fled communist regimes and colonial oppression were granted refugee status on the assumption that repatriation was not an option. Resettlement and local integration were generally regarded as the most viable and strategically desirable durable solutions. With the demise of communism and colonialism,

Preparation for voluntary repatriation of refugees to Angola from the Divuma camp in the Democratic Republic of Congo. (UNHCR/S. Hopper/2003)

however, repatriation became more realistic and attractive for states. Furthermore, the increase since the 1980s in migration from poor to rich countries and the growing association of refugees with migrants fleeing poverty have added to the reluctance of wealthy nations to offer resettlement.[8] As for southern states, in the aftermath of economic adjustment and democratization most of them have been less willing to support local integration. This is in contrast to the situation in the 1960s and 1970s when, in Africa, for instance, rural refugees were allowed a high level of *de facto* local integration.[9]

Consequently, repatriation is now often regarded as the most desirable durable solution—provided that return is genuinely voluntary and sustainable. The 1990s became the decade of repatriation: more than 9 million refugees returned home between 1991 and 1996. However, returns under pressure from host governments—particularly the 1996 return of Rwandan refugees hosted by Zaire (now the Democratic Republic of Congo, or DRC) and Tanzania—have raised fresh questions about the degree of voluntariness and the role of compulsion in 'imposed return'.[10] Moreover, arguably premature repatriations to the former Yugoslav republics and Afghanistan in the early 2000s have renewed debate on sustainable reintegration and its relationship to post-conflict reconstruction.

The recognition, on the one hand, that voluntary repatriation is not always possible and, on the other, that indefinite encampment is unacceptable has led to a profound review of the three durable solutions and how they relate to one another. The need to avoid human degradation while simultaneously safeguarding voluntariness has spurred the development of new methods and approaches.

The period covered in this book saw the culmination of a cycle of reflection within UNHCR on the use of durable solutions, with the debate reinvigorated by new initiatives. The Global Consultations on International Protection with states, academics, NGOs and refugees resulted in the publication of an Agenda for Protection which stressed the need to redouble the search for durable solutions. To further these aspirations, UNHCR and partner states published a Framework for Durable Solutions for Refugees and Persons of Concern (hereafter referred to as the Framework for Durable Solutions). This elaborated the '4Rs': Repatriation, Reintegration, Rehabilitation and Reconstruction, as a process that would bridge the gap between relief and development. It also emphasized the two related concepts of Development Assistance for Refugees and Development through Local Integration.

Subsequently, durable solutions were placed within the context of a multilateral dialogue, which is referred to as the Convention Plus initiative. This led, most notably, to agreement by a range of resettlement and host states on a Multilateral Framework of Understandings on Resettlement. In light of these innovations, this chapter explains UNHCR's new approaches to durable solutions in three areas: first, the targeting of development assistance; second, migratory movements; and third, resettlement. It concludes by discussing the multilateral and political context in which UNHCR has tried to facilitate international cooperation to improve access to durable solutions.

Figure 6.1   Top 10 voluntary repatriation movements, 2004

TO (Country of origin)	FROM (Main countries of asylum)	
Afghanistan	Islamic Rep. of Iran	515,000
	Pakistan	424,000
	Other	760
	Total	**939,760**
Iraq	Islamic Rep. of Iran	57,000
	Lebanon	1,500
	Other	135,000
	Total	**193,500**
Burundi	United Rep. of Tanzania	89,000
	Dem. Rep. of Congo	880
	Other	400
	Total	**90,280**
Angola	Zambia	47,000
	Dem. Rep. of Congo	34,000
	Namibia	8,800
	Other	850
	Total	**90,650**
Liberia	Guinea	22,000
	Côte d'Ivoire	17,000
	Sierra Leone	15,000
	Ghana	1,900
	Other	910
	Total	**56,810**
Sierra Leone	Liberia	13,000
	Guinea	12,000
	Other	690
	Total	**25,690**
Somalia	Ethiopia	9,500
	Djibouti	8,500
	Other	110
	Total	**18,110**
Rwanda	Dem. Rep. of Congo	11,000
	Uganda	2,600
	Other	740
	Total	**14,340**
Dem. Rep. of Congo	Burundi	11,000
	Central African Rep.	2,000
	Other	670
	Total	**13,670**
Sri Lanka	India	9,900
	Other	110
	Total	**10,010**

Note: Figures are based on country of origin and asylum reports.
Source: UNHCR.

Returnee woman at a sewing workshop in Jalalabad, Afghanistan. (UNHCR/M. Shinohara/2004)

Targeting development assistance

Humanitarian assistance and development have usually been seen as distinct areas of national and global governance. However, the gap between refugee- and returnee-assistance programmes and long-term development efforts is a central hurdle in the way of both sustainable repatriation and the promotion of local integration. In this context, drawing on the ideas in the Agenda for Protection, the Framework for Durable Solutions has emerged as a means to better integrate refugees into development planning.[11] It has two explicit aims. The first is to improve international burden-sharing to build refugee-protection and reception capacities in developing states; the second, to improve access to durable solutions. To meet these goals, it sets out a series of concepts related to the targeting of development assistance. These focus on two areas: states of origin, and host states of asylum within regions of origin. In both cases, the principle of government ownership of the projects is paramount.

States of origin

With respect to states of origin, the 4Rs concept of repatriation, reintegration, rehabilitation and reconstruction focuses on improving the sustainability of repatriation. It does this by fostering the capacities and institutional partnerships necessary to ensure the smooth transition from emergency relief to long-term development. Its premise is that repatriation must involve more than transferring refugees across the border; rather, it must strive to create an environment conducive to sustainable return. To succeed in this task it must nurture partnerships with a range of government and development actors. As stipulated by UNHCR's Executive Committee in 2004, it is crucial to ensure that appropriate levels of security, social services and economic opportunity are available to returnees.[12] The idea of addressing the gap between relief and development builds upon the partnerships between UNHCR, the World Bank, UNICEF, UNDP, ILO and WFP. It also ties in to the EU's approach linking relief, reconstruction and development.[13]

The 4Rs concept is now fairly uncontroversial. It simply combines the notion of voluntary repatriation with the idea of post-conflict reconstruction. The latter has been part of mainstream development discourse since the late 1990s. States of origin rarely pose objections to return, while asylum states are keen to emphasize it as the ideal durable solution. For their part, donor states often have specific economic and political interests in reconstruction. As a consequence, major development agencies already have mechanisms focusing on post-conflict reconstruction. Almost everyone is receptive to the idea; the challenge is to build a framework for institutional collaboration to ensure smooth implementation.

There has been significant progress in establishing such a collaborative framework covering various UN agencies. Furthermore, discussions between UNHCR and the World Bank have looked into overlaps between the 4Rs and the Bank's programmes for post-conflict situations and low-income countries. As a result of inter-agency collaboration and commitment by donors, it has been possible to apply the 4Rs in Afghanistan, Sierra Leone and Sri Lanka. In each case, the UN country team has tried to lead a process of integrated planning in relation to return.[14]

The case of Liberia shows how the 4Rs can improve the prospects for sustainable repatriation. Following the end of the 14-year civil war in the country and the exile of former dictator Charles Taylor in 2003, UNHCR began to organize the return of some 320,000 refugees from neighbouring states. The implementation of tripartite agreements between UNHCR, the Liberian Transitional Government and the neighbouring host states began in October 2004. An operations plan for return and reintegration is expected to run until 2007. In order to facilitate reintegration, more than 30 community projects are being implemented in the counties of Bong, Grand Gedeh, Montserrado and Nimba. Given the scale of destruction during the conflict, the projects aim to rebuild local infrastructure, water supplies, schools and sanitation. To ensure local and national ownership of the projects, receiving communities and returnees participate in the planning process. Furthermore, proposals are submitted to district development committees and incorporated within national transition strategies.

The Liberian example demonstrates the extent to which UNHCR's search for durable solutions is drawing on a range of implementing partners, including NGOs. An example of the latter is the Environmental Foundation for Africa, which has been conducting workshops on environmental rehabilitation.[15] Reintegration in Liberia has also drawn upon another innovation related to the 4Rs, the concept of Disarmament, Demobilization, Rehabilitation and Reintegration. Developed by the UN's Department of Peacekeeping Operations as a programme for ex-combatants, it seeks to ease the transition from conflict to peace in a manner conducive to sustainable return. It is particularly important in West Africa, given the number of refugees and internally displaced persons in the region who were combatants or child soldiers.

Host states

While the long-term confinement of refugees to camps and closed settlements is a severe restriction of their rights, it is important to acknowledge the concerns of host states as well. Receiving countries need help to overcome the political and economic obstacles that prevent them from finding alternatives to confining refugees within camps. These states need to be assisted and encouraged to allow refugees greater freedom of movement, access to social services and the right to earn a living. In this context, the two key concepts set out in the Framework for Durable Solutions are Development Assistance for Refugees and Development through Local Integration. Both recognize that refugees need not inevitably be perceived as a burden but could, in the right circumstances, be agents of development.

The concept of Development Assistance for Refugees covers additional development assistance to countries hosting large numbers of refugees; promotion of a better quality of life and self-reliance for refugees pending durable solutions; and a better quality of life for host communities. In other words, it is about empowering the productive capacities and self-reliance of refugees as well as supporting host-country and local-community development. The concept is similar to Development through Local Integration. The latter, however, relates to situations in which the host state provides the opportunity for gradual integration of refugees. Here, additional development assistance would facilitate refugees' economic self-reliance, socio-cultural integration and access to legal rights, culminating in citizenship.[16]

In contrast to the principles behind the 4Rs, on which consensus has come relatively easily, discussions on the last two concepts have advanced more slowly. Whereas repatriation is widely accepted as the most desirable durable solution, local integration is more likely to be resisted by host states. Receiving countries usually have strong concerns about the economic, political, environmental and security implications of moving beyond encampment.[17] Fostering the conditions in which those concerns can be addressed, and at the same time reducing the confinement of refugees to camps, depends on international cooperation and inter-agency coordination.

Development Assistance for Refugees promotes self-sufficiency through local interaction and the provision of services for refugees. While not necessarily according refugees full citizenship, it allows freedom of movement and access to land or employment, provides for education, health facilities and housing, and creates opportunities to form social networks beyond the immediate community. It may ultimately promote repatriation by better equipping refugees with the skills and autonomy they need to return home. That was the case with Angolan refugees in Zambia, whose contribution to the local economy was widely acknowledged. Though they had the right to free movement and to earn a livelihood on land provided by the state, many returned home once conditions there improved.[18]

Both Development Assistance for Refugees and Development through Local Integration build on the legacy of UNHCR's attempts in the 1980s to promote local integration by using development assistance as a burden-sharing tool. Partnerships between UNHCR and development agencies such as UNDP were promoted to help African states host the large refugee populations in their rural areas.[19] The linking of development with local integration also builds upon the experience of UNHCR in Mexico during the 1990s, when a multi-year rural-development programme supported the integration of Guatemalan refugees in the states of Campeche and Quintana Roo. These were one-off applications, but UNHCR is now trying to apply a broad collaborative framework across the UN system.

Development through Local Integration is part of the Zambia Initiative, which supports the host government's policy of local integration for Angolan refugees (see Box 6.1).[20] In Serbia and Montenegro, UNHCR has collaborated with the government and other partners to provide housing, micro-credit facilities and vocational training to locally settled refugees displaced by conflict in the Balkans.[21] Development Assistance for Refugees has most notably been applied to Uganda's Self-Reliance Strategy (see Box 6.1).[22] These cases have been used to demonstrate the potential of targeting development assistance with a focus on host states.

All these initiatives attempt to build on the existing activities of states and organizations. Denmark, for instance, has its own strategy to promote Development Assistance for Refugees. It has agreed to assist Sudanese refugees in northern Uganda to support the host country's self-reliance strategy. Japan, as part of its Trust Fund for Human Security initiative, has agreed to provide development assistance to encourage self-reliance among Somali refugees in Ethiopia.[23] Meanwhile, in 2004 Ecuador emerged as a possible recipient of Development Assistance for Refugees; the UN Assessment Mission to Ecuador's Northern Border Region recommended including Colombian refugees within development plans for the north of the country.

Box 6.1

The Zambia Initiative and the Ugandan Self-Reliance Strategy

The Zambia Initiative and the Ugandan Self-Reliance Strategy exemplify the potential to integrate refugees into national-development plans. They demonstrate that it is not inevitable that refugees will be perceived as burdens that need to be confined to camps or closed settlements. Instead, these cases in Zambia and Uganda highlight the role refugees can play as active agents of development, contributing to the economy and society of the host state. The Zambia Initiative represents the most salient case study for the implementation of Development through Local Integration, while the Ugandan Self-Reliance Strategy shows how interim self-sufficiency can be developed prior to repatriation.

The Zambia Initiative

Due to the longstanding nature of the Angolan civil war, Angolan refugees have been present in Zambia's Western Province for more than 30 years. The local authorities have routinely provided between 6 and 12 fertile acres on which refugees can grow crops. This has allowed the majority of refugees in, for example, Mayukwayukwa and Meheba settlements to become self-sufficient in food and end their dependence on World Food Programme rations. They have also been able to sell their produce in nearby towns and even as far away

as Lusaka, thanks to 30–60 day travel passes provided by the authorities. The refugee populations have therefore lived alongside their local hosts for many years. The significance of these refugees' contribution to the local community is highlighted by the collapse in food production in western Zambia after the repatriation of 220,000 Angolans in 2002.

In June 2001, a joint UNHCR and United Nations Office for Project Services mission to Zambia's Western Province explored the possibility of addressing the needs of the host population as well refugees in the area. After discussions with major donors, partners and stakeholders, it recommended an integrated approach to infrastructure and socio-economic development in refugee-hosting areas that would build upon initiatives already underway in the province. Besides helping host communities, such an approach would be more likely to contribute to an enabling environment and security for refugees. UNHCR has coordinated and monitored the initiative since its inception in 2002.

The initiative rests on two pillars: poverty reduction, with priority given to agriculture, health, education and infrastructure; and empowerment of refugees and their local integration for a durable solution. Progress was to

be reviewed every three months. The project sought to address the strain on local resources and the food deficit which has emerged since 2002 to allow the province to continue to host and integrate refugees while benefiting the local population. The focus of the initiative has been on small-scale, community-based development projects such as wells, food-storage silos, health facilities and rural-credit schemes.

Through the Zambia Initiative, refugees have been integrated within the government's National Development Plan and its poverty-reduction strategy. The initiative has attracted resources through its concept of flexible funding, which allows donors to contribute in line with their own priorities and budget lines. The main contributions have come from Denmark, Sweden, Japan, the United States and the European Union. They total more than US$14 million and benefit some 456,000 people, including 150,000 refugees.

Uganda's Self-Reliance Strategy

Uganda has been hosting refugees since the 1940s. Despite never having formally adopted refugee legislation, a policy of local settlement has

Donor trends

The main obstacle to promoting the widespread application of Development Assistance for Refugees has been the reluctance of donor states to provide more resources. For their part, many southern host states fear that aid destined for them would be diverted to assist refugees. The debate has been somewhat polarized, with host states fearing that initiatives to provide Development Assistance for Refugees are an attempt to shift the burden to regions of origin. In 2004, UNHCR's Executive Committee concluded that assistance to refugee populations and host communities to promote self-reliance is one element of a burden-sharing been in place since the arrival of these early refugees. It is estimated that the government has made more than 3,300 square kilometres of land available to refugees for settlement on the basis of 'right of use for the time that they are in exile'.

The government has attempted to promote self-reliance and local integration by allowing refugees to grow their own crops on the small plots of land provided. Since the influx of nearly 200,000 Sudanese refugees in the late 1980s, it has made large amounts of land available in the northwest Nile Region. When compared with refugees confined to camps, many of those in the settlements have achieved a relatively high degree of free movement and food self-sufficiency. For instance, refugees in the Kiryandongo settlement in northeastern Uganda achieved self-sufficiency by 1995, allowing the phasing-out of food distribution.

Recognizing the role that refugees can play in the development of their own and their host communities, in 1998 the Government of Uganda and UNHCR established the Self-Reliance Strategy. Focusing on the districts of Adjumani, Arua and Moyo in the West Nile region, its goal was to improve the standard of living of all people—including refugees—in those districts. The principal goals of the project were to empower refugees and nationals in the area to support themselves and to integrate services for the refugees with those for nationals. The 1999–2003 strategy planned to phase out all food assistance by 2001. By 2003, it was forecast, the refugees would be able to grow or buy their own food, have access to and pay for basic services, and maintain self-sustaining communities.

The mid-term review of the project, in 2004, revealed the initiative's positive impact and its limitations. The review noted that there had been an increase in food production by both refugees and the local host communities. In certain areas of Adjumani, such as Mogula, where the land is very fertile, surveys suggested that up to 90 per cent self-sufficiency had been achieved, allowing food distribution to be phased out in a number of settlements. Self-sufficiency had also increased the range of foods available. Meanwhile, the integration of refugee children into Uganda's Universal Primary Education initiative had promoted social cohesion and refugees' interaction with host communities. Limited facilities were provided to support youth training in carpentry or brick laying, for example, in Rhino camp in Arua. The review also pointed to improvements in healthcare and water safety.

However, despite these achievements, the review makes clear that the four-year schedule to make the refugees self-reliant was overly ambitious. The small plot sizes and poor soil quality in certain areas have meant that some refugees continue to depend on food rations. This is particularly the case in Arua, where refugees are mainly settled in the Nile Basin area and face irregular rainfall and poor soil. In Adjumani and Moyo districts, soil exhaustion and bad farming practices have had the same results.

The lessons learnt from the project could be applied in the ongoing transition from self-reliance to Development Assistance for Refugees. As part of its strategy to assist refugees in their region of origin, the Danish Government has taken a lead role in the programme. Consequently, it is envisaged that UNHCR will play the part of facilitator, rather than actively coordinating assistance. For its part, the Ugandan government has responded to the mid-term review by seeking to include a wider range of stakeholders and development partners in the existing process.

framework. According to the committee, this could be developed in the context of an international response, particularly to protracted refugee situations.[24]

The inability of donor states to provide new resources is partly attributable to the separation at government level of development and refugee issues. A crucial task for UNHCR, therefore, has been to mobilize donor commitments to support the Framework for Durable Solutions and encourage greater coordination across the branches of national government. In this regard, a number of bilateral and multilateral donor initiatives that look at refugees within a development context have emerged. For example, the World Bank's focus on post-conflict reconstruction is particularly relevant to the 4Rs. Meanwhile, European Union funds for cooperation on migration issues have supported UNHCR's Strengthening Protection Capacity Project.[25]

The commitments of states to the United Nations' Millennium Development Goals are also relevant to the search for durable solutions, given that the levels of human development of refugees often fall below those of non-refugees. Millennium goals such as the eradication of extreme poverty, universal access to primary education, gender equality and reductions in infant mortality are very germane to the need to focus resources on refugees.[26]

The 2002 Monterey Financing for Development Summit saw a number of pledges by states and international organizations to increase financial and technical cooperation for development. In particular, it reiterated the central role of official development assistance (ODA) for states with the lowest capacity to attract private direct investment. It also pointed to the need to target assistance more effectively, and aspired to commit at least 0.7 per cent of the GDP of industrialized states to ODA.[27] In 2005, the Summit on the Millennium Declaration and the G-8 discussions on British Prime Minister Tony Blair's Africa Plan for trade, aid and debt relief highlighted opportunities to mobilize resources. Following the Gleneagles Summit, G-8 countries pledged to increase the overall aid to developing countries by US$50 billion, doubling the aid for Africa by US$25 billion by 2010. In this regard, promoting the productive capacities of refugees and placing security issues within a displacement context could prove to be an extremely effective means of garnering wider development assistance.

Inter-agency collaboration

The UNHCR 2004 review process highlighted the growing links between peace, security, development and humanitarianism.[28] Given this complex inter-connectedness, UNHCR cannot do everything alone. But it has an important role in advocacy and coordination. In implementing the goals of the Framework for Durable Solutions, UNHCR is not aspiring to become a development agency. Rather, it seeks to act as a catalyst, creating the collaborative framework under which other actors can better assist the displaced.

In this context, UNHCR has fostered a number of inter-agency partnerships. Most significantly, it has joined the United Nations Development Group (UNDG). Created by UN Secretary-General Kofi Annan in 1997, the group seeks to improve the effectiveness of development work at the country level. In 2004, the group adopted a Guidance Note on Durable Solutions for Displaced Persons that stresses the need for UN country teams to consider the search for durable solutions for displaced persons.[29] UNHCR collaborates with the Organization for Economic Cooperation and Development, especially with regard to post-conflict development cooperation, and with the World Bank. In the latter case, it advocates more systematic inclusion of population displacement in the Bank's poverty-reduction strategies.[30] These initiatives highlight the importance of mainstreaming the needs of the displaced across the UN system, particularly within a development context.

Secondary movement

As asylum can no longer be entirely disconnected from more general migration issues, UNHCR must deal with the so-called asylum–migration nexus. In the context of industrialized states' growing interest in managed migration and the emergence of exclusion and deterrence policies, UNHCR faces the challenge of protecting *bona fide* refugees within broader migratory movements. Ironically, the current debates on migration control may offer new opportunities in the search for durable solutions for refugees.

An incentive for engagement

A number of EU states, in particular, have begun to make the case that the current spontaneous-arrival asylum system fails to meet the needs of the most vulnerable refugees. The majority of these, it is asserted, remain in their region of origin, without the means to use human smugglers to reach the rich North. The link between spontaneous-arrival asylum in rich countries and the absence of durable solutions in poorer ones is uncertain. But statistics on the origins of asylum applicants in industrialized states imply that a large proportion are fleeing protracted refugee situations in host states in the region of origin. Indeed, a Swiss Migration Forum study of onward secondary movement of Somali refugees reveals that many of them do not wish to move beyond the region of first asylum, but protection issues, lack of social amenities and confinement to camps force them to.[31] This has led to a growing debate over the causes of onward secondary movement. Questions have arisen, for instance, on the circumstances under which it would be legitimate to undertake a secondary movement from the first country of asylum in the region.

Strengthening protection capacities in regions of origin

Restricting the rights of refugees and delaying the attainment of durable solutions cause frustration and tension among refugees and in the host community. In such situations refugees, in particular women and children, become more vulnerable to various forms of exploitation such as trafficking and forced recruitment, and may develop a long-term dependence on humanitarian assistance. Often the result is the marginalization and isolation of refugees, which can lead to an increase in irregular movements and even to security and stability problems for the host state and other states in the region.

As such, states' interests in resolving the issue of onward secondary movement can best be met by providing effective protection in regions of origin. Starting from the premise that northern states are eager to reduce the need for onward movement, the Convention Plus initiative links this to the need to resolve the underlying causes of such movement through international cooperation.[32] It recognizes that many secondary movements are caused by the absence of secure legal status, the non-availability of long-term durable solutions, and the absence of educational or employment opportunities. Solving the problem of secondary movements, it is argued, will require a cooperative framework to strengthen protection in states of first asylum.[33]

Among donors, the European Union and the Netherlands have taken the lead in trying to improve protection capacities within regions of origin. Notably, the EU's 2004–08 budget for external cooperation on migration issues has been expanded to €250 million. In 2004, a small part of this budget was allocated to UNHCR's Strengthening Protection Capacity Project. This one-year scheme focuses on Kenya and Tanzania as states with protracted refugee situations, and Benin and Burkina Faso as emerging resettlement countries.[34]

Labour migration: a durable solution?

In political debate in industrialized states, asylum is generally seen within the wider context of immigration. The asylum–migration nexus is therefore increasingly perceived as a largely disaggregated flow in which asylum claimants are tarnished as bogus. What this view ignores is that migrants can represent productive and enterprising people. The contribution that they can make, whether as refugees or otherwise, depends on their integration within a host society. In this regard, the Declaration of The Hague on the Future of Refugee and Migrant Policy, the culmination of an initiative that coordinated the views of more than 500 people involved and interested in refugee issues, sets out 21 principles to advance the refugee and migration agenda. In particular, the declaration pointed to the need to recognize that managed migration could be in everyone's interests.[35]

Many of the industrialized states now expending vast resources on excluding and deterring asylum seekers will face labour shortages in the future as life expectancies rise and birth rates decline. This paradox may provide a key to improving access to durable solutions not only in a northern context, but also in terms of promoting solutions in the South. For example, UNHCR has begun to explore the possibility that temporary labour-migration visas might be made available to Afghan refugees in Pakistan and Iran. Such an approach highlights the need for the implications of the asylum–migration nexus to be fully explored in the search for durable solutions.

Figure 6.2 **Total number of arrivals of resettled refugees in industrialized countries, 1990-2004**

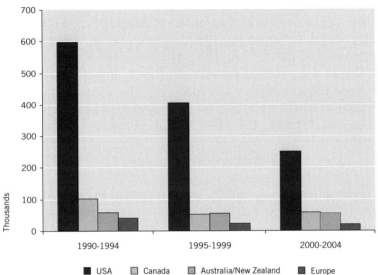

Note: Europe here refers to Denmark, Finland, Iceland, Ireland, the Netherlands, Norway, Sweden and the United Kingdom.

Source: Governments.

Figure 6.3 **Number of arrivals of resettled refugees in industrialized countries, 1990-2004**

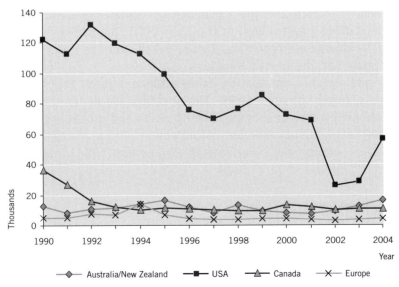

Note: Europe here refers to Denmark, Finland, Iceland, Ireland, the Netherlands, Norway, Sweden and the United Kingdom.

Source: Governments.

Resettlement

Resettlement may be defined as the transfer of refugees from a state in which they have initially sought protection to a third state that has agreed to admit them with permanent-residence status.[36] Until the mid-1980s, resettlement was generally seen by states as the preferred durable solution. In the aftermath of the Second World War it was the primary means by which the International Refugee Organization and, later, UNHCR provided solutions for the displaced. It was used to resettle nearly 200,000 refugees following the 1956 Hungarian revolution, more than 40,000 people expelled from Uganda by Idi Amin in 1972, and 5,000 Latin American refugees facing *refoulement* from Augusto Pinochet's Chile in 1973. Perhaps most notably, resettlement was used to address the problem of the Vietnamese 'boat people', of whom nearly 2 million were resettled as a result of the 1989 Comprehensive Plan of Action (CPA) for Indochina. Yet despite the example of the CPA, resettlement elsewhere was limited to the often-unfilled quotas of a handful of traditional resettlement states. By the 1990s, repatriation had taken centre stage.[37]

However, since the end of the CPA in 1995 there has been ongoing reflection and reassessment of the role of resettlement. Following UNHCR's 1994 Evaluation Report on Resettlement Activities, the Working Group on Resettlement was formed that same year, and shortly afterwards UNHCR's Annual Tripartite Consultations (ATC) on resettlement began. These consultations have become a forum in which resettlement countries, NGOs and UNHCR share information and develop joint strategies to address resettlement needs. Alongside the ATC, the Working Group began to reassess the role of resettlement and promote the emergence of new resettlement countries and the expansion of quotas. As a result, the global resettlement quota grew to nearly 100,000 by 2001. Among the new resettlement countries to emerge are Argentina, Benin, Brazil, Burkina Faso, Chile, Iceland, Ireland, Spain and the United Kingdom.

Policy and practice in relation to resettlement have therefore undergone significant changes in recent years. The strategic use of resettlement and new operational methods such as group identification and processing are enhancing resettlement's traditional function of protection. These innovations have been consolidated within the Multilateral Framework of Understandings on Resettlement, agreed in June 2004.

The functions of resettlement

Resettlement formed a central component of the Global Consultations. In the context of a comprehensive strategy to enhance international protection, discussions on resettlement highlighted that it has three central functions. Its first—and traditional—role is as a tool of international protection for individual refugees. Second, it may serve as a durable solution. This reflects acknowledgement that resettlement can be used alongside other durable solutions as part of a comprehensive strategy to overcome protracted refugee situations. Finally, resettlement may be an expression of international solidarity. Resettlement by third states represents a commitment to a more equitable sharing of responsibility for protection with the developing countries that host the majority of the world's refugees.[38]

However, questions remain about resettlement and its relationship to the other durable solutions. On the one hand, it may be seen as a symbol of extra-regional states' willingness to share responsibility; on the other, it may represent a disincentive to repatriation by encouraging some refugees to remain in the host state hoping to be resettled.

The strategic use of resettlement

The three complementary functions of resettlement—as a protection tool, a durable solution and an expression of international burden-sharing—would indicate that it is most effective when applied as part of a comprehensive approach to international protection. Indeed, it was in the broader multilateral context of the Convention Plus initiative that the Core Group on Resettlement was created. The group drafted the Multilateral Framework of Understandings on Resettlement, building on the prior initiatives of the Working Group on Resettlement and the Global Consultations on International Protection.

In recent years more emphasis has been placed on the strategic use of resettlement. This conceives of 'the planned use of resettlement that maximizes the benefit of resettlement, either directly or indirectly, other than to those being resettled. Those benefits accrue to other refugees, the host States, other States, and the international protection regime in general'.[39] Such strategic use of resettlement acknowledges that it is likely to be most effective when applied alongside the other durable solutions in situation-specific plans of action. For example, this might apply when a small group represents a stumbling block in the way of peace negotiations or a wider repatriation agreement. Here resettlement, even of small groups, may serve as a catalyst in leveraging other solutions.

The group methodology

Aside from presenting many of the general principles underlying resettlement, the Multilateral Framework also elaborated the role of the Group Methodology, developed in 2003 to enhance the use of resettlement. Group resettlement covers not only specific vulnerable individuals, but also groups that are in protracted refugee situations. By focusing on a section of the refugee population on the basis of identity characteristics such as clan, ethnicity, age or gender, for example, it may enhance the search for durable solutions. It would benefit not only the group

Box 6.2

Afghanistan—a complex transition

In mid-2001, the prospects for progress in one of the world's largest and most complex refugee problems were remote. The extremist policies of the Taliban regime, deepening poverty and a crippling three-year drought had generated a major internal displacement problem and driven new population flows across Afghanistan's borders. The new exodus added to the estimated 6 million Afghans that had fled to neighbouring countries since 1980. Moreover, disillusioned by the state of their homeland, increasing numbers of Afghans had left the region and sought asylum throughout the world.

Given such unpromising circumstances, few would have imagined the dramatic change in Afghanistan's fortunes that 12 months later propelled one of the largest repatriation movements in modern history. By the end of 2002, well over 2 million Afghans had returned home from Pakistan and Iran. The repatriation continued throughout 2003 and 2004, with figures passing the half-million mark each year. At the same time, the return of internally displaced persons gathered pace and secondary movements beyond the region declined sharply.

Perhaps the most influential factor behind this remarkable turnaround was the growing confidence that flowed from international re-engagement in Afghanistan. The Bonn Agreement of December 2001 provided a political road map and timetable that presented the most persuasive opportunity for peace and reconciliation in more than a decade. It was underpinned by strong expressions of donor support for economic and social reconstruction at the Tokyo conference on Afghanistan in February 2002. Taken together, these moves renewed interest in the search for a solution to what had seemed an intractable refugee situation.

The huge repatriation movements since 2002 have partially alleviated a humanitarian concern that has persisted for more than two decades. They also provided valuable opportunities for political cooperation between Afghanistan and its neighbours on an issue that has been a source of considerable regional tension. Currently,

the legal and operational framework for the management of voluntary repatriation is provided for by tripartite agreements which are serviced by regular working-level meetings. The confidence-building these exchanges permit will be critical to ensuring continued progress as the full consequences of the protracted displacement from Afghanistan become apparent.

The Governments of Pakistan and Iran, the two countries most affected by the presence of Afghan refugees, have long insisted on repatriation as the preferred solution. They have been steadfast in their opposition to local integration, especially in view of the large numbers involved. At the same time, they have implicitly acknowledged that the nature and composition of the Afghan populations on their territory has changed. Indeed, even before the fall of the Taliban both governments had periodically asserted that Afghans were predominantly economic migrants rather than refugees. They are also aware that long-established Afghan communities have formed close links with their host societies and have considerably expanded pre-conflict patterns of seasonal labour migration.

While the emergence of a recognized government in Afghanistan has partially removed an important obstacle to solutions at the inter-state level, serious economic, social and security concerns remain. These are of a magnitude that may take many years to overcome, and their solution will depend primarily on the establishment of a politically and financially viable state. The problems are reflected in the pattern of return to date, with comparatively few Afghans choosing to return to the south, southeast and central highlands, areas that are especially troubled by insecurity, drought and poverty. Moreover, long exposure to higher standards of living and better public services and employment opportunities have had a profound impact on long-staying Afghan communities in general, and the younger generation in particular. There is reluctance, both among those who are very poor and the comparatively better off, to return to a

country where socio-economic indices are still among the lowest in the world, and where protection and human rights concerns persist.

Recognizing that tensions would eventually emerge over the scope and duration of the agreements on voluntary repatriation, UNHCR launched a policy initiative in mid-2003 to explore more comprehensive approaches. While supporting voluntary return as the preferred durable solution, it argued that a purely humanitarian and refugee-oriented perspective would be insufficient to address the more complex challenges of development, poverty, migration and demography that have emerged.

To this end, it has promoted inclusive consultations with donors, governments, civil society and Afghans themselves to devise policy and management arrangements for the future. There is broad agreement that continuing support for Afghanistan's reconstruction and the management of population movements as part of normalized bilateral and regional relations should be key objectives for the coming years. Progress in these areas would enhance sustainable reintegration and solutions for the remaining Afghan populations in the neighbouring countries. To achieve this, there was agreement that development and technical cooperation funding should increasingly replace humanitarian aid in the years to come.

During this transition period, finding a workable balance between Afghanistan's absorption capacity and the high returns, and between voluntariness and the pressures on asylum space, will remain key protection concerns for UNHCR. In the longer term, the transition from the international policy and solutions architecture of the refugee regime to the regional and bilateral management of population movements should be completed as the concerned states normalize relations. Within this overall perspective, UNHCR will focus increasingly on the identification of those individuals in continuing need of international protection and asylum.

p 6.1   ## Afghan Refugee Repatriation

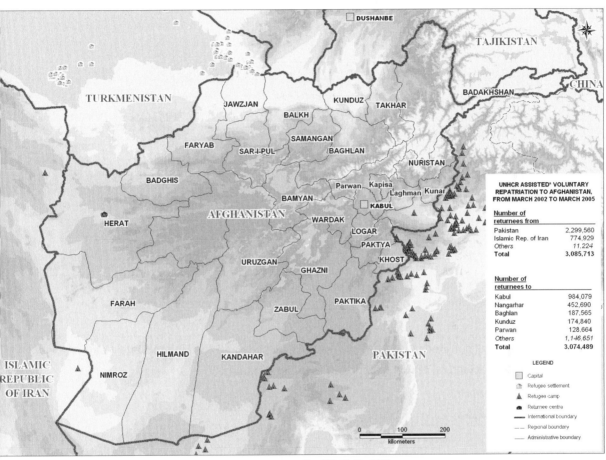

UNHCR ASSISTED[a] VOLUNTARY
REPATRIATION TO AFGHANISTAN,
FROM MARCH 2002 TO MARCH 2005

Number of
returnees from

Pakistan	2,299,560
Islamic Rep. of Iran	774,929
Others	*11,224*
Total	3,085,713

Number of
returnees to

Kabul	984,079
Nangarhar	452,690
Baghlan	187,565
Kunduz	174,840
Parwan	128,664
Others	*1,146,651*
Total	3,074,489

LEGEND

▢	Capital
	Refugee settlement
▲	Refugee camp
	Returnee centre
	International boundary
	Regional boundary
	Administrative boundary

ividuals only from Pakistan and the Islamic Republic of Iran. Statistical data sources: Aims.ORG.AF, May 2005
boundaries and names shown and the designations used on this map do not imply official endorsement or acceptance by the United Nations.
graphical data sources: UNSECOORD, UNHCR, Global Insight digital mapping - © 1998 Europa Technologies Ltd.

in question, but also those not resettled by removing a vulnerable section of the population from a given situation. Group resettlement is designed to supplement traditional resettlement activities. It does not replace the responsibility of UNHCR to identify and process individual resettlement cases based on established criteria.

Resettlement countries and other partners have welcomed the Group Methodology and participated in missions to locations where refugee populations have been identified for possible resettlement. Examples of refugee groups processed for resettlement in 2003–04 include:

- Liberians in Côte d'Ivoire and Sierra Leone resettled in the United States;
- Liberians in Guinea resettled in Australia and the United States;

Figure 6.4   Resettlement arrivals of refugees, 2004

United States*	52,868
Australia	15,967
Canada	10,521
Sweden	1,801
Norway	842
New Zealand	825
Finland	735
Denmark	508
Netherlands	323
United Kingdom	150
Ireland	63
Chile	26
Mexico	11
Jordan	9
Guatemala	1
El Salvador	1
Total	**84,651**

* Refers to US Fiscal Year.
Source: Governments.

- Somalis in Kenya resettled in Australia, Canada and the United States; and
- Ethiopians in Yemen resettled in the United States.[40]

Towards a multilateral approach

The Preamble to the 1951 UN Refugee Convention recognizes the need for international cooperation in order to achieve durable solutions. It states that 'considering that the grant of asylum may place unduly heavy burdens on certain countries . . . a satisfactory solution of a problem . . . cannot therefore be achieved without international cooperation.'[41] However, in contrast to the widely accepted and customary legal norm of *non-refoulement*, the global refugee regime lacks an established legal framework to make states share the responsibility for long-term solutions. Resettlement and financial contributions to support local integration or repatriation have historically been discretionary acts by governments. Rich countries have avoided responsibility through exclusionary or deterrent policies and their distance from regions of refugee origin.

The political engagement of host states, countries of origin and third states within and beyond the region of origin is required if durable solutions are to be attained in situations of mass influx, or where protracted situations remain unresolved. The success of the Indochinese CPA and the International Conference on Central American Refugees (CIREFCA) highlights that the search for durable solutions is most effective when burdens are shared between North and South. In the case of the Indochinese CPA, states of first asylum in the region were willing to offer interim protection and asylum processing in exchange for a commitment from third states outside the region to resettlement and financial support. That kind of commitment was not forthcoming, however, for initiatives such as the International Conferences on Assistance to Refugees in Africa (ICARA I and II). Indeed, resettlement is available to less than 1 per cent of refugees, and the low level of non-earmarked contributions to UNHCR shows that much needs to be done to enhance burden-sharing in the search for durable solutions.

By placing the search for durable solutions within the context of a multilateral dialogue, UNHCR has sought to answer this through three related concepts: appealing to state-specific interests; fostering linkages across previously discrete areas; and attempting to develop a new, normative framework for responsibility-sharing.[42]

Interests

Historically, in the absence of a guiding normative framework, industrialized states have helped provide durable solutions for refugees in poorer states where doing so has accorded with their own interests. During the Cold War, support for refugees was channelled in accordance with strategic interests. In Africa, for instance, this meant support for guerrilla movements in exile waging proxy wars. The success of the Indochinese CPA and CIREFCA in Central America, for example, are in large part attributable to the involvement of the United States in the conflicts in both regions, impelling it towards engagement and political leadership.[43] Meanwhile, in the post-Cold War context there has been a clear correlation between donor states' earmarking of contributions to UNHCR for in-country protection and their interests in containment and security—or their colonial links with strategic partners.[44] It is clear, therefore, that UNHCR must be politically engaged if it is to influence the policies of governments, thus linking states' interests with the search for durable solutions.

UNHCR has appealed to state-specific interests through the strategic use of resettlement and the flexible funding inherent in targeting development assistance, as in the Zambia Initiative (see Box 6.1). This has allowed states to contribute to the search for durable solutions in accordance with their own existing priorities. The drawback of such an approach is that it may encourage greater selectivity and the corresponding neglect of certain groups or situations. On the other hand, reconciling states' interests with the search for solutions and seeking compatibility between different states' contributions may offer incentives for engagement which would otherwise be absent.

However, it is important to recognize that perceptions of state interest can vary, and that in democracies state policies are to a large extent a reflection of electoral will, media representation and the engagement of civil society. Movements such as Live8, the Oxfam-led Make Poverty History campaign in the United Kingdom and the efforts that culminated in the Ottawa Treaty on Landmines highlight the influence of civil society in the search for durable solutions. Initiatives such as the North–South Civil Society Conference on Refugee Warehousing, organized by the United States Committee for Refugees and Immigrants and other NGOs in 2005, offer the potential to raise the profile of refugees.

Linkages

While the end of the Cold War removed many of the incentives for northern states to engage with the South, globalization and the post-11 September 2001 era offer new reasons for involvement in regions of refugee origin. The recognition of global interconnectedness and the non-viability of disengagement—given cross-border flows—are generating new commitments in the areas of development, migration and security. Where initiatives such as the Peacebuilding Commission envisaged by Secretary-General Kofi Annan or the Millennium Development Goals emerge from such interests, it is crucial that UNHCR's advocacy strategy in New York links them to, for instance, making repatriation more sustainable.[45]

These new trends represent both constraints and opportunities for UNHCR. While the willingness of states to accept resettlement has declined since 11 September 2001, there is an emerging consensus that resolving protracted refugee situations through a commitment to durable solutions could help meet wider strategic concerns. By fostering links between development, security, migration management and the global refugee regime, state interests can play a part in overcoming protracted refugee situations.

The interests of northern states in managed asylum entry and the reduction of onward movement are channelled into strengthening protection in regions of origin and resettlement. UNHCR has also tried to create a link between states' prior commitments to the Millennium Development Goals and the Framework for Durable Solutions. From a host-state perspective, such a linkage is evident in Uganda's identification of refugee self-reliance as a means to encourage new development assistance.[46]

Norms

Multilateral discussions under the Convention Plus initiative aimed at creating agreements in each of the three main strands— the strategic use of resettlement, irregular secondary movements and targeted development assistance. These accords would then have been applied collectively to protracted refugee situations through comprehensive plans of action, such as those developed for Somali and Afghan refugees (see Box 2.5, Box 6.2).[47] However, during discussion it became increasingly apparent that states were unwilling to commit to a binding normative framework on, for example, targeted development assistance.

Figure 6.5   **Number of refugees and asylum seekers in top 10 UNHCR donor countries and top 10 hosting countries, 2004**

Top 10 UNHCR donor countries in 2004 (Rank)	Number of refugees and asylum seekers, end-2004	Number of refugees and asylum seekers per 1 USD GDP per capita
Germany (8)	963,000	33.1
United States (1)	685,000 *	18.6
United Kingdom (6)	299,000 *	9.9
Canada (9)	169,000 *	6.4
Netherlands (3)	155,000 *	4.9
Sweden (4)	101,000 *	3.0
Switzerland (10)	66,300	1.5
Denmark (7)	66,200 *	1.7
Norway (5)	44,000 *	0.9
Japan (2)	2,500	0.1

Top 10 hosting countries, end-2004	Number of refugees and asylum seekers, end-2004	Number of refugees and asylum seekers per 1 USD GDP per capita
Islamic Rep. of Iran	1,046,000	530.2
Pakistan	969,000 *	1,858.6
Germany	963,000	33.1
United States	685,000 *	18.6
United Rep. of Tanzania	602,000	2,241.8
China	299,000	278.0
United Kingdom	299,000 *	9.9
Serbia and Montenegro	277,000	140.2
Chad	260,000	971.4
Uganda	252,000	1,154.6

* UNHCR estimate.

Sources: UNHCR; World Bank; United Nations Population Division.

This begs the question of how a normative framework for sharing responsibility might emerge. UNHCR's Executive Committee Conclusion of 2004 on International Cooperation and Burden and Responsibility Sharing in Mass Influx Situations is a step in that direction. It seems clear that situation-specific approaches to areas such as Afghanistan offer the best means to build inter-state consensus. Channelling state interests into resolving protracted refugee situations might facilitate the emergence of a common understanding of what equitable responsibility-sharing means.

Future directions

As all protracted situations or mass influxes have unique characteristics, varied approaches and partnerships have been developed to improve the prospects for durable solutions in specific situations. These range from concepts such as the 4Rs, Development Assistance for Refugees and Development through Local Integration to the strategic use of resettlement. They also include the Group Methodology, the strengthening of protection capacity in regions of origin and managed labour migration. All offer ways to complement and facilitate access to the three traditional durable solutions.

Despite these initiatives, other areas remain to be explored. First, could the Framework for Durable Solutions be applied to internally displaced persons? If so, how would it need to be adapted? Second, how should durable solutions be adapted in the case of urban refugees? For example, would the solutions pertinent to Somali refugees on the Eastleigh Estate in Kenya's capital, Nairobi, be the same as for Somali refugees in the Dadaab camps in the same country? Third, how can refugees' preferences be better taken into account when implementing durable solutions? What types of participatory approaches could be used to ensure choice and compliance with the principle of voluntarism? Fourth, how should diasporas, which in many cases provide support to refugees in camps via remittances, be recognized as stakeholders in the process? And fifth, what is the role of regional approaches, as in the European Union or the West African region, and how might these be reconciled with global standards? Although these questions remain to be resolved, it is clear that the search for solutions must be comprehensive and collaborative. In each case, this means political engagement.

UNHCR's work on durable solutions recognizes the potentially complementary relationship between the three durable solutions and the way in which they can be most effectively applied within the context of comprehensive plans of action. The strategic use of resettlement, in particular, highlights how it is most effective when used not in isolation but to complement other durable solutions. From a political perspective, ensuring that stakeholders provide a combination of the durable solutions may bring previously unattainable solutions within reach. Such comprehensive approaches would need to be developed on a situational basis and be linked to wider peace-building and post-conflict reconstruction initiatives across the UN system. As was the case in 1989, when UNHCR helped to nurture comprehensive agreements relating to Indochina and Central America, achieving political agreements to overcome particular protracted refugee situations will require strong individual and institutional leadership, and a willingness to engage in political facilitation.

In seeking to implement its new approaches, UNHCR has tried to play the role of catalyst, advocating the mainstreaming of displacement issues across the UN system. Rather than confining itself to legal protection, on one extreme, or indefinitely expanding its mandate, on the other, UNHCR may take on a role that is primarily one of innovation, advocacy and facilitation. Issues such as development, migration, peace-building and security all affect the welfare of refugees and the search for durable solutions, yet rely on the collaboration of other UN agencies and NGOs in order to ensure coordinated policy-making. Creating linkages across the issue-areas of global governance represents a crucial means to channel states' existing interests and other UN agencies' expertise in these areas into improving access to durable solutions.

7 Internally displaced persons

They have been forced from their homes for many of the same reasons as refugees, but have not crossed an international border. Often persecuted or under attack by their own governments, they are frequently in a more desperate situation than refugees. They also outnumber refugees two to one. No international agency has a formal mandate to aid them. But they are increasingly at the forefront of the humanitarian agenda. They are sometimes called 'internal refugees', but are more often known as internally displaced persons.

Since the end of the Cold War, the number of people uprooted by conflict, ethnic strife and human rights violations has soared. In 2004 there were between 20–25 million internally displaced persons (see Figure 7.1). By then the number of refugees—those who fled or had been pushed out of their own countries—had declined to 9.2 million from 9.6 million in 2003. This trend was already apparent in 2001 during the war in Afghanistan, when the number of internally displaced persons in the country stood at 2 million. However, in the same year only 200,000 Afghans crossed into Pakistan as refugees.

In 2003, during the war in Iraq, hundreds of thousands of displaced people remained at risk inside the country; only a very small number were able to flee abroad. In some African humanitarian crises, there can be ten internally displaced persons for every refugee. Currently there are an estimated 1.4 million people displaced by conflict in Uganda, at least 1.5 million in the Democratic Republic of Congo (DRC) and 6 million in Sudan. But only 30,000 displaced people from Uganda have gone on to become refugees, while the numbers for the DRC and Sudan are 469,000 and 703,000, respectively.

Sometimes, mountains and rivers impede flight across borders, or people may flee to other parts of their own country to remain in relatively familiar surroundings. Even when they do manage to cross national frontiers, however, the displaced rarely find a welcome. Hostility to refugees and asylum seekers has grown since the end of the Cold War, with many countries seeing it as too costly or destabilizing to admit them. In several recent emergencies, states have closed their borders to refugees or adopted restrictive admission policies. As a result, there is an inverse relationship between the rising number of internally displaced persons and the declining figure for refugees.

The statistics on internally displaced persons generally count only those who are displaced by conflict and persecution.[1] But millions more have been uprooted within their own countries by natural disasters. Indeed, UNHCR helped some of the survivors

Internally displaced women in Seliah camp, West Darfur informing UNHCR about their living conditions.
(UNHCR/H. Caux/2004)

of the Asian tsunami of 2004. By doing so, the agency went beyond its core mandate of assisting refugees. However, it only aided victims in countries where its staff were already present, and then only if it were asked to help.

Even development projects can cause internal displacement. Poor, indigenous and marginalized groups are frequently displaced without consultation to make way for grand national projects. Not only are the rights of such people ignored, they are rarely offered resettlement or adequate compensation.[2] According to the World Bank, 10 million people are forcibly displaced by development projects each year, prompting the Bank and other donors to set standards for the treatment of the 'involuntarily resettled'.

Though displacement has many causes, it is those uprooted by conflict and human rights violations who generally arouse the most concern. The overwhelming need of these people for protection *from* their own governments draws international attention to their plight. Like refugees, they cannot obtain the security and well-being they need in their own countries, and therefore turn to the international community. According to the Global IDP Survey, there are more than 13 million internally displaced persons in Africa, 5–6 million in Asia (including the Middle East), 3 million in Europe and 3–4 million in the Americas.[3]

Figure 7.1 Global number of refugees and internally displaced persons (IDPs), 1990-2004

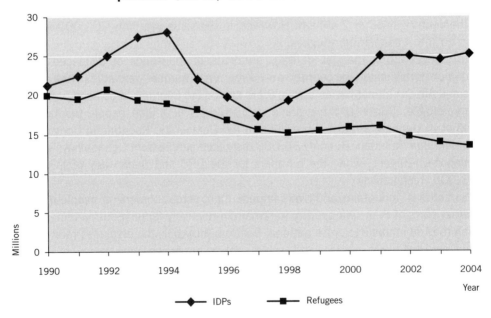

Note: Includes Palestinian refugees under the mandate of the United Nations Relief and Works Agency for Palestine Refugees in the Near East (UNRWA). All figures as at 31 December of each year.

Sources: UNHCR; UNRWA; US Committee for Refugees (1990-2000); The Global IDP Project/Norwegian Refugee Council (2001-2004).

Figure 7.2   Internally displaced persons (IDPs) of concern to UNHCR, 1995-2004

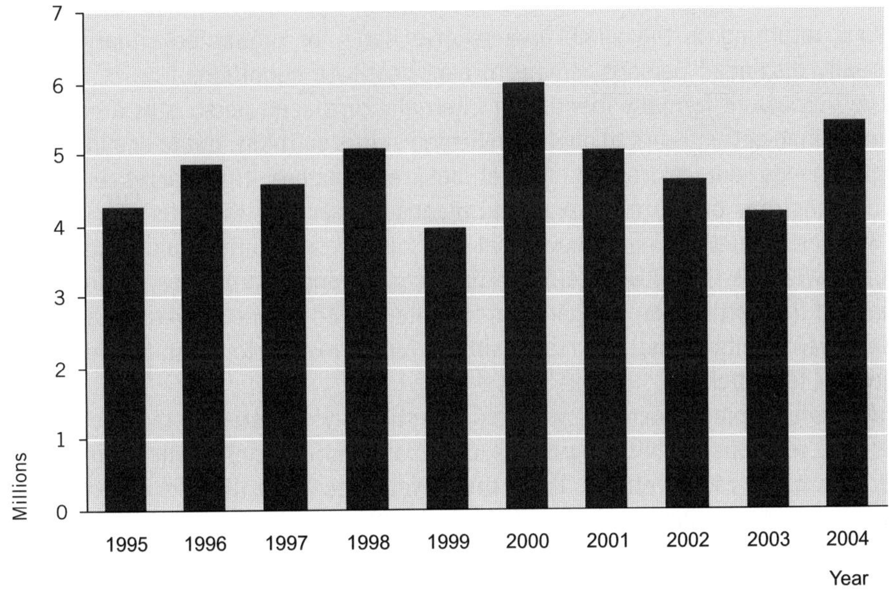

Note: All figures are as at 31 December of each year.
Source: UNHCR.

A special category?

The plight of the internally displaced has been well documented over the past decade. But there is still debate over whether they should be recognized as a special category of persons for humanitarian purposes. The International Committee of the Red Cross (ICRC), for example, provides assistance and protection to *all* civilian victims of armed conflict and prefers to target assistance on the basis of vulnerability, not category. The fear is that singling out one group could lead to discrimination against others, fostering inequity and conflict. Making a distinct category of the displaced, a 2005 donor evaluation warns, could lead to their becoming 'privileged'.[4]

Nonetheless, the displaced do have special needs. Displacement breaks up families and severs community ties. It leads to unemployment and limits access to land, education, food and shelter. The displaced are particularly vulnerable to violence. As an official of ICRC observes: 'It goes without saying that, deprived of shelter and their habitual sources of food, water, medicine and money', internally displaced persons 'have different, and often more urgent, material needs'.[5]

These special needs have often been ignored in 'situational approaches'. As a consequence, the internally displaced frequently suffer the highest mortality rates in humanitarian emergencies.[6] In Uganda, the HIV/AIDS rate among the internally displaced is six times higher than in the general population.[7] Even when the internally displaced and other vulnerable groups such as refugees face the same problems and are in similar circumstances they are not treated the same. For instance, tensions arise when UNHCR gives returning refugees seeds and tools but internally displaced persons returning to the same area receive none. In protracted situations, many internally displaced persons remain in near-destitute conditions.[8]

The purpose of formally identifying internally displaced persons as a category for humanitarian action is not to confer privileged status on them, but to ensure that their unique needs are addressed. Sometimes, approaches that target all affected populations may be the most practical means of reaching the internally displaced. Nonetheless, experience has shown that special attention to particular disadvantaged groups—whether refugees, internally displaced persons, minorities or women—has enhanced their protection. Singling out the internally displaced makes it easier to call upon governments to assume responsibility for them and to press for international action on their behalf.

Internally displaced persons are often intentionally uprooted by their governments on ethnic, religious or political grounds, or as part of counterinsurgency campaigns. In civil wars along racial, ethnic, linguistic or religious lines, the displaced are often perceived as the enemy (see Box 7.1, Box 7.2). They may be associated with an insurgent group or an opposing political party or ideology, or be considered inferior or threatening. In other cases the displaced may be trapped between opposing sides in civil wars or come under direct attack by insurgents, as in Colombia, the DRC and Nepal. Competition over scarce resources or land often aggravates such conflicts, with the displaced bearing the brunt of the violence. When states disintegrate into anarchy, as in Sierra Leone and Somalia, some of the worst atrocities have been inflicted on the internally displaced.

Internal displacement disrupts the lives not only of the individuals and families concerned but of whole communities and societies. Both the areas left behind by the displaced and the areas to which they flee can suffer extensive damage. Socio-economic systems and community structures often break down, impeding reconstruction and development for decades. Conflict and displacement also spill over into neighbouring countries, as has been seen in Central America, the Balkans and West Africa. Clearly, both humanitarian and geo-political reasons prompted UN Secretary-General Kofi Annan's call to the international community to strengthen support for national efforts to assist and protect internally displaced persons.

Sovereignty: barrier or responsibility?

Because internally displaced persons reside within the borders of their own countries and in most cases under the jurisdiction of their own governments, primary responsibility for them rests with their national authorities. As Roberta Cohen and Francis Deng point out in their study, *Masses in Flight*, 'Since there is no adequate replacement in sight for the system of state sovereignty, primary responsibility for

Box 7.1

Lessons from Bosnia and Herzegovina

The brutal campaign of 'ethnic cleansing' waged in Bosnia and Herzegovina during the Balkan wars caused the largest uprooting of populations in Europe since the Second World War. Three months following Bosnia and Herzegovina's declaration of independence in 1992, the number of Bosnian refugees and internally displaced persons soared to 2.6 million. While media coverage was extensive and humanitarian assistance quick to reach needy populations, the international community proved reluctant to address the root causes of the problem or to act militarily to stem the fighting. Instead, it concentrated on sustaining an enormous emergency-relief operation, led by UNHCR. This emphasis on material relief undoubtedly saved many lives. But it did not prevent the forcible uprooting of people from their homes, mass murder and mass rape; nor did it thwart the establishment of concentration camps in which displaced men were starved and beaten as a prelude to 'ethnic cleansing'.

The Bosnia operation was one of the largest relief initiatives ever undertaken. Between 1992 and 1995, UNHCR and its partner NGOs delivered approximately 950,000 metric tons of humanitarian assistance to 2.7 million beneficiaries. UNHCR's role expanded from that of an agency whose sole purpose was to secure asylum for refugees and prevent involuntary return to one of providing humanitarian assistance to large numbers of internally displaced persons and other war-affected people. For the first time, it was called upon to operate in an active war zone where its staff faced unprecedented security risks. The effectiveness with which UNHCR handled this role prompted many subsequent calls for it to enlarge its mandate and take on the protection and assistance of both refugees and internally displaced persons in emergencies (see Box 7.3).

But UNHCR also came under heavy criticism. The organization thought

that if it maintained a 'presence', it would be able to effectively monitor human rights abuses and offer protection to vulnerable populations. While it did manage to take a number of steps to protect the civilian population, its presence did not, and could not, stop the atrocities. Moreover, when it helped evacuate people from life-threatening circumstances it was accused of being an accomplice to 'ethnic cleansing'. Critics also charged that UNHCR's involvement with in-country protection was enabling neighbouring states to stem refugee movements into their countries, although hundreds of thousands of Bosnians were given temporary refuge in European nations.

The humanitarian relief effort was also seen as an alibi and excuse for the international community, allowing it to be seen as doing something without actually having to confront those carrying out ethnic cleansing. Security Council resolutions on Bosnia and Herzegovina—all 46 of them—failed to address the underlying causes of the conflict, concentrating instead on sustaining the humanitarian operation and on creating UN-protected safe areas—without, however, giving the UN Protection Force (UNPROFOR) the mandate, equipment or resources to defend adequately the six Muslim enclaves created. The failure to protect displaced persons in the safe areas was epitomized at Srebrenica, when UNPROFOR stood by as Serb forces overran the safe area and marched off and murdered at least 7,000 Muslim men and boys.

This horrific event became a rallying cry for those opposed to the notion of 'helping people where they are' and who rejected out-of-hand the creation of safe areas in subsequent wars in Kosovo and Afghanistan. Ironically, in those wars safe areas might have been better defended and saved many lives.

It was not until July 1995 that the international community finally undertook the type of decisive

military action that was required in the Balkans. When the Dayton Peace Accords were signed in November of that year, approximately 1.3 million Bosnians remained internally displaced. Since that time, an exceptional international effort to implement the right of displaced people and refugees to return to their homes has resulted in 1 million returns. However, the plight of a significant number of internally displaced persons remains unresolved, in particular those who would be minorities in areas of return.

Bosnia and Herzegovina was a cauldron of experience from which four lessons can be learned. The first is that a humanitarian effort should never be allowed to serve as a substitute for political or military solutions. Protection should be a prerequisite for assistance, since it makes little sense to provide emergency relief to besieged populations only for them to be killed by belligerents. The second is that the trauma of Srebrenica should not be allowed to paralyse all future initiatives to try to protect people in their own countries. Safe areas should be considered for displaced persons when military forces have the capability to protect them. The vast majority of people in most emergencies cannot get out of their countries and need international protection as badly as, if not more than, refugees. Third, a lead humanitarian agency to take charge in an emergency could be useful in dealing with displaced populations. That UNHCR was able to act swiftly and deal comprehensively with all affected populations, whether refugees, internally displaced persons or others, has been thoroughly documented. The fourth and final lesson is that far greater attention must be paid to preventive measures. If the international community had spent as much time devising a plan to stop the war as it spent distributing aid, fewer people would have been uprooted and many more lives could have been saved.

Map 7.1

Internally displaced persons, *1 January 2005*

 Countries with IDPs, as of 1 January 2005

Countries with IDPs assisted by/of concern to UNHCR, as of 1 January 2005

Statistical data sources: The Global IDP Project / Norwegian Refugee Council.
The boundaries and names shown and the designations used on this map do not imply official endorsement o
acceptance by the United Nations.
Geographical data sources: UNHCR, Global Insight digital mapping - © 1998 Europa Technologies Ltd.

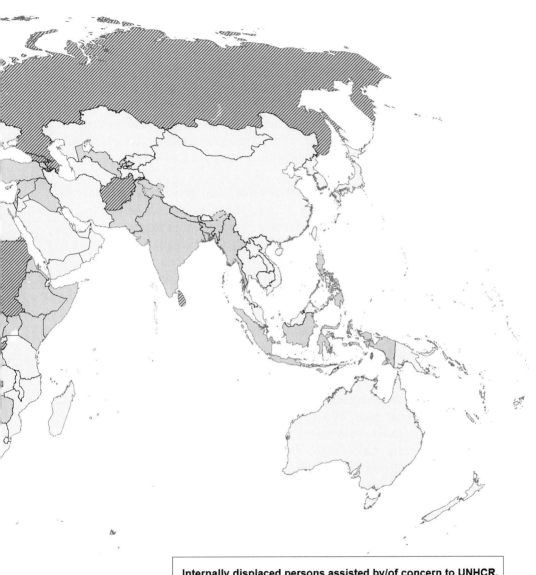

Internally displaced persons assisted by/of concern to UNHCR, as of 1 January 2005

Colombia:	2,000,000	Bosnia and Herzegovina:	309,200
Sudan:	662,300	Serbia and Montenegro:	248,200
Azerbaijan:	578,500	Georgia:	237,100
Liberia:	498,600	Afghanistan:	159,500
Sri Lanka:	352,400	Côte d'Ivoire:	38,000
Russian Federation:	334,800	Croatia:	7,500
		Burundi:	900

Statistical data sources: UNHCR, Governments. Compiled by: UNHCR promoting the security, welfare, and liberty of populations must remain with the state'.[9] Yet, when asked why the United Nations had not been able to do more for internally displaced persons, former High Commissioner for Refugees Sadako Ogata replied: 'The problem is sovereignty'.[10]

Indeed, many countries use sovereignty as a justification for resisting or obstructing international aid efforts. In Myanmar, the government has barred access to the country's internally displaced ethnic minorities, with which it is at war. For many years during the insurgency by the Kurdish PKK group, Turkey barred access to hundreds of thousands of displaced Kurds. In Algeria, no one knows for sure how many internally displaced people there are, or what their needs might be; the government has denied access to them.

Sometimes governments categorize internally displaced persons as 'migrants' or 'terrorists' to avoid responsibility for them, or they fail to develop policies and laws to help the displaced. Getting states to assume their responsibilities can be a challenge for the international community (see Box 7.2). This is particularly so in civil wars, where governments fear that aid to the displaced could strengthen insurgent groups. International efforts to negotiate with insurgents are often obstructed by national governments fearful that such engagement could legitimize the rebels. During the Angolan civil war, the government objected to UN agencies negotiating with the rebel UNITA group. As a result the United Nations had no access to large numbers of displaced persons in insurgent areas. Only in 2002, with a ceasefire, did the widespread starvation and disease plaguing these people come to light.

Nonetheless, over the past 15 years a perceptible shift has occurred in international thinking about the internally displaced. It is now widely recognized that people in need of aid and protection in their own countries have claims on the international community when their governments do not fulfil their responsibilities, or where there is a disintegration of the nation-state. While reaffirming respect for sovereignty, United Nations resolutions have authorized the establishment of relief corridors and cross-border operations to reach people in need. UN Security Council resolutions have demanded access for the delivery of relief in Bosnia and Herzegovina, Darfur (Sudan), northern Iraq, Mozambique, Somalia and Timor Leste, among other places. In exceptional cases the United Nations has authorized the use of force to ensure the delivery of relief and to provide protection.

Today, many governments allow some form of access to their displaced populations. The Government of Sri Lanka has set up welfare centres to provide material assistance to displaced populations in both government- and rebel-held areas. It has also accepted UNHCR's establishment of relief centres on government territory that are open to all groups. Following the 2004 tsunami, the government signed an agreement with the Tamil-separatist leadership to share reconstruction funds for the displaced.

The Turkish government is cooperating with the United Nations and the World Bank in the return and reintegration of its displaced population. In the South Caucasus, the Georgian government encourages international access to its displaced and provides a small allowance for them. Similarly, the Government of Azerbaijan has welcomed international assistance for its large population of internally displaced and considers the phase-down of international aid to have been premature. Many other governments have also welcomed international aid for the internally displaced, among them Colombia, DRC and Uganda. In response to international pressure, the Khartoum government agreed to Operation Lifeline Sudan to allow international aid to reach displaced people under insurgent control in the south.[11]

The former Representative of the Secretary-General on Internally Displaced Persons, Francis Deng, believes that while governments have the primary responsibility to care for their displaced populations, when they are unable to do so they must request and accept outside help. If they refuse, or deliberately obstruct access to the displaced, the international community has a right, even a responsibility, to become involved. International engagement could range from diplomatic dialogue and negotiation of access for relief supplies to political pressure. In exceptional cases, it could lead to sanctions or military action.

While no government has explicitly challenged this concept, states such as China, Egypt, India and Sudan have expressed fears that international humanitarian action could be a pretext for interference by powerful states in the affairs of weaker ones. Nonetheless, the concept of 'a collective responsibility to protect' the displaced when their national authorities are unable or unwilling to do so has gained ground. Indeed, it was most recently upheld in the World Summit document adopted by heads of government in September 2005.[12]

To provide guidance to governments, the Brookings–Bern Project on Internal Displacement has identified the main indicators of national responsibility.[13]

- To begin with, governments are expected to prevent or mitigate displacement. When displacement is unavoidable, they are expected to raise national awareness of the problem, collect data on the numbers, locations and conditions of the displaced and facilitate access to populations at risk, including those under insurgent control.

- Governments are expected to adopt laws and policies to protect displaced populations; train their officials, military and police in the rights of the displaced; and designate an institutional focal point for coordination within the government and with local and international partners.

- Allocating resources in the national budget for the displaced, or creating special funds from oil and other revenues, is another indicator of national responsibility. So too is finding solutions to the plight of the displaced, for instance by giving them the choice to return voluntarily to their homes or to resettle in another part of the country. The displaced should also be assisted to reintegrate and recover, or receive compensation for, lost property.

- Finally, governments are expected to cooperate with international and regional organizations when national capacity is insufficient.

The current Representative of the Secretary-General on the Human Rights of Internally Displaced Persons, Walter Kälin, has been using the framework of national

Box 7.2

Darfur: the challenge of protecting the internally displaced

The Darfur emergency has been called the world's 'worst humanitarian disaster' by UN Under-Secretary-General for Humanitarian Affairs, Jan Egeland. It is a case study of how difficult it is to protect internally displaced persons when their own government has caused the displacement and fails to comply with UN resolutions to provide security. As in Bosnia and Herzegovina a decade earlier (see Box 7.1), the international response in Darfur has largely focused on providing emergency relief. There are more than 11,000 humanitarian workers on the ground in Darfur, but fewer than 100 staff with protection responsibilities, and only a few thousand lightly armed African Union troops with a weak mandate for protection. Recalling how in Bosnia and Herzegovina civilians watched the aid trucks roll in while their neighbours were gunned down, Secretary-General Annan in April 2005 asked: 'Are we now going to stand by and watch a replay in Darfur?'

The crisis in Sudan's western region began in 2003 with an attack on government military outposts by insurgents of the Fur, Masselit and Zaghawa tribes. Their immediate grievance was government favouritism toward Arab herdsmen who were increasingly encroaching on black African farmlands. More fundamentally, the rebels saw an opportunity in the ongoing north–south peace process in Sudan to demand for Darfur the same power and wealth sharing arrangements that black African tribes in the south and centre of the country were obtaining from the Sudanese national authorities.

The government response was swift and brutal. With helicopters and troops supported by Arab militias (the Janjaweed) on the ground, the military set upon the three black African communities, killed up to 70,000 men and deliberately drove from their homes more than 2 million people, most of whom became internally displaced, while 200,000 became refugees in neighbouring Chad. Janjaweed militias then burned their villages, poisoned the

wells and killed animals in a scorched-earth campaign reminiscent of the tactics used in earlier years against the black African tribes of the south.

From 2003 to the present, the number of deaths from starvation, disease and violence in Darfur is estimated at more than 350,000. Almost 2 million people live in squalid camps, totally dependent on international aid and with little or no prospect of returning home due to the insecurity and destruction in their homeland areas. Although overall violence has decreased, military and Janjaweed attacks on black African farming communities and camps of internally displaced people still continue.

International assistance with little protection

The main international achievement to date has been to assure the delivery of humanitarian relief. In July 2004, the UN Security Council demanded an end to the government's obstruction of humanitarian organizations. In an unprecedented move, the UN Secretary-General and other international leaders travelled to the area to reinforce the point. As a result the government lifted most of its restrictions on humanitarian organizations and signed an agreement with the United Nations. By the end of 2004, large-scale famine had been avoided, epidemics contained and malnutrition reduced among many of those in the camps for displaced persons. Food distribution and healthcare were also enhanced. Humanitarian organizations were criticized for being slow to react to the emergency, but by mid-2005 the number of people receiving international food aid exceeded 2 million. However, aid agencies continue to lack access to hundreds of thousands in rural areas under insurgent control.

Far less progress has been made in the area of protection. When the government refused to comply with Security Council requests to stop attacks on the civilian population, little or no effort was made to

enforce the resolutions. The government failed to disarm the Janjaweed, cease helicopter assaults on villages or end the forcible returns of internally displaced persons to their home areas. In addition, some armed groups have been actively seeking to hinder relief and monitoring activities. Yet the Security Council failed to agree on sanctions other than symbolic ones such as travel bans and asset freezes. A no-fly zone was not introduced, nor was a UN protection force created. Arab and Islamic governments opposed pressure on the Sudanese government, while China, the main foreign investor in Sudan's oil industry, threatened to use its veto. Russia, a key supplier of arms, also opposed strong action. Even the United States and European Union did not wish to press the Sudanese government too far, fearing that doing so could jeopardize the signing and implementation of the peace agreement between north and south ending two decades of civil war.

A regional solution

In the absence of international willingness to act, the African Union came forward to try to stop the violence. Indeed, 'African solutions for African problems' became a rallying cry and also proved more acceptable to the Sudanese government. Initially, the Union sent in several hundred unarmed observers under the banner of the African Mission to Sudan, or AMIS, to monitor the April 2004 ceasefire between the Darfur rebels and the government. But it also expanded its forces and mandate in response to the violence against the civilian population. Specifically, it sent in troops and police to contribute to enhancing security throughout Darfur. It indicated that it would monitor and verify security around camps of displaced persons and in areas of their return, protect civilians under imminent threat, protect humanitarian operations and, through its visible military presence, try to deter armed groups from committing hostile acts against the population.

But the language was couched in caveats. AMIS was supposed to protect civilians, but only if it had the resources and the military capability. In fact, it was able to field only 2,700 military observers, troops and police to Darfur (an area the size of France) and could deploy police in only one camp. It has few aircraft or vehicles to transport its police and troops, and insufficient communication facilities and other basic equipment. It has plans to expand its forces to 7,700 by September 2005 and to 12,300 by the spring of 2006, and Western countries have pledged funds and logistical support. But the process is slow, the numbers are small, and the mandate far from robust.

Nonetheless, where AMIS has been present Janjaweed forays into camps of displaced persons have diminished, as have militia attacks on villages and sexual assaults against women gathering firewood and water. AMIS has also enlarged humanitarian access by escorting aid convoys, which in 2005 came under increasing attack, and plans to accompany international human rights observers on their monitoring missions.

International protection mechanisms

In July 2004, the Security Council called for the deployment of human rights observers to Darfur to report on violations, provide assistance to victims and work with local authorities and other actors to enhance the security of civilians. But by March 2005, only 16 were reported to be on the ground, together with 26 international staff with protection responsibilities. By the end of June, the number had risen to 41, but many were reported to have little experience in protection work, were not deployed around the country and often could not travel to areas of conflict where serious violations were occurring. All these factors highlighted the need to reinforce the capacity of the UN High Commissioner for Human Rights to respond rapidly and effectively in humanitarian emergencies.

Since no UN agency had a protection responsibility for internally displaced persons, none came forward to take the overall lead in the area of protection in all three provinces in Darfur. When the United Kingdom's Secretary of State for International Development, Hilary Benn, visited the area in June 2004, he found 'confusion and poor delivery' and observed that 'even now [after more than a year], internally displaced persons are not being protected adequately.' Similarly, UN evaluations acknowledged the failure of the collaborative approach to bring protection to internally displaced persons in Darfur. One notorious example was the management of the camps of displaced persons. The Office for the Coordination of Humanitarian Affairs (OCHA) was unable to find any agency ready to manage the camps in Darfur. OCHA therefore had to turn the responsibility over to NGOs with little prior experience in camp management or protection and insufficient staff.

The Representative of the Secretary-General on the Human Rights of Internally Displaced Persons, Walter Kälin, wrote in the *Forced Migration Review* of May 2005 that 'it is obvious that UNHCR is the organization with the most experience and capacity to protect and assist persons displaced by armed conflict who are in camps or to organize IDP returns . . . Indeed, it is difficult to understand why there should not be at least a presumption that the High Commissioner for Refugees should assume responsibility in such situations.' Today, UNHCR is the lead agency for the protection and return of some 700,000 internally displaced persons in West Darfur, while IOM was given responsibility for North and South Darfur. But IOM's lack of a protection mandate and experience has led some to suggest that UNHCR should assume the entire responsibility.

Human rights advocates believe that the Security Council's decision to refer individual perpetrators of crimes against humanity and acts of genocide in Darfur to the

International Criminal Court will help deter violence against civilians. However, the Sudanese government has rejected the Security Council decision and at the moment there is no assurance that perpetrators of genocide will actually be prosecuted by the court.

Opportunities

Despite the absence of strong international mechanisms to rely upon in internal crises such as Darfur's, there are still positive developments to build upon. One is the North–South peace agreement of January 2005, which offers the possibility of a political resolution of the crisis. The accord provides for the sharing of power and wealth between the Arab government in Khartoum and the black African tribes of the south as well as with other ethnic groups at war with the government. Were the African Union and the United Nations to persuade the government and rebels to extend this agreement to Darfur, it could help resolve the issues at the root of the conflict. Sudan's new unity government, installed in July 2005, has promised to promote a fair and just settlement in Darfur. The designation of Salim Ahmed Salim, former Secretary-General of the Organization of African Unity, as the African Union's Special Envoy to South Sudan has also raised the prospects for peace.

Strengthening the African Union's protection role offers another opportunity to address the crisis. Expanding its forces and mandate could not only enhance security for the displaced but also make possible their return; it would enable them to plant and grow crops and thereby reduce their dependency on international aid. This will require substantial resources and technical support from major donors, but without such steps, the Darfur crisis could become, in the words of Suliman Baldo of the International Crisis Group, 'another never-ending conflict in which donors spend large sums feeding the displaced but otherwise fail to protect civilians and to address the underlying political causes.'

Map 7.2 **Internal Displacement in Darfur,** *November 2004*

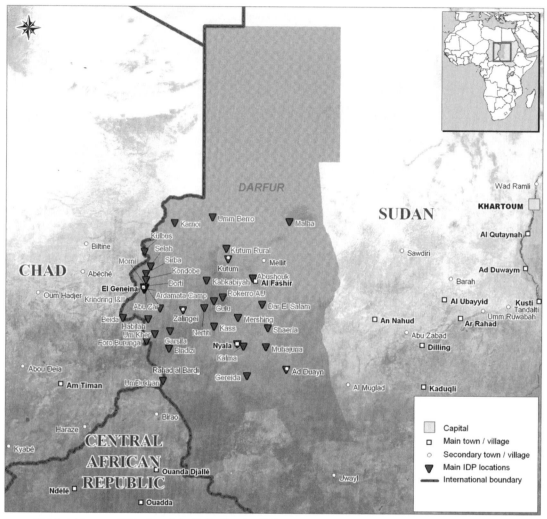

Statistical data source: OCHA - Humanitarian Profile, November 2004
The boundaries and names shown and the designations used on this map do not imply official endorsement or acceptance by the United Nations. Geographical data sources: UNHCR, Global Insight digital mapping - © 1998 Europa Technologies Ltd.

responsibility in his dealings with governments. The Commonwealth too has emphasized national responsibility and drawn up 'best practice guidelines' for its member states.[14] But the efforts of donor governments, regional bodies and the United Nations to encourage states to assume their responsibilities need to be strengthened. So too do initiatives to get rebel armed groups to adhere to international standards in their treatment of those under their control.[15]

Applying the Guiding Principles

Among the more effective tools for addressing situations of internal displacement are the Guiding Principles on Internal Displacement. The principles constitute a comprehensive minimum standard for the treatment of the internally displaced. They set forth the rights of the displaced and the obligations of governments, insurgent groups and other actors toward these populations. The principles are not legally binding but are derived from international human rights treaties and humanitarian law. Since their presentation to the UN Commission on Human Rights in 1998 by Deng, a growing number of governments, regional bodies, UN agencies and NGOs have begun to use them. Resolutions of the Commission and General Assembly regularly refer to them as 'an important tool' and 'standard' for dealing with situations of internal displacement.[16] In the World Summit document of 2005, heads of government recognized the Guiding Principles as 'an important international framework for the protection of internally displaced persons.'[17] United Nations Secretary-General Kofi Annan has called upon states to promote their adoption through national legislation.[18]

Over the past five years, governments have begun to make the Guiding Principles a basis for their policies and laws on internal displacement. Angola based its 2001 law relating to the resettlement of displaced persons on the principles, and Peru used them when developing its 2004 law providing benefits to the internally displaced. Colombia's Constitutional Court based three decisions in support of aid to the displaced on the principles, and Georgia amended its laws and improved its practices on the voting rights of internally displaced persons to conform to them. Burundi, the Philippines, Sri Lanka and Uganda have also based national policies on the principles, and Liberia's president has announced his government's adoption of them.[19]

Regional inter-governmental bodies use the Guiding Principles as a monitoring tool when measuring conditions on the ground and as a framework for their programmes and activities. UN agencies and NGOs provide training in the principles, while local groups in different countries have produced handbooks and illustrated materials to adapt them to conditions on the ground. In Sri Lanka, the Consortium of Humanitarian Agencies published a *Toolkit* based on the principles in three national languages, while lawyers in the South Caucasus and the Russian Federation have evaluated the laws of their countries in terms of the principles.[20] To date, the Guiding Principles have been translated into more than 40 languages.

The Guiding Principles have empowered internally displaced persons and their representatives. In Sierra Leone, displaced persons used the principles to call on UN agencies to provide education in camps. In Sri Lanka, representatives of the internally displaced used the principles to make their concerns known to camp commanders. Even armed rebel groups have acknowledged the value of the Guiding Principles: the southern Sudan People's Liberation Movement and Army (SPLM/A), in collaboration with the UN's Office for the Coordination of Humanitarian Affairs (OCHA) and the UN

Box 7.3

Should UNHCR become a 'displacement agency'?

For more than a decade, influential voices have been calling for the enlargement of UNHCR's mandate to encompass internally displaced persons. In 1993, the Government of the Netherlands proposed at a meeting of UNHCR's Executive Committee that the United Nations assign 'a general competence' for the internally displaced to UNHCR. In 1997, prior to the announcement of the Secretary-General's reform programme, his senior adviser Maurice Strong sounded out UNHCR about becoming the premier assistance agency of the United Nations and assuming responsibility for internally displaced persons. In 2000, after visiting Angola and finding UN agencies in disarray, the US Ambassador to the United Nations at the time, Richard Holbrooke, made a public recommendation: 'The primary mandate for internal refugees should be given to a single agency, presumably the UNHCR.'

In 2004, following a visit to camps for internally displaced persons in Darfur, the UK's Secretary of State for International Development, Hilary Benn, posed the question: 'Is it really

sensible that we have different systems for dealing with people fleeing their homes dependent on whether they happen to have crossed an international border? I have my doubts.' In 2005 in the United States, a Congressionally-mandated bipartisan task force on the United Nations recommended 'redefining' the mandate of UNHCR to ensure the delivery of aid to refugees, internally displaced persons and those affected by natural disasters. Similarly, a report of the US Institute of Peace called upon the United Nations to designate UNHCR the lead agency for internally displaced persons.

UNHCR's long experience with refugees and its comprehensive mandate, encompassing both protection and assistance, makes it an obvious candidate for dealing with the internally displaced. Advocates of a larger role for the organization point to its involvement with the internally displaced since the 1960s, and its more substantial engagement since the 1990s, when a surge in civil conflicts following the Cold War began to produce more internally displaced persons than refugees. Currently, UNHCR is engaged in helping some

5 million internally displaced persons, one-fifth of the world's total. This number includes 1 million people in Africa, the continent most ravaged by conflict and displacement. Those in favour of a 'UNHCR solution' also argue that current institutional arrangements—namely the collaborative approach under the Emergency Relief Coordinator—have failed the internally displaced, especially in protection. As no other agency has the background or experience when it comes to uprooted populations, they see UNHCR as the only realistic alternative for dealing with the problem.

Nonetheless, strong objections to UNHCR assuming the primary responsibility for the internally displaced have been expressed. Indeed, UNHCR itself has long been divided on the issue. Some fear that the agency would be overwhelmed by the magnitude of the problem of internal displacement, and in the process undercut refugee protection. Others point to a conflict of interest between protecting people in their own countries and defending the right of people to leave and seek asylum abroad. In the former Yugoslavia, for

Children's Fund (UNICEF), has drafted a policy on internal displacement based on them.

But are the Guiding Principles actually improving conditions on the ground? No comprehensive study has yet been undertaken to evaluate their impact. Governments may announce laws and policies based on the principles but not necessarily implement them. As Deng observed in 2002, 'while the Guiding Principles have been well received at the rhetorical level, their implementation remains problematic, and often rudimentary.'[21] Much is needed in the way of monitoring, advocacy and the engagement of international and local actors to promote their implementation.

It is frequently asked whether compliance would be greater if there were a legally binding treaty on internal displacement. Egypt, India and Sudan have pointed out that the Guiding Principles were not negotiated by governments or formally adopted by the UN General Assembly. Those who favour a treaty argue that it would hold states accountable if they disregarded its provisions. However, others point out that the example, UNHCR was criticized for paying too little attention to gaining asylum and resettlement for victims of violations while at the same time failing to provide effective in-country protection. States have also used UNHCR's in-country protection activities as a pretext for refusing to grant asylum. Moreover, the prospect of UNHCR taking on responsibility for the internally displaced has triggered fears that other UN agencies would be sidelined and their roles diminished. Finally, many donor governments continue to favour the collaborative approach despite criticisms that it is ineffective when it comes to the internally displaced.

The debate need not be framed as a zero sum game, however. UNHCR could not possibly take on *all* internally displaced persons, millions of whom are displaced by natural disasters and millions more by development projects. Moreover, many of those displaced by conflict are integrated into cities, may be in protracted situations for decades and may not be able to avail themselves of the kind of support UNHCR can provide. The more pertinent question is whether UNHCR can enlarge its

role. In 2005, OCHA's Internal Displacement Division proposed that UNHCR carve out areas of responsibility for which it could be relied upon in emergencies. For example, drawing upon its expertise, it could take the lead in designing protection strategies and managing camps. By assuming responsibility for specific functions, it could help make the overall UN response more predictable and the collaborative approach work better. UNHCR's greater involvement, moreover, would not diminish other agencies' roles since it and they would have to work together, just as they do now when protecting refugees.

In 2005, senior UNHCR officials articulated a more expansive outlook, speaking of the organization's 'predisposition' to help the internally displaced and 'a generous and more flexible application of UNHCR policy criteria' in deciding when to become involved with those uprooted in their own countries. In support of an enlarged role, the positive consequences of UNHCR's involvement have been pointed out. Countries of asylum might be more inclined to maintain their asylum policies if

something is being done to alleviate the suffering of the internally displaced, reduce their need to seek asylum and create conditions conducive to their return. Moreover, UNHCR could expand its role gradually to enable it to monitor the impact of its actions on refugee protection and to assure other agencies of their continued roles.

UNHCR's 12 September 2005 agreement to assume lead responsibility for protection, camp management and emergency shelter for internally displaced persons, endorsed by the Inter-Agency Standing Committee, marks a milestone in the evolution of UN policy on this issue. Beginning in January 2006, UNHCR will take on this role in two or three countries. If it performs effectively, calls to expand its mandate will no doubt continue, and so will the debate on the best way to deal institutionally with the needs of internally displaced persons.

Guiding Principles do have 'legal significance' and are being applied internationally by a growing number of states.[22]

Human rights treaty-making at the international level can take decades, with no guarantee that states will ratify instruments or observe their obligations. The process could also lead to watering-down of the accepted provisions of international law on which the principles are based. Until the international community is ready to adopt a binding instrument that accords with the protection level set forth in the Guiding Principles, the majority opinion is that the best approach is to expand the application of the principles at the national level.[23] Nonetheless, at the regional level the African Union is using the principles to develop a treaty on internal displacement for the continent.

Whatever the outcome of this debate, for the time being the Guiding Principles fill a major gap in the international protection system for internally displaced persons. They provide the displaced with a document to turn to when they are denied their rights. For their part, governments and other actors have guidelines to follow in designing national policies and laws on behalf of the displaced. Indeed, some experts are building upon the Guiding Principles to spell out issues related to restitution, compensation and land use for the displaced in more detail.[24]

Institutional arrangements: the 'collaborative approach'

A multitude of international organizations offer protection to internally displaced persons and help them with aid for reintegration and development. First come the various UN agencies, ranging from UNHCR to UNICEF to OCHA. Others in the field are the ICRC, the International Organization for Migration and many NGOs. The overall UN response is the responsibility of the Emergency Relief Coordinator, who heads OCHA. Since 1997 he has served as the United Nations' 'focal point' for internally displaced persons. In addition, the Representative of the Secretary-General on the Human Rights of Internally Displaced Persons serves as principal 'advocate' for the internally displaced.

Under this 'collaborative approach', all agencies share the responsibility for responding to situations of internal displacement. The system was decided upon by default. Neither the political will nor the resources existed to create a new agency to address the needs of the internally displaced. Such a new entity, it was feared, would duplicate the work of other agencies and almost certainly meet with opposition from governments that object to international involvement with their displaced populations. A second, frequently suggested option—the enlargement of UNHCR's mandate to enable it to assume the responsibility—was also rejected (see Box 7.3). The scale of the problem, it was argued, was too large for one agency. Even the 'lead agency' option, in which one agency assumes the main role in the field (see Box 7.1), was largely sidelined by the collaborative approach, which substituted coordination by the Emergency Relief Coordinator at headquarters and by Resident/Humanitarian Coordinators (RC/HCs) in the field.

Most UN and independent evaluations have found the collaborative approach inadequate to the task and difficult to implement.[25] Critics charge that UN agencies regularly resist coordination and that there is no real centre of responsibility for the displaced in the field. 'Co-heads are no-heads,' quipped Richard Holbrooke, former US Ambassador to the United Nations, after visiting camps for internally displaced persons in Angola.[26] Critics also point to the lack of predictability, since the different agencies basically pick and choose the situations in which they wish to become involved on the basis of their mandates, resources and interests. For instance, most agencies rushed to South and Southeast Asia to help those displaced by the 2004 tsunami, but only a limited international presence could be mobilized for northern Uganda, where tens of thousands of children are at risk each night of abduction or maiming. The Humanitarian Coordinator lacks both the authority and resources to assign responsibilities. His only tool is persuasion. But can 'persuasion without authority over budgets and operations' be sufficient, asks Georgetown University's Susan Martin.[27]

In response to these widely publicized deficiencies, a special office was created in OCHA in 2002, devoted exclusively to internal displacement. Upgraded to a division in 2004—the Inter-Agency Internal Displacement Division (IDD)—and with staff largely drawn from the different international agencies, it has sought to ensure that UN agencies in the field, under the leadership of RC/HCs, develop and implement a strategic action plan to meet the needs of internally displaced persons. To help with this, the IDD put together a policy package on the internally displaced which all the major agencies and NGOs agreed to.[28]

But ensuring the implementation of action plans around the world soon proved to be beyond the capacity of one small non-operational office. The cooperation of the powerful operational agencies was needed to develop and carry out the plans. Yet there was no agreed division of labour among agencies, so that at the beginning of each new emergency it was unclear which agency or combination of agencies would become involved and which responsibilities they would assume.

To rectify this, the IDD came up with a proposal for a 'sectoral' approach, whereby agencies would be expected to carve out areas of responsibility (e.g. protection, camp coordination and management, emergency shelter, nutrition, water and sanitation) based on their expertise, and fulfil them in emergencies.

The most challenging sector by far is protection. While agencies regularly provide food, medicine and shelter to internally displaced persons, they are not well equipped to defend the physical safety and human rights of those endangered. Providing material aid while ignoring the fact that the displaced are being beaten, raped or killed too often leads to the tragic description of the victims as the 'well-fed dead' (see Box 7.1). Where national protection does not exist, international agencies may be called upon to set up early warning systems, negotiate access with governments and insurgent groups, deploy staff among threatened communities and protect women and children from rape and abduction. They may also be called on to arrange relocations and evacuations, intercede with authorities to assure that the displaced are not forcibly returned to conditions of danger, or accompany the displaced home.

These initiatives go beyond the mandates and expertise of most international field staff. Still, many are trying to enhance protection by reporting protection problems, becoming more engaged with the displaced and designing assistance programmes in ways that reinforce protection. They have also been working more closely with displaced communities to build the latter's coping skills. But the dangers are considerable. In some emergencies in recent years more aid workers have been attacked or killed than peacekeepers. This has sometimes led to assistance by 'remote control' (i.e., through local organizations) which has diminished protection, whether in Chechnya, Iraq or Somalia.[29]

Only two agencies, the ICRC and UNHCR, have a specific legal mandate to carry out protection work. But even here there are limits. ICRC cannot always become involved

Box 7.4

Internal displacement in Colombia

With 2 to 3 million displaced persons, Colombia presents the highest number of internally displaced people in the western hemisphere, and the second largest displaced population in the world after Sudan. Most of the displacement is related to the country's four-decade-long internal armed conflict, the most protracted in Latin America. This 'dirty war' is a complex conflict fought primarily between left-wing guerrillas, right-wing paramilitaries and Colombian armed forces. But it also involves drug traffickers, landowners, and other legal and illegal interests.

More than 40,000 people, most of them civilians, have been killed in Colombia as a result of the armed conflict since 1990 alone. In recent years, Colombians have been fleeing over the country's borders in increasing numbers, most notably to Costa Rica and Ecuador (but also Panama and Venezuela) in the region, as well as to the United States and Europe. Since 2000, more than 100,000 Colombians have sought asylum abroad. But since 11 September 2001, states have adopted increasingly restrictive asylum policies, making it harder for Colombians to claim asylum. Although over 250,000 Colombians are thought to be currently seeking asylum abroad, many others have sought refuge abroad without seeking asylum.

However, the vast majority of those forced to flee are civilians who do not cross an international border, but become displaced within their own country. More than 1.5 million displaced persons are registered with the Colombian government, but NGOs estimate that the real figure is more than double this. Many

displaced people within Colombia do not register for fear of being attacked, stigmatized or displaced again. Official sources claim that 74 per cent of the internally displaced are women and children. The Consultancy for Human Rights and Displacement estimated that 288,000 Colombians were newly displaced during 2004, 39 per cent more than in 2003.

The vast majority of those displaced are dispersed rather than living in organized camps, and many seek anonymity in the country's big cities. Almost 40 per cent of the internally displaced have settled in and around the ten largest cities. Without official registration and proper identity documents, internally displaced persons often face difficulty in accessing basic government assistance, employment, healthcare and education. It has been estimated that only one in eight internally displaced pupils have returned to school after having been displaced. Displaced girls are more vulnerable to sexual exploitation and pregnancy than other teenagers.

Displacement has often been an end in itself rather than just a by-product of Colombia's conflict. For many years, both guerrillas and paramilitaries have depopulated rural areas and appropriated the land for political, economic and strategic gain. Upon seizing control of an area, armed groups often kill or displace civilians they suspect of supporting the opposing side. Human rights defenders frequently suffer a similar fate.

In recent years, indigenous communities and their leaders have increasingly been targeted by the irregular armed groups, who favour

action against the civilian population over direct military confrontation. Although indigenous people represent only 2 to 3 per cent of Colombia's total inhabitants, they make up as much as 8 per cent of the county's internally displaced population. If the current trend persists, there is even concern that some of the smaller and more vulnerable groups may disappear altogether.

And the story does not end with initial displacement. In some areas, there have been reports of internally displaced young men being forcibly recruited into irregular armed groups. In the cities, large sections of the population are increasingly being drawn into gang warfare which replicates war allegiances and divisions at the national level, bringing with it intra-urban displacements. Internally displaced persons are becoming displaced a second and even a third time.

Colombia's legislation on internal displacement is among the most advanced in the world. The country's 1997 Law on Internal Displacement (Law 387) is consistent with the UN Guiding Principles on Internal Displacement, requiring the state to create policies and adopt measures for displacement prevention, attention and protection. But the problem is implementation, and in February 2004, Colombia's Constitutional Court issued a landmark judgement, which deemed government policy in this regard inadequate and unconstitutional.

The government does not register or recognize in official statistics those displaced by the fumigation campaign, those unwilling or unable to apply for assistance and those rejected under its strict criteria. The return of internally displaced persons, a priority for the administration of President Alvaro Uribe, has sometimes taken place despite the fact that the conditions which caused the displacements remain unchanged. Many return areas continue to be under the control of at least one irregular armed group and numerous returned internally displaced persons have been killed in recent years.

UNHCR established a permanent presence in Colombia in 1998. Uniquely, the organization's mandate in the country is concerned with the protection of internally displaced people, as well as with refugees and others of concern. UNHCR's work focuses on capacity-building activities, notably in strengthening the protection regime through documentation campaigns, human rights training, pedagogy projects and integration initiatives. Rather than provide emergency assistance for internally displaced persons itself, UNHCR reinforces civil society organizations that address these needs. In particular, NGOs and church groups have long played a crucial role in assisting internally displaced persons in Colombia.

UNHCR follows a collaborative response to internal displacement by chairing the UN Thematic Group on Displacement. Partnerships have also been established with ECHO, ICRC, IOM, UNIFEM, several government departments including the one with responsibility for assisting the internally displaced (the Social Solidarity Network), and numerous NGOs. UNHCR's overall objective in relation to internally displaced persons in Colombia is to promote a comprehensive and coordinated response to the humanitarian crisis.

Many of Colombia's internally displaced people look for anonymity in the country's big cities. Of the 90,000 people living in Comuna 2 in northwest Medellín, up to 15 per cent are estimated to be displaced. (UNHCR/S. Loughna/2005)

in situations below the threshold of armed conflict—and sometimes is denied entry into conflict areas. UNHCR's mandate focuses primarily on refugees and restricts its involvement with the internally displaced under criteria which can range from a specific request from the Secretary-General and the agreement of the state concerned to adequate resources or a 'link factor' to refugees.

Given UNHCR's long experience in protecting uprooted populations (see Box 7.3), on 12 September 2005 the UN Inter-Agency Standing Committee assigned it lead responsibility for the protection of the internally displaced (as well as responsibility for camp management and emergency shelter). Its enlarged protection role will require it to ensure that joint steps are taken by all agencies in the field to enhance the security of the displaced. Special partnerships will be needed with the Office of the High Commissioner for Human Rights (OHCHR), which has largely stayed clear of operational engagement with internally displaced persons, and UNICEF, whose protection role with internally displaced children could be strengthened. A protection policy paper adopted by the Inter-Agency Standing Committee sets forth in detail the protection steps international agencies can take.[30] Currently under discussion are ideas for 'protection coalitions', 'interagency mobile protection advisory teams' as well as a 'protection standby force'.[31]

UNHCR will also have to navigate a collaborative system that often resists involvement with the security and human rights of internally displaced persons. As the Brookings–OCHA study, *Protect or Neglect*, found, the majority of RC/HCs, who direct the collaborative response in the field, are reluctant 'to advocate for the rights of the displaced in an effective and assertive manner'.[32] Many fear that doing so could compromise their relationships with governments, threaten relief programmes or even lead to their expulsion. Moreover, RC/HCs in many countries report to Special Representatives of the Secretary-General who often put political concerns over humanitarian and human rights objectives.[33]

Despite the obvious limits on the role outsiders can play in providing protection, how the humanitarian community deals with this major gap in the international response system will in large measure determine whether the collaborative approach will be successful or whether alternative arrangements will be needed.

The effectiveness of the collaborative approach will also depend on adequate resources. The UN's Consolidated Appeals Process (CAP) for emergencies now targets internally displaced persons. But the amounts allotted are often insufficient, and when it comes to protection and human rights initiatives, woefully inadequate.[34] Donors often lavish aid on areas of the world in which they have strategic interests, such as Afghanistan, the Balkans or Iraq, but seriously underfund humanitarian crises, especially in Africa, where the needs of vulnerable populations may be far greater.[35] Calls for international trust funds for emergency action and post-conflict reconstruction continue to be under discussion. In 2005 the World Summit approved the expansion of the UN Central Emergency Revolving Fund (CERF) to enable UN humanitarian organizations to receive 'instant' funds when a new disaster strikes and to inject 'equity' into the system.[36]

The role of the military

In her book *The Turbulent Decade: Confronting the Refugee Crises of the 1990s*, Sadako Ogata describes UNHCR's initial hesitance to accept military cover for its humanitarian activities and its subsequent recognition of the importance of such support. Without it, UNHCR would not have been able to get supplies to displaced people in central Bosnia, undertake the Sarajevo airlift or make airdrops to besieged towns and villages.[37] Similarly, in Afghanistan in 2001, relief agencies found that working with the military benefited displaced populations: the WFP was able to position millions of metric tons of food in surrounding countries, truck them inside Afghanistan and thereby avert widespread famine. In Liberia in 2003, UN troops helped UNHCR to relocate thousands of internally displaced persons from public buildings in Monrovia to proper camps or settlements.

But humanitarian involvement with the military comes at a price. For the ICRC the cardinal principles of impartiality and neutrality, which aid agencies are bound to uphold, are compromised by 'blending' humanitarian action with military operations. NGOs such as *Médecins Sans Frontières* have pointed out that unless military and humanitarian action are separate, humanitarian workers can become identified with one side to the conflict, endangering both aid deliveries and humanitarian staff. Reportedly, camps of displaced persons in Macedonia became military targets when NATO involved itself in setting up tents and providing camp security. In Afghanistan, humanitarian workers were put in danger when Western military forces, wearing civilian clothes, did humanitarian and development work.

Nonetheless, it has become clear that the complete independence of humanitarian and military action is not possible in most emergencies, and may even prove perilous to the displaced populations the international community is trying to protect. In the words of Major-General William Nash, a veteran of the Balkan wars, 'Although the demand for independent humanitarian action is admirable, more important is an effective strategy to assist those who are in need'.[38] The importance of humanitarian, development and military actors working together has led UN agencies and a number of NGOs to call for better communication with military actors, including sharing of information and joint planning and strategizing. Currently, the United Nations is studying how best to organize 'integrated missions'.[39]

Since the 1990s, UN Security Council resolutions have called upon peacekeepers to undertake a variety of protection responsibilities for the internally displaced, ranging from facilitating the delivery of relief and establishing and maintaining secure humanitarian areas to ensuring protection in camps, monitoring and reporting the conditions of the displaced and enabling their safe return home. Whether in the Balkans, the DRC, Haiti, Iraq, Liberia, Rwanda, Sierra Leone or Timor Leste, peacekeepers have been specifically charged with providing assistance or protection to internally displaced persons. Most recently, African Union troops have been called upon to enhance security for internally displaced persons in Darfur, Sudan (see Box 7.2).

But the record has been mixed. Whereas peacekeeping forces have generally been effective in preventing mass starvation by ensuring delivery and distribution of food through logistical support, they have been less effective when it comes to protecting the physical security of the internally displaced and other affected populations. In most cases, UN forces have not had enough troops to provide adequate protection, clear mandates to allow them to engage in robust action or the necessary training and equipment to do their jobs adequately. The lack of political will in the Security Council often contributed to this outcome.

An outstanding exception was Iraq in 1991, where multinational forces succeeded in creating a safe haven for internally displaced Kurds under attack in the wake of the Gulf War. This refuge existed for more than a decade. But in Bosnia and Herzegovina, the overrunning of the 'safe area' of Srebrenica in 1995 stands as one of the most ignominious examples of the international failure to provide protection to internally displaced persons. So too is what happened in Kibeho, Rwanda that same year, when UN forces stood by while several thousand internally displaced persons in camps were killed by the Rwandan army. Worse yet, earlier in this decade UN peacekeepers in the DRC and Sierra Leone were raping and sexually exploiting internally displaced women and children they were supposed to protect—using humanitarian supplies as bait.

Despite these well-publicized failures, there remain many instances where peacekeepers have provided security for displaced populations in internal conflict situations. East Timor, where a multinational force saved many lives and enabled the return of tens of thousands of refugees and internally displaced persons, is a good example. In Kosovo, Liberia, Mozambique and Rwanda, peacekeeping troops effectively facilitated the return of displaced persons. A 2004 report on the role of peacekeepers with internally displaced persons identified impressive 'best practices' in different countries in protecting the internally displaced.[40] In particular, military training has begun to focus on how to protect internally displaced persons, greater efforts are being made to deploy civilian police, protection mandates have been strengthened, and in some instances peacekeepers have taken a bolder approach toward protecting civilians. The United Nations also has begun to implement its 'zero tolerance' policy toward sexual exploitation.

But fundamental problems remain. Most internally displaced persons in need of protection are in Africa, yet most of the UN peacekeeping missions deployed there are understaffed and without sufficient resources. Even in the DRC, where 16,700 troops are on the ground, the mission is reported to have insufficient resources to fulfil its mandate, which includes protecting internally displaced persons in camps. Moreover, developed countries with well-trained, experienced and heavily-armed troops have been proving increasingly unwilling to offer their forces or resources to UN operations when their national interests are not at stake—currently less than 10 per cent of peacekeepers come from Western armies.[41] Nor is there agreement among the major powers on creating a standing UN force that could be rapidly deployed in emergencies both for prevention and protection. Heads of government at the World Summit urged only the 'further development of proposals' to build up reserves for rapid deployment, although they endorsed a standing police capacity which could prove valuable in protection.[42]

Military intervention and humanitarian relief alone, however, are but stopgap measures. They can never substitute for the political settlements needed to resolve the conflicts that produce internal displacement. When peacekeepers and humanitarian workers are left on the front lines without efforts to resolve these conflicts, they can even unwittingly prolong them. Therefore, strong leadership is needed both from UN headquarters and from the international community to manage and mediate disputes and lay the foundation for transitions out of conflict.

The road ahead

Over the past fifteen years, international involvement with internally displaced persons has become an increasingly accepted course of action when governments are unable or unwilling to provide for the welfare and security of their displaced populations. One of the reasons for this change has been evolving notions of sovereignty. Although the World Summit in September 2005 did not go so far as to affirm *automatic* international protection of populations at risk, it did posit a collective 'responsibility to protect' when civilians are subject to ethnic cleansing, crimes against humanity or genocide.[43] This can be built upon to reinforce both national and international responsibility for internally displaced persons.

Similarly, the legal framework contained in the Guiding Principles on Internal Displacement has increasingly been guiding governments and international organizations in addressing situations of displacement, influencing how the displaced are perceived and treated at the national and international levels.

Less effective have been the institutional arrangements developed, but here too progress is discernible. The UN's decision to assign responsibilities to specific agencies has the potential to bring predictability and clarity to the international response system for the displaced. UNHCR's role in the new division of labour is pivotal because it is focused on protection, the biggest gap in the system. Indeed, UNHCR is at a critical juncture in its 55-year history, having agreed to substantially expand its role to encompass the internally displaced. For the first time since the end of the Second World War, a comprehensive regime is being designed to address the needs of forced migrants on both sides of the border. As High Commissioner António Guterres put it, the international community has finally awakened to its 'biggest failure in terms of humanitarian action' and decided to act in defence of those who 'have not crossed a frontier'.[44]

8 Looking to the future

Globalization poses new challenges in all domains of international life, and the world of forced migration is no exception. In the coming decades states, international agencies and NGOs face multiple challenges in relation to the problem of human displacement. How effectively they surmount these hurdles will determine the viability of international refugee protection in the years to come.

The challenges ahead can be listed as follows. First, states must be persuaded to reconsider their restrictive asylum policies. Second, it must be ensured that the core principles of international refugee law, particularly that of *non-refoulement*, are not eroded. Third, the security of refugees, particularly women and children, and humanitarian workers, must be enhanced. Fourth, problems relating to protracted situations and the 'warehousing' of refugees must be resolved. Fifth, host states must be prevented from undermining the principle of voluntary repatriation in the absence of responsibility-sharing by the international community. Sixth, the problem of smuggling and trafficking of asylum seekers must be addressed. Seventh, the root causes of refugee flows must be given more attention than they receive at present. Eighth, UNHCR must respond to numerous supervisory, accountability and partnership challenges, besides clearly defining its role vis-à-vis internally displaced people.

A number of initiatives have already been taken by states and international agencies, and in particular by UNHCR, to meet these challenges. This book has attempted to assess such efforts in the context of key political and socioeconomic developments over the past few years. Decolonization, the end of the Cold War, rapid globalization, the growing North-South divide, the proliferation of internal conflicts and the so-called 'war on terror' have all affected the policies of states towards refugees and internally displaced persons. They have also led to a change in perceptions of the role of international agencies, including UNHCR, in dealing with displaced people.

Despite these efforts, much remains to be done. This chapter highlights some of the key areas in need of immediate attention: ensuring the security of refugees, improving mechanisms to better identify those in need of international protection, and finding durable solutions—especially to resolve protracted situations. These and other challenges can only be met through adequate responsibility-sharing. The chapter also looks into various mechanisms for achieving it. A separate section is devoted to identifying the challenges facing UNHCR in providing protection and assistance for refugees and, increasingly, internally displaced people.

Sri Lankan internally displaced returnees at Thadadeli Welfare Centre. (UNHCR/S. Boness/2000)

Key concerns

Threats to the physical security of refugees are a growing problem.[1] They emanate from armed criminals, aberrant military and police forces, non-state armed actors, local populations and elements within the refugee community, and can lead to the killing of refugees and the abuse of women and children. A number of measures are being taken to address the problem. These include establishing refugee camps at a distance from volatile borders, separating combatants from civilian elements, providing safe access to food and water and training local police and refugee leaders on security issues. Some of these measures call for assistance from UN peacekeepers and collaboration with other agencies. For instance, UNHCR has teamed up with other UN organizations in a group called Coordinating Action on Small Arms to help reduce threats to the physical security of refugee populations.

As enshrined in international humanitarian law, the physical security of refugees remains primarily the responsibility of the host state, whereas the security of internally displaced people must be ensured by their own state. When the state fails to provide adequate protection, be it due to lack of capacity or unwillingness, the international community should intervene. But such intervention is often constrained by sensitivities over the sovereignty of the state concerned and the political agendas of other states. Consequently, interventions are usually too late, poorly funded and restricted by limited mandates. These problems have been illustrated during the Darfur crisis. More effective responses can only come about when there is the political will backed up by sufficient resources.

Another key on-going concern is the asylum-migration nexus. Asylum seekers and refugees have increasingly been resorting to illegal means of entry into states. In turning to smugglers to get them to their destinations, some of them fall victim to people traffickers. While illegal migration is a problem that no state can afford to ignore, policies to combat it should distinguish between illegal migrants seeking better economic conditions and individuals in need of international protection. Such a distinction exists in principle but in practice it is blurred. In many states asylum seekers and refugees endure the same treatment as illegal migrants, and in the process their right to international protection is often violated. This tendency has been fuelled by political agendas appealing to xenophobic sentiments.

Efforts to combat smuggling and trafficking in recent years include the adoption of treaties, notably the UN Convention against Transnational Organized Crime (2000), its Protocol to Prevent, Suppress and Punish Trafficking in Persons, Especially Women and Children, as well as its Protocol against the Smuggling of Migrants by Land.[2] The two protocols call upon states to take a range of measures to combat the smuggling of migrants and trafficking in persons, in particular women and children. For example, the protocol against migrant-smuggling requires member states to make it a criminal offence under national laws, adopt special measures to crack down on migrant-smuggling by sea, and boost international cooperation to seek out and prosecute smugglers and traffickers.

In an attempt to protect asylum seekers and refugees, the protocols maintain that the rights, responsibilities and obligations of states and individuals contained in the 1951 UN Refugee Convention, and other instruments of international humanitarian law and international human rights law, must be upheld. In so doing, the protocols reinforce states' obligations to respect the principle of *non-refoulement* and refrain from imposing penalties on asylum seekers for illegal entry, as mentioned in Article 31 of the 1951 UN Refugee Convention. While this represents a step forward, more has to be done at the national level to identify those in need of international protection.

Recent years have witnessed renewed efforts to reach durable solutions. Still, the majority of today's refugees remain in situations of protracted displacement. The three classic durable solutions are voluntary repatriation, local integration in the country of first asylum and resettlement in a third country. But the history of durable solutions shows that a particular durable solution becomes the dominant solution in particular times.[3] Resettlement in third countries was the durable solution for much of the Cold War period; today it is voluntary repatriation.

While it is still recognized that resettlement is a vital instrument of international solidarity and responsibility-sharing, some states today are increasing the quotas of people they accept for resettlement, as a substitute for allowing spontaneous arrivals to apply for asylum.[4] The durable solution of resettlement needs to be strengthened. It is therefore encouraging to see the 'internationalization of resettlement', with new countries such as Argentina, Benin, Brazil, Burkina Faso, Chile, Iceland and Ireland agreeing to annual resettlement quotas, however small. In this respect, the adoption of the Multilateral Framework of Understandings on Resettlement by a range of resettlement and host states is helpful as it codifies standard principles and practices. The framework could be actively supported through the creation of a Refugee Resettlement Fund.[5]

Efforts to achieve the durable solution of return in security and dignity have underlined the importance of development assistance. Such assistance formed an element of Convention Plus in tandem with international support for the implementation of the 4Rs (Repatriation, Reintegration, Rehabilitation and Reconstruction) in the country of origin.[6] Another purpose of targeting development assistance is to promote local integration. While the idea is to encourage self-reliance among refugees, it can also become a means by which third states reduce the pressure for asylum and resettlement in their territories.

The targeting of development assistance for durable solutions is not a new concept. However, the success of initiatives launched over the past five years remains to be seen. The evaluations of the Uganda Self-Reliance Strategy and the Zambia Initiative for local integration will be important in assessing the potential of the continued targeting of development assistance for durable solutions. In the case of protracted refugee situations, the focus on development assistance for durable solutions should not overlook the importance of addressing and resolving political problems.

Need for greater responsibility-sharing

Institutionalizing dialogue

In the last few years, concrete policy initiatives to address the global refugee problem have come either from concerned states or UNHCR. The initiatives coming from states are essentially a response to the concerns of their citizens that they have become a soft touch for 'bogus' asylum seekers.[7] In tandem with growing xenophobia, restrictive administrative and legal measures have sharply reduced the number of asylum applications in many Western states. Such policies have led to the general erosion of the core principles of international refugee law, in particular the principle of *non-refoulement.* New initiatives proposed include 'extraterritorial processing of refugees' and 'protection in the region of origin'. Broadly based on the Pacific Solution, they seek to limit the number of refugees entering industrialized states by establishing a deterrent asylum regime.

Indeed, developing countries often point to Western-country policies to justify their increasingly restrictive asylum practices. In recent years, these practices have included the more frequent detention of asylum seekers, while encampment and restrictions on freedom of movement have been stepped up. Furthermore, in many developing countries no distinction is made between asylum seekers and refugees on the one hand, and illegal migrants on the other. As a result, the rights of the former are often violated due to the indiscriminate implementation of measures aimed at combating illegal migration.

Concerned about these developments around the world, UNHCR has in recent years launched two important initiatives—the Global Consultations on International Protection and Convention Plus—to address global refugee problems. The Global Consultations represented UNHCR's bid to rise to the new challenges confronting refugee protection and shore up support for the international framework of protection principles. It was also an effort by the organization to enhance protection through new approaches which address the concerns of states and other actors, as well as the inadequate asylum practices of states.[8]

Both the Global Consultations process and the Convention Plus initiative were based on the assumption that the policy responses of states and international organizations would be effective if they arose from dialogue between all the relevant actors.[9] These include developed and developing states, international agencies, the refugee community and NGOs, all of whom play a role in protecting and assisting refugees.

The Convention Plus initiative was informed by the understanding that developed states can take on greater responsibility for the protection of refugees within the ambit of international human rights law. The initiative highlighted the need for developed nations to respond to the concerns of the developing states that host most of the world's refugees. In short, the two initiatives recognized that for a solution to the refugee problem to succeed it must be reached through dialogue between all the stakeholders, in particular developed and developing countries, on the basis of *shared interests.*[10]

Both the Global Consultations and Convention Plus moved the dialogue on the refugee problem forward. The former led to the reaffirmation of the 1951 UN Refugee Convention by states and also helped clarify core aspects of international refugee law. The process 'encouraged a cooperative spirit in tackling refugee issues' and 'roused an interest in multilateral dialogue to find solutions to an increasingly internationalized set of problems'.[11] It led to the adoption of UNHCR's Agenda for Protection, a comprehensive programme to tackle the various issues besetting refugee protection in today's complex environment.[12]

Among the tangible achievements of the Convention Plus initiative was the adoption of a Multilateral Framework of Understandings on Resettlement in September 2004. It also led to dialogue on a number of elements including resettlement, targeting development assistance and irregular secondary movements to give concrete shape to the principle of international responsibility-sharing. These three elements were brought together in efforts to formulate comprehensive solutions for Afghanistan and Somalia.[13]

To the extent initiatives such as Convention Plus acknowledge growing North-South interconnectedness in areas such as migration, security and development, they take a step forward. But the substantive achievements of Convention Plus in terms of new commitments by states to responsibility-sharing and thus to refugee protection have been very few. This is largely due to the limited timeframe of the initiative and initial scepticism towards it because of its association with the concept of asylum transit processing and protection in regions of origin.[14]

Regional solutions: exclusive or complementary?

Any proposed mechanism for responsibility-sharing must, if it is to yield favourable results, be a dialogic and a global model. Both the dialogic and global dimensions are neglected when a regional solution to refugees is recommended as *the* model to respond to the global refugee problem. This is the approach of states that propose protection in the regions of origin. From a global perspective the regional solution can be adopted either as a complementary or an exclusive solution. The exclusive approach is often advocated to help reduce the burden of the refugee problem on affluent regions of the world.[15]

The efficiency and culture arguments used to justify an exclusively regional approach are being used without any serious attempt to conceptualize their meaning and implications.[16] Moreover, the idea of refugee-resources exchange (where rich states compensate poor states for hosting refugees) that informs cruder versions of the efficiency argument is ethically problematic; it treats refugees as commodities. It also ignores the possible social, security and environmental costs to developing host countries from such an exchange.

The other premise, that cultural similarities facilitate the hosting of refugees in regions of origin, is also debated. Quite often the assumption of cultural similarities is a myth. For instance, it is often presumed—erroneously—that all Africans share a

Map 8.1   Average number of refugees per 1 USD GDP per capita, 2000-2004

500 or more
50 - 500
less than 50
data not available

Statistical data sources: UNHCR (refugees)/World Bank (GDP)/United Nations Population Division (national populations). Compiled by: UNHCR.
The boundaries and names shown and the designations used on this map do not imply official endorsement or acceptance by the United Nations.
Geographical data sources: UNHCR, Global Insight digital mapping - © 1998 Europa Technologies Ltd.

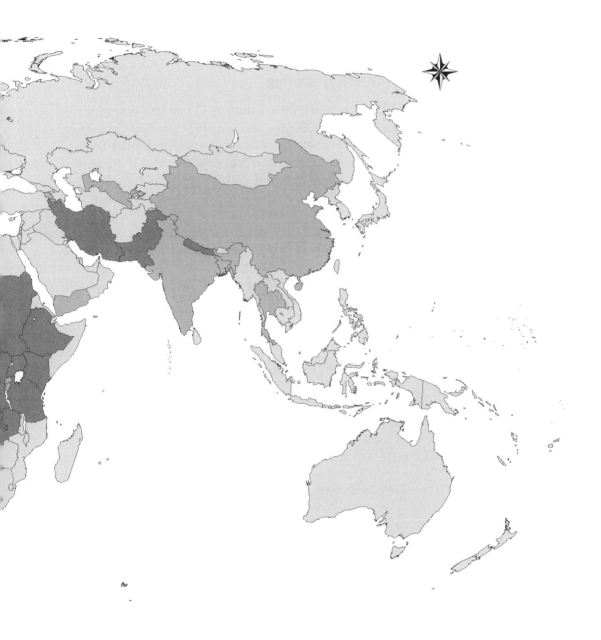

common culture, language and traditions.[17] Furthermore, geographical proximity cannot be the basis for advocating an exclusively regional approach.

A regional solution is therefore better used as a complement to a global approach. The regional approach can, however, put in place structures that facilitate preventive action, ensure a quick response to the need for humanitarian assistance and help parcel out responsibility for specific refugee groups.

Models for greater responsibility-sharing

Both the Agenda for Protection and UNHCR's Executive Committee conclusion of 2004 on International Cooperation and Burden and Responsibility-Sharing in Mass Influx Situations recognize the need for global responsibility-sharing arrangements to take some of the load off first-asylum countries.[18] But how are these to be worked out in a concrete manner? An approach based on dialogue would require that responsibility-sharing be defined in accordance with criteria that are acceptable from the perspective of all parties involved.[19] A global approach would anticipate that responsibility is shared both in hosting the displaced and providing the funds required to offer them durable solutions. Keeping these views in mind, there are three possible ways to define global norms for responsibility-sharing.

First, agree on situation-specific comprehensive plans of action that respond to particular mass influx situations. This is the kind of agreement that was envisaged in the Convention Plus initiative. It will have a limited objective, and to yield positive results it must be based upon an acceptance of responsibility-sharing as a principle of customary international law.

Second, go beyond specific mass influx situations to adopt general rules of responsibility-sharing. Such a multilateral framework will take a more holistic approach and bring within its sights all practices that are not in line with the spirit of international responsibility-sharing, such as the restrictive asylum policies of some states. For this option to be effective, restrictive asylum practices have to be moderated so as to allow persons in need of international protection to have access to it.

Third, arrive at a multilateral framework that formulates rules that not only automatically come into play in situations of mass influx but also apply to protracted refugee situations. Such a framework will define the obligations of states more clearly and make the response of the international community more predictable by removing the element of discretion from the scheme of things. This can only be achieved by: the recognition of the need for effective and equitable responsibility-sharing in situations where developing countries are hosting large numbers of refugees; the provision of greater relief and reconstruction aid to post-conflict societies; and a common understanding based on shared interests.

All three models would define the criteria and modalities for burden-sharing and the role of states involved. They would focus on providing effective protection within the framework of international human rights and refugee law. They should not, however, lay down any particular formula for sharing the burden of asylum; rather, states would be expected to respond appropriately in light of the global refugee situation and the specific refugee flow.

Financial aspects

An important aspect of effective responsibility-sharing is financial burden-sharing, whereby the financial cost to countries hosting great numbers of the displaced is shared. Unfortunately, the provision of humanitarian assistance does not necessarily permit appropriate relief to be provided to states in need. In some cases, the political interests of states override humanitarian concerns based on needs. As a result, a number of critical refugee crises remain under-funded while other less urgent situations are allocated a surplus of funds.[20]

Furthermore, prompted by foreign policy and domestic political considerations, major donor states have increasingly channelled much of their humanitarian aid through large NGOs.[21] This has led to the 'bilateralization' of humanitarian assistance. Donors also have begun to earmark much funding so as to gain visibility and political influence.[22] In the process they have overlooked the comparative advantages and legitimacy of UN agencies.[23] These developments have led to a certain degree of incoherence contributing to the inability to get relief to those who need it.

Responding to criticism, in June 2003 concerned states launched the Good Humanitarian Donorship initiative to enhance the effectiveness and accountability of their actions.[24] Donor states agreed to certain principles and good practice, as well as to allocate funding in proportion to needs, to support development, UN leadership and coordination. They also agreed to explore ways to reduce the earmarking of humanitarian aid.

UNHCR: challenges ahead

The supervision challenge

In the course of UNHCR's Global Consultations on International Protection, the supervisory responsibility (under Article 35 of the 1951 UN Refugee Convention) of the organization was discussed by a gathering of distinguished experts. There was agreement that 'the identification of appropriate mechanisms should seek to preserve, even strengthen, the pre-eminence and authority of the voice of the High Commissioner. Anything that could undermine UNHCR's supervisory authority should be avoided'.[25]

On the other hand, some experts have been recommending that an independent committee be established with the task of ensuring the accountability of states under the 1951 UN Refugee Convention. These experts argue that UNHCR is unable to perform its supervisory role because of its financial dependence on donor countries and the absence of a clear procedure in the Convention on how the supervisory task assigned to it is to be carried out.

The challenge can be met if UNHCR takes steps identified in the course of the Global Consultations to strengthen its supervisory role.[26] Its adoption of a dialogic model in recent initiatives is a move in the right direction as it allows all stakeholders, including the refugee community, to express their concerns.

The partnership challenge

Within the UN system the primary responsibility for providing assistance and protection to refugees lies with UNHCR. In recognition of the expertise that other actors can bring in responding to and resolving refugee situations, in recent years UNHCR has worked to strengthen partnerships with governments, other UN agencies, NGOs, the private sector and the refugee community. It has continued to work with other UN agencies to assist refugees where their mandates meet. It has also invested particular efforts to strengthen collaboration with local and international NGOs, which are its main operational partners.

While much has been achieved, to identify and fill protection gaps the organization should go further in involving all relevant actors, including host governments, in assessing the needs of displaced people and in planning and implementing effective responses. By bringing in the expertise of others, UNHCR will complement its own work and capacity and therefore ensure that minimum standards of protection and assistance are met.

The accountability challenge

Critics of the organization contend that its internal accountability mechanisms are inadequate for 'they neither offer adequate sanctions nor remedies when fundamental rights of refugees and stateless persons have been directly violated by an act or omission of the UNHCR'.[27] While the practicalities of such a proposal may be questioned, more can certainly be done to increase the transparency and accountability of the organization.

Considering the fact that UNHCR is constantly making decisions that affect the lives of hundreds of thousands of displaced people, there is a real and vital need for the organization to be more accountable to its beneficiaries. One concrete area that requires attention is refugee status determination (RSD) conducted by UNHCR. The number of applications received by UNHCR offices worldwide nearly doubled from 1997 (45,000 persons) to 2004 (86,000 persons). In 2004, UNHCR eligibility decisions affected 54,000 persons in over 80 countries, two-thirds of which are parties to the 1951 UN Refugee Convention. UNHCR conducts RSD mostly in developing countries. In some of these, it conducts RSD 'jointly' with the national authorities, in a gradual process of building national asylum systems. In states where national RSD procedures are in place without yet offering the necessary safeguards,

UNHCR closely monitors the processing of asylum claims by reviewing some claims in order to influence the decision of contracting states who may not otherwise grant refugee status to individuals deserving international protection. In other countries still, UNHCR carries out RSD as no national procedures yet exist.

RSD conducted by UNHCR may directly influence decisions regarding an asylum seeker's deportation, release from detention, resettlement to a third country or eligibility for humanitarian assistance. Researchers and refugee-rights advocates have noted several problems in the RSD process and detailed the standards that a fair, efficient and open RSD procedure should meet to comply with international human rights law.[28] UNHCR has responded positively to academic and NGO criticism and has drafted and started implementing in November 2003 its Procedural Standards for RSD under UNHCR's mandate, which were made public in September 2005.

The funding challenge

UNHCR has lacked sufficient core funding in recent years because nearly 85 per cent of the contributions to it have been earmarked.[29] International agencies need the freedom to allocate about 25 per cent of their funds freely if they are to function effectively.[30] Tight earmarking has also reduced the organization's flexibility, weakening its ability to balance financing between regions, countries and emergencies. Consequently, some refugee crises, mainly in Africa, received far less funding than was available for the crises in Afghanistan, the Balkans and Iraq. The organization has found itself reacting to donor demand instead of assessed needs.[31]

In addition, at the end of the 1990s, UNHCR also started experiencing funding shortages as contributions fell well behind the budgeted needs approved by its Executive Committee.[32] The organization's funding situation had substantially improved by 2004. The agency raised sufficient funding for all its programmes as donors responded positively in 2004 to appeals for flexible, early and prompt funding. In addition, several donors have increased their unrestricted contributions.[33] However, by the end of 2005, UNHCR's financial situation had deteriorated once again.

The IDP challenge

The need for clarity and consistency in UNHCR's response to internally displaced persons has been recognized.[34] On 12 September 2005, the Inter-Agency Standing Committee decided that when responding to situations of internal displacement certain agencies will lead preparedness and response on a global basis in nine sectors. Known as the Collaborative Approach, this is an important marker in a process to improve the overall humanitarian response to internal displacement, by reaching more systematic, predictable and less ad hoc responses.

UNHCR will be the leading agency for protection, camp coordination and management, and emergency shelter. Its role is pivotal because it addresses protection, an important gap in the system. There are, however, limitations on UNHCR's involvement. Its lead role in the three sectors would not apply where internal displacement is caused solely or very substantially by natural disasters or human-made calamities (such as a nuclear accident or any major ecological disaster). In addition, its involvement with internally displaced persons and affected populations will be limited or cease when such involvement poses a serious threat to the safety and security of refugees, its staff and operations.

Having agreed to expand its role to encompass the internally displaced, the organization is at a critical juncture after more than 50 years of existence. The effectiveness of the Collaborative Approach and the role of UNHCR remain to be seen. While UNHCR has extensive experience in dealing with refugee emergencies and providing refugee protection, it has limited experience with crises of internal displacement. In the context of UNHCR's new role within the Collaborative Approach, the organization will have to formulate guidelines on how to operationalize 'protection' in situations of internal displacement and train its staff accordingly. Additionally, the organization needs to develop its camp coordination function and devise operating standards. Furthermore, given that the number of internally displaced persons is substantially higher than that of refugees, UNHCR needs to strengthen and extend its emergency response capacity to meet the additional caseload. The fulfilment of these requirements depends on the availability of substantial funding.

The staff security challenge

Over the past few years the 'humanitarian space' for aid workers has been shrinking. Personnel of humanitarian agencies have increasingly become the target of violent attack. In September 2000, three UNHCR field workers were killed in Atambua, West Timor by rampaging militiamen.[35] To address this issue UNHCR has undertaken a review of its own security policies, and sought to implement measures to enhance staff security. These include security training and the deployment of more security advisors. In 2005, the UN General Assembly established a new Department of Safety and Security for all 400,000 UN staff and dependants.[36] These developments will go some way to safeguard those on whom the effective protection of displaced people depends.

An overriding consideration

Refugees and internally displaced people reflect the shortcomings of political systems. A primary objective of states and their governments is to protect their citizens against violence and persecution. Governments are obliged to ensure respect for human rights. When a government fails to fulfill this duty, the result is often forced displacement. In situations where such displacement involves crossing international borders, the provision of protection is the responsibility of the international community. This is also the case in situations of displacement within national borders when the government concerned fails to provide protection and assistance. Through various forms of intervention, the international community should then provide appropriate responses.

Governments remain the primary protectors, but also violators, of human rights as enshrined in international law. Consequently, attempts to fortify the international protection regime are contingent upon the respect and implementation of states' obligations under international humanitarian law as well as human rights and refugee law.

In recent years, the elevated security concerns of states have increasingly led to practices that ignore international human rights standards. In the process, the international protection regime has been undermined. Therefore, future efforts to meet the on-going challenges in the provision of adequate protection and assistance to those in need, would yield limited results in a world where international law is increasingly under threat.

Endnotes

Introduction

1 This section draws on speeches and statements by the UN High Commissioner for Refugees António Guterres, and former High Commissioner Ruud Lubbers, as well as the Director of UNHCR Department of International Protection, Erika Feller.

Chapter 1

1 UNHCR, *The State of the World's Refugees: The Challenge of Protection*, Penguin Books, Middlesex, 1993, Figure A (Global Number of Refugees: 1960–1992); *Refugees by Numbers* (2005 web edition).

2 M. Marshall and T. Gurr, *Peace and Conflict 2005: A Global Survey of Armed Conflicts, Self-Determination Movements, and Democracy*, Center for International Development and Conflict Management, University of Maryland, 2005, pp. 1–2.

3 Ibid., pp. 44–5.

4 S. Jackson, 'Fortunes of War: the Coltan Trade in the Kivus', in S. Collinson (ed), *Power, Livelihoods and Conflict: Case Studies in Political Economy Analysis for Humanitarian Action*, Humanitarian Policy Group Report No.13, Overseas Development Institute, London, 2003, pp. 21–36.

5 UNHCR, *Global Report 2004*, pp. 476–77.

6 See, for example, Memorandum submitted by the United Nations Children's Fund (UNICEF) to the UK's International Development Committee October 2001 inquiry into the humanitarian crisis in Afghanistan. International Development Committee, *First Report: The Humanitarian Crisis in Afghanistan and the Surrounding Region. Volume II: Minutes of Evidence.* HC 300-II, Session 2001-02, The Stationery Office, London, 2001.

7 International Development Committee, *First Report: The Humanitarian Crisis in Afghanistan and the Surrounding Region. Volume I: Report and Proceedings of the Committee.* HC 300-I, Session 2001-02, The Stationery Office, London, 2001, paras. 39 and 40. See also *Volume II* (HC 300-II), Ev 124 (Annex F) for estimated numbers of IDP populations and additional populations dependent on aid as at 13 November 2001, included in the Memorandum submitted to the inquiry by Clare Short, Secretary of State for International Development.

8 UNHCR, *Refugees by Numbers* (2004 edition), pp. 9 and 14.

9 R. Zetter, D. Griffiths, S. Ferretti and M. Pearl, *An Assessment of the Impact of Asylum Policies in Europe 1990–2000*, Home Office Research Study 259, Home Office, Development and Statistics Directorate, London, June 2003, pp. x and 117.

10 Notably France and the ten new EU Member States. UNHCR, *Asylum Levels and Trends in Industrialized Countries, 2004. Overview of Asylum Applications Lodged in Europe and Non-European Industrialized Countries in 2004*. UNHCR, Geneva, 1 March 2005, p. 5.

11 Ibid., pp. 3–4.

12 Ibid., pp. 6-7.

13 R. Zetter et al., *An Assessment of the Impact of Asylum Policies in Europe 1990–2000*, pp. xvii, 8, 83, and 125.

14 Ibid., pp. xi–xvi.

15 UNHCR, *Global Report 2004*, p. 451.

16 UNHCR, *Statistical Yearbook 2001*, p. 32 (Table 1.2); and *Statistical Yearbook 2002*, p. 36 (Table II.1).

17 UNHCR, *Global Report 2004*, p. 459; *Refugees by Numbers* (2005 web edition).

18 The main countries of resettlement of refugees in 2003 were the United States, Australia, Canada, Norway, Sweden, New Zealand, Finland, Denmark, Netherlands and Ireland. Around 90 per cent of resettled refugees were admitted by the United States, Australia and Canada. UNHCR, *Refugees by Numbers* (2004 edition), pp. 16–17.

19 UNHCR, *Global Report 2004*, p. 14.

20 UNHCR, *The State of the World's Refugees: In Search of Solutions*, Oxford University Press, Oxford, 1995, Annex II, Table 1.

21 UNHCR, *Refugees by Numbers* (2005 web edition).

22 UNHCR, *Global Report 2004*, p. 183.

23 Global IDP Project, *Internal Displacement: Global Overview of Trends and Developments in 2004*, Norwegian Refugee Council, Geneva, 2005, p. 9.

24 UNHCR, *Global Report 2004*, pp. 332 and 421.

25 Global IDP Project, *Internal Displacement*, p. 13.

26 UNHCR, *Global Report 2004*, pp. 238 and 288.

27 UNHCR, *Refugees by Numbers* (2005 web edition).

28 J. Macrae, 'Aiding Peace ... and War: UNHCR, Returnee Reintegration and the Relief–Development Debate', *New Issues in Refugee Research*, Working Paper No.14, UNHCR, 1999, p. 1.

29 S. Petrin, 'Refugee Return and State Reconstruction: a Comparative Analysis', *New Issues in Refugee Research*, Working Paper No.66, UNHCR, 2002. See also 'Reintegration Challenges for Burundi', *Forced Migration Review*, Issue 21, September 2004, pp. 26–7.

30 M. De Vriese and S. Sperl, 'From Emergency Evacuation to Community Empowerment: Review of the Repatriation and Reintegration Programme in Sierra Leone', Evaluation and Policy Analysis Unit, UNHCR, February 2005, p. 12.

31 UNHCR, *Global Report 2004*, p. 343.

32 UNHCR, *Statistical Yearbook 2003*, p. 54.

33 UNHCR, 'Refugee Children', Report of the Global Consultations on International Protection, 4th Meeting, EC/GC/02/9, 25 April 2002, p. 1.

34 UNHCR, *Statistical Yearbook 2003*, p. 54.

35 UNHCR, *Statistical Yearbook 2002*, p. 58.

36 UNHCR, *Statistical Yearbook 2003*, p. 54.

37 Save the Children, *State of the World's Mothers 2003: Protecting Women and Children in War and Conflict*, May 2003, p. 5.

38 P. Spiegel, 'HIV/AIDS among Conflict-Affected and Displaced Populations: Dispelling Myths and Taking Action', *Disasters*, vol. 28, no. 3, 2004, p. 325.

39 R. Wexler, 'HIV and the Internally Displaced: Burundi in Focus', *Forced Migration Review*, Issue 16, January 2003, pp. 11–13.

40 UNHCR, *Statistical Yearbook 2003*, p. 55.

41 Global IDP Project, *Internal Displacement*, pp. 13 and 15–16.

42 International Organization for Migration, *World Migration Report 2005*, p. 13.

43 M. Bhatia, J. Goodhand with H. Atmar, A. Pain and M. Suleman, 'Profits and Poverty: Aid, Livelihoods and Conflict in Afghanistan', in S. Collinson (ed), *Power, Livelihoods and Conflict*, p. 73.

44 S. Dick, *Responding to Protracted Refugee Situations: A Case Study of Liberian Refugees in Ghana*, Evaluation and Policy Analysis Unit, UNHCR, July 2002, p. 6.

45 International Organization for Migration, *World Migration Report 2005*, p. 94.

46 Ibid., p. 37.

47 Integrated Regional Information Networks (IRIN), *Disaster Reduction and the Human Cost of Disaster*, IRIN Web Special, UN Office of the Coordination of Humanitarian Affairs (OCHA), www.IRINnews.org, June 2005, pp. 3 and 7.

48 Ibid.

49 E. Hedman, 'The Politics of the Tsunami Response', *Forced Migration Review*, Special Issue, July 2005, pp. 4–5.

50 A. Roy, 'The Greater Common Good', in A. Roy (ed), *The Cost of Living*, Flamingo, London, 2000.

51 M. Colchester, *Dams, Indigenous People and Vulnerable Ethnic Minorities*, WCD Thematic Review, Social Issues I.2, prepared as an input to the World Commission on Dams, Cape Town, November 2000, p. 16.

52 C. McDowell, *Understanding Impoverishment: The Consequences of Development-induced Displacement*, Berghahn Books, Providence and Oxford, 1996.

53 C. de Wet, 'Improving Outcomes in Development-Induced Displacement and Resettlement Projects', *Forced Migration Review*, Issue 12, January 2002, pp. 6–12.

54 T. Downing, 'Creating Poverty: the Flawed Economic Logic of the World Bank's Revised Involuntary Resettlement Policy', *Forced Migration Review*, Issue 12, January 2002, pp. 13–14.

55 M. Cernea and C. McDowell, *Risks and Reconstruction: Experiences of Resettlers and Refugees*, World Bank, Washington DC, 2000.

56 S. Castles and N. Van Hear, *Developing DFID's Policy Approach to Refugees and Internally Displaced Persons*, Consultancy Report and Policy Recommendations, Volume 1, Refugee Studies Centre, Oxford, February 2005, p. 14.

Chapter 2

1 UNHCR, *Note on International Protection*, Executive Committee of the High Commissioner's Programme, 55th session, A/AC.96/989, 7 July 2004, para. 11.

2 Amnesty International, *Afghanistan: Continuing Need for the Protection and Standards for Return of Afghan Refugees*, AI Index: ASA 11/014/2002, 25 July 2002.

3 US Committee for Refugees, 'USCR Calls on Rwanda to End Forced Return of Congolese Refugees', Press Release, 26 September 2002; UNHCR, 'Pressure Continues for DR Congolese Refugees in Rwanda to Go Home', News Stories, 20 September 2002.

4 UNHCR, 'Malaysia: UNHCR Extremely Concerned by Deportation of Acehnese', UNHCR Briefing Notes, 5 September 2003; Human Rights Watch, 'Malaysia: Don't Return Indonesian Asylum Seekers', Press Release, 29 August 2003.

5 Amnesty International, 'Panama/Colombia: Border Security Must Not Violate International Refugee Law', Press Release AI Index: AMR 23/034/2003, 28 April 2003.

6 G. S. Goodwin-Gill, 'Article 31 of the 1951 Convention Relating to the Status of Refugees: Non-Penalization, Detention, and Protection', in E. Feller, V. Türk, F. Nicholson (eds) *Refugee Protection in International Law. UNHCR's Global Consultations on International Protection*, Cambridge University Press, Cambridge, 2003, pp. 186–8.

7 UNHCR, *Note on International Protection*, Executive Committee of the High Commissioner's Programme, 52nd session, A/AC.96/951, 13 September 2001, paras. 17–8.

8 UNHCR, *Note on International Protection*, Executive Committee of the High Commissioner's Programme, 53rd session, A/AC.96/965, 11 September 2002, paras. 17–8; *Note on International Protection*, Executive Committee of the High Commissioner's Programme, 54th session, A/AC.96/975, 2 July 2003, paras. 13–4. See also C. Costello, 'The Asylum Procedures and the Proliferation of Safe Country Practices: Deterrence, Deflection and Dismantling of International Protection?', *European Journal of Migration and Law*, vol. 7, no. 1 March 2005, pp. 35–70.

9 'Extraterritorial processing' is not a new idea. It draws upon earlier practices, notably in the United States' use of its naval base in Guantanamo Bay to process Haitian asylum seekers. For further reading see G. Noll, 'Visions of the Exceptional: Legal and Theoretical Issues Raised by Transit Processing Centres and Protection Zones', *European Journal of Migration and Law*, vol. 5, no. 3, November 2003, pp. 303-341.

10 S. Castles, H. Crawley and S. Loughna, *States of Conflict: Causes and Patterns of Forced Migration to the EU and Policy Responses*, Institute of Public Policy Research, London 2003, p. 46.

11 See G. Goodwin-Gill, *The Refugee in International Law*, Clarendon Press, Oxford, 1996, pp. 161–7. See also UNHCR, B*ackground Note on the Protection of Asylum-Seekers and Refugees Rescued at Sea, and UNHCR, Rescue-at- Sea. Specific Aspects Relating to the Protection of Asylum-Seekers and Refugees, Expert Roundtable. Summary of Discussions*, Lisbon 25–26 March 2002.

12 *La vicenda della nave "Cap Anamur" all'esame dei Ministri dell'Interno Pisanu e Schily. Incontro a margine della riunione informale a Sheffield*. Comunicato stampa del 06/07/2004. Available at: http://www.interno.it/.

13 In July 2004, UNHCR raised its concerns at the way the cases had been subsequently handled, and which resulted in the deportation of 25 persons to Ghana and 5 to Nigeria in July, while one person received a temporary residence permit without going through the asylum procedure. UNHCR News Stories, 23 July 2004.

14 UNHCR, 'Conclusion on Protection Safeguards in Interception Measures', Executive Committee 54th Session, Executive Committee Doc No. 97 (LIV) – 2003.

15 UNHCR, *Note on International Protection*, 2004, para. 11.

16 UNHCR, *Note on International Protection*, 2002, paras. 43–5.

17 UNHCR, *Note on International Protection*, Executive Committee of the High Commissioner's Programme, 56th session, A/AC.96/1008, 4 July 2005, para. 18.

18 See UNHCR's *Notes on International Protection* for 2000 to 2005. Also see Amnesty International, *Protection Gaps: Amnesty International's Concerns to UNHCR's Standing Committee*, 8–11 March 2005.

19 UNHCR, *Note on International Protection*, 2003, paras. 4–5.

20 UNHCR, 'Asylum Processes (Fair and Efficient Asylum Procedures)', Document prepared for the 2nd Meeting of the Global Consultations on International Protection, Doc EC/GC/01/12, 31 May 2001.

21 M. A. Kate, 'The Provision of Protection to Asylum Seekers in Destination Countries', *New Issues in Refugee Research*, Working Paper No. 114, UNHCR, Geneva, May 2005, pp. 1–2.

22 R. Lubbers, UN High Commissioner for Refugees, 'Talking Points for the Informal Justice and Home Affairs Council', Luxembourg, 29 January 2005.

23 UNHCR, *Note on International Protection*, 2001, paras. 38–40.

24 J. Crisp, 'No Solution in Sight: The Problem of Protracted Refugee Situations in Africa', *New Issues in Refugee Research*, Working Paper no. 75, Geneva: UNHCR, 2003, pp. 11–2.

25 The outcomes of the 'second track' are published in E. Feller, V. Türk, F. Nicholson (eds) *Refugee Protection in International Law. UNHCR's Global Consultations on International Protection*, Cambridge University Press, Cambridge, 2003.

26 The papers produced within the 'third track' are published in *Refugee Survey Quarterly*, vol. 22, no. 2/3, October 2003.

27 Adopted on 13 December 2001 in Geneva at the Ministerial Meeting of States Parties to the 1951 Convention and/or its 1967 Protocol relating to the Status of Refugees, UNHCR Doc. HCR/MMSP/2001/09 16 January 2002.

28 UNHCR, *Agenda for Protection*, UN Doc. A/AC.96/965/Add.1, 26 June 2002.

29 Memorandum of Understanding between the African Commission on Human and Peoples' Rights and the United Nations High Commissioner for Refugees, published in the *Sixteenth Annual Activity Report of the African Commission on Human and Peoples' Rights 2002–2003*, Annex IV, pp. 25–9.

30 UNHCR, ICRC, APU, and IPU, *Refugees in Africa: The Challenges of Protection and Solutions*, 2004, p. 1–23.

31 Mexico Declaration and Plan of Action to Strengthen the International Protection of Refugees in Latin America, Mexico City, 16 November 2004.

32 UNHCR, *The State of the World's Refugees. Fifty Years of Humanitarian Action*, Oxford University Press, Oxford, 2000, pp. 155-183.

33 UN Security Council Resolution, UN Doc. S/RES/1373 (2001), 28 September 2001, paras. (f) and (g).

34 Similar language can be found in later resolutions, most recently UN Security Council Resolution 1566 (2004), of 8 October 2004 and the General Assembly Resolution 59/195 of 22 March 2005.

35 V. Türk, 'Forced Migration and Security', *International Journal of Refugee Law*, vol. 15, no. 1, January 2003, pp. 115–6.

36 G. Gilbert, 'Current Issues in the Application of the Exclusion Clauses', in E. Feller et al. (eds) *Refugee Protection in International Law*, 2003, p. 428.

37 See for instance, S. Grey, 'United States: Trade in Torture', *Le Monde Diplomatique*, April 2005; Amnesty International, USA: *Human dignity denied: Torture and accountability in the 'war on terror'*, AMR 51/145/2004, 27 October 2004, pp. 181-190; Amnesty International, *USA/Jordan/Yemen. Torture and secret detention: Testimony of the 'disappeared' in the 'war on terror'*, AMR 51/108/2005, 4 August 2005.

38 European Commission, *Commission Working Document. The Relationship between Safeguarding Internal Security and Complying with International Protection Obligations and Instruments*, COM(2001) 743 final, of 5 December 2001, para. 2.3.1; and C. Dyer, 'Ministers Seek to Overturn Torture Rule in Deportations', *The Guardian*, 3 October 2005.

39 Global Commission on International Migration, *Migration in an Interconnected World: New Directions for Action*, Global Commission on International Migration, Geneva, October 2005, p. 40.

40 Ibid., p. 7.

41 Ibid., p. 33.

42 UNHCR, *Asylum Levels and Trends in Industrialized Countries 2004*, 1 March 2005, pp. 3-4.

43 Global Commission on International Migration, *Migration in an Interconnected World: New Directions for Action*, 2005, p. 41.

44 See Preamble and Recommendation D to the 1951 UN Refugee Convention.

45 Letter from the UK Government to the Greek Presidency of the EU, 10 March 2003. Available at: http://www.statewatch.org/news/2003/apr/blair-simitis-asil e.pdf. This proposal constitutes a revised version of the one presented at the European Conference on Asylum that discussed ways to develop a common asylum procedure and a uniform status valid throughout the European Union, held in Lisbon in June 2000 under the auspices of the Portuguese Presidency of the European Union and the European Commission. J. Straw, *'Towards a Common Asylum Procedure'*, in *Towards a Common European Asylum System. European Conference on Asylum*. Lisbon: Serviço de Estrangeiros e Fronteiras, 2000, pp 133–9.

46 Amnesty International, *UK/EU/UNHCR Unlawful and Unworkable – Amnesty International's views on proposals for extraterritorial processing of asylum claims*, IOR 61/004/2003, 18 June 2003.

47 A. Betts, 'The International Relations of the "New" Extraterritorial Approaches to Refugee Protection: Explaining the Policy Initiatives of the UK Government and UNHCR', *Refuge*, vol. 22, no. 1, March 2004, p. 61.

48 Commission of the European Communities, *Communication from the Commission to the Council and the European Parliament: Towards more Accessible, Equitable and Managed asylum Systems*, COM(2003) 315 final, of 3 June 2003, p. 13.

49 Commission of the European Communities, *Communication from the Commission to the Council and the European Parliament on the Managed Entry in the EU of Persons in Need of International Protection and the Enhancement of the Protection Capacity of the Regions of Origin 'Improving' access to Durable Solutions*, COM(2004) 410 final, of 4 June 2004, para. 8.

50 Commission of the European Communities, *Communication from the Commission to the Council and the European Parliament on Regional Protection Programmes*, COM(2005) 388 final, of 1 September 2005, para. 5.

51 The state of activities for each country, as well as the gaps analysis reports can be found in UNHCR's website: http://www.unhcr.ch/.

52 UNHCR, *The Strengthening Protection Capacity (SPC) Project. Summary of Activities*, 31 August 2005.

53 UNHCR, *2004 Global Refugee Trends*, Geneva, 20 June 2005, pp. 2–5.

Chapter 3

1 N. Van Hear, 'Recasting Societies in Conflict', COMPAS Working Paper No. 22, University of Oxford, Oxford, 2005, pp. 1-5.

2 G. Loescher, 'Refugees as Grounds for International Action', in E. Newman and J. van Selm (eds), *Refugees and Forced Displacement: International Security, Human Vulnerability, and the State*, United Nations University Press, Tokyo, 2003, pp. 31-6.

3 H. Arendt, *The Origins of Totalitarianism*, Meridian, New York, 1957, p. 288.

4 G. Loescher, *The UNHCR and World Politics: A Perilous Path*, Oxford University Press, Oxford, 2001, p. 125; J. Crisp, 'Africa's Refugees: Patterns, Problems and Policy Challenges', *New Issues in Refugee Research*, Working Paper No. 28, UNHCR, Geneva, 2000, p. 9.

5 B. Posen, 'Military Responses to Refugee Disasters', *International Security*, vol. 21, no. 1, 1996, pp. 72-111; M. Weiner, 'Bad Neighbors, Bad Neighborhoods:

An Inquiry into the Causes of Refugee Flows',
International Security, vol. 21, no. 1, 1996, pp. 5-42.

6 V. Türk, 'Forced Migration and Security', *International Journal of Refugee Law*, vol. 15, no. 1, 2003, p. 117.

7 See Ministry of Foreign Affairs of Japan, 'Efforts to Tackle Various Global Issues to Promote Human Security', *Japan's Foreign Policy in Major Diplomatic Fields, 2004*, p. 184, www.mofa.go.jp/policy/human_secu/index.html; see also Canada's Human Security Website, Foreign Affairs Canada, www.humansecurity.gc.ca/menu-en.asp.

8 Commission on Human Security, *Human Security Now*, New York, 2003, pp. 49-50.

9 Ibid.

10 T. G. Weiss, *Military-Civilian Interactions: Humanitarian Crises and the Responsibility to Protect*, Rowman and Littlefield, Lanham, Maryland, 2005, pp. 137-8.

11 G. Goodwin-Gill, 'Editorial: Refugees and Security', *International Journal of Refugee Law*, vol. 11, no. 1, 1999, p. 3; G. Loescher, 'Refugees as Grounds for International Action', pp. 39-40.

12 A. Hammerstad, 'Making or Breaking the Conflict Cycle: The Relationship between Underdevelopment, Conflict and Forced Migration', in S. Castles and N. Van Hear, *Developing DFID's Policy Approach to Refugees and Internally Displaced Persons*, Final Report, University of Oxford, Oxford, 2005, pp. 14-18.

13 H. Adelman, 'The Use and Abuse of Refugees in Zaire', in S. J. Stedman and F. Tanner (eds), *Refugee Manipulations: War, Politics, and the Abuse of Human Suffering*, Brookings Institution Press, Washington DC, 2003, pp. 95-134.

14 G. Loescher, 'Refugees as Grounds for International Action', p. 35.

15 Ibid., p. 34.

16 United Nations, 'Recent Killings of Humanitarian Workers Demonstrate Changing Landscape for UN Operations, Security Council Told by Humanitarian Affairs Head: Briefs on Challenges Faced in Protecting Civilians in Conflict Areas', Security Council 4877th meeting, UN Doc. Press Release SC/7947, 9 December 2003.

17 S. Ogata, *The Turbulent Decade: Confronting the Refugee Crises of the 1990s*, W. W. Norton, New York, 2005, p. 327.

18 J. Crisp, 'A State of Insecurity: The Political Economy of Violence in Refugee-Populated Areas of Kenya', *New Issues in Refugee Research*, Working Paper No. 16, UNHCR, Geneva, 1999, p. 13, footnote 36.

19 United Nations, Resolution 1208 adopted by the Security Council at its 3954th meeting on 19 November 1998, UN Doc. S/RES/1208 (1998), 19 November 1998; United Nations, Resolution 1296 adopted by the Security Council at its 4130th meeting on 19 April 2000, UN Doc. S/RES/1296 (2000), 19 April 2000.

20 UNHCR, Regional Symposium on Maintaining the Civilian and Humanitarian Character of Asylum, Refugee Status and other Locations, Pretoria, Southern Africa, 26-27 February, 2001, p. 2, www.unhcr.ch/cgi-bin/texis/vtx/global-consultations.

21 UNHCR, 'The Security, and Civilian and Humanitarian Character of Refugee Camps and Settlements', Executive Committee Doc, EC/49/SC/INF.2, 14 January 1999, pp. 2-4; UNHCR, 'The Security, Civilian and Humanitarian Character of Refugee Camps and Settlements: Operationalizing the "Ladder of Options",' in *Refugee Survey Quarterly*, vol.19, no. 1, 2000, pp. 93-8.

22 W. Lewis, E. Marks and R. Perito, 'Enhancing International Civilian Police in Peace Operations', Special Report 85, US Institute of Peace, April 22, 2002, p. 3.

23 UNHCR, 2004 Annual Protection Report: Nepal, p. 2.

24 R. da Costa, 'Maintaining the Civilian and Humanitarian Character of Asylum', Legal and Protection Policy Research Series, Department of International Protection, UNHCR, June 2004, p. 63.

25 Ibid, p. 54.

26 V. Türk, 'Forced Migration and Security', pp. 115-6.

27 J-F. Durieux, 'Preserving the Civilian Character of Refugee Camps: Lessons from the Kigoma Programme in Tanzania', *Track Two*, vol. 9, no. 3, November 2000.

28 UNHCR, 2005 Country Operations Report: Kenya.

29 UNHCR, *Handbook for Emergencies*, Second Edition, 2000, p. 137.

30 UNHCR, 'Hot Spots Brief on Guinea', July 17, 2003.

31 UNHCR, 2004 Annual Protection Report: Panama, p. 12.

32 Commission on Human Security, *Human Security Now*, pp. 124-5.

33 Ibid., pp. 1-12.

Chapter 3 boxes

i The overall death toll recorded by the study was 375, which included UN peacekeepers (88 cases) as well as deaths due to disease and natural causes (31). See Mani Sheik et al., 'Deaths among Humanitarian Workers', *British Medical Journal*, no. 321, July 2000, pp. 166-8.

ii ECHO, *Report on Security of Humanitarian Personnel*, Brussels, 2004, www.europa.eu.int/comm/echo/other_files/security/echo_security_ report_en.doc.

iii Centre for Humanitarian Dialogue (CHD), *No Relief*, Geneva, 2005, www.hdcentre.org.

iv Ibid.

v D. King, 'Chronology of Humanitarian Aid Workers Killed in 1997-2003', 15 January 2004, www.vranet.com/Govt1027/Docs/chron1997-2003.html.

vi M. Sheik et al., 'Deaths among Humanitarian Workers'.

vii D. King, 'Chronology of Humanitarian Aid Workers'; CHD, *No Relief*.

Chapter 4

1 UNHCR, 'Strengthening UNHCR's Emergency Response Capacity', UNHCR Policy Paper, July 2005, p. 3.

2 UNHCR, *The State of the World's Refugees: Fifty Years of Humanitarian Action*, Oxford University Press, Oxford, 2000, p. 5.

3 Ibid., p. 37.

4 Ibid., p. 7.

5 G. Loescher, *The UNHCR and World Politics: A Perilous Path*, Oxford University Press, Oxford, 2001, p. 13.

6 J. Eriksson with contributions by H. Adelman, J. Borton, H. Christensen, K. Kumar, A. Suhrke, D. Tardif-Douglin, S. Villumstad and L. Wohlgemuth, *The International Response to Conflict and Genocide: Lessons from the Rwanda Experience, Synthesis Report*, Joint Evaluation of Emergency Assistance to Rwanda, Copenhagen, 1996, p. 52.

7 Fritz Institute, 'Logistics and the Effective Delivery of Humanitarian Relief', San Francisco, 2005, p. 9.

8 UNHCR, 'Strengthening UNHCR's Emergency Response Capacity', p. 7.

9 Ibid., p. 5.

10 Ibid.

11 United Nations, *Strengthening of the Coordination of Humanitarian Assistance of the United Nations*, General Assembly Economic and Social Council, UN Doc. A/60/87-E/2005/78, 23 June 2005, p. 6.

12 A. Suhrke, M. Barutciski, R. Garlock and P. Sandison, 'The Kosovo Refugee Crisis: An Independent Evaluation of UNHCR's Emergency Preparedness and Response', Evaluation and Policy Analysis Unit, UNHCR, Geneva, 2000, p. x.

13 G. Loescher, *The UNHCR and World Politics*, p. 14.

14 UNHCR, 'Strengthening UNHCR's Emergency Response Capacity', p. 6.

15 S. Vieira de Mello, 'Empowerment, Responsibility and Accountability', in Inter-Agency Standing Committee, *Humanitarian Action in the Twenty First Century*, Inter-Agency Standing Committee, New York, 2000, p. 11.

16 G. Dunkley, M. Kunieda and A. Tokuri, 'The Tokyo eCentre and Jakarta Partnership: Evaluation of UNHCR's Contribution to Emergency Preparedness, Contingency Planning and Disaster Management in the Asia Pacific region (2000-2003)', Evaluation and Policy Analysis Unit, UNHCR, Geneva, 2004, pp. 7-8, 46-7.

17 E. Lauterpacht and D. Bethlehem, 'The Scope and Content of the Principle of Non-Refoulement: Opinion', in E. Feller, V. Türk and F. Nicholson (eds), *Refugee Protection in International Law*, Cambridge University Press, Cambridge, 2003, pp. 89-93.

18 J. Crisp and E. Stigter, 'Real-Time Evaluation of UNHCR's Response to the Afghanistan Emergency', UNHCR, Evaluation and Policy Analysis Unit, Bulletin no. 2, 2001, p. 3.

19 UNHCR, *The State of the World's Refugees: Fifty Years of Humanitarian Action*, p. 239.

20 Fritz Institute, 'Logistics and the Effective Delivery of Humanitarian Relief', p. 3.

21 UNHCR, 'Lessons Learned from the Rwanda and Burundi Emergencies', UNHCR Evaluation Report, December 1996, para. 10.

22 Fritz Institute, 'Logistics and the Effective Delivery of Humanitarian Relief', pp. 2 and 8.

23 L. Gustavsson, 'Humanitarian Logistics: Context and Challenges', *Forced Migration Review*, Issue 18, September 2003, pp. 6-7.

24 D. Bartsch and N. Belgacem, 'Real-Time Evaluation of UNHCR's Response to the Emergency in Chad', Evaluation and Policy Analysis Unit, UNHCR, Geneva, 2004, p. 13.

25 Ibid.

26 L. Gustavsson, 'Humanitarian Logistics: Context and Challenges', pp. 6-7.

27 D. Bartsch and N. Belgacem, 'Real-time Evaluation of UNHCR's Response to the Emergency in Chad', pp. 3 and 7.

28 A. Jamal, 'The Sudan/Eritrea Emergency, May-July 2000: An Evaluation of UNHCR's Response', Evaluation and Policy Analysis Unit, UNHCR, February 2001, p. 6.

29 J. Borton, M. Buchanan-Smith and R. Otto, 'Support to Internally Displaced Persons: Learning from Previous Experience', Swedish International Development Agency, 1 May 2005, p. 16.

30 G. Loescher, *The UNHCR and World Politics*, p. 15; J. Borton et al., 'Support to Internally Displaced Persons: Learning from Previous Experience', pp. 12-3.

31 United Nations, *Strengthening of the Coordination of Humanitarian Assistance of the United Nations*, p. 4.

32 E. Schenkenberg van Mierop, 'Improving the Quality of Humanitarian Response', in *Response Strategies of the Internally Displaced: Changing the Humanitarian Lens*, Seminar Proceedings, Norwegian Refugee Council, Oslo, 9 November 2001, p. 27; H. Slim, *Not Philanthropy but Rights: Rights-Based Humanitarianism and the Proper Politicisation of Humanitarian Philosophy in War*, Oxford Brookes University, Oxford, 2001, p. 3.

33 V. Guarnieri, 'Food Aid and Livelihoods: Challenges and Opportunities in Complex Emergencies', *Forced Migration Review*, Issue 20, May 2004, pp. 15-18.

34 J. Ward, 'If Not Now, When? Addressing Gender-Based Violence in Refugee, Internally Displaced and Post-Conflict Settings: A Global Overview', Reproductive Health for Refugees Consortium, New York, 2002, p. 15.

35 World Food Program, 'Reaching People in Situations of Displacement: Framework for Action', Executive Board Annual Session 2001, Agenda Item 4 (WFP/EB.A/2001/4-C), Rome, p. 6.

36 C. Linnér, 'Introduction', *Refugee Survey Quarterly*, vol. 23 no. 2, 2004, pp. 1-6. This edition is entirely focused on refugee children.

37 S. Collinson, 'Lessons Learned from Specific Emergency Situations: A Synthesis,' in *Developing DFID's Policy Approach to Refugees and Internally Displaced Persons*, Volume II, February 2005, p. 22.

38 A. Harmer and J. Macrae, 'Humanitarian Action and the "Global War on Terror": A Review of Trends and Issues', HPG Briefing Paper, no. 9, Overseas Development Institute, London, July 2003, p. 4.

39 J. Macrae and N. Leader, 'Shifting Sands: The Search for "Coherence" between Political and Humanitarian Responses to Complex Emergencies,' HPG Report 8, Overseas Development Institute, London, August 2000, p. 4.

40 Ibid.

41 J. Macrae and N. Leader, 'The Politics of Coherence: Humanitarianism and Foreign Policy in the Post-Cold War Era,' HPG Briefing, no. 1, Overseas Development Institute, London, July 2000, p. 5.

42 A. Suhrke et al., 'The Kosovo Refugee Crisis', p. x.

43 A. Donini, L. Minear and P. Walker, 'The Future of Humanitarian Action: Mapping the Implications of Iraq and Other Recent Crises', *Disasters*, vol. 28, no. 2, 2004, pp. 260-72.

44 OCHA Business Contributions to the UN Emergency Relief Efforts: An Orientation Guide. ochaonline2.un.org/OCHAonline/ochabusinessguid/Impact ofCrises/tabid/296/Default.aspx 14/10/2005.

45 J. Borton et al., 'Support to Internally Displaced Persons', pp. 17-18.

46 For example, in 2000 the Sphere Project published a handbook, *The Humanitarian Charter and Minimum Standards in Disaster Response*, which was revised in 2004.

47 G. Frerks and D. Hilhorst, 'Evaluation of Humanitarian Assistance in Emergency Situations', Working Paper No. 56, Evaluation and Policy Analysis Unit, UNHCR, Geneva, 2002, pp. 4-5.

48 United Nations, 'Humanitarian Response Review', an independent report commissioned by the Office of the Coordination of Humanitarian Affairs (OCHA), New York and Geneva, 2005, p. 9.

49 C. Buchanan and R. Muggah, 'No Relief: Surveying the Effects of Gun Violence on Humanitarian and Development Personnel', Centre for Humanitarian Dialogue, Geneva, 2005, pp. 7-9.

50 Ibid.

Chapter 5

1 G. van Heuven Goedhart, 'Refugee Problems and Their Solutions', Geneva, UNHCR, 1955, cited in G. Loescher, *The UNHCR in World Politics: A Perilous Path*, Oxford: Oxford University Press, 2001, p. 75.

2 Ibid., p. 62.

3 UNHCR, 'Protracted Refugee Situations', Executive Committee of the High Commissioner's Programme, Standing Committee, 30th Meeting, UN Doc. EC/54/SC/CRP.14, 10 June 2004, p. 2.

4 Ibid., p. 1.

5 Ibid., p. 2.

6 Ibid.

7 Ibid., p. 1.

8 For example, in 1999 it was reported that UNHCR spent about US$0.11 per refugee per day in Africa, compared to an average of US$1.23 per refugee per day in the Balkans. See: G. Loescher, *The UNHCR in World Politics*, p. 322; J. Vidal, 'Blacks Need, but Only Whites Receive: Race Appears to Be Skewing the West's Approach to Aid', *The Guardian (UK)*, 12 August 1999.

9 See US Committee for Refugees and Immigrants, *World Refugee Survey 2005*, Washington DC, US Committee for Refugees and Immigrants, 2005, p. 13.

10 See M. Smith, 'Warehousing Refugees: A Denial of Rights, a Waste of Humanity', *World Refugee Survey 2004*, Washington, US Committee for Refugees, 2004.

11 UNHCR, 'Addressing Protracted Refugee Situations', Paper prepared for the Informal Consultations on New Approaches and Partnerships for Protection and Solutions in Africa, Geneva, December 2001, p. 1.

12 UNHCR, 'Protracted Refugee Situations', p. 3.

13 Ibid.

14 Ibid.

15 See: K. Jacobsen, 'Can Refugees Benefit the State? Refugee Resources and African State-Building', *Journal of Modern African Studies*, vol. 40, no. 4, 2002.

16 UNHCR, 'Economic and Social Impact of Massive Refugee Populations on Host Developing Countries, as well as Other Countries', UN Doc. EC/54/SC/CRP.5, Geneva, 18 February 2004, para. 12, p. 3.

17 For a more detailed consideration of the political and security implications of protracted refugee situations, see G. Loescher and J. Milner, *Protracted Refugee Situations: Domestic and International Security Implications*, Adelphi Paper no. 375, Routledge, London, 2005.

18 UNHCR, *The State of the World's Refugees: Fifty Years of Humanitarian Action*, Oxford University Press, Oxford, 2000, p. 49.

19 See: M. Ayoob, *The Third World Security Predicament: State Making, Regional Conflict and the International*

System, Lynne Rienner Publishers, Boulder CO, 1995;
B. Job (ed), *The Insecurity Dilemma: National Security of Third World States*, Lynne Rienner Publishers, Boulder CO, 1992.

20 Y. Zarjevski, *A Future Preserved: International Assistance to Refugees*, Pergamon Press for the Office of the United Nations High Commissioner for Refugees, Oxford, 1988, pp. 88–90; G. Loescher, *The UNHCR and World Politics*, pp. 89–91.

21 Statement by the UN High Commissioner for Refugees at Meeting of American Immigration Conference, 28 October 1958, UNHCR Archives HCR/1/7/5/USA/CAN.

22 UNHCR, *State of the World's Refugees*, 2000, p. 84.

23 See UNHCR, 'International Conference on Indo-Chinese Refugees: Report of the Secretary-General [Annex: Declaration and Comprehensive Plan of Action (CPA)],' 1989.

24 See S. Bari, 'Refugee Status Determination under the Comprehensive Plan of Action (CPA): A Personal Assessment', *International Journal of Refugee Law*, vol. 4, no. 4, 1992; W. Courtland Robinson, *Terms of Refuge: The Indochinese Exodus and the International Response*, Zed Books, London, 1998; A. Suhrke, 'Burden Sharing during Refugee Emergencies: The Logic of Collective versus National Action', *Journal of Refugee Studies*, vol. 11, no. 4, 1998.

25 UNHCR, 'International Conference on Central American Refugees: Report to the Secretary-General', 1989, and UNHCR, 'Comprehensive and Regional Approaches to Refugee Problems', EC/1994/SCP/CRP.3, 3 May 1994.

26 UNHCR, *Agenda for Protection,* Preamble, Goal 5.

27 The Refugee Policy Group in Washington, DC produced reports on protracted refuge settlements in Africa outlining many of the problems confronting long-staying refugees at that time. T. Betts, R. Chambers and A. Hansen, among others, conducted research on some of these groups in Africa and assessed the international community's policy responses, particularly programmes aimed at promoting local integration. See: Refugee Policy Group, 'Older Refugee Settlements in Africa', Washington DC, 1985.

28 A. Jamal, 'Minimum Standards and Essential Needs in a Protracted Refugee Situation: A Review of the UNHCR Programme in Kakuma, Kenya', Evaluation and Policy Analysis Unit, UNHCR, EPAU/2000/05, 2001.

29 T. Kaiser, 'A Beneficiary-Based Evaluation of UNHCR's Programme in Guinea, West Africa', Evaluation and Policy Analysis Unit, UNHCR, EPAU/2001/02, 2001.

30 T. Kuhlman, 'Responding to Protracted Refugee Situations: A Case Study of Liberian Refugees in Côte d'Ivoire', Evalution and Policy Analysis Unit, UNHCR, EPAU/2002/07, 2002.

31 S. Dick, 'Responding to Protracted Refugee Situations: A Case study of Liberian Refugees in Ghana', Evaluation and Policy Analysis Unit, UNHCR, EPAU/2002/06, 2002.

32 J. Crisp, 'No Solution in Sight: The Problem of Protracted Refugee Situations in Africa', *New Issues in Refugee Research*, Working Paper No. 75, UNHCR, 2003.

33 Ibid., p. 26.

34 See UNHCR, 'Addressing Protracted Refugee Situations'.

35 UNHCR, 'Discussion Paper on Protracted Refugee Situations in the African Region', Background paper prepared for the 52nd Session of UNHCR's Executive Committee, October 2001, p. 1.

36 See UNHCR, 'Chairman's Summary: Informal Consultations on New Approaches and Partnerships for Protection and Solutions in Africa', Geneva, December 2001. For a consideration of the historical and political context of protracted refugee situations in Africa, see: G. Loescher and J. Milner, 'The Long Road Home: Protracted Refugee Situations in Africa', *Survival*, vol. 47, no. 2, Summer 2005.

37 UNHCR, 'Protracted Refugee Situations'.

38 UNHCR, 'Making Comprehensive Approaches to Resolving Refugee Problems More Systematic', Paper prepared for the High Commissioner's Forum, FORUM/2004/7, 16 September 2004.

39 See UNHCR 'Chairman's Summary', High Commissioner's Forum, 12 March 2004.

40 United Nations, 'World Leaders Pledge Wide-Ranging Steps on Poverty, Terrorism, Human Rights', Press release, Department of Public Information, UN Doc. GA/10385, 16 September 2005.

Chapter 6

1 R. Lubbers, High Commissioner for Refugees, Statement to the European Conference on Migration, Brussels, 2001.

2 J. Crisp, 'No Solutions in Sight? The Problem of Protracted Refugee Situations in Africa', *New Issues in Refugee Research*, Working Paper No. 75, UNHCR, Geneva, 2003.

3 M. Smith, 'Warehousing Refugees: A Denial of Rights, a Waste of Humanity', *World Refugee Survey*, 2004, pp. 40–1.

4 A. Helton, *The Price of Indifference*, Oxford University Press, Oxford, 2002, pp. 154–62.

5 UNHCR, 'Protracted Refugee Situations', Executive Committee of the High Commissioner's Programme, Standing Committee, 30th Meeting, UN Doc. EC/54/SC/CRP.14, 10 June 2004.

6 R. Black and K. Koser, 'The End of the Refugee Cycle?' in R. Black, K. Koser (eds), *The End of the Refugee*

Cycle? Refugee Repatriation and Reconstruction,
Berghahn Books, Oxford, 1999.

7   Statute of the Office of the United Nations High
Commissioner for Refugees, Chapter 1, para. 1, General
Assembly Resolution 428, December 1950.

8   B. S. Chimni, 'From Resettlement to Involuntary
Repatriation: Towards a Critical History of Durable
Solutions to Refugee Problems', *New Issues in Refugee
Research*, Working Paper No. 2, UNHCR, Geneva, 1999.

9   J. Milner, 'The Politics of Asylum in Africa: The Cases
of Kenya, Tanzania and Guinea', Paper presented at the
Refugee Studies Centre, Oxford, 9 March 2005,
unpublished manuscript.

10 G. Loescher, *The UNHCR and World Politics: A Perilous
Path*, Oxford University Press, Oxford, 2001.

11 UNHCR, *Framework for Durable Solutions for Refugees
and Persons of Concern*, UNHCR, Geneva, 2003.

12 UNHCR, 'Conclusion on Legal Safety Issues in the
Context of Voluntary Repatriation of Refugees',
Executive Committee Conclusion No. 101 (LV)–2004,
8 October 2004.

13 S. Castles and N. Van Hear, *Developing DFID's Policy
Approach To Refugees and Internally Displaced Persons*,
Final Report, Refugee Studies Centre, Oxford, 2005.

14 B. Lippman, 'The 4Rs: The Way Ahead?'
Forced Migration Review, Issue 21, 2004, pp. 9–11.

15 UNHCR, 'Repatriation and Reintegration Operations in
Liberia', UNHCR, Geneva, 2004.

16 UNHCR, *Framework for Durable Solutions for Refugees
and Persons of Concern*.

17 F. Stepputat, 'Refugees, Security and Development',
Working Paper no. 2004/11, Danish Institute for
International Studies, Copenhagen, 2004.

18 O. Bakewell, 'Repatriation and Self-Settled Refugees in
Zambia: Bringing Solutions to the Wrong Problems',
Journal of Refugee Studies, vol. 13, no. 4, 2000,
pp. 356–73.

19 A. Betts, 'International Cooperation and Targeting
Development Assistance for Refugee Solutions: Lessons
from the 1980s', *New Issues in Refugee Research*,
Working Paper No.107, UNHCR, Geneva, 2004.

20 UNHCR, 'In Pursuit of Sustainable Solutions for
Refugees in Zambia', UNHCR, Geneva, 2004.

21 UNHCR, 'Serbia and Montenegro: Development through
Local Integration', RLSS/DOS Mission Report 2004/10,
Geneva, 2004.

22 UNHCR, 'Report of the Mid-Term Review: Self-Reliance
Strategy for Refugee Hosting Areas in Moyo, Arua and
Adjumani Districts, Uganda', RLSS Mission Report
2004/03, Geneva, 2004.

23 UNHCR, 'Progress Report: Convention Plus', 3rd
Convention Plus Forum, FORUM/2004/5, 16/09/04,
www.unhcr.ch.

24 UNHCR, 'Conclusion on International Cooperation and
Burden and Responsibility Sharing in Mass Influx
Situations', Executive Committee Conclusion No. 100
(LV)–2004, 8 October 2004.

25 UNHCR, 'Convention Plus: Issues Paper on Targeting of
Development Assistance', Annex II, 2004, pp 13–15.

26 UNHCR, 'Putting Refugees on the Development Agenda:
How Refugees and Returnees Can Contribute to
Achieving the Millennium Development Goals',
FORUM/2005/4, 2005.

27 United Nations, 'Report of the International Conference
on Financing for Development', A/Conf.198/11,
www.un.org, 2002.

28 United Nations General Assembly, 'Strengthening the
Capacity of the Office of the United Nations High
Commissioner for Refugees to Carry out its Mandate',
58th Session, Agenda item 112, A/58/410, 2003.

29 United Nations Development Group, 'UNDG Guidance
Note on Durable Solutions for Displaced Persons',
UNDG: New York, www.undg.org, 2004.

30 UNHCR, 'Poverty Reduction Strategy Papers:
A Displacement Perspective', UNHCR, Geneva,
www.unhcr.ch, 2004.

31 Swiss Migration Forum, 'Movements of Somali Refugees
and Asylum Seekers and States' Responses thereto',
presented at Convention Plus Forum, Geneva, 2005.
On file with the author.

32 UNHCR, 'Basic Propositions on Irregular Secondary
Movements', para. 7, 2004.

33 UNHCR, 'Convention Plus Issues Paper on Addressing
Irregular Secondary Movements of Refugees and Asylum
Seekers', FORUM/CG/SM/03, para. 15, www.unhcr.ch,
2004.

34 UNHCR, 'The Strengthening Protection Capacity Project:
Project Description', www.unhcr.ch, 2004.

35 United Nations Press Release, 'Secretary-General
Stresses Clear Need for International Cooperation on
Refugee, Migration Policy', Doc SG/SM/8522, 22 Nov.
2002.

36 J. van Selm, 'The Strategic Use of Resettlement',
Refuge, vol. 22, no. 1, 2004, p. 40.

37 J. Milner, 'Resettlement', in M. Gibney and R. Hansen
(eds), *Immigration and Asylum: From 1900 to the
Present*, ABC-Clio, Santa Barbara, 2005.

38 J. Milner, 'Recent Developments in International
Resettlement Policy: Implications for the UK
Programme', in V. Gelthorpe and L. Herlitz (eds),
*Listening to the Evidence: the Future of UK
Resettlement*, Home Office, London, 2003.

39 UNHCR, 'Convention Plus: Framework of
Understandings on Resettlement', FORUM/CG/RES/04,
www.unhcr.ch, 2003.

40 UNHCR, *Resettlement Handbook*, UNHCR, Geneva,
Chapter 7, www.unhcr.ch, 2004.

41 The 1951 Convention relating to the Status of Refugees, Preamble, para. 4.

42 A. Betts, 'International Cooperation between North and South to Enhance Refugee Protection in Regions of Origin', Working Paper No. 25, Refugee Studies Centre, Oxford, 2005, pp. 40–63.

43 A. Suhrke, 'Burden-Sharing during Refugee Emergencies: The Logic of Collective Action versus National Action', Journal of Refugee Studies, vol. 11, no. 4, 1998, pp. 396–415.

44 A. Betts, 'Public Goods Theory and the Provision of Refugee Protection: The role of the Joint-Product Model in Burden-Sharing Theory', Journal of Refugee Studies, vol. 16, no. 3, 2003, pp. 290–1.

45 UNHCR, 'Briefing Note on UNHCR New York for the High-Commissioner-elect', on file with the author, 2005.

46 Betts, 'International Cooperation between North and South', pp. 50–3.

47 UNHCR, 'Making Comprehensive Approaches to Resolving Problems More Systematically', 3rd Convention Plus Forum, FORUM/2004/7, 16/09/04, www.unhcr.ch.

Chapter 7

1 See the database of the Global IDP Project of the Norwegian Refugee Council (www.IDPProject.org) and the World Refugee Survey of the US Committee for Refugees and Immigrants.

2 W. C. Robinson, Risks and Rights: the Causes, Consequences and Challenges of Development-Induced Displacement, Brookings-SAIS Project on Internal Displacement, May 2003.

3 See www.IDPProject.org. The figures are largely 'guesstimates'. They include both people who are in a state of vulnerability and need international attention and those who may be well integrated, even well-off, in their countries, but who cannot return to the areas of the country from which they originally came and where they have property claims. These figures may also include children and grandchildren of originally displaced persons. Criteria for deciding when displacement ends are currently being developed by the Representative of the Secretary-General on the Human Rights of Internally Displaced Persons in response to a request from the Emergency Relief Coordinator.

4 J. Borton, M. Buchanan-Smith and R. Otto, Support to Internally Displaced Persons – Learning from Evaluations, Swedish International Development Cooperation Agency, 2005, pp. 14–15.

5 J-D. Tauxe, 'We Should Have Humanitarian Access to Displaced Civilians,' International Herald Tribune, 1 March 2000. For a full discussion of internally displaced persons as a special category, see E. Mooney,

'The Concept of Internal Displacement and the Case for Internally Displaced Persons as a Category of Concern,' Refugee Survey Quarterly, September 2005.

6 R. Cohen and F. M. Deng, Masses in Flight: the Global Crisis of Internal Displacement, Brookings Institution, 1998, pp. 2, 27.

7 'HIV Prevalence among IDPs Stands at 35 Percent', The Monitor, Africa News, 30 June, 2005.

8 S. B. Holtzman and T. Nezam, Living in Limbo, The World Bank, 2004.

9 R. Cohen and F. M. Deng, Masses in Flight, p. 275.

10 D. A. Korn, Exodus within Borders, Brookings Institution, 1999, p. 49.

11 Office for the Coordination of Humanitarian Affairs, Internal Displacement Unit, No Refuge: The Challenge of Internal Displacement, United Nations, 2003, pp. 68–9.

12 United Nations General Assembly, 2005 World Summit Outcome Resolution A/RES/60/1, 15 September 2005, para. 139.

13 Addressing Internal Displacement: A Framework for National Responsibility, Brookings Institution–University of Bern Project on Internal Displacement, April 2005.

14 Report of the Expert Group Meeting on Internal Displacement in the Commonwealth: Common Themes and Best Practice Guidelines, Commonwealth Secretariat, 12–21 May 2003.

15 Office for the Coordination of Humanitarian Affairs, No Refuge: The Challenge of Internal Displacement, pp. 64–7.

16 See UN Commission on Human Rights Resolution 2003/51, 23 April 2003, and General Assembly Resolution 58/177, 22 December 2003.

17 United Nations, 2005 World Summit Outcome Resolution, para. 132.

18 K. Annan, In Larger Freedom: Towards Development, Security and Human Rights for All, United Nations, New York, 2005, para. 210.

19 R. Cohen, 'The Guiding Principles on Internal Displacement: An innovation in International Standard Setting', Global Governance, vol. 10, no. 4, October–December 2004, pp. 459–80. For Georgia, see E. Mooney and B. Jarrah, Internally Displaced Persons' Voting Rights in the OSCE Region, Brookings Institution, 2004, pp. 32–41.

20 See R. Cohen, W. Kälin and E. Mooney, The Law of the South Caucasus and the Guiding Principles on Internal Displacement, American Society of International Law and Brookings Institution, 2004, and Memorial, Annotations to the Guiding Principles, Moscow, 2005.

21 United Nations, Commission on Human Rights, Report of the Representative of the Secretary-General on Internally Displaced Persons, F. M. Deng, UN Doc. E/CN.4/2002/95, 16 January 2002, para. 98.

22 See W. Kälin, 'How Hard is Soft Law?' in *Recent Commentaries about the Nature and Application of the Guiding Principles on Internal Displacement*, Brookings–CUNY Project on Internal Displacement, April 2002.

23 *International Symposium on the Mandate of the Representative of the UN Secretary-General on Internally Displaced Persons: Taking Stock and Charting the Future*, hosted by the governments of Austria and Norway, Brookings Institution–SAIS Project on Internal Displacement, Vienna, Austria, 12–13 December 2002, pp. 8–II, 21.

24 United Nations Sub-Commission on the Promotion and Protection of Human Rights, Principles on Housing and Property Restitution for Refugees and Displaced People, E/CN.4/Sub.2/2005/17, 28 June 2005.

25 See United Nations, Commission on Human Rights, Report of the Representative of the Secretary-General on Internally Displaced Persons, Francis M. Deng, which reports on the results of four major studies on the collaborative approach, UN Doc. E/CN.4/2004/77, 4 March 2004, paras. 24–33.

26 R. Holbrooke, 'Forgotten people: a borderline difference', *The Washington Post*, 8 May, 2000.

27 S. Martin, *Refugee Women*, 2nd edition, Lexington Books, pp. 154–5.

28 Inter-Agency Standing Committee, *Implementing the Collaborative Response to Situations of Internal Displacement: Guidance for UN Humanitarian and/or Resident Coordinators and Country Teams*, September 2004.

29 Office for the Coordination of Humanitarian Affairs, *No Refuge*, pp. 42–3.

30 Inter-Agency Standing Committee, *Protection of Internally Displaced Persons*, Policy Paper Series, No. 2, New York, United Nations, 2000.

31 S. Bagshaw and D. Paul, *Protect or Neglect: Towards a More Effective United Nations Approach to the Protection of Internally Displaced Persons*, The Brookings–SAIS Project on Internal Displacement and Office for the Coordination of Humanitarian Affairs, p. 10, www.brookings.edu/fp/projects/idp/protection_survey.htm.

32 S. Bagshaw and D. Paul, *Protect or Neglect*, p. 4.

33 R. Cohen, 'UNHCR: Expanding its Role with IDPs', *Forced Migration Review*, Supplement, October 2005, p. 10.

34 See Office for the Coordination of Humanitarian Affairs, *No Refuge*, pp. 65–6, and S. Bagshaw and D. Paul, *Protect or Neglect*, pp. 75–6.

35 Refugees International, 'Funding shortfalls plague global humanitarian response', 13 June 2005.

36 J. Egeland, 'Towards a stronger humanitarian response system', *Forced Migration Review*, October 2005, p.5.

37 S. Ogata, *The Turbulent Decade: Confronting the Refugee Crises of the 1990s*, W.W. Norton & Co., New York/London, 2005, pp. 50–171.

38 Major-General W. L. Nash (Ret.) at a meeting on 'Independent Humanitarian Action: A Thing of the Past?' Brookings Institution, 16 April 2004.

39 See for example a recent study commissioned by the UN, prepared by E. B. Eide, A. T. Kaspersen, R. Kent and K. von Hippel, *Report on Integrated Missions: Practical Perspectives and Recommendations*, May 2005.

40 See W. G. O'Neill, *A New Challenge for Peacekeepers: The Internally Displaced*, Brookings–SAIS Project on Internal Displacement, April 2004, pp. 6–7, 8–9, 24–39.

41 M. Lacey, 'UN Forces Using Tougher Tactics to Secure Peace', *New York Times*, 23 May 2005.

42 United Nations, 2005 World Summit Outcome, paras. 92–3.

43 Ibid. para. 139.

44 'UN refugee boss says world tackling past failures', *News* 1, New Brisbane, Australia, 27 September 2005.

Chapter 8

1 See the special issue of *Refugees* on 'How Secure Do You Feel?' 2005, vol. 2, no. 139.

2 The first two agreements entered into force in 2003 and the last in 2004. For the list of signatories and precise dates of entry into force see http://www.unodc.org/unodc/en/crime_cicp_signatures.html.

3 B.S. Chimni, 'From Resettlement to Repatriation: Towards a Critical History of Durable Solutions', UNHCR Research Papers No. 2, 1999.

4 UNHCR, 'Multilateral Framework of Understandings on Resettlement', High Commissioner's Forum Forum/2004/6, 16 September 2004.

5 Ibid., p. 4.

6 UNHCR, 'Progress Report: Convention Plus', 16 September 2004, pp. 4-5.

7 For a discussion of the response of Western states see M. Gibney, *The Ethics and Politics of Asylum: Liberal Democracy and the Response to Refugees*, Cambridge University Press, Cambridge, 2004.

8 E. Feller, 'Preface' in E. Feller, V. Turk and F. Nicholson (eds), *Refugee Protection in International Law: UNHCR's Global Consultations on International Protection*, Cambridge University Press, Cambridge, 2003, p. xvii.

9 B.S. Chimni, 'Reforming the International Refugee Regime: A Dialogic Model', *Journal of Refugee Studies* vol. 14, no. 2, 2001, pp. 151-68.

10 UNHCR, 'Progress Report: Convention Plus', High Commissioner's Forum /2004/5, 16 September 2004, footnote 5.

11 E. Feller, 'Preface' in E. Feller et al. (eds), *Refugee Protection in International Law*, p. xviii.

12 Ibid.

13 A. Betts, 'Convention Plus: Continuity or Change in North-South Responsibility Sharing', paper prepared for 'New Asylum Paradigm?' workshop, COMPAS, 14 June 2005, p. 7.

14 Ibid., pp. 1, 5, 12.

15 G. Noll, 'Securitizing Sovereignty? States, Refugees and the Regionalization of International Law', in E. Newman and J. van Selm (eds), *Refugees and Forced Displacement: International Security, Human Vulnerability, and the State*, UN University Press, Tokyo, 2003, p. 292.

16 A. Betts, 'What Does "Efficiency" Mean in the Context of the Global Refugee Regime?', Working Paper No.9 (2005), Centre on Migration, Policy and Society, University of Oxford, Oxford.

17 A. Appiah, *In My Father's House*, Harvard University Press, Harvard, 1992, p. 26.

18 UNHCR, Executive Committee Conclusion on International Cooperation and Burden and Responsibility Sharing in Mass Influx Situations, No. 100 (LV) - 2004, 8 October 2004; UNHCR, Standing Committee, 33rd Meeting, International Cooperation and Burden and Responsibility Sharing in Mass Influx Situations, EC/55/SC/CRP.14, 7 June 2005, para. 1.

19 J. Habermas, 'Struggles for Recognition in the Democratic Constitutional State' in A. Gutman (ed), *Multiculturalism*, Princeton University Press, New Jersey, 1994, p. 142.

20 For example, in 1999 European Community Humanitarian Office (ECHO) funding for former Yugoslavia and Kosovo 'was four times the funding for all 70 African, Caribbean and Pacific countries'. Inter-Agency Standing Committee, *Global Humanitarian Assistance 2000*, United Nations, pp. 64-5.

21 The largest bilateral donors work together through the OECD's official Development Assistance Committee (DAC): they include the United States, the United Kingdom, Germany, Sweden, the Netherlands, Japan, Norway, Italy, France and Switzerland.

22 G. Everts, *Guide for UNHCR Field Offices on Donor Relations and Resource Mobilisation*, UNHCR, 2003, p. 28; I. Smillie and L. Minear, *The Quality of Money: Donor Behavior in Humanitarian Financing; An Independent Study*, Feinstein International Famine Center, Tufts University, Boston, 2003.

23 R. Kent et al., *Changes in Humanitarian Financing: Implications for the United Nations*, Inter-Agency Standing Committee, United Nations, 2003.

24 The International Meeting on Good Humanitarian Donorship was held in Stockholm, 16-17 June 2003; conclusions are available at http://www.reliefweb.int.

25 E. Feller et al. (eds), *Refugee Protection in International Law*, p. 668.

26 See 'Summary Conclusions: Supervisory Responsibility', ibid., pp. 670-1.

27 Hoi Trinh, 'UNHCR and Accountability: the Non-reviewability of UNHCR Decisions' in A. Bolesta (ed.), *Forced Migration and the Contemporary World: Challenges to the International System*, Libra, Bialystok, 2003, p. 51.

28 For detailed recommendations see M. Alexander, 'Refugee Status Determination Conducted by UNHCR', *International Journal of Refugee Law*, vol. 11, no. 2, 1999, pp. 286-7.

29 I. Smillie and L. Minear, *The Quality of Money*, p. 21.

30 G. Everts, *Guide for UNHCR Field Offices*, p. 32.

31 Ibid.

32 See UNHCR, *Global Report 2003* and Everts, *Guide for UNHCR Field Offices*, p. 7.

33 UNHCR, *Global Report 2004*, p. 25.

34 V. Mattar and P. White, *Consistent and Predictable Responses to IDPs: A review of UNHCR's Decision Making Processes*, UNHCR, Evaluation and Policy Analysis Unit, EPAU/2005/2, March 2005, p. 1.

35 UNHCR, *Refugees*, vol. 2, no. 139, p. 8.

36 Ibid., p. 9.

Endnotes

Annexes

Technical notes on statistical information

Most countries have adopted the refugee definition contained in the 1951 UN Refugee Convention, but there are important national differences in refugee registration and determination. In industrialized countries, where UNHCR usually relies on data provided by the authorities, information on individual asylum requests is the main source of statistical data.

In much of the developing world, however, refugees are often accepted on a group basis. In such cases, maintaining a credible refugee registration for the provision of material assistance becomes a priority. These registers, often maintained by UNHCR at the request of the host governments, form an important source of refugee data. Refugee registers are often verified and supplemented with information from health records and surveys.

For the purposes of UNHCR statistics, people of concern to UNHCR include the following categories:

- **Refugees** include: persons recognized under the 1951 Convention relating to the Status of Refugees, its 1967 Protocol and the 1969 OAU Convention Governing the Specific Aspects of Refugee Problems in Africa; those recognized in accordance with the UNHCR Statute; persons allowed to stay for humanitarian reasons; and persons granted temporary protection.

The UNHCR mandate covers all refugees, except Palestinian refugees residing in areas of operation of the United Nations Relief and Works Agency for Palestine Refugees in the Near East (UNRWA). These Palestinian refugees are not included in UNHCR's statistics. However, Palestinian refugees living outside the UNRWA areas of operation fall under the responsibility of UNHCR.

- **Asylum seekers** are persons who have applied for asylum or refugee status, but who have not yet received a final decision on their application. A distinction should be made between the number of asylum seekers who have submitted a request during *a certain period* ('asylum applications submitted') and the number of asylum seekers whose asylum request has not yet been decided *at a certain date* ('backlog of undecided or pending cases').

- In recent years, UNHCR's involvement with **internally displaced persons** (IDPs) has increased. IDPs are often displaced for the same reasons as refugees. However, because IDPs have not crossed an international border, their legal situation as well as the international response to their plight differs significantly from that of refugees. Moreover, statistical data on IDPs is less reliable than on refugees.

UNHCR statistics are limited to IDPs to whom UNHCR extends protection or assistance. As such, UNHCR statistics do not provide a comprehensive picture of global internal displacement.

- **Returnees**, 'returned refugees' and 'returned IDPs', refer to refugees and IDPs who have returned home but continue to receive assistance from UNHCR. For statistical purposes, only refugees and IDPs who have returned during the last 12 months, are included in the population of concern to UNHCR. In practice, however, operations may assist returnees for longer periods.

- In addition to protecting persons who are or have been recently displaced, UNHCR extends support to **stateless persons** by seeking to avoid and reduce statelessness. A stateless person is someone who is not considered a national by any state under its law. Statistics on stateless persons, in particular those who are not displaced, are difficult to obtain.

While efforts have been undertaken to make the statistics as comprehensive as possible, some populations and movements may remain unrecorded due to lack of information. In particular, precise figures on refugee returns and on those who are internally displaced are difficult to obtain due to unregistered movements and lack of access to those people. The data on return presented in Annex 2 are generally based on arrival data from countries of origin.

For industrialized countries which do not keep track of recognized refugees, UNHCR has adopted a simple method to estimate the refugee population, based on recent arrivals of refugees and/or recognition of asylum seekers, including those allowed to remain on humanitarian grounds. For Australia, Canada, New Zealand and the United States, recent refugee population estimates are based on the number of resettled refugees and recognized asylum seekers over a five-year period. For most European countries, a 10-year period has been applied, taking into account the longer period it takes in these countries for refugees to obtain citizenship (see Annex 3).

The regional classification adopted in the annexes is that of the Population Division of the United Nations Secretariat. Asia includes much of the 'Middle East' (though not North Africa), as well as Turkey. Annex 1 shows the classification of countries by region. In the tables, figures are below 1,000 are rounded to the nearest 10, whereas figures of 1,000 and above are rounded to the nearest 100. A dash (-) indicates that the value is zero, rounded to zero or not applicable. Two dots (..) indicate that the value is not available.

Most data used in this publication are derived from the UNHCR Statistical Yearbook and other statistics reports (see http://www.unhcr.org/statistics).

States party to the 1951 UN Refugee Convention, the 1967 Protocol, the 1969 OAU Refugee Convention, the 1954 and 1961 Statelessness Conventions and members of UNHCR's Executive Committee (ExCom), end-2004

United Nations member states	1951 UN Refugee Convention a	1967 Protocol b	1969 OAU Refugee Convention c	1954 Statelessness Convention d	1961 Statelessness Convention e	UNHCR's ExCom members f
Afghanistan						
Albania	1992	1992		2003	2003	
Algeria	1963	1967	1974	1964		1963
Andorra						
Angola	1981	1981	1981			
Antigua and Barbuda	1995	1995		1988		
Argentina	1961	1967		1972		1979
Armenia	1993	1993		1994	1994	
Australia	1954	1973		1973	1973	1951
Austria	1954	1973			1972	1951
Azerbaijan	1993	1993		1996	1996	
Bahamas	1993	1993				
Bahrain						
Bangladesh						1995
Barbados				1972		
Belarus	2001	2001				
Belgium	1953	1969		1960		1951
Belize	1990	1990				
Benin	1962	1970	1973			
Bhutan						
Bolivia	1982	1982		1983	1983	
Bosnia and Herzegovina	1993	1993		1983	1996	
Botswana	1969	1969	1995	1969		
Brazil	1960	1972		1996		1951
Brunei Darussalam						
Bulgaria	1993	1993				
Burkina Faso	1980	1980	1974			
Burundi	1963	1971	1975			
Cambodia	1992	1992				
Cameroon	1961	1967	1985			
Canada	1969	1969			1978	1957
Cape Verde		1987	1989			
Central African Rep.	1962	1967	1970			
Chad	1981	1981	1981	1999	1999	
Chile	1972	1972				2000
China	1982	1982				1958
Colombia	1961	1980				1955
Comoros						
Congo	1962	1970	1971			
Costa Rica	1978	1978		1977	1977	
Côte d'Ivoire	1961	1970	1998			2000
Croatia	1992	1992		1992		
Cuba						
Cyprus	1963	1968				2003
Czech Rep.	1993	1993		2004	2001	
Dem. People's Rep. of Korea						
Dem. Rep. of the Congo	1965	1975	1973			1979
Denmark	1952	1968		1956	1977	1951
Djibouti	1977	1977				
Dominica	1994	1994				

United Nations member states	1951 UN Refugee Convention [a]	1967 Protocol [b]	1969 OAU Refugee Convention [c]	1954 Statelessness Convention [d]	1961 Statelessness Convention [e]	UNHCR's ExCom members [f]
Dominican Rep.	1978	1978				
Ecuador	1955	1969		1970		2002
Egypt	1981	1981	1980			2004
El Salvador	1983	1983				
Equatorial Guinea	1986	1986	1980			
Eritrea						
Estonia	1997	1997				
Ethiopia	1969	1969	1973			1993
Fiji	1972	1972		1972		
Finland	1968	1968		1968		1979
France	1954	1971		1960		1951
Gabon	1964	1973	1986			
Gambia	1966	1967	1980			
Georgia	1999	1999				
Germany	1953	1969		1976	1977	1951
Ghana	1963	1968	1975			2005
Greece	1960	1968		1975		1955
Grenada						
Guatemala	1983	1983		2000	2001	
Guinea	1965	1968	1972	1962		2002
Guinea-Bissau	1976	1976	1989			
Guyana						
Haiti	1984	1984				
Holy See (the) g	1956	1967				1951
Honduras	1992	1992				
Hungary	1989	1989		2001		1993
Iceland	1955	1968				
India						1995
Indonesia						
Iraq						
Ireland	1956	1968		1962	1973	1996
Islamic Rep. of Iran	1976	1976				1955
Israel	1954	1968		1958		1951
Italy	1954	1972		1962		1951
Jamaica	1964	1980				
Japan	1981	1982				1979
Jordan						
Kazakhstan	1999	1999				
Kenya	1966	1981	1992			2003
Kiribati				1983	1983	
Kuwait						
Kyrgyzstan	1996	1996				
Lao People's Dem. Rep.						
Latvia	1997	1997		1999	1992	
Lebanon						1963
Lesotho	1981	1981	1988	1974	2004	1979
Liberia	1964	1980	1971	1964	2004	
Libyan Arab Jamahiriya			1981	1989	1989	
Liechtenstein	1957	1968				
Lithuania	1997	1997		2000		
Luxembourg	1953	1971		1960		
Madagascar	1967					1963
Malawi	1987	1987	1987			
Malaysia						
Maldives						
Mali	1973	1973	1981			

United Nations member states	1951 UN Refugee Convention [a]	1967 Protocol [b]	1969 OAU Refugee Convention [c]	1954 Statelessness Convention [d]	1961 Statelessness Convention [e]	UNHCR's ExCom members [f]
Malta	1971	1971				
Marshall Islands						
Mauritania	1987	1987	1972			
Mauritius						
Mexico	2000	2000		2000		2001
Micronesia (Federated States of)						
Monaco	1954					
Mongolia						
Morocco	1956	1971	1974 h			1979
Mozambique	1983	1989	1989			1999
Myanmar						
Namibia	1995	1995				1982
Nauru						
Nepal						
Netherlands	1956	1968		1962	1985	1955
New Zealand	1960	1973				2002
Nicaragua	1980	1980				1979
Niger	1961	1970	1971		1985	
Nigeria	1967	1968	1986			1963
Norway	1953	1967		1956	1971	1955
Oman						
Pakistan						1988
Palau						
Panama	1978	1978				
Papua New Guinea	1986	1986				
Paraguay	1970	1970				
Peru	1964	1983				
Philippines	1981	1981				1991
Poland	1991	1991				1997
Portugal	1960	1976				
Qatar						
Rep. of Korea	1992	1992		1962		2000
Rep. of Moldova	2002	2002				
Romania	1991	1991				2005
Russian Federation	1993	1993				1995
Rwanda	1980	1980	1979			
Saint Kitts and Nevis	2002					
Saint Lucia						
Saint Vincent and the Grenadines	1993	2003		1999		
Samoa	1988	1994				
San Marino						
Sao Tome and Principe	1978	1978				
Saudi Arabia						
Senegal	1963	1967	1971			
Serbia and Montenegro	2001	2001		2001		2002
Seychelles	1980	1980	1980			
Sierra Leone	1981	1981	1987			
Singapore						
Slovakia	1993	1993		2000	2000	
Slovenia	1992	1992		1992		
Solomon Islands	1995	1995				
Somalia	1978	1978				1988
South Africa	1996	1996	1995			1997
Spain	1978	1978		1997		1994
Sri Lanka						
Sudan	1974	1974	1972			1979

United Nations member states	1951 UN Refugee Convention [a]	1967 Protocol [b]	1969 OAU Refugee Convention [c]	1954 Statelessness Convention [d]	1961 Statelessness Convention [e]	UNHCR's ExCom members [f]
Suriname	1978	1978				
Swaziland	2000	1969	1989	1999	1999	
Sweden	1954	1967		1965	1969	1958
Switzerland	1955	1968		1972		1951
Syrian Arab Rep.						
Tajikistan	1993	1993				
TfYR Macedonia	1994	1994		1994		
Thailand						1979
Timor-Leste	2003	2003				
Togo	1962	1969	1970			
Tonga						
Trinidad and Tobago	2000	2000		1966		
Tunisia	1957	1968	1989	1969	2000	1958
Turkey	1962	1968				1951
Turkmenistan	1998	1998				
Tuvalu	1986	1986				
Uganda	1976	1976	1987	1965		1967
Ukraine	2002	2002				
United Arab Emirates						
United Kingdom	1954	1968		1959	1966	1951
United Rep. of Tanzania	1964	1968	1975			1963
United States		1968				1951
Uruguay	1970	1970		2004	2001	
Uzbekistan						
Vanuatu						
Venezuela		1986				1951
Viet Nam						
Yemen	1980	1980				2003
Zambia	1969	1969	1973	1974		2004
Zimbabwe	1981	1981	1985	1998		
Total	**142**	**142**	**45**	**57**	**29**	**68**

[a] Year of ratification, accession and/or succession to the 1951 UN Refugee Convention.
[b] Year of accession and/or succession to the 1967 Protocol.
[c] Year of ratification of the 1969 Refugee Convention of the Organization of African Unity (OAU).
[d] Year of ratification, accession and/or succession to the 1954 Convention relating to the Status of Stateless Persons.
[e] Year of ratification, accession and/or succession to the 1961 Convention on the Reduction of Statelessness.
[f] Refers to Executive Committee of the High Commissioner's Programme.
[g] Not member state of the United Nations.
[h] Morocco withdrew from the OAU and its obligations in 1984.
Situation as on 31 December 2004.

Annex 2

Total population of concern to UNHCR, end-2004

Region and country/territory of asylum/residence[1]	Refugees[2]	Asylum seekers[3]	Returned refugees[4]	Others of concern				Total population of concern
				IDPs of concern to UNHCR[5]	Returned IDPs[6]	Stateless[7]	Various[8]	
Burundi	48,808	10,712	90,321	855	-	-	-	150,696
Djibouti	18,035	-	-	-	-	-	-	18,035
Eritrea	4,240	449	9,893	-	-	7	-	14,589
Ethiopia	115,980	40	7	-	-	-	-	116,027
Kenya	239,835	9,474	1	-	-	-	-	249,310
Malawi	3,682	3,335	-	-	-	-	-	7,017
Mozambique	623	4,892	-	-	-	-	-	5,515
Rwanda	50,221	3,248	14,136	-	-	-	-	67,605
Somalia	357	334	18,069	-	-	-	-	18,760
Uganda	250,482	1,809	91	-	-	-	-	252,382
United Rep. of Tanzania	602,088	166	2	-	-	-	-	602,256
Zambia	173,907	84	-	-	-	-	-	173,991
Zimbabwe	6,884	-	-	-	-	-	-	6,884
Eastern Africa Total	**1,515,142**	**34,543**	**132,520**	**855**	**-**	**7**	**-**	**1,683,067**
Angola	13,970	929	90,246	-	-	-	-	105,145
Cameroon	58,861	6,123	-	-	-	-	-	64,984
Central African Rep.	25,020	2,748	368	-	-	-	-	28,136
Chad	259,880	-	184	-	-	-	-	260,064
Congo	68,536	3,232	1,035	-	-	-	-	72,803
Dem. Rep. of the Congo	199,323	354	13,843	-	-	-	-	213,520
Equatorial Guinea	-	-	1	-	-	-	-	1
Gabon	13,787	4,839	-	-	-	-	-	18,626
Middle Africa Total	**639,377**	**18,225**	**105,677**	**-**	**-**	**-**	**-**	**763,279**
Algeria	169,048	6	1	-	-	-	-	169,055
Egypt	90,343	8,752	-	-	-	113	-	99,208
Libyan Arab Jamahiriya	12,166	200	-	-	-	-	-	12,366
Morocco	2,121	177	-	-	-	4	-	2,302
Sudan	141,588	4,271	290	662,302	-	-	37,416	845,867
Tunisia	90	12	-	-	-	-	-	102
Northern Africa Total	**415,356**	**13,418**	**291**	**662,302**	**-**	**117**	**37,416**	**1,128,900**
Botswana	2,839	1,034	-	-	-	-	-	3,873
Namibia	14,773	2,155	-	-	-	-	-	16,928
South Africa	27,683	115,224	-	-	-	-	-	142,907
Swaziland	704	306	-	-	-	-	-	1,010
Southern Africa Total	**45,999**	**118,719**	**-**	**-**	**-**	**-**	**-**	**164,718**
Benin	4,802	1,053	-	-	-	-	-	5,855
Burkina Faso	492	518	-	-	-	-	-	1,010
Côte d'Ivoire	72,088	2,111	7,594	38,039	-	-	-	119,832
Gambia	7,343	602	-	-	-	-	-	7,945
Ghana	42,053	6,010	-	-	-	-	-	48,063
Guinea	139,252	6,317	2	-	-	-	-	145,571
Guinea-Bissau	7,536	141	-	-	-	-	-	7,677
Liberia	15,172	5	56,872	498,566	33,050	-	35	603,700
Mali	11,256	1,085	-	-	-	-	-	12,341
Mauritania	473	117	-	-	-	-	29,500	30,090
Niger	344	41	-	-	-	-	-	385
Nigeria	8,395	1,086	364	-	-	-	-	9,845
Senegal	20,804	2,412	-	-	-	-	-	23,216
Sierra Leone	65,437	138	26,271	-	-	-	-	91,846
Togo	11,285	390	120	-	-	-	-	11,795
Western Africa Total	**406,732**	**22,026**	**91,223**	**536,605**	**33,050**	**-**	**29,535**	**1,119,171**
Africa Total	**3,022,606**	**206,931**	**329,711**	**1,199,762**	**33,050**	**124**	**66,951**	**4,859,135**

Region and country/territory of asylum/residence[1]	Refugees[2]	Asylum seekers[3]	Returned refugees[4]	Others of concern				Total population of concern
				IDPs of concern to UNHCR[5]	Returned IDPs[6]	Stateless[7]	Various[8]	
China	299,375	44	-	-	-	-	-	299,419
Hong Kong SAR, China	1,868	670	-	-	-	-	-	2,538
Japan	1,967	496	-	-	-	-	-	2,463
Rep. of Korea	44	247	-	-	-	-	-	291
Eastern Asia Total	**303,254**	**1,457**	**-**	**-**	**-**	**-**	**-**	**304,711**
Afghanistan	30	29	940,469	159,549	27,391	-	-	1,127,468
Bangladesh	20,449	10	-	-	-	250,000	-	270,459
India	162,687	314	-	-	-	-	-	163,001
Islamic Rep. of Iran	1,045,976	48	698	-	-	-	-	1,046,722
Kazakhstan	15,844	9	-	-	-	58,291	-	74,144
Kyrgyzstan	3,753	453	-	-	-	-	-	4,206
Nepal	124,928	654	-	-	-	-	10,737	136,319
Pakistan*	960,617	8,157	-	-	-	-	-	968,774
Sri Lanka	63	48	10,040	352,374	33,730	-	-	396,255
Tajikistan	3,306	458	80	-	-	-	-	3,844
Turkmenistan	13,253	3	-	-	-	-	-	13,256
Uzbekistan	44,455	477	-	-	-	-	-	44,932
South-central Asia Total	**2,395,361**	**10,660**	**951,287**	**511,923**	**61,121**	**308,291**	**10,737**	**4,249,380**
Cambodia	382	316	-	-	-	-	-	698
Indonesia	169	59	-	-	-	-	16,397	16,625
Malaysia	24,905	10,322	-	-	-	-	62,311	97,538
Myanmar	-	-	210	-	-	-	-	210
Philippines	107	44	-	-	-	-	1,829	1,980
Singapore	1	3	-	-	-	-	-	4
Thailand	121,139	1,044	-	-	-	-	5	122,188
Timor-Leste	3	10	-	-	-	-	-	13
Viet Nam	2,360	-	13	-	-	-	-	2,373
South-eastern Asia Total	**149,066**	**11,798**	**223**	**-**	**-**	**-**	**80,542**	**241,629**
Armenia	235,235	68	-	-	-	-	125	235,428
Azerbaijan	8,606	1,231	-	578,545	-	30,000	430	618,812
Bahrain	-	6	-	-	-	-	-	6
Cyprus	531	10,028	-	-	-	-	-	10,559
Georgia	2,559	11	117	237,069	406	32	-	240,194
Iraq	46,053	1,353	193,997	-	-	-	-	241,403
Israel	574	-	-	-	-	-	-	574
Jordan	1,100	12,453	-	-	-	-	-	13,553
Kuwait	1,519	157	-	-	-	80,000	21,000	102,676
Lebanon	1,753	681	-	-	-	-	-	2,434
Occupied Palestinian Territory	-	-	32	-	-	-	-	32
Oman	7	24	-	-	-	-	-	31
Qatar	46	24	-	-	-	6,000	-	6,070
Saudi Arabia	240,552	170	-	-	-	-	-	240,722
Syrian Arab Rep.	15,604	785	158	-	-	300,000	-	316,547
Turkey	3,033	3,929	16	-	-	-	-	6,978
United Arab Emirates	105	52	-	-	-	-	-	157
Yemen	66,384	1,270	39	-	-	-	-	67,693
Western Asia Total	**623,661**	**32,242**	**194,359**	**815,614**	**406**	**416,032**	**21,555**	**2,103,869**
Asia Total	**3,471,342**	**56,157**	**1,145,869**	**1,327,537**	**61,527**	**724,323**	**112,834**	**6,899,589**
Belarus	725	68	-	-	-	10,465	2,458	13,716
Bulgaria	4,684	920	-	-	-	-	-	5,604
Czech Rep.	1,144	1,119	-	-	-	-	-	2,263
Hungary	7,708	354	-	-	-	-	-	8,062
Poland	2,507	3,743	-	-	-	-	-	6,250
Rep. of Moldova	57	184	-	-	-	-	-	241
Romania	1,627	210	-	-	-	400	-	2,237

Region and country/territory of asylum/residence[1]	Refugees[2]	Asylum seekers[3]	Returned refugees[4]	Others of concern				Total population of concern
				IDPs of concern to UNHCR[5]	Returned IDPs[6]	Stateless[7]	Various[8]	
Russian Federation	1,852	315	54	334,796	19,019	10,755	297,761	664,552
Slovakia	409	2,916	-	-	-	7	-	3,332
Ukraine	2,459	1,838	-	-	-	77,760	2,809	84,866
Eastern Europe Total	**23,172**	**11,667**	**54**	**334,796**	**19,019**	**99,387**	**303,028**	**791,123**
Denmark	65,310	840	-	-	-	-	-	66,150
Estonia	11	6	-	-	-	150,536	-	150,553
Finland	11,325	-	-	-	-	-	-	11,325
Iceland	239	19	-	-	-	-	-	258
Ireland	7,201	3,696	-	-	-	-	-	10,897
Latvia	11	1	-	-	-	452,176	-	452,188
Lithuania	470	28	-	-	-	9,028	-	9,526
Norway	44,046	-	-	-	-	923	-	44,969
Sweden	73,408	28,043	-	-	-	-	-	101,451
United Kingdom	289,054	9,800	-	-	-	-	-	298,854
Northern Europe Total	**491,075**	**42,433**	**-**	**-**	**-**	**612,663**	**-**	**1,146,171**
Albania	51	36	-	-	-	-	-	87
Bosnia and Herzegovina	22,215	454	2,447	309,240	17,948	-	-	352,304
Croatia	3,663	33	7,468	7,540	5,026	14	-	23,744
Greece	2,489	7,375	-	-	-	-	3,000	12,864
Italy	15,674	-	-	-	-	886	-	16,560
Malta	1,558	141	-	-	-	-	-	1,699
Portugal	377	-	-	-	-	-	-	377
Serbia and Montenegro	276,683	40	8,143	248,154	9,456	-	85,000	627,476
Slovenia	304	323	-	-	-	584	-	1,211
Spain	5,635	-	-	-	-	14	-	5,649
TfYR Macedonia	1,004	1,232	726	-	-	5,761	6	8,729
Southern Europe Total	**329,653**	**9,634**	**18,784**	**564,934**	**32,430**	**7,259**	**88,006**	**1,050,700**
Austria	17,795	38,262	-	-	-	524	-	56,581
Belgium	13,529	22,863	-	-	-	93	-	36,485
France	139,852	11,600	-	-	-	708	-	152,160
Germany	876,622	86,151	-	-	-	10,619	-	973,392
Liechtenstein	149	68	-	-	-	-	-	217
Luxembourg	1,590	-	-	-	-	-	-	1,590
Netherlands	126,805	28,452	-	-	-	-	-	155,257
Switzerland	47,678	18,633	-	-	-	25	-	66,336
Western Europe Total	**1,224,020**	**206,029**	**-**	**-**	**-**	**11,969**	**-**	**1,442,018**
Europe Total	**2,067,920**	**269,763**	**18,838**	**899,730**	**51,449**	**731,278**	**391,034**	**4,430,012**
Cuba	795	5	2	-	-	-	-	802
Caribbean Total	**795**	**5**	**2**	**-**	**-**	**-**	**-**	**802**
Belize	732	31	-	-	-	-	-	763
Costa Rica	10,413	223	-	-	-	-	-	10,636
El Salvador	235	1	-	-	-	-	-	236
Guatemala	656	4	8	-	-	-	-	668
Honduras	23	21	-	-	-	-	-	44
Mexico	4,343	161	-	-	-	-	-	4,504
Nicaragua	292	1	2	-	-	-	-	295
Panama	1,608	271	-	-	-	-	-	1,879
Central America Total	**18,302**	**713**	**10**	**-**	**-**	**-**	**-**	**19,025**
Argentina	2,916	990	4	-	-	-	-	3,910
Bolivia	524	22	1	-	-	-	-	547
Brazil	3,345	446	-	-	-	-	-	3,791
Chile	569	85	-	-	-	-	-	654
Colombia	141	36	67	2,000,000	-	-	-	2,000,244
Ecuador	8,450	1,660	3	-	-	-	-	10,113
Paraguay	41	6	-	-	-	-	-	47

Region and country/territory of asylum/residence[1]	Refugees[2]	Asylum seekers[3]	Returned refugees[4]	IDPs of concern to UNHCR[5]	Returned IDPs[6]	Stateless[7]	Various[8]	Total population of concern
Peru	766	232	2	-	-	-	-	1,000
Uruguay	97	10	-	-	-	-	-	107
Venezuela	244	3,904	-	-	-	-	26,350	30,498
South America Total	**17,093**	**7,391**	**77**	**2,000,000**	**-**	**-**	**26,350**	**2,050,911**
Latin America and the Caribbean Total	**36,190**	**8,109**	**89**	**2,000,000**	**-**	**-**	**26,350**	**2,070,738**
Canada	141,398	27,290	-	-	-	-	-	168,688
United States	420,854	263,710	-	-	-	-	-	684,564
Northern America Total	**562,252**	**291,000**	**-**	**-**	**-**	**-**	**-**	**853,252**
Australia	63,476	5,022	-	-	-	-	-	68,498
New Zealand	5,350	746	-	-	-	-	-	6,096
Australia-New Zealand Total	**68,826**	**5,768**	**-**	**-**	**-**	**-**	**-**	**74,594**
Papua New Guinea	7,627	198	-	-	-	135	-	7,960
Melanesia Total	**7,627**	**198**	**-**	**-**	**-**	**135**	**-**	**7,960**
Oceania Total	**76,453**	**5,966**	**-**	**-**	**-**	**135**	**-**	**82,554**
Various	-	-	103	-	-	-	-	103
Grand Total	**9,236,763**	**837,926**	**1,494,610**	**5,427,029**	**146,026**	**1,455,860**	**597,169**	**19,195,383**

Notes
The data are generally provided by Governments, based on their own definitions and methods of data collection.
A dash (-) indicates that the value is zero, not available or not applicable.
[1] Regional classification as per the United Nations Secretariat. In the absence of Government figures, UNHCR has estimated the refugee population in many industrialized countries, based on recent resettlement arrivals and recognition of asylum seekers. For Canada, USA, Australia and New Zealand, estimates are based on arrivals/recognition during the past five years, whereas for most European countries a 10-year period has been applied. These periods reflect the different naturalization rates for refugees.
[2] Persons recognized as refugees under the 1951 UN Convention/1967 Protocol, the 1969 OAU Convention, in accordance with the UNHCR Statute, persons granted a humanitarian status and those granted temporary protection.
[3] Persons whose application for asylum or refugee status is pending at any stage in the procedure or who are otherwise registered as asylum seekers.
[4] Refugees who have returned to their place of origin during the year. Source: Country of origin and asylum.
[5] Persons who are displaced within their country and to whom UNHCR extends protection and/or assistance, generally pursuant to a special request by a competent organ of the United Nations.
[6] IDPs of concern to UNHCR who have returned to their place of origin during the year.
[7] Persons who are not considered as a national by any state under the operation of its law. The data should be considered as indicative only due to the limited availability of statistics on stateless persons. Stateless refugees and asylum seekers are included in the categories Refugees and Asylum seekers.
[8] Persons of concern to UNHCR not included in the previous columns including forced migrants (Russian Federation), local residents-at-risk (Kosovo, Serbia and Montenegro), Sahrawis (Mauretania), Afghan asylum seekers (Russian Federation, UNHCR est.), rejected Eritreans following cessation (Sudan), Filipino Muslims (Malaysia) and Colombians (Venezuela).
* The refugee population in Pakistan is a UNHCR estimate. The figure only includes refugees living in camps.
Sources: UNHCR, Governments.

Refugees by UN major area and sub-region of asylum, 1995-2004 (end-year)

UN major area	Sub-region	1995	1996	1997	1998	1999	2000	2001	2002	2003	2004
Africa	Eastern Africa	2,029,000	1,584,000	1,563,000	1,505,000	1,615,000	1,662,000	1,626,000	1,629,000	1,600,000	1,515,000
	Middle Africa	1,545,000	790,000	414,000	379,000	475,000	603,000	612,000	610,000	603,000	639,000
	Northern Africa	876,000	598,000	561,000	575,000	575,000	606,000	540,000	592,000	410,000	415,000
	Southern Africa	104,000	26,000	10,000	15,000	24,000	47,000	54,000	48,000	50,000	46,000
	Western Africa	1,419,000	1,364,000	941,000	872,000	834,000	710,000	452,000	464,000	473,000	407,000
Africa Total		**5,973,000**	**4,362,000**	**3,489,000**	**3,346,000**	**3,523,000**	**3,628,000**	**3,284,000**	**3,343,000**	**3,136,000**	**3,022,000**
Asia	Eastern Asia	295,000	297,000	298,000	298,000	299,000	299,000	300,000	301,000	304,000	303,000
	South-central Asia	3,753,000	3,695,000	3,611,000	3,510,000	3,418,000	4,290,000	4,487,000	2,948,000	2,500,000	2,395,000
	South-eastern Asia	147,000	148,000	190,000	204,000	328,000	294,000	251,000	208,000	142,000	149,000
	Western Asia	691,000	673,000	637,000	735,000	738,000	500,000	732,000	731,000	697,000	624,000
Asia Total		**4,886,000**	**4,813,000**	**4,736,000**	**4,747,000**	**4,783,000**	**5,383,000**	**5,770,000**	**4,188,000**	**3,643,000**	**3,471,000**
Europe	Eastern Europe	53,000	294,000	253,000	143,000	92,000	41,000	34,000	34,000	30,000	23,000
	Northern Europe	413,000	416,000	423,000	428,000	437,000	478,000	520,000	545,000	522,000	491,000
	Southern Europe	971,000	825,000	746,000	617,000	644,000	578,000	485,000	414,000	343,000	330,000
	Western Europe	1,653,000	1,730,000	1,518,000	1,399,000	1,426,000	1,277,000	1,273,000	1,343,000	1,312,000	1,224,000
Europe Total		**3,090,000**	**3,265,000**	**2,940,000**	**2,587,000**	**2,599,000**	**2,374,000**	**2,312,000**	**2,336,000**	**2,207,000**	**2,068,000**
Latin America and the Caribbean	Caribbean	2,800	2,400	2,000	1,800	1,700	1,600	1,000	1,000	840	800
	Central America	75,000	69,000	66,000	57,000	53,000	28,000	27,000	29,000	23,000	18,000
	South America	16,000	17,000	15,000	6,500	6,900	8,600	8,800	11,000	14,000	17,000
Latin America and the Caribbean Total		**93,800**	**88,400**	**83,000**	**65,300**	**61,600**	**38,200**	**36,800**	**41,000**	**37,840**	**35,800**
Northern America	Northern America	775,000	745,000	689,000	653,000	644,000	635,000	645,000	615,000	586,000	562,000
Northern America Total		**775,000**	**745,000**	**689,000**	**653,000**	**644,000**	**635,000**	**645,000**	**615,000**	**586,000**	**562,000**
Oceania	Australia-New Zealand	66,000	71,000	70,000	74,000	70,000	65,000	63,000	65,000	62,000	69,000
	Melanesia	12,000	12,000	9,000	8,400	6,700	5,900	4,900	4,900	7,500	7,600
Oceania Total		**78,000**	**83,000**	**79,000**	**82,400**	**76,700**	**70,900**	**67,900**	**69,900**	**69,500**	**76,600**
Grand Total		**14,895,800**	**13,356,400**	**12,016,000**	**11,480,700**	**11,687,300**	**12,129,100**	**12,115,700**	**10,592,900**	**9,679,340**	**9,235,400**

Note:
For detailed explanations, consult UNHCR statistical yearbooks.
In the absence of Government figures, UNHCR has estimated the refugee population in many industrialized countries, based on recent resettlement arrivals and recognition of asylum seekers. For Canada, USA, Australia and New Zealand, estimates are based on arrivals/recognition during the past five years, whereas for most European countries a 10-year period has been applied. These periods reflect the different naturalization rates for refugees.
Sources: UNHCR, Governments.

Refugee population by country of asylum, 1995-2004 (end-year)

Country of asylum[1]	1995	1996	1997	1998	1999	2000	2001	2002	2003	2004
Afghanistan	19,605	18,775	5	-	-	-	6	3	22	30
Albania	4,720	4,925	30	22,332	3,930	523	292	17	26	51
Algeria	192,489	190,267	170,746	165,226	165,249	169,656	169,422	169,233	169,033	169,048
Angola	10,884	9,381	9,364	10,605	13,071	12,086	12,250	12,250	13,382	13,970
Argentina	10,314	10,430	10,522	2,270	2,345	2,396	2,396	2,439	2,642	2,916
Armenia	218,950	218,950	219,000	310,012	296,216	280,591	264,337	247,550	239,289	235,235
Australia	62,145	67,313	66,074	69,745	64,918	60,246	57,895	59,436	56,258	63,476
Austria	34,385	89,116	84,394	80,300	82,081	15,492	14,390	14,130	16,109	17,795
Azerbaijan	233,682	233,692	233,715	221,635	221,643	287	367	458	326	8,606
Bahamas	8	48	60	80	100	100	-	-	-	-
Bahrain	-	-	-	-	1	1	1	-	-	-
Bangladesh	51,118	30,692	21,603	22,277	22,210	21,627	22,173	22,025	19,792	20,449
Belarus	28,988	30,525	50	75	260	458	584	618	638	725
Belgium	31,691	36,060	36,060	15,509	16,760	18,832	12,265	12,578	12,595	13,529
Belize	8,750	8,534	8,387	3,483	2,891	1,250	1,129	1,049	861	732
Benin	23,843	5,960	2,918	2,903	3,657	4,296	4,799	5,021	5,034	4,802
Bolivia	681	698	333	349	350	351	347	350	527	524
Bosnia and Herzegovina	-	-	40,000	40,000	65,645	38,152	32,745	28,022	22,517	22,215
Botswana	266	214	281	2,137	1,296	3,551	3,581	2,805	2,838	2,839
Brazil	2,050	2,212	2,260	2,347	2,378	2,722	2,884	3,182	3,193	3,345
Bulgaria	1,320	1,430	390	240	547	1,474	3,004	3,658	4,068	4,684
Burkina Faso	29,777	28,381	1,801	564	675	696	457	457	466	492
Burundi	173,017	20,733	22,028	25,093	22,109	27,136	27,896	40,533	40,971	48,808
Cambodia	15	16	14	21	21	34	50	200	76	382
Cameroon	45,781	46,407	47,057	47,826	49,227	43,680	41,186	58,288	58,583	58,861
Canada	152,125	138,435	125,184	119,371	123,316	126,991	129,224	129,950	133,094	141,398
Central African Rep.	33,856	36,564	38,499	43,013	49,314	55,661	49,239	50,725	44,753	25,020
Chad	100	100	302	8,810	23,478	17,692	12,950	33,455	146,400	259,880
Chile	283	313	276	305	323	364	389	413	466	569
China	288,309	290,100	291,507	292,345	293,299	294,110	295,325	297,277	299,354	299,375
Colombia	218	220	223	226	230	239	210	205	186	141
Comoros	-	-	-	-	9	11	13	-	-	-
Congo	19,404	20,451	20,697	27,174	39,870	123,190	119,147	109,201	91,362	68,536
Costa Rica	24,226	23,176	23,114	22,986	22,903	5,519	8,104	12,433	13,508	10,413
Côte d'Ivoire	297,908	327,696	208,502	151,182	138,429	120,691	126,239	44,749	75,971	72,088
Croatia	198,647	165,395	68,863	29,027	28,374	22,437	21,875	8,392	4,387	3,663
Cuba	1,829	1,694	1,280	1,067	967	954	1,036	1,005	836	795
Cyprus	55	49	43	84	117	76	83	173	349	531
Czech Rep.	2,655	2,266	1,731	1,805	1,232	1,186	1,216	1,297	1,516	1,144
Dem. Rep. of the Congo	1,433,760	675,973	297,538	240,214	285,270	332,509	362,012	332,978	234,033	199,323
Denmark	64,844	66,373	68,122	69,015	69,006	71,035	73,284	73,597	69,858	65,310
Djibouti	27,310	25,076	23,590	23,582	23,271	23,243	23,176	21,702	27,034	18,035
Dominican Rep.	985	640	638	614	625	510	-	-	-	-
Ecuador	202	211	227	248	314	1,602	1,715	3,240	6,381	8,450
Egypt	5,407	6,035	6,493	6,276	6,553	6,840	7,230	80,494	88,749	90,343
El Salvador	154	150	109	33	24	59	69	74	246	235
Eritrea	1,083	2,106	2,606	2,501	2,972	1,984	2,272	3,619	3,889	4,240
Estonia	-	-	-	-	-	4	11	10	12	11
Ethiopia	393,479	390,528	323,067	262,160	257,689	197,959	152,554	132,940	130,274	115,980
Fiji	9	9	-	-	-	-	-	-	-	-
Finland	10,191	11,382	12,017	12,290	12,869	13,276	12,728	12,490	10,843	11,325
France	155,245	151,329	146,558	140,215	129,722	132,508	131,601	132,182	130,838	139,852
Gabon	791	798	862	1,124	15,070	17,982	15,581	13,473	14,005	13,787
Gambia	6,599	6,924	7,279	10,320	17,219	12,016	8,133	12,120	7,465	7,343
Georgia	100	95	162	20	5,180	7,620	7,901	4,192	3,864	2,559

Country of asylum[1]	1995	1996	1997	1998	1999	2000	2001	2002	2003	2004
Germany	1,267,900	1,266,000	1,049,000	949,200	975,500	906,000	903,000	980,000	960,395	876,622
Ghana	83,200	35,617	22,858	14,557	13,261	12,720	11,792	33,515	43,947	42,053
Greece	4,428	5,780	5,520	6,145	6,283	6,653	6,948	2,788	2,771	2,489
Guatemala	1,496	1,564	1,508	815	732	720	729	733	715	656
Guinea	672,298	663,854	435,300	482,467	501,544	427,206	178,444	182,163	184,341	139,252
Guinea-Bissau	15,350	15,401	15,982	6,604	7,120	7,587	7,332	7,639	7,551	7,536
Guyana	-	-	1	-	-	-	-	-	-	-
Honduras	63	63	9	9	9	12	20	29	23	23
Hong Kong SAR, China	1,481	1,348	1,229	1,039	974	983	1,390	1,496	1,902	1,868
Hungary	11,394	7,537	5,890	3,504	4,990	5,064	4,710	6,088	7,023	7,708
Iceland	197	232	260	294	254	244	213	207	239	239
India	227,480	233,370	223,073	185,516	180,031	170,941	169,549	168,855	164,757	162,687
Indonesia	19	61	34	47	162,506	122,618	73,551	28,596	233	169
Iraq	116,722	112,957	104,032	104,022	128,913	127,787	128,142	134,190	134,190	46,053
Ireland	400	69	430	600	2,835	2,543	3,598	5,380	5,971	7,201
Islamic Rep. of Iran	2,071,988	2,030,359	1,982,553	1,931,332	1,835,688	1,868,000	1,868,000	1,306,599	984,896	1,045,976
Israel	-	-	-	27	128	4,075	4,168	4,179	4,179	574
Italy	74,302	64,711	66,620	5,473	6,024	6,849	8,571	10,060	12,841	15,674
Jamaica	23	25	33	37	37	38	-	-	-	-
Japan	5,435	5,278	4,851	4,492	4,235	3,752	3,200	2,657	2,266	1,967
Jordan	698	874	733	777	1,012	1,072	1,067	1,199	1,196	1,100
Kazakhstan	15,561	15,577	15,577	8,338	14,795	20,574	19,531	20,610	15,831	15,844
Kenya	234,665	223,640	232,097	238,187	223,696	206,106	239,221	233,671	237,512	239,835
Kuwait	3,306	3,831	3,787	4,182	4,334	2,776	1,255	1,521	1,518	1,519
Kyrgyzstan	13,407	16,707	15,276	14,560	10,849	10,609	9,296	7,708	5,591	3,753
Lao People's Dem. Rep.	-	-	-	2	-	-	-	-	-	-
Latvia	-	-	-	2	6	7	8	7	17	11
Lebanon	1,867	2,408	3,062	3,684	4,172	2,672	2,815	2,820	2,522	1,753
Lesotho	-	-	-	-	1	-	39	-	-	-
Liberia	120,080	120,061	126,886	96,317	96,317	69,315	54,760	64,956	33,997	15,172
Libyan Arab Jamahiriya	3,973	7,747	8,481	10,558	10,535	11,543	11,664	11,666	11,897	12,166
Liechtenstein	-	-	-	-	-	70	141	128	149	149
Lithuania	-	-	6	34	44	55	287	368	403	470
Luxembourg	700	700	700	700	700	759	1,201	1,201	1,201	1,590
Macao SAR, China	8	-	-	-	-	-	-	-	-	-
Madagascar	-	-	-	-	28	50	34	-	-	-
Malawi	1,018	1,268	280	1,245	1,700	3,900	6,200	2,166	3,202	3,682
Malaysia	5,278	5,309	5,285	50,614	50,517	50,487	50,466	50,612	7,424	24,905
Mali	17,916	18,234	12,552	13,598	8,302	8,412	8,439	9,095	10,009	11,256
Malta	416	367	343	296	271	190	176	307	895	1,558
Mauritania	34,394	15,880	7,511	26	223	350	365	405	475	473
Mauritius	-	-	-	-	43	-	14	-	-	-
Mexico	38,717	34,569	31,908	28,251	24,511	18,451	15,455	12,962	6,075	4,343
Morocco	55	51	57	901	901	2,105	2,091	2,127	2,121	2,121
Mozambique	128	198	72	52	220	207	207	207	311	623
Namibia	1,682	2,204	2,511	3,820	7,612	27,263	30,885	21,651	19,800	14,773
Nepal	124,754	126,815	129,157	126,101	127,940	129,237	130,945	132,436	123,667	124,928
Netherlands	79,960	102,588	118,071	131,490	138,646	146,180	151,928	148,362	140,886	126,805
New Zealand	3,758	3,788	3,646	4,097	4,800	4,923	5,264	5,757	5,807	5,350
Nicaragua	577	557	465	474	471	332	325	325	300	292
Niger	27,622	25,845	7,376	3,691	350	58	83	296	328	344
Nigeria	8,118	8,486	9,071	6,780	6,941	7,270	7,200	7,355	9,171	8,395
Norway	47,607	48,409	47,381	45,334	43,440	47,693	50,128	50,432	46,109	44,046
Oman	-	-	-	-	-	-	-	-	-	7
Pakistan	1,202,493	1,202,703	1,202,734	1,202,462	1,202,015	2,001,466	2,198,797	1,227,433	1,124,298	960,617
Panama	867	867	622	1,188	1,321	1,313	1,474	1,573	1,445	1,608
Papua New Guinea	9,601	10,176	8,198	8,198	6,666	5,863	4,941	4,941	7,491	7,627

Country of asylum[1]	1995	1996	1997	1998	1999	2000	2001	2002	2003	2004
Paraguay	60	53	47	30	19	21	21	21	28	41
Peru	610	663	750	433	702	687	683	688	718	766
Philippines	783	691	311	307	170	176	136	114	108	107
Poland	600	600	835	898	942	1,020	1,311	1,591	1,836	2,507
Portugal	248	308	319	339	379	433	449	462	418	377
Qatar	-	-	-	-	6	31	67	46	46	46
Rep. of Korea	5	6	3	1	7	6	7	17	25	44
Rep. of Moldova	-	-	-	-	8	68	159	173	102	57
Romania	194	269	640	989	1,242	1,685	1,805	1,857	2,011	1,627
Russian Federation	-	246,691	237,720	128,574	80,060	26,265	17,970	14,969	9,899	1,852
Rwanda	7,792	25,257	34,227	33,403	34,365	28,398	34,786	30,863	36,608	50,221
Saint Lucia	-	-	3	-	-	-	-	-	-	-
Saudi Arabia	13,169	9,852	5,833	5,531	5,562	5,309	245,268	245,290	240,835	240,552
Senegal	66,769	65,044	57,229	60,823	21,539	20,766	20,707	20,711	20,726	20,804
Serbia and Montenegro	650,700	563,215	550,061	502,037	501,262	484,391	400,304	354,402	291,403	276,683
Sierra Leone	4,675	13,532	13,011	9,866	6,570	6,546	10,501	63,494	61,194	65,437
Singapore	112	10	5	5	1	-	2	2	1	1
Slovakia	2,339	1,387	746	424	443	457	472	444	414	409
Slovenia	22,314	10,014	5,135	3,465	4,382	2,816	2,415	390	2,069	304
Solomon Islands	2,000	2,000	800	210	-	-	-	-	-	-
Somalia	626	700	622	337	130	558	589	199	368	357
South Africa	101,408	22,645	6,819	8,388	14,538	15,063	18,605	23,344	26,558	27,683
Spain	5,852	5,688	5,532	5,939	6,714	6,987	6,806	6,780	5,900	5,635
Sri Lanka	16	14	26	29	21	16	17	28	30	63
Sudan	674,071	393,874	374,415	391,496	390,995	414,928	349,209	328,176	138,163	141,588
Suriname	-	-	11	-	-	-	-	-	-	-
Swaziland	712	575	592	592	616	690	690	653	686	704
Sweden	199,212	191,171	186,725	178,795	159,513	157,220	146,491	142,193	112,167	73,408
Switzerland	82,943	84,413	83,203	81,903	82,298	57,653	58,494	54,113	50,144	47,678
Syrian Arab Rep.	36,222	27,759	22,704	20,974	6,474	3,463	3,351	2,918	3,681	15,604
Tajikistan	620	1,166	2,174	3,634	4,541	15,364	15,346	3,437	3,306	3,306
TfYR Macedonia	9,048	5,089	3,500	1,700	21,200	9,050	4,363	2,816	193	1,004
Thailand	106,565	107,962	169,154	138,332	100,133	104,965	110,711	112,614	119,053	121,139
Timor-Leste	-	-	-	-	-	-	-	1	3	3
Togo	10,876	12,589	12,682	11,816	12,113	12,223	12,257	12,294	12,395	11,285
Tunisia	199	176	506	528	454	436	97	102	99	90
Turkey	12,841	8,166	2,446	2,528	2,815	3,103	3,472	3,301	2,490	3,033
Turkmenistan	23,323	15,580	15,787	14,625	18,464	14,188	14,005	13,693	13,511	13,253
Uganda	229,350	264,294	188,513	204,545	218,191	236,622	199,736	217,302	230,903	250,482
Ukraine	5,193	3,591	4,564	6,101	2,697	2,951	2,983	2,966	2,877	2,459
United Arab Emirates	407	464	519	529	501	562	556	163	160	105
United Kingdom	90,909	98,577	107,933	121,716	148,922	186,248	233,389	260,687	276,522	289,054
United Rep. of Tanzania	829,671	498,732	570,367	543,881	622,203	680,862	646,900	689,373	649,770	602,088
United States	623,294	607,024	563,837	533,969	521,143	508,222	515,853	485,171	452,548	420,854
Uruguay	132	138	133	163	87	79	90	99	91	97
Uzbekistan	2,627	2,900	3,159	1,071	1,014	38,350	39,579	44,936	44,682	44,455
Venezuela	1,613	1,596	301	158	188	132	59	58	58	244
Viet Nam	34,400	34,400	15,000	15,000	15,000	15,945	15,945	15,945	15,360	2,360
Yemen	53,453	53,546	40,964	61,382	60,477	60,545	69,468	82,803	61,881	66,384
Zambia	129,965	131,139	165,072	168,564	206,386	250,940	284,173	246,765	226,697	173,907
Zimbabwe	514	595	806	1,655	2,071	4,127	8,706	9,432	12,721	6,884
Grand Total	14,896,087	13,357,087	12,015,350	11,480,860	11,687,226	12,129,572	12,116,835	10,594,055	9,680,265	9,236,763

Note:
For detailed explanations, consult UNHCR statistical yearbooks.
[1] In the absence of Government figures, UNHCR has estimated the refugee population in many industrialized countries, based on recent resettlement arrivals and recognition of asylum seekers. For Canada, USA, Australia and New Zealand, estimates are based on arrivals/recognition during the past five years, whereas for most European countries a 10-year period has been applied. These periods reflect the different naturalization rates for refugees.
Sources: UNHCR, Governments.

Annex 5

Refugee population by origin, 1995-2004 (end-year)

Origin	1995	1996	1997	1998	1999	2000	2001	2002	2003	2004
Afghanistan	2,679,133	2,674,236	2,676,674	2,667,115	2,601,691	3,587,336	3,809,767	2,510,294	2,136,043	2,085,522
Albania	5,803	5,785	5,379	5,353	6,288	6,802	7,626	10,761	10,385	10,470
Algeria	1,520	2,247	3,418	5,727	7,151	8,034	8,418	12,107	11,667	10,691
Andorra	2	3	1	2	3	2	1	10	10	3
Angola	246,657	249,687	267,696	319,430	353,478	433,760	470,625	435,421	329,583	228,838
Antigua and Barbuda	-	-	1	2	2	1	4	5	5	13
Argentina	330	217	159	142	586	609	659	771	784	796
Armenia	201,442	203,231	203,690	193,150	193,231	5,786	7,207	13,249	13,162	13,422
Australia	1	1	2	1	3	3	1	10	15	13
Austria	49	52	55	60	48	35	29	72	66	47
Azerbaijan	200,520	236,086	234,950	329,657	311,131	284,277	268,759	260,214	253,255	250,581
Bahamas	-	-	-	1	1	1	-	1	1	1
Bahrain	71	63	82	97	129	95	46	50	52	52
Bangladesh	56,956	57,959	44,373	4,658	4,468	5,401	5,548	5,808	5,565	5,731
Barbados	3	2	3	5	4	8	7	9	11	7
Belarus	84	501	303	290	1,507	2,519	3,696	6,364	7,815	8,244
Belgium	3	5	10	14	16	19	13	27	40	45
Belize	8	3	-	-	11	12	-	1	10	9
Benin	54	46	46	56	52	54	55	232	282	309
Bermuda	-	-	-	1	1	1	1	1	-	-
Bhutan	104,750	106,822	108,703	105,689	107,619	108,945	110,845	112,523	103,978	105,255
Bolivia	180	177	161	183	174	175	156	219	264	285
Bosnia and Herzegovina	769,753	993,868	849,241	640,075	598,193	504,981	447,321	406,448	300,006	229,339
Botswana	25	23	17	16	10	3	2	5	5	6
Brazil	53	85	104	136	196	224	254	441	378	403
Brunei Darussalam	3	-	-	-	-	-	-	2	1	1
Bulgaria	4,156	3,246	3,048	3,122	2,653	2,404	2,121	2,841	2,567	2,215
Burkina Faso	63	72	118	103	106	130	98	978	853	582
Burundi	350,582	428,680	519,123	502,568	527,449	568,084	553,999	574,557	531,637	485,773
Cambodia	61,225	62,244	103,246	76,576	38,320	36,855	34,759	33,456	31,407	18,121
Cameroon	2,017	2,109	2,258	1,348	1,654	2,062	2,724	5,225	6,206	7,629
Canada	4	8	11	15	18	26	4	51	60	56
Cape Verde	1	2	2	1	2	2	4	8	9	8
Central African Rep.	242	240	149	173	196	139	28,704	25,376	35,400	31,069
Chad	59,727	58,445	55,025	61,298	58,797	54,962	46,294	47,349	52,275	52,663
Chile	14,273	12,805	9,776	7,011	1,543	860	834	1,709	1,555	1,194
China	104,693	105,810	106,738	109,402	111,952	110,975	117,409	132,115	132,406	134,724
Colombia	1,902	2,168	2,377	3,538	4,413	9,279	17,938	30,625	37,995	47,357
Comoros	10	13	10	33	31	28	26	43	58	50
Congo	177	221	21,147	17,143	27,302	27,579	24,237	28,002	28,958	28,152
Costa Rica	211	139	90	54	76	57	86	98	92	138
Côte d'Ivoire	201	268	360	537	562	773	858	23,741	33,637	23,655
Croatia	245,572	310,088	349,307	338,089	353,725	335,199	290,279	274,818	230,189	215,475
Cuba	24,854	25,462	24,913	23,559	23,328	20,084	18,959	18,043	16,093	15,657
Cyprus	9	10	8	11	16	11	5	7	5	2
Czech Rep.	2,039	977	698	1,934	1,243	810	1,179	6,984	6,702	4,542
Dem. People's Rep. of Korea	7	11	1	9	13	13	19	259	304	343
Dem. Rep. of the Congo	89,738	158,794	173,995	158,833	255,950	371,713	392,146	421,362	453,465	462,208
Denmark	18	34	33	28	25	25	3	8	10	10
Djibouti	18,095	18,101	8,142	3,219	1,879	1,910	452	471	522	495
Dominica	-	1	1	1	3	2	5	6	17	25
Dominican Rep.	30	29	47	42	45	47	46	83	92	97
Ecuador	206	221	217	512	496	671	653	822	730	727
Egypt	872	1,202	1,722	2,612	3,491	3,953	4,678	6,443	5,735	5,376
El Salvador	23,535	19,639	17,126	12,591	12,410	7,756	7,150	6,632	5,658	4,497

Origin	1995	1996	1997	1998	1999	2000	2001	2002	2003	2004
Equatorial Guinea	343	397	473	420	429	509	529	552	591	549
Eritrea	286,712	332,225	319,077	346,781	347,138	376,851	333,229	318,176	124,121	131,131
Estonia	351	1,310	1,266	792	633	455	479	1,060	1,027	855
Ethiopia	100,987	96,270	84,401	70,680	71,055	66,410	58,997	61,240	62,677	63,147
Fiji	222	305	326	301	328	401	731	1,072	1,087	1,281
Finland	1	1	2	6	6	5	2	9	7	3
France	15	44	61	64	63	78	44	90	110	110
French Guiana	5	5	5	5	5	-	-	-	-	-
Gabon	25	24	19	28	26	26	27	37	39	53
Gambia	161	310	421	570	677	750	734	861	746	684
Georgia	308	48,489	47,164	35,669	29,878	21,821	17,498	16,975	12,497	6,633
Germany	386	420	443	688	1,298	1,183	1,033	928	725	78
Ghana	13,592	15,095	14,775	13,633	13,293	14,775	14,556	15,686	15,879	14,767
Greece	222	250	178	174	164	125	97	301	270	224
Grenada	6	11	12	20	36	24	53	73	77	99
Guatemala	42,899	40,342	37,508	32,747	28,082	20,711	16,867	13,888	6,696	4,376
Guinea	441	523	648	924	1,151	1,497	2,019	3,418	3,871	4,782
Guinea-Bissau	830	856	868	8,887	3,185	886	927	986	975	1,018
Guyana	62	55	38	41	49	36	36	49	78	194
Haiti	13,925	15,118	15,481	13,538	8,766	7,561	7,248	7,718	7,547	9,208
Holy See	-	-	-	-	-	-	-	-	-	2
Honduras	1,219	1,259	1,246	1,101	1,070	903	781	673	604	484
Hong Kong SAR, China	205	105	50	42	20	13	7	5	9	8
Hungary	2,348	3,083	2,669	1,242	800	518	953	3,517	3,395	2,749
Iceland	-	4	5	5	5	5	-	13	12	10
India	5,011	7,550	8,924	9,663	9,845	11,399	11,571	14,349	13,706	13,345
Indonesia	9,836	11,365	8,799	9,053	9,020	9,149	8,970	9,906	16,240	27,919
Iraq	718,719	714,730	707,338	675,030	642,886	526,179	530,511	422,512	368,580	311,878
Ireland	2	2	1	-	-	3	3	7	6	3
Islamic Rep. of Iran	112,364	104,129	93,993	89,979	86,855	88,278	92,491	138,364	132,544	115,149
Israel	937	1,126	987	835	478	416	363	564	625	672
Italy	121	112	112	79	52	48	34	224	207	192
Jamaica	10	18	21	27	33	37	37	147	259	350
Japan	3	2	2	3	3	5	5	19	19	21
Jordan	513	708	719	899	973	919	775	1,287	1,162	1,169
Kazakhstan	139	40,163	40,774	20,459	9,057	2,537	2,803	6,315	6,559	6,121
Kenya	9,327	9,390	9,570	6,046	6,138	2,373	2,559	3,098	3,163	3,847
Kiribati	-	-	-	-	-	-	-	3	16	32
Kuwait	762	854	825	830	992	692	701	709	616	398
Kyrgyzstan	22	17,118	16,320	7,449	4,003	748	685	2,950	3,141	3,292
Lao People's Dem. Rep.	58,193	46,909	37,367	29,017	21,396	16,094	12,631	11,235	10,363	16,114
Latvia	160	1,958	1,915	1,013	907	491	619	3,082	3,177	2,826
Lebanon	13,515	10,890	10,235	9,786	7,685	10,215	8,763	26,320	24,932	19,866
Lesotho	-	2	3	3	3	4	1	4	6	7
Liberia	744,637	784,008	493,340	365,398	294,694	266,930	244,608	275,422	353,344	335,467
Libyan Arab Jamahiriya	624	281	274	433	568	619	888	1,456	1,570	1,720
Lithuania	109	662	649	282	258	163	216	1,371	1,541	1,482
Luxembourg	-	-	-	-	-	-	-	-	-	1
Macao SAR, China	-	1	1	1	1	6	8	15	15	20
Madagascar	79	79	76	66	54	54	40	53	88	135
Malawi	37	39	34	28	34	33	25	48	59	94
Malaysia	79	103	87	90	86	82	79	119	239	292
Maldives	-	1	1	2	3	4	3	3	1	3
Mali	77,219	55,198	18,015	3,702	387	364	311	531	461	483
Malta	13	18	14	17	22	16	7	8	7	3
Martinique	1	1	1	-	-	-	-	-	-	-
Mauritania	84,312	83,234	70,294	70,224	29,948	29,752	29,862	30,137	30,525	31,131

Origin	1995	1996	1997	1998	1999	2000	2001	2002	2003	2004
Mauritius	13	13	3	15	8	35	35	43	61	19
Mexico	361	520	665	1,016	1,359	1,291	1,594	1,670	1,652	1,744
Monaco	-	1	1	1	1	1	-	1	1	-
Mongolia	4	7	9	19	25	23	60	280	324	442
Morocco	301	297	310	353	377	392	363	1,269	1,291	1,319
Mozambique	125,562	34,657	33,652	59	35	30	46	130	111	104
Myanmar	152,298	143,017	135,772	133,407	131,663	137,128	145,856	148,501	151,384	161,013
Namibia	13	12	2	1,902	701	2,308	2,297	1,302	1,293	1,314
Nauru	-	-	-	-	3	3	-	-	3	-
Nepal	27	44	52	101	186	235	306	902	1,231	1,416
Netherlands	89	176	198	181	157	152	4	256	271	48
New Zealand	-	-	-	-	-	-	-	2	1	3
Nicaragua	23,938	22,820	22,494	21,389	20,573	5,071	4,399	4,050	3,983	1,822
Niger	10,291	10,361	2,788	423	514	493	483	834	728	689
Nigeria	1,939	4,754	3,059	3,999	4,441	5,742	6,084	24,572	24,428	23,890
Norway	1	1	3	4	4	4	3	5	6	5
Occupied Palestinian Territory[1]	72,768	80,215	76,821	77,524	100,602	110,640	349,161	428,782	427,862	350,617
Oman	10	10	10	11	11	5	5	19	11	18
Pakistan	5,277	7,502	5,985	6,864	8,015	10,133	12,324	23,163	24,389	25,949
Panama	160	149	122	85	72	67	37	44	30	40
Papua New Guinea	2,000	2,008	808	220	9	8	8	16	18	18
Paraguay	51	44	20	21	18	19	8	31	32	37
Peru	5,904	6,696	6,610	7,066	7,206	6,944	6,502	6,430	5,581	4,769
Philippines	516	598	525	45,598	45,520	45,482	45,467	45,608	412	434
Poland	19,732	12,869	7,294	1,880	1,245	865	3,191	16,712	15,211	10,677
Portugal	25	217	213	18	15	23	17	62	55	47
Puerto Rico	12	12	-	-	-	-	-	-	-	-
Qatar	30	18	19	23	8	1	-	8	13	10
Rep. of Korea	30	42	48	65	75	73	83	245	237	272
Rep. of Moldova	529	5,829	5,141	2,754	2,407	2,657	3,737	10,130	11,146	11,937
Romania	16,978	11,871	8,951	10,921	8,558	7,348	6,052	8,847	8,387	5,916
Russian Federation	207,034	173,723	198,063	172,730	28,314	40,310	45,156	91,626	96,420	107,967
Rwanda	1,819,366	469,136	68,003	77,743	88,944	119,056	84,513	75,257	75,263	63,812
Saint Kitts and Nevis	-	-	-	-	-	-	-	2	1	1
Saint Lucia	2	2	3	5	9	11	9	10	16	34
Saint Vincent and the Grenadines	7	13	13	24	36	48	67	81	105	181
Samoa	-	-	1	1	1	1	1	-	-	-
San Marino	-	-	2	4	4	4	-	3	1	1
Sao Tome and Principe	36	49	43	42	30	25	23	39	42	39
Saudi Arabia	260	242	358	362	233	77	35	109	236	214
Senegal	17,592	17,631	17,163	9,716	11,606	11,088	8,559	12,069	8,351	8,332
Serbia and Montenegro	86,120	103,967	106,654	115,292	172,509	146,748	144,231	327,587	296,632	236,999
Seychelles	339	138	33	39	29	23	13	44	38	44
Sierra Leone	379,495	375,104	329,327	406,077	490,061	402,807	179,113	141,475	70,580	41,801
Singapore	9	19	22	23	25	22	16	39	35	36
Slovakia	26	57	70	143	178	220	191	595	667	619
Slovenia	12,860	3,368	3,414	3,302	3,295	3,284	765	858	610	582
Solomon Islands	34	34	34	34	34	34	42	54	60	61
Somalia	638,698	636,985	608,094	557,959	524,613	475,655	440,134	432,316	402,336	389,314
South Africa	488	290	244	188	193	168	123	275	288	272
Spain	36	218	215	60	53	80	48	58	53	49
Sri Lanka	107,589	109,578	122,287	114,976	116,709	124,160	122,420	133,239	122,010	114,050
Stateless	26,139	23,692	23,334	7,114	11,814	6,434	7,161	14,476	13,861	14,008
Sudan	445,280	475,305	364,589	390,013	485,460	494,363	489,950	508,877	606,242	730,650
Suriname	817	754	663	491	411	334	237	103	70	51
Swaziland	15	17	20	30	28	16	15	19	5	14
Sweden	25	38	40	41	31	18	5	28	32	29

Origin	1995	1996	1997	1998	1999	2000	2001	2002	2003	2004
Switzerland	27	33	55	77	91	70	61	56	35	12
Syrian Arab Rep.	7,994	8,609	8,653	8,126	6,695	5,871	4,869	18,913	20,276	21,439
Tajikistan	58,956	107,503	75,878	56,349	45,167	59,940	56,108	63,267	58,936	56,780
TfYR Macedonia	12,883	13,041	12,747	1,939	2,089	2,176	12,197	8,107	5,982	5,106
Thailand	211	284	272	295	318	217	94	344	296	319
Tibetans	20,035	20,037	20,506	21,229	21,040	20,968	20,720	20,631	20,039	20,040
Timor-Leste	-	-	-	-	162,472	122,202	73,042	28,097	127	221
Togo	93,155	25,593	7,187	3,506	3,692	4,016	4,354	10,448	10,614	10,819
Tonga	-	3	3	2	2	3	1	8	12	5
Trinidad and Tobago	14	16	21	26	25	24	16	35	38	41
Tunisia	333	406	698	932	1,240	1,207	1,368	2,543	2,563	2,518
Turkey	44,866	50,354	47,341	45,019	44,012	47,155	47,090	193,704	185,687	174,574
Turkmenistan	47	2,937	3,181	1,562	1,051	300	310	801	840	812
Tuvalu	3	3	3	3	3	3	3	3	3	3
Uganda	24,166	28,339	55,241	13,301	13,937	32,414	40,141	40,425	35,247	31,963
Ukraine	1,701	6,107	6,348	4,596	12,236	19,312	26,716	85,265	94,148	89,579
United Arab Emirates	-	-	4	7	7	15	18	31	20	71
United Kingdom	77	73	79	92	106	113	109	164	149	144
United Rep. of Tanzania	68	65	66	102	118	313	378	580	711	985
United States	245	143	75	51	41	176	219	383	395	451
Uruguay	262	201	89	74	39	51	46	61	57	81
Uzbekistan	143	69,747	69,069	51,729	45,533	3,628	3,458	6,881	7,391	7,288
Venezuela	476	557	608	570	556	471	466	526	598	1,256
Viet Nam	543,541	518,340	476,795	435,437	405,377	370,758	353,224	373,741	363,179	349,780
Western Sahara	165,000	166,328	166,099	165,967	165,868	165,810	165,910	165,884	165,729	165,731
Yemen	369	1,154	1,721	1,935	2,022	2,113	1,985	1,600	1,597	1,606
Zambia	20	40	63	77	87	98	62	92	100	124
Zimbabwe	36	34	38	42	43	109	257	4,030	7,162	9,568
Various/unknown	2,166,465	1,412,730	1,065,663	1,070,493	1,236,702	1,119,235	1,099,539	289,540	319,996	342,322
Grand Total	**14,896,087**	**13,357,087**	**12,015,350**	**11,480,860**	**11,687,226**	**12,129,572**	**12,116,835**	**10,594,055**	**9,680,265**	**9,236,763**

Note:
Data includes estimates for most industrialized countries. Complete breakdown by origin not always available.
For detailed explanations, consult UNHCR statistical yearbooks.
[1] Palestinian refugees under UNHCR mandate only.
Sources: UNHCR, Governments.

Refugee population by origin and country/territory of asylum, end-2004

Origin	Country/territory of asylum		Origin	Country/territory of asylum	
Afghanistan	Pakistan[1]	960,041	Central African Rep.	Chad	29,683
Afghanistan	Islamic Rep. of Iran	952,802	Central African Rep.	Various/unknown	1,386
Afghanistan	Germany	38,576	**Central African Rep. Total**		**31,069**
Afghanistan	Netherlands	25,907	Chad	Cameroon	39,290
Afghanistan	United Kingdom	22,494	Chad	Sudan	5,023
Afghanistan	Canada	15,242	Chad	Nigeria	3,195
Afghanistan	United States	9,778	Chad	Various/unknown	5,155
Afghanistan	India	9,761	**Chad Total**		**52,663**
Afghanistan	Australia	8,037	China	India	94,349
Afghanistan	Denmark	6,437	China	United States	18,957
Afghanistan	Uzbekistan	5,238	China	Canada	8,071
Afghanistan	Sweden	3,903	China	Germany	6,914
Afghanistan	Norway	3,693	China	Netherlands	2,288
Afghanistan	Tajikistan	3,304	China	Various/unknown	4,145
Afghanistan	Hungary	2,497	**China Total**		**134,724**
Afghanistan	Austria	2,482	Colombia	United States	14,920
Afghanistan	Various/unknown	15,330	Colombia	Canada	9,441
Afghanistan Total		**2,085,522**	Colombia	Costa Rica	8,750
Angola	Dem. Rep. of the Congo	98,383	Colombia	Ecuador	8,270
Angola	Zambia	88,842	Colombia	Various/unknown	5,976
Angola	Namibia	12,618	**Colombia Total**		**47,357**
Angola	South Africa	5,774	Congo	Gabon	11,988
Angola	Congo	3,632	Congo	Dem. Rep. of the Congo	5,277
Angola	United Kingdom	3,349	Congo	Various/unknown	10,887
Angola	Netherlands	3,296	**Congo Total**		**28,152**
Angola	Germany	3,272	Côte d'Ivoire	Liberia	12,408
Angola	France	2,146	Côte d'Ivoire	Guinea	4,735
Angola	Switzerland	2,129	Côte d'Ivoire	Mali	2,704
Angola	Brazil	2,005	Côte d'Ivoire	Various/unknown	3,808
Angola	Various/unknown	3,392	**Côte d'Ivoire Total**		**23,655**
Angola Total		**228,838**	Croatia	Serbia and Montenegro	180,117
Azerbaijan	Armenia	235,101	Croatia	Bosnia and Herzegovina	19,213
Azerbaijan	Germany	9,150	Croatia	United States	4,732
Azerbaijan	United States	2,559	Croatia	Germany	2,900
Azerbaijan	Various/unknown	3,771	Croatia	Australia	2,689
Azerbaijan Total		**250,581**	Croatia	Sweden	2,050
Bhutan	Nepal	104,915	Croatia	Various/unknown	3,774
Bhutan	Various/unknown	340	**Croatia Total**		**215,475**
Bhutan Total		**105,255**	Dem. Rep. of the Congo	United Rep. of Tanzania	153,474
Bosnia and Herzegovina	Serbia and Montenegro	95,297	Dem. Rep. of the Congo	Zambia	66,248
Bosnia and Herzegovina	United States	39,393	Dem. Rep. of the Congo	Congo	58,834
Bosnia and Herzegovina	Germany	30,083	Dem. Rep. of the Congo	Burundi	48,424
Bosnia and Herzegovina	Denmark	22,176	Dem. Rep. of the Congo	Rwanda	45,460
Bosnia and Herzegovina	Netherlands	13,518	Dem. Rep. of the Congo	Uganda	14,982
Bosnia and Herzegovina	Sweden	7,177	Dem. Rep. of the Congo	Angola	13,510
Bosnia and Herzegovina	Switzerland	6,553	Dem. Rep. of the Congo	South Africa	9,516
Bosnia and Herzegovina	Norway	3,875	Dem. Rep. of the Congo	France	7,665
Bosnia and Herzegovina	Croatia	3,204	Dem. Rep. of the Congo	Germany	6,668
Bosnia and Herzegovina	France	2,642	Dem. Rep. of the Congo	United Kingdom	5,973
Bosnia and Herzegovina	Various/unknown	5,421	Dem. Rep. of the Congo	Canada	5,069
Bosnia and Herzegovina Total		**229,339**	Dem. Rep. of the Congo	Zimbabwe	3,614
Burundi	United Rep. of Tanzania	443,706	Dem. Rep. of the Congo	Central African Rep.	3,447
Burundi	Dem. Rep. of the Congo	19,400	Dem. Rep. of the Congo	United States	3,262
Burundi	Rwanda	4,719	Dem. Rep. of the Congo	Kenya	2,367
Burundi	South Africa	2,075	Dem. Rep. of the Congo	Netherlands	2,097
Burundi	Various/unknown	15,873	Dem. Rep. of the Congo	Various/unknown	11,598
Burundi Total		**485,773**	**Dem. Rep. of the Congo Total**		**462,208**

Origin	Country/territory of asylum	
Eritrea	Sudan	110,927
Eritrea	Ethiopia	8,719
Eritrea	Germany	2,974
Eritrea	United Kingdom	2,404
Eritrea	Various/unknown	6,107
Eritrea Total		**131,131**
Ethiopia	Sudan	14,812
Ethiopia	United States	12,980
Ethiopia	Kenya	12,595
Ethiopia	Germany	6,669
Ethiopia	Canada	3,549
Ethiopia	United Kingdom	2,542
Ethiopia	Various/unknown	10,000
Ethiopia Total		**63,147**
Indonesia	Malaysia	15,181
Indonesia	Papua New Guinea	7,626
Indonesia	United States	3,107
Indonesia	Various/unknown	2,005
Indonesia Total		**27,919**
Iraq	Islamic Rep. of Iran	93,173
Iraq	Germany	68,071
Iraq	Netherlands	27,622
Iraq	United Kingdom	22,763
Iraq	Sweden	22,028
Iraq	Syrian Arab Rep.	14,391
Iraq	Denmark	11,500
Iraq	Australia	11,471
Iraq	United States	8,583
Iraq	Norway	8,265
Iraq	Canada	5,402
Iraq	Switzerland	3,208
Iraq	Various/unknown	15,401
Iraq Total		**311,878**
Islamic Rep. of Iran	Germany	39,904
Islamic Rep. of Iran	United States	20,541
Islamic Rep. of Iran	Iraq	9,500
Islamic Rep. of Iran	United Kingdom	8,044
Islamic Rep. of Iran	Netherlands	6,597
Islamic Rep. of Iran	Canada	6,508
Islamic Rep. of Iran	Sweden	5,258
Islamic Rep. of Iran	Norway	3,465
Islamic Rep. of Iran	Australia	2,766
Islamic Rep. of Iran	Various/unknown	12,566
Islamic Rep. of Iran Total		**115,149**
Liberia	Guinea	127,256
Liberia	Côte d'Ivoire	70,402
Liberia	Sierra Leone	65,433
Liberia	Ghana	40,853
Liberia	United States	19,555
Liberia	Nigeria	2,932
Liberia	Various/unknown	9,036
Liberia Total		**335,467**
Mauritania	Senegal	19,778
Mauritania	Mali	6,185
Mauritania	France	3,391
Mauritania	Various/unknown	1,777
Mauritania Total		**31,131**

Origin	Country/territory of asylum	
Myanmar	Thailand	120,814
Myanmar	Bangladesh	20,402
Myanmar	Malaysia	9,601
Myanmar	United States	5,342
Myanmar	Various/unknown	4,854
Myanmar Total		**161,013**
Nigeria	Cameroon	16,686
Nigeria	United Kingdom	2,012
Nigeria	Various/unknown	5,192
Nigeria Total		**23,890**
Occupied Palestinian Territory[2]	Saudi Arabia	240,007
Occupied Palestinian Territory[2]	Egypt	70,245
Occupied Palestinian Territory[2]	Iraq	22,711
Occupied Palestinian Territory[2]	Libyan Arab Jamahiriya	8,873
Occupied Palestinian Territory[2]	Algeria	4,005
Occupied Palestinian Territory[2]	Various/unknown	4,776
Occupied Palestinian Territory[2] Total		**350,617**
Pakistan	Canada	9,662
Pakistan	Germany	8,656
Pakistan	United Kingdom	3,609
Pakistan	Various/unknown	4,022
Pakistan Total		**25,949**
Russian Federation	Germany	45,030
Russian Federation	United States	15,891
Russian Federation	Kazakhstan	13,684
Russian Federation	Azerbaijan	8,367
Russian Federation	Austria	4,152
Russian Federation	France	3,991
Russian Federation	Georgia	2,543
Russian Federation	Norway	2,249
Russian Federation	Canada	2,118
Russian Federation	Various/unknown	9,942
Russian Federation Total		**107,967**
Rwanda	Uganda	18,902
Rwanda	Dem. Rep. of the Congo	11,816
Rwanda	Congo	5,852
Rwanda	Zambia	5,791
Rwanda	Various/unknown	21,451
Rwanda Total		**63,812**
Serbia and Montenegro	Germany	142,681
Serbia and Montenegro	United Kingdom	20,527
Serbia and Montenegro	Sweden	11,844
Serbia and Montenegro	Switzerland	10,956
Serbia and Montenegro	Canada	6,472
Serbia and Montenegro	France	6,292
Serbia and Montenegro	Australia	5,366
Serbia and Montenegro	Denmark	4,876
Serbia and Montenegro	Austria	4,715
Serbia and Montenegro	Netherlands	3,748
Serbia and Montenegro	Norway	3,527
Serbia and Montenegro	Bosnia and Herzegovina	2,991
Serbia and Montenegro	Italy	2,302
Serbia and Montenegro	Hungary	2,251
Serbia and Montenegro	Various/unknown	8,451
Serbia and Montenegro Total		**236,999**

Origin	Country/territory of asylum	
Sierra Leone	Guinea	7,165
Sierra Leone	United States	6,885
Sierra Leone	Gambia	5,955
Sierra Leone	United Kingdom	4,118
Sierra Leone	Netherlands	3,737
Sierra Leone	Liberia	2,735
Sierra Leone	Various/unknown	11,206
Sierra Leone Total		**41,801**
Somalia	Kenya	153,627
Somalia	Yemen	63,511
Somalia	United Kingdom	36,700
Somalia	United States	31,110
Somalia	Djibouti	17,331
Somalia	Ethiopia	16,470
Somalia	Netherlands	11,239
Somalia	Denmark	7,788
Somalia	South Africa	7,118
Somalia	Norway	6,242
Somalia	Canada	4,894
Somalia	Egypt	3,809
Somalia	Switzerland	3,747
Somalia	Eritrea	3,523
Somalia	Germany	3,423
Somalia	Libyan Arab Jamahiriya	2,938
Somalia	Sweden	2,932
Somalia	United Rep. of Tanzania	2,867
Somalia	Various/unknown	10,045
Somalia Total		**389,314**
Sri Lanka	India	57,274
Sri Lanka	France	15,304
Sri Lanka	Germany	12,850
Sri Lanka	Canada	12,062
Sri Lanka	United Kingdom	8,064
Sri Lanka	Switzerland	2,952
Sri Lanka	Various/unknown	5,544
Sri Lanka Total		**114,050**
Sudan	Chad	224,924
Sudan	Uganda	214,673
Sudan	Ethiopia	90,451
Sudan	Kenya	67,556
Sudan	Dem. Rep. of the Congo	45,226
Sudan	Central African Rep.	19,470
Sudan	United States	17,994
Sudan	Australia	16,365
Sudan	Egypt	14,904
Sudan	Canada	6,312
Sudan	Netherlands	3,618
Sudan	United Kingdom	2,426
Sudan	Various/unknown	6,731
Sudan Total		**730,650**

Origin	Country/territory of asylum	
Syrian Arab Rep.	Germany	16,184
Syrian Arab Rep.	Various/unknown	5,255
Syrian Arab Rep. Total		**21,439**
Tajikistan	Uzbekistan	39,202
Tajikistan	Turkmenistan	12,085
Tajikistan	Kyrgyzstan	3,472
Tajikistan	Various/unknown	2,021
Tajikistan Total		**56,780**
Tibetans	Nepal	20,000
Tibetans	Various/unknown	40
Tibetans Total		**20,040**
Turkey	Germany	128,419
Turkey	Iraq	13,353
Turkey	France	9,387
Turkey	United Kingdom	8,602
Turkey	Switzerland	5,613
Turkey	Canada	2,632
Turkey	Various/unknown	6,568
Turkey Total		**174,574**
Uganda	Dem. Rep. of the Congo	18,953
Uganda	Sudan	7,901
Uganda	Various/unknown	5,109
Uganda Total		**31,963**
Ukraine	Germany	57,693
Ukraine	United States	28,484
Ukraine	Various/unknown	3,402
Ukraine Total		**89,579**
Viet Nam	China	299,287
Viet Nam	Germany	21,006
Viet Nam	United States	12,382
Viet Nam	France	9,132
Viet Nam	Switzerland	2,214
Viet Nam	Various/unknown	5,759
Viet Nam Total		**349,780**
Western Sahara	Algeria	165,000
Western Sahara	Various/unknown	731
Western Sahara Total		**165,731**

Note:
This table shows the origin for refugee populations of 20,000 or more. Countries of asylum are listed if they host 2,000 or more refugees from that country/territory of origin.
In the absence of Government figures, UNHCR has estimated the refugee population in many industrialized countries, based on recent resettlement arrivals and recognition of asylum seekers. For Canada, USA, Australia and New Zealand, estimates are based on arrivals/recognition during the past five years, whereas for most European countries a 10-year period has been applied. These periods reflect the different naturalization rates for refugees.
For detailed explanations, consult UNHCR statistical yearbooks.
[1] UNHCR estimate.
[2] Palestinian refugees under UNHCR mandate only.

Refugees per 1,000 inhabitants: top 40 countries, end-2004

Country of asylum	Refugees per 1,000 inhabitants		Country of asylum	Refugees per 1,000 inhabitants
Armenia	78.0		Switzerland	6.6
Chad	26.7		Burundi	6.5
Serbia and Montenegro	26.3		Central African Rep.	6.2
Djibouti	22.7		Pakistan	6.1
Congo	17.1		Bosnia and Herzegovina	5.7
United Rep. of Tanzania	15.7		Rwanda	5.6
Islamic Rep. of Iran	15.0		Algeria	5.1
Zambia	14.9		United Kingdom	4.8
Guinea	14.8		Gambia	4.8
Denmark	12.0		Guinea-Bissau	4.8
Sierra Leone	11.8		Liberia	4.6
Germany	10.6		Nepal	4.6
Gabon	10.0		Canada	4.4
Saudi Arabia	9.8		Liechtenstein	4.3
Norway	9.5		Côte d'Ivoire	4.0
Uganda	8.7		Sudan	3.9
Sweden	8.1		Malta	3.9
Netherlands	7.8		Cameroon	3.6
Namibia	7.3		Dem. Rep. of the Congo	3.5
Kenya	7.0		Luxembourg	3.4

Note: Data includes estimates for refugee populations in most industrialized countries. For detailed explanations, consult UNHCR statistical yearbooks.
Sources: UNHCR; United Nations, Department of Economic and Social Affairs, *World Population Prospects, The 2004 Revision*, New York, 2005.

Asylum applications and total admissions in industrialized countries, 1995-2004

Country of asylum or resettlement	New asylum claims submitted[1]	1951 Convention refugee status granted[1]	Allowed to remain for humanitarian reasons[1]	Arrival of resettled refugees[1]	Temporary protection; Other[2]	Total admissions[3]	New asylum claims submitted per 1,000 inhabitants		Total admissions per 1,000 inhabitants	
							Total	Rank	Total	Rank
Australia	83,174	22,127	-	106,267	-	128,394	4.1	22	6.4	8
Austria[4]	198,296	16,798	994	-	20,278	38,070	24.2	3	4.6	10
Belgium	211,728	15,758	750	-	-	16,508	20.3	6	1.6	18
Bulgaria	13,159	1,352	3,336	-	-	4,688	1.7	27	0.6	24
Canada	303,482	131,197	-	109,265	-	240,462	9.4	14	7.5	7
Cyprus[5]	20,019	514	113	-	-	627	24.0	5	0.8	23
Czech Rep.	69,263	1,144	-	-	-	1,144	6.8	18	0.1	28
Denmark[6]	76,398	15,207	35,800	6,567	7,736	65,310	14.1	11	12.0	2
Estonia	96	4	3	-	-	7	0.1	35	0.0	37
Finland	22,262	137	4,869	6,319	-	11,325	4.2	21	2.2	16
France	382,841	83,576	-	-	-	83,576	6.3	19	1.4	20
Germany[7]	866,562	133,248	22,227	-	330,000	485,475	10.5	13	5.9	9
Greece	38,705	1,214	1,288	-	-	2,502	3.5	23	0.2	26
Hungary[8]	48,996	1,694	5,635	-	377	7,706	4.9	20	0.8	22
Iceland	400	1	45	194	-	240	1.4	29	0.8	21
Ireland[9]	63,402	6,841	381	1,264	102	8,588	15.3	10	2.1	17
Italy[10]	110,777	9,018	6,660	-	68,527	84,205	1.9	26	1.4	19
Japan	2,378	122	191	851	-	1,164	0.0	37	0.0	35
Latvia	137	6	10	-	-	16	0.1	36	0.0	36
Liechtenstein[11]	1,138	-	239	-	63	302	33.0	2	8.7	4
Lithuania	1,715	34	178	-	-	212	0.5	33	0.1	33
Luxembourg	11,195	300	851	-	-	1,151	24.1	4	2.5	15
Malta[12]	3,028	540	1,008	-	10	1,558	7.5	17	3.9	12
Netherlands	292,146	32,702	91,336	2,767	-	126,805	17.9	9	7.8	6
New Zealand	12,557	2,855	-	7,541	-	10,396	3.1	24	2.6	14
Norway[13]	91,050	2,123	25,143	15,229	5,882	48,377	19.7	7	10.5	3
Poland	43,191	1,647	856	-	-	2,503	1.1	30	0.1	32
Portugal	2,600	82	307	-	-	389	0.2	34	0.0	34
Rep. of Korea	416	33	7	-	-	40	0.0	38	0.0	38
Romania	12,240	948	679	-	-	1,627	0.6	32	0.1	31
Slovakia	44,401	409	-	-	-	409	8.2	15	0.1	30
Slovenia	15,311	41	112	-	-	153	7.8	16	0.1	29
Spain	65,619	2,646	2,991	-	-	5,637	1.5	28	0.1	27
Sweden	175,880	5,826	54,766	12,816	-	73,408	19.5	8	8.1	5
Switzerland[14]	245,797	29,197	81,187	-	53,496	163,880	33.9	1	22.6	1
Turkey	48,901	21,748	-	-	-	21,748	0.7	31	0.3	25
United Kingdom	677,029	169,669	104,556	240	-	274,465	11.3	12	4.6	11
United States[15]	606,992	200,952	-	654,495	-	855,447	2.0	25	2.9	13
Total	**4,863,281**	**911,710**	**446,518**	**923,815**	**486,471**	**2,768,514**	**4.4**		**2.5**	

Country of asylum or resettlement	New asylum claims submitted[1]	1951 Convention refugee status granted[1]	Allowed to remain for humanitarian reasons[1]	Arrival of resettled refugees[1]	Temporary protection; Other[2]	Total admissions[3]	New asylum claims submitted per 1,000 inhabitants		Total admissions per 1,000 inhabitants	
							Total	Rank	Total	Rank
- European Union (15)	3,195,440	493,022	327,776	29,973	426,643	1,277,414	8.3		3.3	
- European Union (25)	3,441,597	499,055	335,691	29,973	427,030	1,291,749	7.5		2.8	
- Western Europe	3,533,425	524,342	434,345	45,202	486,084	1,489,973	8.9		3.8	
- Central Europe	246,561	7,235	10,618	-	377	18,230	2.6		0.2	
- Europe	3,854,282	554,424	446,320	45,396	486,471	1,532,611	6.7		2.7	
- Northern America	910,474	332,149	-	763,760	-	1,095,909	2.8		3.3	
- Australia/New Z.	95,731	24,982	-	113,808	-	138,790	4.0		5.7	

Note:
For detailed explanations on methodology and data limitations, consult UNHCR statistical yearbooks.
[1] These four columns concern annual arrivals.
[2] The figures included in this column concern both annual arrivals and population estimates (stocks). A second major difference with the previous three columns is that temporary protection has ended for most refugees and that many of these refugees have returned.
[3] Number of persons granted refugee or humanitarian status, refugees admitted under resettlement programmes and refugees provided temporary protection. Due to the temporary nature of some forms of protection (e.g. humanitarian status, temporary protection), not all those who are admitted stay indefinetely.
[4] Column 6 includes temporary protection for Bosnians in 1995 (18,685) and Kosovars in 1999 (1,593), but excludes aliens permits granted to Bosnians in 1996 (62,700).
[5] Columns 2 to 4 include asylum applications lodged (1,065), refugees recognized (307) and humanitarian status granted (46) under the UNHCR mandate during 2002-2004.
[6] Column 6 includes refugees recognized at embassies (458), persons granted a special humanitarian residence permit (1,002), persons admitted for exceptional reasons (1,395) and Bosnians, Kosovars and Serbs granted temporary protection (4,881).
[7] Column 6 refers to temporary protection granted to Bosnians in 1996.
[8] Column 2 includes asylum applications lodged under the UNHCR mandate (2,141) and column 6 refers to refugees recognized under the UNHCR mandate (1995-1998).
[9] Column 6 refers to persons granted temporary leave to remain (TLR) outside the asylum procedure in 2000 and 2003.
[10] Column 6 refers to persons from the former Yugoslavia (58,500) and Somalia (10,000) granted temporary protection during 1995-1997.
[11] Column 6 refers to Bosnians granted temporary protection outside the asylum procedure in 2001.
[12] Column 6 refers to refugees recognized under the UNHCR mandate during 2001.
[13] Column 6 refers to Bosnians (1,896), Iraqi (2,019) and Kosovars (1,967) granted temporary protection during 1995-2000.
[14] Column 6 refers to persons granted temporary protection under special cantonal and other regulations.
[15] Columns 2 and 3 refer to the number of cases.
Sources: Governments, UNHCR.

Main origin of asylum seekers in selected European countries, 1995-2004

Origin	1995	1996	1997	1998	1999	2000	2001	2002	2003	2004	Total
Serbia and Montenegro	51,800	38,400	48,400	98,300	121,300	45,900	28,200	33,400	27,100	23,700	516,500
Iraq	18,200	26,300	40,400	40,800	35,100	44,400	47,800	51,300	25,100	10,500	339,900
Turkey	41,400	38,400	33,100	21,800	19,700	28,500	30,100	28,800	24,200	15,600	281,600
Afghanistan	11,700	12,500	16,400	18,600	23,800	32,800	51,400	28,100	13,800	9,000	218,100
Islamic Rep. of Iran	11,000	11,600	10,200	10,300	16,200	32,000	17,700	13,200	14,600	11,600	148,400
Russian Federation	4,700	4,900	5,500	5,800	8,000	14,300	18,300	19,400	34,100	29,600	144,600
Somalia	12,300	8,100	9,000	12,100	14,300	11,000	11,900	12,600	15,100	9,000	115,400
Sri Lanka	12,800	13,100	14,100	12,300	12,700	13,500	11,200	8,400	4,100	4,100	106,300
China	3,900	4,300	6,900	6,000	11,000	13,400	8,800	13,100	15,600	11,800	94,800
Bosnia and Herzegovina	17,200	6,500	8,200	10,200	6,700	11,300	10,700	8,100	5,500	5,400	89,800
Dem. Rep. of the Congo	7,800	7,900	8,700	7,000	7,200	8,000	9,300	12,500	10,800	8,800	88,000
India	9,100	7,400	5,800	4,800	6,500	9,200	10,900	11,300	11,000	9,900	85,900
Nigeria	8,900	6,400	5,300	5,700	4,700	7,300	9,400	13,300	13,300	11,500	85,800
Romania	14,500	9,800	10,600	8,800	8,600	9,200	7,400	7,300	3,800	3,600	83,600
Algeria	8,700	5,200	6,900	8,200	8,000	7,900	10,400	9,700	7,900	8,600	81,500
Pakistan	9,800	7,800	8,300	6,600	8,100	8,900	7,400	7,200	7,800	9,500	81,400
Armenia	5,700	7,000	6,100	5,300	8,600	6,900	6,600	6,900	5,700	4,600	63,400
Georgia	3,200	3,100	4,400	4,100	3,400	3,600	6,000	8,200	8,200	8,700	52,900
Bangladesh	2,800	3,000	4,000	3,400	4,800	5,700	5,300	5,300	6,600	5,900	46,800
Ukraine	1,800	2,100	2,700	1,800	4,100	6,100	10,000	6,800	5,400	4,900	45,700
Sierra Leone	2,600	1,300	3,300	4,000	7,000	7,800	9,500	5,300	2,500	1,400	44,700
Albania	1,300	1,500	7,900	6,700	5,400	6,200	3,800	3,800	3,000	2,400	42,000
Angola	3,200	2,500	2,100	2,200	4,300	4,900	7,900	7,200	4,300	2,700	41,300
Viet Nam	3,700	2,800	3,500	3,500	2,900	3,600	6,000	5,000	4,300	3,500	38,800
Syrian Arab Rep.	2,200	3,100	3,000	3,300	4,200	5,000	4,200	3,600	3,200	3,200	35,000
Stateless	3,100	3,600	3,700	3,700	4,200	4,000	2,100	2,500	3,600	3,500	34,000
Rep. of Moldova	1,200	1,600	1,300	1,100	2,600	3,600	5,200	5,600	5,500	5,700	33,400
Azerbaijan	600	1,200	1,700	3,200	6,000	3,800	3,400	3,900	3,800	4,100	31,700
Sudan	2,800	2,200	2,300	3,300	2,900	2,800	2,400	3,800	3,700	3,600	29,800
Bulgaria	3,800	3,800	4,000	1,700	1,700	2,700	2,900	3,800	2,400	2,700	29,500
TfYR Macedonia	4,200	2,300	2,300	1,100	1,200	910	6,200	4,700	2,500	2,400	27,810
Slovakia	780	620	1,000	1,700	5,000	4,500	2,800	4,200	3,100	1,900	25,600
Guinea	630	1,000	1,100	1,700	1,800	3,200	4,000	3,100	3,100	3,300	22,930
Cameroon	560	780	1,000	1,300	1,700	2,200	2,600	4,000	4,000	2,900	21,040
Ethiopia	2,500	2,200	2,100	1,500	1,700	1,800	2,200	2,600	2,600	1,800	21,000
Various/unknown	44,100	38,600	37,600	39,000	77,300	67,500	71,000	82,200	68,700	54,000	580,000
Total	**334,570**	**292,900**	**332,900**	**370,900**	**462,700**	**444,410**	**455,000**	**450,200**	**380,000**	**305,400**	**3,828,980**

Note:
Countries of asylum included are Austria, Belgium, Bulgaria, Cyprus, Czech Rep., Denmark, Estonia, Finland, France, Germany, Greece, Hungary, Iceland, Ireland, Italy, Latvia, Liechtenstein, Lithuania, Luxembourg, Malta, Netherlands, Norway, Poland, Portugal, Romania, Slovakia, Slovenia, Spain, Sweden, Switzerland, Turkey and the United Kingdom (number of cases 1995-2003).
For detailed explanations, consult UNHCR statistical yearbooks.
Sources: Governments, UNHCR.

Industrialized countries

Industrialized countries	Industrialized countries (regions)	Industrialized countries (regions)	Industrialized countries (regions)
All	*Europe*	*Western Europe*	*European Union (25)*
Australia	Austria	Austria	Austria
Austria	Belgium	Belgium	Belgium
Belgium	Bulgaria	Denmark	Cyprus
Bulgaria	Cyprus	Finland	Czech Republic
Canada	Czech Rep.	France	Denmark
Cyprus	Denmark	Germany	Estonia
Czech Rep.	Estonia	Greece	Finland
Denmark	Finland	Ireland	France
Estonia	France	Italy	Germany
Finland	Germany	Liechtenstein	Greece
France	Greece	Luxembourg	Hungary
Germany	Hungary	Netherlands	Ireland
Greece	Iceland	Norway	Italy
Hungary	Ireland	Portugal	Latvia
Iceland	Italy	Spain	Luxembourg
Ireland	Latvia	Sweden	Lithuania
Italy	Liechtenstein	Switzerland	Malta
Japan	Lithuania	United Kingdom	Netherlands
Latvia	Luxembourg		Poland
Liechtenstein	Malta		Portugal
Lithuania	Netherlands	*European Union (15)*	Slovakia
Luxembourg	Norway	Austria	Slovenia
Malta	Poland	Belgium	Spain
Netherlands	Portugal	Denmark	Sweden
New Zealand	Romania	Finland	United Kingdom
Norway	Slovakia	France	
Poland	Slovenia	Germany	
Portugal	Spain	Greece	*Northern America*
Rep. of Korea	Sweden	Ireland	Canada
Romania	Switzerland	Italy	United States
Slovakia	Turkey	Luxembourg	
Slovenia	United Kingdom	Netherlands	
Spain		Portugal	
Sweden		Spain	
Switzerland	*Central Europe*	Sweden	
Turkey	Bulgaria	United Kingdom	
United Kingdom	Czech Rep.		
United States	Hungary		
	Poland		
	Romania		
	Slovakia		
	Slovenia		

Source: UNHCR.

United Nations major areas

Africa	Asia	Latin America and the Caribbean	Europe
Algeria	Afghanistan	Antigua and Barbuda	Albania
Angola	Armenia	Argentina	Andorra
Benin	Azerbaijan	Bahamas	Austria
Botswana	Bahrain	Barbados	Belarus
Burkina Faso	Bangladesh	Belize	Belgium
Burundi	Bhutan	Bolivia	Bosnia and Herzegovina
Cameroon	Brunei Darussalam	Brazil	Bulgaria
Cape Verde	Cambodia	Cayman Islands	Croatia
Central African Rep.	China	Chile	Czech Rep.
Chad	Cyprus	Colombia	Denmark
Comoros	Dem. People's Rep. of Korea	Costa Rica	Estonia
Congo	Georgia	Cuba	Faeroe Islands
Côte d'Ivoire	Hong Kong SAR, China	Dominica	Finland
Dem. Rep. of the Congo	India	Dominican Rep.	France
Djibouti	Indonesia	Ecuador	FYR Macedonia
Egypt	Iraq	El Salvador	Germany
Equatorial Guinea	Islamic Rep. of Iran	French Guiana	Greece
Eritrea	Israel	Grenada	Hungary
Ethiopia	Japan	Guatemala	Iceland
Gabon	Jordan	Guyana	Ireland
Gambia	Kazakhstan	Haiti	Italy
Ghana	Kuwait	Honduras	Latvia
Guinea	Kyrgyzstan	Jamaica	Liechtenstein
Guinea-Bissau	Lao People's Dem. Rep.	Mexico	Lithuania
Kenya	Lebanon	Nicaragua	Luxembourg
Lesotho	Macao SAR, China	Panama	Malta
Liberia	Malaysia	Paraguay	Monaco
Libyan Arab Jamahiriya	Maldives	Peru	Netherlands
Madagascar	Mongolia	Puerto Rico	Norway
Malawi	Myanmar	Saint Kitts and Nevis	Poland
Mali	Nepal	Saint Lucia	Portugal
Mauritania	Occupied Palestinian Territory	Saint Vincent and the Grenadines	Rep. of Moldova
Mauritius	Oman	Suriname	Romania
Morocco	Pakistan	Trinidad and Tobago	Russian Federation
Mozambique	Philippines	Turks and Caicos Islands	San Marino
Namibia	Qatar	Uruguay	Serbia and Montenegro
Niger	Rep. of Korea	Venezuela	Slovakia
Nigeria	Saudi Arabia		Slovenia
Rwanda	Singapore	**Oceania**	Spain
Sao Tome and Principe	Sri Lanka	Australia	Sweden
Senegal	Syrian Arab Rep.	Fiji	Switzerland
Seychelles	Tajikistan	Kiribati	Ukraine
Sierra Leone	Thailand	Micronesia (Federated States of)	United Kingdom
Somalia	Timor-Leste	Nauru	
South Africa	Turkey	New Zealand	
Sudan	Turkmenistan	Palau	
Swaziland	United Arab Emirates	Papua New Guinea	
Togo	Uzbekistan	Samoa	
Tunisia	Viet Nam	Solomon Islands	
Uganda	Yemen	Tonga	
United Rep. of Tanzania		Tuvalu	
Western Sahara	**Northern America**	Vanuatu	
Zambia	Bermuda		
Zimbabwe	Canada		
	United States		

Source: United Nations Population Division, United Nations Statistics Division, New York.

Index